CHRISTIANITY AND THE RELIGIONS

CHRISTIANITY AND THE RELIGIONS

From Confrontation to Dialogue

Jacques Dupuis, S.J.

Translated by Phillip Berryman

ORBIS BOOKS

Maryknoll, New York 10545

DARTON·LONGMAN+TODD

Imprimi potest:
Francisco J. Egaña, S.J., Vice-Rector of the Gregorian University, Rome, June 3, 2001

Founded in 1970, Orbis Books endeavors to publish works that enlighten the mind, nourish the spirit, and challenge the conscience. The publishing arm of the Maryknoll Fathers and Brothers, Orbis seeks to explore the global dimensions of the Christian faith and mission, to invite dialogue with diverse cultures and religious traditions, and to serve the cause of reconciliation and peace. The books published reflect the views of their authors and do not represent the official position of the Maryknoll Society. To obtain more information about Maryknoll and Orbis Books, please visit our website at www.maryknoll.org.

Published by Orbis Books, Maryknoll, NY 10545-0308, and Darton, Longman and Todd Ltd., 1 Spencer Court, 140–142 Wandsworth High Street, London, SW18 4JJ.
English translation copyright © 2002 by Orbis Books.

This book was first published as *Il cristianesimo e le religioni: Dallo scontro all'incontro* copyright © 2001 by Edizioni Queriniana, Brescia.

Manufactured in the United States of America

Library of Congress Cataloging-in-Publication Data

Dupuis, Jacques, 1923-
   [Cristianesimo e le religioni. English]
   Christianity and the religions : from confrontation to dialogue /
Jacques Dupuis ; translated by Phillip Berryman.
     p. cm.
   Includes index.
   ISBN 1-57075-440-3 (pbk.)
   1. Theology of religions (Christian theology) 2. Christianity and other religions. 3. Catholic Church – Relations. I. Title.
BT83.85 .D87 2002
261.2 – dc21

                          2002010234

ISBN (USA) 1-57075-440-3
ISBN (GB) 0-232-52482-3

Dedicated to His Eminence Cardinal Franz König
Archbishop Emeritus of Vienna, Austria

The servility of the sycophants (branded by the genuine prophets of the Old Testament as "false prophets"), of those who shy from and shun every collision, who prize above all their calm complacency, is not true obedience . . . What the Church needs today, as always, are not adulators to extol the status quo, but men whose humility and obedience are no less than their passion for truth: men who brave every misunderstanding and attack as they bear witness; men who, in a word, love the Church more than ease and the unruffled course of their personal destiny.

—Josef Ratzinger
"Free Expression and
Obedience in the Church"*

---

*Taken from Hugo Rahner, ed., *The Church: Readings in Theology* (New York: P. J. Kenedy, 1963), 212.

CONTENTS

INTRODUCTION

IT MAY SEEM PRETENTIOUS, even rash, for an author to write three books on the same subject. Hence some explanation is called for by way of justification. Over ten years have already gone by since I wrote a book titled *Jesus Christ at the Encounter of World Religions.*[1] It took the form of a monograph. After having studied closely how Hindu scholars and theologians look at the historic person of Jesus of Nazareth, I was proposing what was then called a "theocentric Christocentrism" as a more appropriate model for a Christian theology of religions. That book remained quite limited in scope. Almost ten years later, at the request of other publishers, I undertook a much more ambitious project. The aim this time was to present a fresh general introduction to the theology of religions updated in terms of the new context created by noteworthy developments of theological reflection on the matter. This entailed first examining the concrete stances and theological assessments of official church teaching and theologians vis-à-vis other religions over the centuries of Christianity, and then, making a concise exposition of the core theological problems that are raised within a serious encounter between Christianity and the other religions of the world. This second work, published as *Toward a Christian Theology of Religious Pluralism,*[2] proposes as a model for such a renewed theology of religions what I called a model of a "Trinitarian and pneumatic Christology." Such a model, by clearly holding on to and affirming unhesitatingly what is considered to be the central core of Christian faith, that is, faith in Jesus Christ as "constitutive" universal Savior of all humankind, made it possible to acknowledge a positive meaning and salvific value in other religious traditions for their adherents, within the sole divine plan for humankind. Even though it generally met with a positive "reception," that work also raised serious questions on the part of some theologians in the many book reviews that appeared in theological periodicals in various languages, primarily Italian, French, and English. I have devoted three articles to a detailed and thorough response to the various theological questions courteously addressed to me by my fellow theologians.[3] Hence there is no need to return to those explanations here. Suffice it to say that in this new book I have scrupulously

1. *Jesus Christ at the Encounter of World Religions* (Maryknoll, N.Y.: Orbis Books, 1991). The French original, *Jésus-Christ à la rencontre des religions,* was published by Desclée de Brouwer, Paris, 1989.

2. *Toward a Christian Theology of Religious Pluralism* (Maryknoll, N.Y.: Orbis Books, 1997; reprints: 1998, 1999, 2000, 2001, 2002).

3. Jacques Dupuis, "La teologia del pluralismo religioso rivisitata," *Rassegna di Teologia* 40, no. 5 (1999): 669–93; idem, " 'The Truth Will Make You Free': The Theology of Religious Pluralism

avoided all expressions that could raise any misunderstanding or create ambiguity over either the content of the faith or my own thought.

After the publication of that second work in 1997, the editors asked me for another book on the same topic, one less ponderous, more accessible, and aimed at an audience broader than the circle of specialists and the academy. However, this new book does not seek to merely offer a handy summary of the previous one. It proceeds in a different way. A quick glance at the table of contents suffices to show how different it is from the previous work. Some chapters are completely new; others have been reorganized. Throughout the entire work, more subtle theological discussions regarded as less relevant have been put aside; the references in notes have been reduced to only those absolutely necessary. The work is thus presented in a more readable and easier form.

While not specializing in the theology of religions, and perhaps not aware of the discussions on the matter today, the broader audience to which the new work is addressed cannot but ask often pressing questions about the relationship between Christianity and the other world religions, what possible meaning the other religions might have in the divine plan for humankind, and more generally, what difference it makes in one's personal life to belong to one religious tradition or another. Why am I a Christian? Is it due only to the accident of birth? How should I take on the fact that I am attached to the "way" of Jesus? As a privilege or as a responsibility in God's eyes? Is being a Christian a grace or a task — or both? And what should be my attitude toward so many people that I am now encountering in the street or at work? We are living in a new world, one that has now become multiethnic, multicultural, and multireligious. Negative attitudes toward the "others" and biased evaluations of their traditions that have characterized many centuries of Christian history are now inappropriate; they in fact constitute a past that demands that we repent and ask God and human beings for forgiveness. What then should our real attitude be today, and what should be our theological assessment? As is clear, the scope of the book is more pastoral than academic, more concrete than abstract. The intention is to help Christians of our time to discover more deeply the scope of God's plan for humankind, infinitely more beautiful and deeper than perhaps we had ever thought.

THREE THEOLOGICAL PERSPECTIVES

From a theoretical standpoint, it is possible to distinguish the various successive perspectives or ways of focusing in the way in which Christian theology has approached the problem of other religions. For many centuries the issue was the possibility of the salvation of "others" in Jesus Christ. Starting from the clear affirmation of faith that Jesus Christ is the universal Savior, the question was whether others could attain salvation in him or not. It must be acknowledged —

Revisited," *Louvain Studies* 24, no. 3 (1999): 211–63; idem, "Religious Pluralism: A Provisional Assessment," unpublished.

with due shame on our part — that for many centuries both theology and the official teaching of the church gave a mainly negative response to that question. The axiom *Extra ecclesiam nulla salus,* understood rigidly starting in the fifth century, found its way into documents of popes and church councils until the fifteenth century. Today we ask how such negative opinions could prosper and remain received doctrine for so long. We wonder what idea was being entertained of the God of revelation, the God who created all humans, the one who, according to the revealed message in the Old and New Testament, "is not partial" (Deut 10:17), the one with whom "there is no partiality" (Rom 2:11), the one who "shows no preference for persons" (Acts 10:34) — was not that God perhaps reduced to a narrow and partial god in the work of those churchmen? How could he have allowed the majority of the human beings in the world, all created by him with the same destiny of union with him, to have been lost forever? Furthermore, how could he have allowed his universal plan of salvation to thereby be deprived of realization in the history of humankind?

In any case it is understandable that, especially after the discovery of the "new world" in 1492, it was no longer possible for theologians to think and teach that one who had not come to explicit faith in Jesus Christ could not be saved. St. Thomas Aquinas, the great thirteenth-century theologian, still held that after the historic event of Jesus Christ, explicit faith was necessary for the salvation of any human being. Such opinions were no longer sustainable. At this point various theories were developed whereby implicit faith is sufficient for attaining salvation in Jesus Christ. This is not the place to give lengthy consideration to these various more or less satisfactory theories. What is important is to note that until almost the mid-twentieth century the same perspective remained the usual way theologians dealt with the issue, and was the common teaching of the church about the theological problem of the salvation of members of other religions. The profound insufficiency of such a perspective should not be ignored. Even as the possibility of the salvation of human beings who had not come to know the gospel was being affirmed, each particular case in which this happened seemed like an exception to the divine disposition which in itself was rigid and restricted. Could not God have provided more generously for the salvation of the bulk of humankind? Did a disposition that would unilaterally favor a Christian minority — currently one billion and a half out of six billion human beings — in terms of the possibility of salvation in Jesus Christ seem just and worthy of a God of universal love? And could it sincerely be thought that God's "universal will" that all humans be saved, clearly affirmed in the New Testament — "God . . . who desires everyone to be saved and to come to the knowledge of the truth" (1 Tim 2:4) — was serious and efficacious?

The theological perspective of the possibility or not of salvation for the members of other religions — which was answered negatively for a long time, and then positively, albeit under restrictive conditions — continued to be the common approach to the theology of the religions up to the last decades leading up to Vatican II (1962–65). Beginning in the 1950s, some theologians searched for a more positive and more open prospect for the "others." Various theories were developed, offering an approach that was not so exclusively individualistic but was socially oriented. The problem was no longer limited to the possibility of individual salvation for particular persons who were not members of the church, but it turned to recognizing the positive values in the religious traditions themselves which in some way could affect the personal salvation of their adherents. Here important distinctions would have to be made with regard to the way in which the positive values that they recognized in religious traditions were conceived and evaluated by the various theologians. Suffice it to say that for some those positive elements represented only the divine gifts placed in human nature, whereas for others these were specifically elements or seeds of "truth and grace," which figured as God's personal gifts to the people and could be discovered in their traditions. In the former case, humans by themselves could attain a "natural" knowledge of God, without thereby ever being able to establish a real contact with him; in the latter case, God had manifested himself in some manner to the people through their history, and their religious traditions continued the memory of that authentic experience of God. The religious traditions therefore had something to do with the mystery of the salvation of their adherents in Jesus Christ. Obviously, the distance between the first interpretation and the second is significant. In the first case, humans remain powerless vis-à-vis their salvation; in the second, God holds out his hand to them through their religious tradition. In the first case, they can be saved outside of and despite their belonging to such a religious tradition; in the second, it is in it, and somehow through it. The second interpretation represents the more positive and open form of the second theological perspective about which we are speaking.

In recent years, however, scholars have opened up a third perspective on this issue. No longer does it suffice to ask whether and what religious traditions have to do with the mystery of the salvation of their adherents in Jesus Christ. More positively and profoundly, the question is what positive meaning the religious traditions themselves have in God's single overall plan of salvation. Without a pretense of being able to fully discern the divine plan for humankind, the question is nevertheless posed of whether the religious pluralism in our world today does not perhaps have a positive meaning, albeit hidden and mysterious, in that plan. In short, the question is whether the divine design for humankind might not be much more vast and deep than we had ever thought before. Is it still to be thought today, as was once thought spontaneously — not without some negative prejudices against the religious traditions — that all men are destined by God to become explicitly Christians, even if most of them do not reach this destiny of theirs, while the reality in which we are living seems to indicate just the opposite? Is not God perhaps "greater than our hearts" (1 Jn 3:20) — and his plan of salvation larger than our theological ideas? It is easy to foresee that this new prospect will open previously unheard questions and demand of us a broader assessment of the religious traditions as well as a different attitude in dealing with their adherents. My intention has been to place *Toward a Christian Theology of Religious Pluralism* in this latter perspective, as the title clearly indicates. My aim now is to place this present book in that same perspective, by developing new aspects and highlighting different nuances. It is in fact presented as a collection of monograph studies of the theology of the religions, written from the standpoint of a religious pluralism envisioned by God in his sole design of salvation for humankind.

FROM CONFRONTATION TO DIALOGUE

I have subtitled this new book *From Confrontation to Dialogue.* It may indeed be asked whether a true encounter between the various religious traditions is already under way in our multireligious world and to what extent. The various kinds of difficulties that such endeavors must overcome in order to become a concrete reality should not be concealed. Without wishing to enter into protracted descriptions of the conflictive situations that have occurred among the various religious traditions over centuries now distant from us, it suffices to recall the crimes against humanity that the century just completed has witnessed — often enough with complicity of the religious traditions involved in the conflicts. It has been suggested that this past century has perhaps been the cruelest in human history. Be that as it may, it is clear that a true purification of the memory — and of memories — even for recent events is needed by all parties, if we wish to reach a mutual renewed attitude, characterized by a true and sincere encounter between the various religious traditions. One example suffices: in the context of the *Shoah* and of the inhuman massacre of millions of Jews in World War II, a battered people have asked where God was during such massacres and what he was doing, and the question is still being asked; and, in any case, how after the *Shoah* suffered by the chosen people could one still speak of a providential God of the covenant? And further, how could one give credence to the claim of the Christian message, according to which the world in which we are living is a world already redeemed and saved once and for all in Jesus of Nazareth? Reality seems to refute the claims of faith.

Purification of memory is not at all easy. Peoples and religious communities cannot be asked to forget how much they have suffered, even at the hand of Christianity, if not in the extermination of their populations, often in any case to the point of the destruction of their cultural and religious heritage. For them forgetting would be tantamount to betrayal. The personal identity of a human group is built up from a concrete historic past that in any case cannot be annulled, even if there were a will to do so. But even while not forgetting, memory can be healed and purified through a shared determination to begin new constructive mutual relations of dialogue and collaboration, of encounter.

Besides the often hostile attitudes toward people, the traditional negative appraisals of both their religious or cultural heritage over the centuries must also be kept in mind. After becoming first an accepted religion in the Roman empire, and then officially the state religion, in the fourth century Christianity developed an exclusivist attitude combined with a negative assessment of other religions. The claim of being the only *true* religion is expressed ideologically in the afore-mentioned axiom: *Extra ecclesiam nulla salus.* The church was considered the only "ark of salvation" — outside of it human beings were lost. The theological termi-nology used even today by many Christian preachers and even theologians still retains clear traces of a pejorative vocabulary toward the "others." Hence along with purification of memory, theological language also needs to be purified. To-day there is still talk of "pagans," even of "infidels" or of "nonbelievers." The very term "non-Christians" is today considered offensive. What would we think if the "others" were to consider us "non-Hindu" or "non-Buddhist"? What people are called should be based on how they understand themselves, not on a foreign and often prejudiced understanding.

More deeply, how can it be announced to the "others," as "good news" of the gospel for everyone, that we Christians are "God's new people"? The question is not imaginary, since Vatican II itself has considered it appropriate to use that expression, which is injurious at least to the people of Israel (cf. *Lumen Gentium* §9). While speaking clearly of a "new covenant" (2 Cor 3:6; Heb 9:15; 12:14) and of the church as "people of God" (1 Pet 2:9–11), the New Testament never uses the expression "new people of God" for the church. Recent exegesis rightly reacts against a linguistic abuse by which the advent of the church would prevent Israel from still being God's people. In reality, the New Testament is not about one people of God being replaced by another, but about the expansion of the people of God beyond its own limits through the extension of the church which is now part of it, to the nations in the Hellenistic ambit. Indeed, the use of the expression "people of God" or "new people of God" to refer to the church has a negative effect on relations between Christianity and the other religious tra-ditions, even more harmful than that produced in the field of relations between Christianity and Judaism. Is it enough to subsume under a single expression of "people of God" — albeit in different ways — the Jewish people and the church, while continuing to exclude all the "others"? Without denying God's special elec-tion of the people of Israel, an election that has been extended in Jesus Christ and brought to completion in the church, can the "other" peoples be regarded as excluded from the divine election? Or, on the contrary, should it be said that the divine election is extended in some fashion to all peoples, and should it therefore be said that all are "chosen peoples"? Perhaps there is insufficient sensitivity to the legacy of exclusivism or triumphalism of which the people-of-God eccle-siology may be a vehicle with regard to the relationship between Christianity and the other religious traditions. "This impossible people of God," exclaimed a theologian familiar with interreligious dialogue! Nor can it be forgotten that M. K. Gandhi, the father of the Indian nation, used the term *harijan*, that is, "people of God," to refer to his country's "untouchables," those despised and re-jected by people as "nonpersons." Was his theology of the people of God perhaps closer to that of Jesus than is a traditional Christian theology? In any case, the expression "people of God" is not an isolated case where theological language must be purified. Another case — to which we will turn later — is that of the traditional theological identification between the Reign of God announced by Jesus and the Christian church. Does such an identification, which at least implicitly excludes "others" from the Reign of God, fit with the thought of the historic Jesus?

Openness to positive relations of encounter thus requires from us — albeit not exclusively — that memory and language be purified. How mutual relations between the religions and Christianity have been formulated over the centuries may be summarized in a few words. In the modern age with some effort there has been a shift from the confrontation and open opposition that have characterized a good many centuries to a certain passive tolerance, leading in turn in more recent times to a more or less peaceful coexistence. Today's multiethnic, multicultural, and multireligious world requires from all parts a qualitative leap proportional to our situation, if we wish to have in the future open and positive mutual relations between the peoples, cultures, and religions of the world, relations, in other words, of dialogue and collaboration — in short of encounter rather than the confrontation of a past now behind us. No more biased interpretations of data and facts about others and about the religious traditions of others; no more stubborn misunderstandings due to ignorance or malice. The aim is a conversion to the other that can open the way to sincere and profitable relations. Nothing short of a true conversion of persons will suffice for achieving true peace between the religions of the world, which is a necessary and essential condition for peace between peoples. So what does such a mutual conversion mean?

To begin with, it means a true sym-pathy, or "em-pathy," that helps understand others as they understand themselves, not as we, often according to stubborn traditional prejudices, think we know who they are. In a word, it entails unrestricted acceptance of "others" even in their difference, in their irreducible personal identity. The challenge — but at the same time the grace — of interreligious dialogue consists in this acceptance of the difference of the others. Interpersonal encounter necessarily takes place between different persons, and the wealth of communion is built on the mutual complementarity between different persons. The same is true of religions. Union does not mean uniformity, nor does communion mean conformity. The grace of the dialogue between religions consists, as will be said explicitly further ahead, in the possibility of mutual enrichment.

Yet all this does not mean that the new perspective in which we seek to insert our work can be allowed to leave the past behind or to ignore it. This approach must no doubt go beyond the theological solutions of the past that do not suit reality, and leave behind the negative attitudes that have characterized centuries of Christian relations with other religions. At the same time, it must remain in contact with the living tradition of the church — which itself is the result of past tradition — and build on what in the Christian centuries, first in the revealed word and then in authentic postbiblical tradition, has been shown to be of value by means of an open attitude suited for leading toward a positive assessment of the religions. Lack of consideration leads to contempt; familiarity to critical appreciation.

FROM INTERRELIGIOUS DIALOGUE
TO A THEOLOGY OF RELIGIOUS PLURALISM

Theology has traditionally used a dogmatic and deductive method. Starting from the church's dogmatic pronouncements, based on suitably selected scripture quotes, ever more precise theological conclusions were built up. The process consisted of starting from general principles in order to apply them concretely to problems today. The danger of such a method lay in the fact that the more conclusions were drawn from abstract principles, the greater the risk of being cut off from reality. With regard to the theology of religions, taking as a starting point the dogmatic datum of the universal salvation of humankind in Jesus Christ, itself based on a few key isolated New Testament texts (Acts 4:12; 1 Tim 2:4–5), it was concluded with astonishing ease that the other religions had no saving value. They represented — at best — the expression of some vague human aspiration for union with the divine that was ineffective in any case. There was no concern whatsoever with becoming informed about the self-understanding of the "others" or of the faith content of their traditions. Outside reality was prejudged dogmatically. Thus, upon being asked how he could know and state with such certainty that the other religions were nothing but an idolatrous human pretension of self-justification, Karl Barth answered with unswerving arrogance: I know it a priori.

A methodological advance occurred with the gradual introduction of an opposite method, one that could be defined as inductive. With such a method, the problem is no longer that of coming down from principles to concrete applications, but rather — moving in the opposite direction — that of starting from reality as now experienced with all the problems that it entails, in order to seek a Christian solution to such problems in the light of the revealed message and through theological reflection. With regard to the theology of religions, the "first act" of doing theology must be a serious practice of interreligious dialogue and taking seriously the religious experience met personally in the lives of the "others" with whom one comes in contact through such interreligious dialogue. That encounter, if true and authentic, cannot fail to raise serious questions for a Christian believer. These are indeed the questions — not abstract but quite concrete — that demand of the theology of religions a detailed response based on a sincere reinterpretation of the revealed datum. It is interesting to note that, while having a limited knowledge of other religious traditions — he left that task to historians of religions — Karl Rahner, on the basis of his philosophical and theological analysis of the "supernatural existential" innate in the very humanity of every human being, was able to counter Karl Barth rather explicitly with his assertion that "elements of truth and grace" exist and may be found in every religious tradition in the world — their fullness is found in the incarnate Word (cf. Jn 1:14, 17) — placed there by God. How did he know? He too claimed to know it a priori. It may be noted in passing that the Rahnerian expression, the "elements of truth and grace," used in an essay originally published in 1961,[4] was taken up by Vatican II — even though most of the member bishops were unaware of it! — in *Ad Gentes* §9 (1965).

Today the talk is of "contextualizing" theology — a principle that goes beyond that of adaptation or even inculturation[5] — and of the theological model to which it gives rise under the rubric of "hermeneutical" (i.e., interpretive) theology. Adopting an inductive method means starting from lived historic reality, letting oneself be questioned by it, and attempting to cast the light of the revealed word on it. It means, in other words, starting from the concrete context in which the church lives its faith and interpreting the surrounding reality with the help of the gospel message. Basically, it means contextualization and hermeneutics (interpretation).

Claude Geffré has rightly defined "hermeneutical theology" as "a new act of interpretation of the Jesus Christ event on the basis of a critical correlation between the fundamental Christian experience, attested by the received tradition and contemporary human experience."[6] This new interpretation of the Christian message emerges out of the "circularity between a believing reading of the founding texts which bear testimony to the originating Christian experience, on the one hand, and Christian existence today, on the other" (p. 75).

Christian existence is everywhere conditioned by the historic context in which it is lived, with its cultural, economic, social, political, and religious components. Hermeneutic theology will accordingly consist of a continuous progressive back-and-forth movement between the present contextual experience and the witness of the founding experience entrusted to the memory of the church's tradition — and vice versa. This ongoing movement back and forth between "context" and "text," between present and past, is known as the "hermeneutic circle."

Actually what is happening here is not a circularity between two members, but rather a triangularity and an interaction of three points: the "text" or the "datum" of faith, the concrete historic "context," and the contemporary "interpreter."[7] The circle imagery could then be usefully replaced with a drawing of a triangle. But each of the three poles composing it — each constitutive element of the triangle — is seen in the full complexity of its reality.

The term "text" covers everything that goes under the name of "Christian memory": the objective tradition based on sacred scripture. "Context" refers to that complex reality that includes sociopolitical, economic, cultural, and religious

---

4. Karl Rahner, "Christianity and the Non-Christian Religions," in *Theological Investigations* (London: Darton, Longman & Todd, 1966), 5:115–34.

5. Jacques Dupuis, "Méthode théologique et théologies locales: Adaptation, inculturation, contextualisation," *Seminarium* 32, no. 1 (1992): 61–74.

6. Claude Geffré, *Le christianisme au risque de l'interprétation* (Paris: Cerf, 1983), 71.

7. Jacques Dupuis, *Who Do You Say That I Am? Introduction to Christology* (Maryknoll, N.Y.: Orbis Books, 1994), 8–9.

aspects. Strictly speaking, the "interpreter" is not understood to be the individual theologian but rather the church community to which he or she belongs and at whose service he or she is placed. It has to do with the local church, a believing people who live their faith experience in diachronic communion with the apostolic church and in synchronic communion with all the local churches — a communion presided over in charity by the bishop of Rome. The hermeneutical triangle between "text," "context," and "interpreter" therefore consists of the interaction between Christian memory, the surrounding cultural reality, and the local church. The context acts on the interpreter by raising specific questions; this influences the preunderstanding of faith with which the interpreter reads the text. The latter in turn acts on the interpreter, whose reading of the text will supply guidance for Christian practice. As is evident, the interaction between text and context, or between memory and culture, takes place in the interpreter, and hence in the local church.

Applying these principles to the theology of the religions enables us to say the following. It must be admitted that those Western theologians who have taken up the theology of the religions, even those whose efforts have been more successful, have more often than not utilized a purely deductive method. They start from certain New Testament statements that they judge to have a clear and indisputable meaning, and then they ask what concessions Christian faith can make to other religious traditions. Do the premises of revelation allow us to attribute to those traditions a positive value for the salvation of their adherents? Taking a further step, which of these premises allow Christians to regard such traditions as ways of salvation — not ways parallel to that opened by God in Jesus Christ, but yet genuine ways of salvation by virtue of a relationship that they can have with the Christian way? It must be acknowledged that on the basis of an exclusively deductive method, they have reached somewhat positive answers to such questions with difficulty and great parsimony.

The reaction to an exclusively deductive method, a method that is a priori and, as such, inevitably inadequate, has emerged — as could be expected — in those churches in which coexistence with the other religious traditions is an integral part of everyday life, where the great world religions mingle on an everyday basis, especially in Africa, and even more in Asia. Recently, however, even in the West — as religious pluralism has gradually emerged as normal — theologians have found themselves advocating a rigorously inductive method. The starting point is the practice of interreligious dialogue between the various traditions (experienced on both sides, each within its own faith, as it should be), and only then, as "second act," is there theological reflection on the relationship between those traditions. The priority is given to interreligious dialogue, as the absolutely necessary basis for theological discourse. The a priori procedure has to be replaced with one that is a posteriori, which alone can bring positive results. Engaging in a broad experience of the practice of encounter and dialogue is thus regarded as decisive; indeed, a theological reflection from a distance cannot actually be very promising, that is, a discourse "on others" without having met them and listened to them, without having been in close contact with their religious life and "firm belief," which often, as Pope John Paul II recognized in his first encyclical, "can make Christians ashamed" (*Redemptor Hominis* §6). Is it not perhaps the lived reality of ongoing encounter between Christianity and the other religious traditions that explains the undeniable fact that the documents published by gatherings of Asian bishops clearly attest to an attitude that is plainly more open and positive than is usually found in the documents of the church's central magisterium? As long ago as 1974, during the plenary assembly of the Federation of Asian Episcopal Conferences, held in Taipei, Taiwan, the Asian bishops declared in a somewhat rhetorical and emphatic tone: "How can we not recognize in the religious traditions of our peoples the way in which God has sought them through their history?"

If the principles of contextualization and interpretative theological method are applied seriously to the religious reality of the world, it immediately becomes clear that the theology of religions cannot be seen simply as a new argument or topic for theological consideration. When the "theology of the religions" or of "religious pluralism" is under discussion, the genitive is understood not only as the objective genitive, i.e., as though it had to do with a new object for theological consideration. The theology of religions is not seen so much as a new issue for theological consideration but rather as a new way of doing theology in an interreligious context: a new method for doing theology in a situation of religious pluralism. This hermeneutical "interreligious" theology is a call to broaden the horizon of theological discourse; it ought to lead to a deeper discovery of the cosmic dimensions of the mystery of God and God's design for all humankind. The aim is to do theology not for a billion Catholics in the world, or even for a billion and a half Christians, but for the six billion human beings who share the same "global village" on our planet.

The theology of religions or of religious pluralism thus represents a new method for doing theology. Its point of departure is a practice of interreligious dialogue, on the basis of which it goes in search of a Christian interpretation of the surrounding manifold religious reality. It constitutes a new way of theologizing. Indeed, this theology does not simply observe the practice of interreligious dialogue as a necessary condition, as a premise, or even as a first step of its own activity; it maintains a dialogical stance at every stage of its reflection. It is theological reflection on dialogue and in dialogue; it is "dialogical interreligious theology."

OUTLINE AND DEVELOPMENT
OF THIS BOOK

In the past the negative assessments of the religions that can be found in the scriptures, both Old and New Testaments, were rather unilaterally given prominence. Without wishing to deny the existence of such negative judgments, they should be placed in their context and should be interpreted properly. It seems essential to distinguish clearly between the revealed message about the religions considered in themselves and perversions of them by human beings, which are vehemently rejected, for example, in the condemnation of idolatry strongly accented by the Old Testament prophets. If that distinction is kept in mind, various open attitudes and several positive doctrinal elements on the matter, contained in the revealed datum, can be highlighted. It should be added that in the renewed context of the encounter between the religions, it does not suffice to clearly mention the positive elements that can be found in the revealed datum; those data must also be submitted to a contextual interpretation in contemporary reality.

Here we will be considering only the New Testament, but the scope of chapter 1 is twofold. First, there is an effort to see and to discover — or rediscover — what stance the Jesus of history took toward "foreigners" who did not belong to the people of Israel, and what he may have thought about their religious ideas and practices. Was it a negative and condemnatory attitude, or a behavior of opening and sympathy? The second part of the chapter moves with the same question from the historical Jesus to the apostolic church, attested to in the New Testament writings. The question is whether the concrete attitude toward the "others" and the theoretical appreciation of their religious traditions is positive or negative, open or closed. We also ask whether the early Christian church might not have undergone a certain evolution in the sense of a conversion in the matter, moving, in other words, through providential events, from a narrow resistance toward a certain openness. The chapter is accordingly titled "Jesus, the Apostolic Church, and the Religions."

This offers us something to build on. But the aim here will not be to follow the whole course taken in Christian tradition, either positively with the "seeds of the Word" and the "covenants of God" in the writings of the second-century fathers, or negatively with the "ark-of-salvation" church and the consequent adage "Outside the church no salvation," which, starting in the fifth century, underwent an increasingly narrow interpretation leading to an exclusivism that is anything but Christian. Nor will we trace here the "gospel surrogates," that is, the various ways in which after the path of narrow ecclesiocentric exclusivism could no longer be taken, theologians endeavored to discover various replacement solutions. These are the various theories of "implicit faith," which then came to be seen by them as sufficient for salvation in Jesus Christ. Anyone wishing to pursue this long journey comprised of positive and negative elements, of ups and downs, may refer to the ample treatment that was made in *Toward a Christian Theology of Religious Pluralism.*[8] The stress here is on moving directly to recent times, that is, to the typical perspective on the theology of religions primarily in the Catholic Church, in the years leading up to Vatican II, and then to ask what has been the exact import of the conciliar event, and to gauge the true, albeit limited, openness

---

8. See the whole first part, especially 84–129.

of the church's recent magisterium. Based on its central focus, chapter 2 is titled "At the Crossroads of Vatican II."

Continuing our route, we reach our own era in terms of the theology of religions with a rapid, but substantially complete, consideration of the range of theological positions toward the saving value of other religious traditions or lack of it, of their positive significance or lack of it in the divine plan for the salvation of humankind and their possible relationship with Christianity. There is no longer any need to reaffirm that alongside the "way" that is in Jesus, people encounter other "ways" claiming to lead them to salvation, even in the Western world. It is therefore not so surprising if alongside more traditional positions at issue, new theories are being developed toward a theology of the religions or even of religious pluralism. As we will have occasion to note in chapter 3, even "religious pluralism" actually has quite different meanings, within which it will be important to make the necessary distinctions, in order to avoid improperly confusing theories irreconcilable with the content of Christian faith — the pluralist paradigm of the theologians known as "pluralists" — with those theological efforts which, while they unhesitatingly retain the central core of faith, attempt to discern a positive meaning in the other religious traditions of the world within the divine plan for humankind. Chapter 3, "Christianity and the Religions in Recent Theology," thus brings us up-to-date on the contemporary debate on the theology of the religions.

After three chapters that could be termed "positive theology," there follow some chapters that I place under the rubric of "synthetic theology," thereby avoiding the term "systematic theology," or that of "dogmatic theology." I have earlier explained the insufficiency of a "dogmatic" way of doing theology; moreover, it is obvious that the divine mystery and the mystery of God's design for humankind are beyond any theological "systematization"; at every stage and in every situation, our knowledge and comprehension of that mystery remain limited, partial, and provisional. In any case, the primary and more pressing questions that are raised within the theology of religions today are considered under the rubric of "synthetic theology." The aim in posing the issues in a way that is serious and seeks to be open is to lay the foundations for a Christian theology of the religions and of religious pluralism that can open the door to a profitable interreligious dialogue. The first question dealt with in chapter 4 is that of the breadth of the "history of salvation" or of "salvation in history." Under the title "The God of the Covenant and the Religions," we ask whether the God revealed in the Hebrew tradition and in Jesus Christ may have made some saving covenant with the "Gentiles" and other peoples, such that they too may and should be called "peoples of God," and "peoples of the God of the covenant." We furthermore ask whether such "cosmic" covenants remain in effect even today, so as to ground even today a personal relationship between God and the peoples, the initiative for which must always be placed in God's universal saving will and in his indiscriminate love.

Along with the problem of whether the "others" are part of the history of salvation and whether they have a covenant bond with the living God, there is the problem of the "many and various ways" in which God manifested and revealed himself to human beings through their history, before being revealed "in these last days...through his Son" (Heb 1:1–2). There is no questioning the fact that the author of the Letter to the Hebrews was referring solely to revelation of God through the prophets of the Hebrew tradition. Nevertheless, we may ask whether the perspective opened by that text may not be extended to the entire history of humankind. If all peoples are included in the economy of divine covenants and in the history of salvation, may it perhaps not be concluded that in some manner, if only incipiently and incompletely, God manifests himself in their history, through revealed words and saving gestures? Chapter 5 attempts to answer such questions positively, under the title "In Many and Various Ways." The suggestion is that in the other religious traditions, in the written memory of their sacred books and the living memory of their religious practices, are traces of divine words and gestures of salvation, "diverse faces of the divine," to be drawn out, discovered, and honored.

Jesus Christ represents the peak of God's self-manifestation to humankind. In the Word of God made man in Jesus of Nazareth, God has spoken his decisive word to humankind and has embodied the mystery of the salvation of humankind and the world. The revelation of God in Jesus Christ is unsurpassed and unsurpassable in the history of divine revelations: that is so because of the personal identity of the man Jesus with the only-begotten Son of God made man. A universal saving value must likewise be attributed to the human life of Jesus, and specifically to the paschal mystery of his death and resurrection. That does not mean, however, that the human consciousness of Jesus exhausts — or could exhaust — the divine mystery, and consequently that the revelation of God that took place in him is exhaustive of the divine mystery. Nor does it mean that the life, death, and resurrection of Jesus are the only real and possible expression of the saving power of the Word of God. Chapter 6, "The Word of God, Jesus Christ, and the Religions of the World," seeks to explain and clarify in what sense the Word of God as such can act salvifically, beyond the humanity of Jesus, now risen and glorified, but ever in "union" with it. Indeed, the chapter insists on the close connection within the sole divine plan for the salvation of humankind, between that illuminating and saving action of the Word as such and the mystery of salvation realized by God in the historical Jesus Christ event. It also highlights the significance and relevance of the saving action of the Word as such for an open theology of the religions.

Chapter 7, "The 'One Mediator' and 'Participated Mediations,'" follows closely from the preceding chapter. It intends to show that the "one mediation" of Jesus Christ between God and human beings, clearly affirmed in New Testament revelation (1 Tim 2:5), does not in fact rule out the "participated mediations" at work in other religious traditions. In other words, the mystery of salvation carried out in Jesus Christ may reach human beings in various ways, through different mediations, which represent different types of the sacramental visibility of the mystery. Such shared mediations must not be placed on a level of equality with that at work in the church — which itself also shares in the one mediation of Jesus Christ. It must be maintained that the church, founded on the Christ event, and whose Head and Lord is Christ, represents more completely the sacramental visibility of the mystery of salvation in Jesus Christ; but it is not the only possible way. A true, albeit incomplete, mediation of the mystery is also at work in the other religious traditions, enabling them to serve as "ways" or "paths" of salvation for their members. In any case such effectiveness of other religious traditions in the order of human salvation is always to be situated in the overall plan of God for humankind which culminates in the Jesus Christ event.

Chapter 8 is concerned more closely with the relationship between the church, the Reign of God, and the religions, and is appositely titled "The Reign of God, the Church, and the Religions." The aim is to show clearly that the Reign of God announced by Jesus is something broader than the church. God has established his Reign in Jesus, in his life, in his words and in his deeds, and decisively in the paschal mystery of his death and resurrection. The Reign of God present in history cannot be identified with the church. The Reign of God represents the mystery of salvation present and operative in the world and in history. It is a universal reality in which the adherents of other religious traditions can share with full title alongside Christians. The church is therefore not the Reign; it is the "sacrament" of it, insofar as it signals, witnesses, and announces as "good news" for all human beings the operative presence of the Reign of God in the world and in history. This chapter highlights the relevance and importance for the theology of religions of the fact that all human beings, Christians and "others" together, share in the Reign of God.

Such a doctrine also serves in a special way as the theological foundation for interreligious dialogue. Chapter 9 is called "Interreligious Dialogue in a Pluralistic Society." Since all human beings, regardless of their adherence to one religious tradition or another, are fellow members of the Reign of God and together called by God to make his Reign grow in history toward eschatological fullness, it is clear that a deep communion between Christians and the "others" already exists. We discover that the differences of religious obedience that keep us separated are of less weight in God's eyes than the deep reality in which we are already united even before our common action. The endeavor of interreligious dialogue involves making operational that deep union between Christians and adherents of the other religious traditions. The chapter explains how the practice of dialogue can lead to a mutual enrichment between the various traditions, as well as a collaboration and shared effort on behalf of a more human, and therefore more divine, world.

Chapter 10 is closely connected to the preceding one. In the context of inter-religious dialogue it asks whether a practice of shared prayer between Christians and members of the other religious traditions is possible and perhaps desirable. The chapter is entitled "Interreligious Prayer." As a first step we ask what might be the theological foundation for such a shared prayer in principle, that is, in-dependently of which religious traditions might be specifically involved in it.

Taking a further step, bearing in mind the specific religious traditions that might be involved, whether monotheistic or otherwise, we ask what the specific grounds for such a practice might be. Some concrete suggestions are made about putting interreligious prayer into practice.

It has been observed before that the issue of the theology of religions in recent times is posed under the sign of religious pluralism. At the end of this journey, the question is raised of whether or not it is allowable from the standpoint of Christian theology to speak not simply of a de facto pluralism but of a religious pluralism in principle, i.e., whether or not it can be stated theologically that the plurality of religions characteristic of our contemporary world has as such a positive meaning in the divine plan for humankind. There must be clarity about the proper meaning of the question — which has nothing to do with surreptitiously adopting the "pluralist paradigm" of the pluralist theologians, or some sort of doctrinal "relativism." Rather the question has to do with whether, in the entirety of the single design chosen and established by God in his eternity for the entire human race and carried out in our history, the plurality of the religions in the world might not perhaps have, in the eyes of God himself, a positive but hidden meaning that we have yet to discover. As I try to show in this book, God has become involved in seeking human beings in their history, before they could seek him. Is it not possible, in the case of all those who have not come to knowledge of Jesus Christ, that the way "known to God" (cf. *Gaudium et Spes* §22) by which "the Holy Spirit offers to all the possibility of being made partners . . . in the paschal mystery" of salvation is indeed the historic "ways" by which they have sought God, because he had sought them first? Are not those "ways" perhaps God's ways? If the message of Sacred Scripture — as will be noted explicitly further on — sees in all the religions of the world "gifts of God to the peoples," does it not perhaps follow that the multiplicity of the religious traditions has a positive meaning in the divine design for humankind? It is this "religious pluralism in principle" that is here regarded as valid.

To Father Gerald O'Collins, S.J., who has studied the manuscript with great care and has provided useful suggestions for improving it, I express my profound gratitude as I complete this study on March 31, 2000.

Chapter One

JESUS,
THE APOSTOLIC CHURCH,
AND THE RELIGIONS

I N CONCLUDING a very thorough examination of the "biblical foundations of mission,"[1] Donald Senior and Carroll Stuhlmueller observe that the Bible does not contain "any comprehensive solution" to the troubling question that challenges the contemporary church in terms of Christianity's relationship to the other religions. Among the "indications" that can be deduced from the Bible to provide a solution to that question, the authors cite the following points: (1) Biblical religion is deeply rooted in the religions and the cultures around Israel. (2) The clear self-awareness that Israel had of its own religious identity as chosen people gave rise to negative judgments on other religious systems considered to be vain idolatry. (3) In the New Testament that same powerful sense of identity and authority often produced equally negative judgments upon the other religions, in which no validity was conceded to religious systems other than Judaism and Christianity. (4) The attitude of the Bible toward Gentiles as individuals covers the full range of positions from hostility to admiration; some biblical writers recognize a genuine religious experience in individual "pagans." (5) Some biblical writers, including Paul, would come to recognize the possibility of "natural religion," "whereby the true God could be detected in the order and beauty of his creation," but for a biblical writer it remains inconceivable "to express admiration for a full-blown cult or nonbiblical religion."

These results are rather meager and reveal a predominantly negative attitude. Nevertheless, bearing in mind the profound changes that have affected the contemporary world, and the consequent shift in how the problem is posed, these authors draw attention to some biblical themes that might lead to a more positive assessment of nonbiblical religions.

> Many of the biblical themes we have discussed, such as the expansive nature of the religious experience, the revelation of God in creation, the recognition of the Gentiles' capacity to respond to the gospel, and the awed awareness that God and his Spirit range far beyond the boundaries

---

1. D. Senior and C. Stuhlmueller, *The Biblical Foundations for Mission* (Maryknoll, N.Y.: Orbis Books, 1983), 344–47.

of human expectations, are some aspects of the biblical data that suggest positive links with non-Christian religions.[2]

That may serve to indicate the complexity of the biblical data on the religions of the "Gentiles," and the need to handle the data with caution. The biblical sources often tend to be implicit rather than clearly formulated; they wend their way over an extensive period of time and affect different situations, which lead to varying assessments and attitudes; moreover, they are often ambivalent, if not seemingly contradictory. Particular attention is reserved for the organic relationship existing between the Old and New Testaments and to the relationship of continuity and discontinuity that runs between them. The Christ event, the interpretation of it given in the apostolic church as attested in the New Testament, and the consequent self-understanding of the apostolic church itself have notably influenced the appraisal that the church has made of the religious traditions — initially Jewish then Hellenistic — that it has found itself facing.

Even while admitting the complexity of the objective situation, it must honestly be recognized that in the past attention has often focused one-sidedly on the biblical data that could provide the basis for a negative assessment, or even on the statements most contemptuous of nonbiblical religious traditions. Thus the unequivocal Old Testament condemnations of the idolatrous practices of the nations and the foolishness, or even nonexistence, of the gods they adored were repeatedly emphasized. These condemnations of idolatry seemed to provide an unequivocal basis for a negative theological appraisal of those traditions. The openly negative attitude professed by the Christian church toward the other religions, as well as the very prudent albeit more tolerant position adopted in more recent times by the "official" church, have naturally inclined theologians to place great emphasis on the negative data.

In the new situation brought about by the pursuit of mutual understanding and openness to dialogue, however, it seems proper, in fact urgent, that a theological presentation of the biblical appraisal of the religions of the nations properly highlight those positive elements capable of providing, in a changed context, a valid basis for a more generous theological appreciation of the other religious traditions in the world. But there is more to be said. It must be acknowledged that the traditionally negative appraisals of the biblical data on the religious traditions of the world were often based on one-sided and biased interpretations of the data and the texts. The texts have often been interpreted out of context, thereby making the statements even more negative. One is left with the impression that what was of utmost importance was the apologetic claim of the uniqueness of Christianity as the "true religion"; a negative appraisal of other religious traditions found in the Bible seemed to offer a necessary foundation for that claim. The "exclusivist" theological positions of the past on the religions were often based on such dubious interpretations of the texts. Some biblical statements about the

---

2. Ibid., 346.

unique positive significance of Christianity were easily interpreted in an exclusive sense to the detriment of the other religions. In such a situation it is not enough to highlight — as the authors mentioned earlier sought to do — some positive elements that can be found in the Old and New Testaments about the religions. On the contrary, the data and texts of the Bible must be reexamined and reinterpreted with a fresh understanding, bearing in mind the different contexts, that of the biblical past and that of the present time, so as to be able to propose a renewed biblical theology of the religions in the contemporary context of the theological reassessment of the religions. That is what Giovanni Odasso set out to do in a recent book, *Bibbia e religioni: Prospettive bibliche per la teologia delle religioni,*[3] which will be cited often in the pages ahead.

The scope of this chapter is much more modest. It is limited to the New Testament, and in it, to some core texts that are often ignored in the context of the biblical discussion of the religions, or that have been given an unduly negative interpretation with regard to the religions. However, in dealing with the New Testament message about the surrounding religions, two moments or two stages should be clearly distinguished. First, we must pull together what sort of attitude and mind the historical Jesus himself had toward the personal religious life of the "pagans" with whom he came in contact during his earthly "mission," and what, insofar as it can be drawn from the texts, was his appraisal of the religious traditions to which they adhered. The second moment consists in asking how the apostolic church assessed, in the light of its new faith in the risen Christ — whom God had constituted "Lord and Christ" (Acts 2:36) through his resurrection — the situation in which the "Gentiles" surrounding them stood in terms of divine salvation, and of any human or saving value that it might be possible to discover in their religions. Let us note at the outset that the memory of Jesus, insofar as it can be recovered from the New Testament texts, and the theology of the apostolic church contained in the New Testament tell us directly and formally of the concrete situations in which persons found themselves and do not construct theories of the theological relationship between Christianity and the world religions. In terms of both the Jesus of history and the apostolic church, the horizon remains existential and concrete; a long reflection process emerging out of lived experience will be needed in order to develop theological theories about the religions of the world.

The chapter thus unfolds in two main sections. The first, "Jesus and the Religions," studies the personal attitude of the Jesus of history toward persons who did not belong to the "chosen" people of Israel, and his appreciation of their religious life. The second section, "The Apostolic Church and the Religions," asks how, on the basis of its paschal faith in Christ, the apostolic church went about situating the "peoples" vis-à-vis the mystery of salvation in him, and how consequently it appraised their religious traditions.

---

3. Giovanni Odasso, *Bibbia e religioni: Prospettive bibliche per la teologia delle religioni* (Rome: Urbaniana University Press, 1998).

JESUS AND THE RELIGIONS

Thanks to various recent studies, often with input from Jewish scholars, theology has rediscovered the deeply Jewish identity of the Jesus of history. Jesus of Nazareth was really a Jew, born of the lineage of Judah, "the son of David, the son of Abraham" (Mt 1:1). The whole gospel attests to his deep-rootedness in the religious tradition of his people. Jesus clearly declared that he had not come to abolish but to confirm, bring to perfection, and purify the covenant relationship established by God with his people: "Do not think that I have come to abolish the law or the prophets; I have come not to abolish but to fulfill" (Mt 5:17). The covenant and the Law that seals it remain, and yet a new order of justice, higher than the previous one, is established: "For I tell you, unless your righteousness exceeds that of the scribes and Pharisees, you will never enter the kingdom of heaven" (Mt 5:20). Jesus has come to bring God's covenant with his people to completion. That intention of renewal is the direct and primary cause of the opposition that his activity will stir up among those holding religious power in his people. The gospel tells the story of the clash that develops through the ministry of Jesus between his desire for a renewal of the religious tradition of Israel and the legalistic and oppressive stance of those who wield power in his religious community. Jesus intended to revitalize the true religious spirit that he shared with his people, and to inspire a new vision of God's saving action not only within the confines of the Jewish religious world, but beyond it, in the broader world. This aspect of Jesus' design will be considered later.

What should be noted immediately is the intention of continuity and discontinuity in the attitude and the religious design of Jesus. He does not intend to overcome Judaism and replace it by setting up a new "religion." What he seeks is to establish adoration of God "in spirit and truth" (Jn 4:23) by all human beings. It is not our task here to enter into the issue of the origin of the Christian church in Jesus.[4] However, it seems legitimate to think that the origin of the Christian church goes back principally to the risen Christ, rather than to the Jesus of history. The most important thing to note here is that the early church does not automatically separate itself from the Judaism of its origins after the resurrection of its Lord. For decades it continues to remain within the Jewish lineage and only gradually will there develop within it the awareness of a distinctive religious identity and eventually a break from its origins. Christianity will then understand itself as a different "way," but one springing from Israel. In whichever way the origin of the Christian church in Christ ought to be conceived, it can confidently be said that the Jesus of history had no formal intention of a separation into two "religions," one Jewish and the other Christian. His personal attitude toward the "pagans" with whom he came into contact and his assessment of their religious life were inspired by his aim of a spiritual renewal of religion. Indeed, the thought horizon of the Jesus of history was not the church as a distinct religion, but the Reign of God that God was establishing in his life, through his words and deeds.

---

4. Cf. among others, J. Guillet, *Entre Jésus et l'Eglise* (Paris: Seuil, 1985).

THE HORIZON OF THE REIGN OF GOD

The Reign of God unquestionably stands at the center of the preaching and mission of Jesus, his thought and life, his words and actions. The "sermon on the mount" and the beatitudes are the constitution of the Reign of God. All Jesus' parables refer to it: the miracles show that it is already present and at work.[5] It is also certain that the Reign that God had begun to set up in the world through the earthly life of Jesus became really present through the mystery of his death and resurrection. There is no solution of continuity here between the "regno-centered" character of the proclamation of Jesus and the "Christocentrism" of the kerygma of the apostolic age. The gospel moreover attests that for Jesus himself, the Reign announced by him and already present had to unfold toward its fullness.

Certainly, the Reign of God places God himself at the origin and heart of Jesus' activity. The Reign of God actually means God himself, as God begins to act decisively in the world, manifesting himself and ordering his creation through the human actions of Jesus. Jesus' initial mission is accompanied by miracles, and it would not be correct to understand them and treat them simply as though they were displaying his credentials as a prophet of the Reign of God. The healing miracles and exorcisms (similar to healing) that generally figure among the unassailable historical data of the initial ministry of Jesus, as indeed the raising of the dead, are signs and symbols of the fact that, through Jesus, God is establishing his dominion over the earth, subjugating the destructive forces of death and sin. In short, the miracles are the first fruits of the operative presence of the Reign of God among human beings.

The Reign of God is the dominion of God among human beings. That requires completely reorienting human relations and organizing human society in accordance with God's intention. The values that, in keeping with the Lordship of God, ought to characterize human relations can be summarized in a few words: freedom, brother- and sisterhood, peace, justice, and love. Along these lines, through his missionary activity, Jesus denounces everything that violates these values in the society of his time. That fact puts him at odds with various categories of his people: he castigates the oppressive legalism of the scribes, the exploitation of the people in the hands of the priestly class, and the arrogant hypocrisy of the Pharisees. Jesus is not a conformist, but a subversive on behalf

---

5. Jacques Dupuis, *Who Do You Say That I Am? Introduction to Christology* (Maryknoll, N.Y.: Orbis Books, 1994), 42–46. Within the abundant literature on the question, the following titles may be consulted: G. R. Beasley-Murray, *Jesus and the Kingdom of God* (Exeter: Paternoster Press, 1986); N. Perrin, *The Kingdom in the Teaching of Jesus* (London: SCM Press, 1963), and *Rediscovering the Teaching of Jesus* (London: SCM Press, 1967); Rudolf Schnackenburg, *God's Rule and Kingdom* (London: Burns and Oates, 1968); J. Fuellenbach, *The Kingdom of God: The Central Message of Jesus' Teaching in the Light of the Modern World* (Manila: Logos Publications, 1993), and *The Kingdom of God: The Message of Jesus Today* (Maryknoll, N.Y.: Orbis Books, 1995); J. Schlosser, *Le Règne de Dieu dans les dits de Jésus*, 2 vols. (Paris: Gabalda, 1980); N. F. Fisher, *The Parables of Jesus: Glimpses of God's Reign* (New York: Crossroad, 1990); W. Willis, ed., *The Kingdom of God in Twentieth-Century Interpretation* (Peabody, Mass.: Hendrickson, 1987); C. S. Song, *Jesus and the Reign of God* (Minneapolis: Fortress Press, 1993); G. Iammarrone, *Gesù di Nazaret Messia del Regno* (Padua: Messagero, 1996).

of God's power: he refuses to accept the unjust structures and stereotypes of the society in which he lives, and prefers to be associated with sinners and tax collectors, heretical Samaritans and the poor, i.e., with all those groups despised by the society of his time. To those categories of people, Jesus announces that the Reign of God has arrived, and he invites them to enter it by being converted and redirecting their lives.

Jesus is the "eschatological prophet" in whom the Reign of God not only is announced but arrives. His entire mission is centered on the Reign of God, that is, on God himself as the one who is establishing his dominion on the earth through his messenger. Because he is centered on God's Reign, Jesus is centered on God. In him there is no distance between one and the other: "Regnocentrism" and "theocentrism" coincide. The God whom Jesus calls "Father" is the center of his message, his life, and his person: Jesus did not speak primarily about himself, but he came to proclaim God and the advent of his Reign and to place himself at its service. God is at the center, not the messenger!

The Jesus of history, however, enjoyed a special and unique relationship of sonship toward the God of the Reign whom he called his Father (*Abbà*). He was likewise aware of his messianic vocation, which consisted in the renewal and fulfillment of the religion of the covenant established by God with his people. Indeed, that renewal and fulfillment constituted the establishment of God's reign in the world through his life. That was the horizon — that was the perspective — on the basis of which Jesus thought about and understood the situation, not only of the members of the people of the covenant, but of the "pagans" as well, of the "peoples," of the "foreigners," vis-à-vis the God of salvation and the Kingdom. As mysterious as the situation of the "others" might be with regard to the God of salvation, for Jesus, in any case, that God was the God of all human beings, who according to the scriptures does not make differences between persons: "God...who is not partial" (cf. Deut 10:17). Thus he could not share the tendency toward a certain "exclusivism" which the very identity as chosen people was ever in danger of stamping on the mind of the members of Israel. Jesus on the contrary would have thought that God's salvation is intended for all human beings alike, and for all peoples. The universal scope of salvation goes hand in hand with the universal God of the Reign.

Thus it is striking, in view of the testimony of the gospel, that the historic mission of Jesus seems to be directed principally, if not exclusively, at Israel. In Matthew 15:24 he explicitly declares that he has been sent only "to the lost sheep of the house of Israel." When he sent the twelve out on a mission, he ordered them to go "nowhere among the pagans," and to "enter no town of the Samaritans," but rather to go to "to the lost sheep of the house of Israel" (Mt 10:5–6). In all likelihood, these scriptural data are substantially authentic,[6] but they do create a problem to which we will have to turn further on. Yet there are

6. L. Legrand, *Le Dieu que vient: La mission dans la Bible* (Paris: Desclée, 1988), 69–92. Cf. also J. Jeremias, *Jesus' Promise to the Nations* (London: SCM Press, 1958).

occasions in the gospel when Jesus comes explicitly into contact with foreigners. These episodes serve as occasions in which Jesus reveals his thinking on the God of salvation and on the universality of that salvation. These episodes deserve close examination.

ENTRY OF THE GENTILES
INTO THE REIGN OF GOD

A first episode is that of the centurion of Capernaum who comes to Jesus, pleading for his paralyzed servant to be healed (Mt 8:5–13). Jesus is seen to be full of admiration for the faith of the centurion: "Truly I tell you, in no one in Israel have I found such faith" (Mt 8:10). Finding such faith in a pagan offers Matthew the occasion to mention the saying by Jesus that many, coming from the east and the west, will be admitted into the Kingdom of heaven (Mt 8:11–12). The entry of the "others" is not purely eschatological: it takes place first of all in history, as attested by the parable of the banquet (Mt 22:1–14; Lk 14:15–24). Indeed it is already operative and present. On this last point, however, interpreters have varying opinions. In the view of J. Jeremias, Jesus was expecting the incorporation of pagans into the people of God or into the Reign of God, as an eschatological act of the power of God.[7] L. Legrand disagrees to some extent and says that "attention must be paid to the realization of eschatology which is already taking place. The eschatological gathering of the Nations has already begun in the ministry of Jesus... Access into the Reign takes place through faith and conversion (Mk 1:15) and not through mere ethnic belonging (cf. Mt 3:8). Where faith appears, the Reign is present."[8] The universality of the Reign of God already operative during the historic mission of Jesus is affirmed even more clearly by C. S. Song. With regard to the parable of the "great banquet" (Lk 14:15–24; Mt 22:1–14), he notes that after the "outcasts" of Israel, even people from the foreign regions, i.e., the Gentiles, are called by the lord of the banquet. He tells his servant: "Go out into the roads and lanes, and compel people to come in, so that my house may be filled" (Lk 14:23). "This great banquet embodies Jesus' vision of God's reign. It is a global vision. It is a vision inspired by God, the creator of heaven and earth, God who created human beings in God's image."[9]

The participation of all in the banquet symbolizes the participation of all in God's salvation. For Jesus, therefore, the faith and conversion that lead to salvation do not entail moving to any different religion, but mean conversion to the God of life, love, and freedom, that is, to the God of the Reign of God, of all human beings. The full house of the banquet symbolizes the universality of belonging to the Reign of God: the banquet becomes a banquet for the people — even the "outcasts" and "foreigners." It is a celebration of the people. Those invited, "compelled to enter," will certainly represent a variety of faiths and religions. "We

7. Jeremias, *Jesus' Promise to the Nations*, 71.
8. Legrand, *Le Dieu que vient*, 85.
9. Song, *Jesus and the Reign of God*, 26.

must learn from Jesus' message of God's reign in order to realize who God is. It is to this God of God's reign, and not to the God of our religious tradition, certainly not to the God of our own making, that Jesus wants to direct our thoughts and commitment" (p. 38).

Another instance of Jesus marveling at the faith of pagans is the case of the Canaanite woman in Matthew 15:21–28. During some "excursions" into the Syro-Phoenician region, Jesus comes into contact with persons who do not belong to the chosen people. Again he is amazed at the faith of these "pagans," and for them he performs the healing miracles that they request of him. Tyre and Sidon are cited various times in the gospel. According to Matthew 15:21–28, Jesus there heals the possessed daughter of a Canaanite woman, at whose faith he marvels: "Woman, great is your faith! Let it be done for you as you wish." It must be kept clearly in mind that the miracles worked by Jesus for "foreigners" have the very same meaning that he gives to all of his other miracles. They mean that the Reign of God is already present and at work (cf. Mt 11:4–6; Lk 4:16–22; Mt 12:25–28). The healing miracles and exorcisms performed for the "others" are thus indications that God's Reign is present and at work among them as well; it extends to all those who approach God through faith and conversion (cf. Mk 1:15). In the case of the Canaanite woman, C. S. Song notes that when confronted with human suffering Jesus must have realized immediately that a distinction could not be made between Jews and Gentiles, nor between his ministry to his own people and his mission to the Gentiles. "The two ministries are in fact two aspects of one and the same ministry and mission. Human suffering is suffering whether it happens to Jews or to Gentiles . . . The foreign woman becomes the occasion for Jesus to cross the frontiers of faith and truth! . . . That Canaanite woman is playing a role in the enlarging of his vision of God's saving activity in the world!"[10] People outside his own religion were also capable of true and authentic faith, of that faith that saves. Indeed, their faith could be stronger and deeper than that with which he was familiar in his own religious community. The incident reminds us of the episode of the faith of the Roman centurion, recalled earlier, and of Jesus' admiring reaction: "Truly I tell you, in no one in Israel have I found such faith" (Mt 8:10; cf. Lk 7:9).

Both stories took place outside of Jesus' own religious community. A genuine faith is thus possible anywhere in this world, which is God's world. C. S. Song concludes, "Jesus crossed the frontier that separates Jews from Gentiles, the frontier that divides the Jewish community and Gentile communities, the frontier that keeps God's saving truth within one particular religion in exclusion of other religions" (p. 80). One who does not belong to Jesus' religious community — like one who is not a member of the Christian community — may really have faith in God's saving power. That should not be surprising, if it is true that the God of salvation is not only the God of Jews — and Christians — but of all peoples (cf. Rom 3:29–30), all of them being peoples of God. The Reign of

---

10. C. S. Song, *Jesus in the Power of the Spirit* (Minneapolis: Fortress Press, 1994), 77–78.

God, established by God in Jesus and proclaimed by Jesus as present and at work through his own life, his words and deeds, and ultimately realized in his death and resurrection, represents the universal reality of salvation present in the world. All human beings, in all the circumstances of life, may enter it through faith and conversion.

THE UNIVERSALITY OF THE REIGN OF GOD

What connection did the Jesus of history maintain between the Reign of God announced by him and the movement created by him, which after him was destined to become the "Christian" church? If the Reign of God really represents universal salvation, attainable by all people through faith and conversion to the God of the Reign, what function would the "Christian" movement have with regard to the Reign, in Jesus' mind? The fact that Jesus refers to the church only indirectly makes it all the more difficult to answer this question. As is known, the term *ekklèsia* is found only twice in the gospels, both times in Matthew. The "prediction of the church" in Matthew 16:18 has been retouched editorially in the light of the paschal event; in Matthew 18:18, *ekklèsia* indicates a local community of "disciples" without necessarily having any technical significance. Nevertheless it remains true that Jesus chose "the twelve" and entrusted to them the primary responsibility for continuing his mission of proclaiming the gospel for the sake of the Reign of God. Through the event of the resurrection of Christ and the gift of the Spirit at Pentecost, "the twelve" would become, along with others, the "apostles."[11] The "movement" begun by Jesus, destined to be transformed into the church in which he had instituted a competent authority, was nevertheless not identified by him with the Reign of God that he went about proclaiming; rather it was intended to serve the Reign of God, to help it to grow, to give witness to its presence in the world, to announce it as "good news" for all people.

Thus Jesus cannot be said to have identified the Reign with the "movement" that he was creating and that was destined to become the church.[12] Rather it should be acknowledged that when he sent the "twelve" on mission, charging them to proclaim the advent of the Reign (Mt 10:5–7), he was in anticipation placing the church at the service of the Reign. The "good news" that would be proclaimed after the resurrection (cf. Mk 16:15) was the same as that proclaimed by Jesus during his earthly life: the coming of the Reign (Mk 1:15). The church is intended to proclaim not itself, but God's Reign.

As will be seen in part two of this chapter, the theology of the New Testament will continue to be situated in this perspective of the Jesus of history, despite the well-known fact that "Reign of God," an expression so often on Jesus' lips, according to the synoptic gospels, partially disappears — albeit not completely — in

---

11. Cf. Guillet, *Entre Jésus et l'Eglise.*
12. On the universality of the Reign of God in the thought of Jesus, cf. C. S. Song, *Jesus and the Reign of God,* 3–38, and *Jesus in the Power of the Spirit,* 196–226.

the rest of the New Testament. It is noteworthy that, after Christianity had existed for decades, a time during which Paul had founded numerous local churches, at the end of the Acts of the Apostles, when Paul is "testifying" in Rome, he proclaims "the Reign of God" to all and teaches them "the facts about the Lord Jesus Christ" (Acts 28:30–31; cf. 28:23). The Reign of God and the Lord Jesus coincide. Even though by then it has become less common, the expression "the Reign of God" continues to be present in a fresh way, that of the Lordship of the risen Christ, which continues the Reign of God. That Lordship extends not simply to the church but to the entire world. But in terms of the Jesus of history, what still remains to be underscored is the universality of the Reign of God, extending beyond the people of the covenant, and beyond the movement created by Jesus and his "disciples," to the whole world, including foreigners, "pagans," Gentiles.

There are some episodes in the gospel that attest to the universalization of the Reign of God in Jesus' thinking. Let us recall some. In the gospel of John, while returning to Galilee — presumably after celebrating the Passover in Jerusalem — Jesus crossed Samaria and came to a city called Sychar (Jn 4:1–6).[13] The text in John shows him conversing with a Samaritan woman. This in itself had to cause amazement among the disciples — and the gospel does not fail to point it out: "Jews do not get along well with Samaritans" (Jn 4:9), whom they regard as foreigners. What amazes Jesus, by contrast, is the woman's openness to faith and her thirst for "living water" (Jn 4:7–15). He does not even reject Samaritan worship on Mount Garazim, as opposed to that in Jerusalem: rather he tells the woman that "the hour is coming when you will worship the Father neither on this mountain nor in Jerusalem . . . [the hour] when true worshipers will worship the Father in spirit and truth, for the Father seeks such as these to worship him" (Jn 4:20–23). All worship, not simply foreign but even Jewish, must give way to true spiritual adoration. C. S. Song notes that Jesus did not have to cross Samaria to return to Galilee. He could have avoided Samaria by choosing to go through Perea. "It must have been not human necessity but divine necessity, not human accident but divine providence, that prompted him to take the road leading to Samaria."[14] Jesus must have been compelled by the Spirit to cross the border into the region of Samaria. The dialogue that took place between Jesus and the Samaritan woman, as recorded by the evangelist John, is a "theological dialogue." "Having initiated it, Jesus led it step by step to a vision that sees the fulfillment of human religious efforts in the abolition of them." Neither Mount Garazim, the center of the religious world of the Samaritans, nor Jerusalem, the navel of the spiritual cosmos of the Jews, has a permanent meaning in God's presence. Both of them are symbols, images, to be surpassed. Indeed, they have been surpassed in Jesus himself, who is the image of the loving God and the symbol of God's reign.

---

13. It should be noted that while the apostolic church certainly evangelized Samaria (cf. Acts 8:5, 14–17), the story of the encounter between Jesus and the Samaritan woman in John seems to be a "retrojection" of that evangelizing activity.

14. Song, *Jesus in the Power of the Spirit,* 103.

Jesus aims at changing, transforming, revitalizing life with images and symbols that disclose and reveal for all the true nature of the Reign of God.[15]

It should not pass unnoticed that there are other times in the life of Jesus when people belonging to the Samaritan people are explicitly mentioned, and they serve as examples and models for an attitude of the faith and of brotherly and sisterly charity through which the Reign of God is entered. It is no coincidence that Jesus contrasts the attitude of the "good Samaritan," in the parable that bears his name, to that of a priest and a Levite (Lk 10:29–37). "A man was going down from Jerusalem to Jericho, and fell into the hands of robbers, who stripped him, beat him, and went away, leaving him half dead" (Lk 10:30). While the priest and the Levite passed by "on the other side" (Lk 10:31–32), "a Samaritan while traveling came near him; and when he saw him, he was moved with pity . . . and took care of him" (Lk 10:33–35). The gospel goes into details, explaining what was entailed in taking care of the injured man. The conclusion is that of the three, the Samaritan was the one who was the "neighbor to the man who fell into the hands of the robbers" (Lk 10:36). Jesus then proposes him as an example to the Jews: "Go and do likewise" (Lk 10:37).

Nor is it a coincidence that when Jesus was crossing Galilee and Samaria on the way to Jerusalem and he healed ten lepers in a village (Lk 17:11–14), it was only a Samaritan who, "when he saw that he was healed, turned back, praising God with a loud voice . . . [and] prostrated himself at Jesus' feet and thanked him" (Lk 17:15–16). Then Jesus asked: "Was none of them found to return and give praise to God except this foreigner?" and he said to the Samaritan: "Get up and go on your way; your faith has made you well" (Lk 17:18–19).

It is therefore clear that, for Jesus, saving faith is available to "pagans" and "foreigners" not only from afar; it is really at work in their midst. Analogously, even foreigners can belong ultimately to the Reign of God, the call to which extends beyond the confines of the chosen people of Israel. Belonging ethnically to the chosen people is irrelevant. This attitude stands in sharp contrast to Jesus' explicit statement — noted above — about being sent exclusively "to the lost sheep of the house of Israel" (Mt 15:24).

Another episode affirms even more provocatively, for anyone seeking to understand it correctly, the borderless universality of the Reign of God and of divine salvation operative in the world, as well as God's welcome to all people, independently of any belonging of theirs to a chosen people. It is the episode in which Jesus' disciples seek to prevent one "who is not one of us" from driving out demons "in the name of Jesus" (Mk 9:38–39). It is noteworthy that the episode closely follows another in which Jesus' disciples have not been able to heal a boy "possessed by a mute spirit" (Mk 9:14–29; cf. Mt 17:14–21; Lk 9:37–43). The failure of Jesus' disciples to heal the boy possessed by a spirit makes the success of a foreigner in driving out demons "in the name of Jesus" even more ironic, striking, and provocative. The "foreign exorcist" who drives out demons in the

---

15. Ibid., 103–6.

name of Jesus shows that the boundaries between belonging to the Reign and the workings of salvation do not follow the boundaries of a privileged people. They are borderless. The disciples who are scandalized at the success of the foreigner "have not understood that Jesus' name is not to be used to define the range of his fellowship, to set limits to his community, and to restrict the boundary of his activity."[16] Should not perhaps the company of Jesus — and the church — submit to God's authority in determining who are the "people of God," and how and where God is performing his saving works? Such powers belong personally to Jesus himself, not to his followers. The foreign exorcist, as reported by John, was capable of having that faith in God that was lacking in the disciples (cf. Mk 9:28–29). "John said to him, 'Teacher, we saw someone casting out demons in your name, and we tried to stop him, because he was not one of us'" (Mk 9:38). The reason that the foreign exorcist was capable of such faith is that God is not only the God of the Jews — and Christians — but of all peoples. The Reign of God for which Jesus lived and died can be made manifest inside and outside of his community alike. Consciously or unconsciously, the foreign exorcist, while he was driving out demons in the name of Jesus, was taking part in Jesus' mission for the Reign of God. The disciples were to be left even more amazed when Jesus explained to them why the exorcist must not be stopped: "Do not stop him; for no one who does a deed of power in my name will be able soon afterward to speak evil of me. Whoever is not against us is for us" (Mk 9:39–40). It does not matter whether one is a Jew, a Samaritan, a Gentile, or any person who is not part of the community of men and women who follow Jesus. Jesus is going beyond the bounds of race, religion, and tradition, during his life and his ministry.

In the light of his attitude, should we not perhaps also understand better the relationship to Jesus and the God of salvation of the people and peoples who remain beyond the community in which his name is claimed exclusively? "Whoever is not against us is for us" (Mk 9:40; cf. Lk 9:50b). Indeed, Jesus' entire life, his choices and his deeds, exhibit what C. S. Song calls "the centrifugal force" of this word of his. In this regard, he writes, "The more Jesus is repelled from the center of power held by the religious authorities, the more he is drawn to the women, men, and children in his community excluded from that center, and even to those outside his own religious community. The people whom the religious authorities considered to be beyond salvation have come to occupy the central place in his ministry of God's reign."[17] In the power of the Spirit, Jesus has launched the ministry of the Reign of God in such a way as to restructure the human community, and especially the religious community, not on the basis of the traditional religious boundaries, but on the basis of the demands and challenges of the Reign of God. "We Christians, theologians, and churches must open our eyes, hearts, and church doors to the saving activity of God in the world

---

16. Ibid., 207; cf. 200–226.
17. Ibid., 222.

of nations and peoples, in the community of people of other religions as well as in the community of Christians" (p. 226).

THE REIGN OF GOD AND THE RELIGIONS

Thus far we have limited ourselves to showing that in the thought of Jesus, men and women who do not belong to the people of the covenant can enter the Reign of God through faith and conversion to the God of the Reign, and be fully members: the God of the Reign is a "God . . . who does not show partiality" (Deut 10:17). As the ministry of Jesus demonstrated, the Reign of God goes beyond all human boundaries of any kind: ethnic, national, religious. However, we still have to ask what can be concluded about the value of the religious traditions in themselves. Jesus did not propose a theology of the religious traditions of the "others." He was content to make it clear that his deepest teaching was not addressed solely to a privileged group of disciples and friends, but was open to all, regardless of their attachment to any cultural or religious group.

That is what emerges from a careful study of the beatitudes of Jesus (Mt 5:3–12; Lk 6:20b-23) and of the sermon on the mount — or on the plain — of which they form a part (Mt 5:1–7:29; Lk 6:17–49). There can be no doubt that the beatitudes contain the heart of Jesus' teaching. But while some exegetes are inclined to consider them as the charter for the life of the close disciples and the inner circle of the followers of Jesus, others — rightly, it seems — see in them the charter of the Reign of God in its universality and openness to whoever is willing to enter it. Moreover, while some interpreters think that the sermon on the mount, as it appears in the texts, was preached by Jesus to a single gathering, others are probably more correct to see it as a compilation of "sayings" issued by Jesus at different times and in different places, sometimes to individuals, sometimes to various groups. C. S. Song pursues this second opinion even further.[18] He includes among the hearers of the sermon on the mount "the crowd" which is explicitly mentioned in Matthew (cf. Mt 5:1), or even better, the "great crowd of his disciples and a great multitude of people from all Judea, Jerusalem, and the coast of Tyre and Sidon. They had come to hear him and to be healed of their diseases" (Lk 6:17). This observation has major consequences for Jesus' own thought about the intended audience for even his more personal and deeper teaching. Indeed, that teaching is not intended solely for a select group of friends and disciples, chosen in accordance with various human criteria; on the contrary, it is addressed to all human beings who want to listen to it, all of them being destined by the God of the Reign for the praxis of the "values of the Reign" in their respective life circumstances.

Let us then consider the beatitudes, keeping in mind the unlimited assembly, whether religious or not, for which they are intended in Jesus' thinking. "Blessed are you who are poor, for yours is the kingdom of God" (Lk 6:20). The Lucan form of the "first beatitude" clearly establishes that the Reign of God is intended

---

18. Ibid., 214–20.

primarily for the poor, and the second-person address ("you who are poor") indicates that this version is closer to Jesus' words than Matthew's: "Blessed are the poor in spirit, for theirs is the kingdom of heaven" (Mt 5:3). So is there a change in perspective from one version to the other? Should it be thought that Jesus' preference for the poor, because of its apparently scandalous nature, has been lowered in tone after him to the point of being reduced to a "spiritual poverty" or to an "openness" to God that are within the reach of all, even the rich? Or does the Matthean formula suggest an adaptation to a privileged religious group as a whole? That does not seem to be the case; on the contrary, it can be thought that there is continuity between both versions: the true poor are also the "simple," those who are open to God and to his Reign. It seems clear that in both Matthew and Luke Jesus has addressed his speech to a significant group of poor among his hearers, the disinherited who turn to God as their only recourse. Undoubtedly, there would have been many "foreigners" among them.

In his discourse as it is reported, Jesus also tells his listeners: "Blessed are those who hunger and thirst for righteousness, for they will be filled" (Mt 5:6). According to Luke, Jesus says: "Blessed are you who are hungry now, for you will be filled" (Lk 6:21). Jesus' speech in Matthew's text should not be understood to mean that those who can boast a piety and religious observance in a privileged religious group are "those who hunger and thirst for righteousness" and so have a right to the Reign of God. In both cases, the beatitude refers to the poor, with a difference: in Luke the text returns to the idea of the first beatitude according to which the Reign of God is intended preferentially for the poor; in Matthew, there is added the beatitude of those who seek justice in its full scope, which includes justice on behalf of the poor; those, in other words, who make the "preferential option for the poor," and struggle against the unjust structures that maintain the status quo of injustice. In that effort on behalf of justice for the poor, Jesus sees a manifestation of the Reign of God in our midst, independent of any personal religious attachment. And so it goes, through the other beatitudes.

It has in fact been suggested that there is only one beatitude, namely that of poverty, of simplicity of gaze, of openness to God's will, of personal availability to the God of the Reign and to other human beings. This beatitude is attainable by all people of goodwill, open to faith and conversion. As stated earlier, it should also be clear that Jesus' personal attitude toward injustice and poverty goes beyond what the Old Testament prophets said about them. Speaking on behalf of the poor and oppressed and in defense of their rights, they clearly indicated God's intention on their side: his predilection for the poor and his divine wrath over the injustice inflicted on them. Yet Jesus not only shows a "preferential option" for the poor, he is not simply "on their side," but he personally identifies and associates preferentially with them: he is not simply *for* the poor, but *belongs* to them, and is *with* them. In this belonging to, and associating with, the poor by Jesus, God's preferential love for them reaches its apex: Jesus' attitude not only indicates God's thought on behalf of the poor, but personifies God's commitment to them, and his involvement in their condition.

Through Jesus' ministry, the Reign announced by him and initiated in him by God in the world reaches all humankind. Here is the "good news" for all human beings on earth, whatever their ethnic group or religious tradition. Such sharing of the Reign of God among all human beings from all parts of the world, and from all religions, is at the center of Jesus' message; it is what he has disclosed most clearly about foreign religious traditions. The God of Jesus is the God of all human beings; his Reign is intended for all.

THE APOSTOLIC CHURCH
AND THE RELIGIONS

As noted earlier, the horizon of the thinking of the Jesus of history was that of the universality of the Reign of God, which God was establishing in the world through his life and works; it was also that of the opening of all human beings toward the Reign of God through faith and conversion. The thought horizon of the early Christian apostolic church was its experience of the resurrection of Jesus and of the outpouring of the Holy Spirit. According to the apostolic kerygma, God has resurrected the Jesus who was crucified and has made him "both Lord and Christ" (Acts 2:36). That is the fundamental faith of the church. The paschal event of the death and resurrection of Jesus offers Christians a new perspective for understanding not only their religious situation, but that of all humankind, including people who belong to other religious traditions. The paschal mystery of the death and resurrection of Jesus represents the salvation effected in him by God for all of humankind. But while the death of Jesus was an event contained within the limits of history, his resurrection, although it took place at a precise time in history, transcends history and is essentially a transcendent event. Having been constituted by God "the Christ," Jesus has become "transhistoric." As such, for the Christian church he is now the key to understanding the mystery of salvation for all human beings. That is the basis of the apostolic faith according to which he is Mediator between God and human beings in the order of salvation (cf. 1 Tim 2:5). In the risen Christ, God has established a new order in his relationships with humankind, the consequences of which reach all human beings in their different situations. The community of Jesus' disciples which has begun to be shaped on the basis of paschal faith lives this relationship of salvation with God in Jesus Christ consciously and explicitly; but it is also convinced of the saving significance of the paschal event for all humankind. That persuasion will determine the Christian church's self-understanding of its mission and of its function in God's plan of universal salvation. In this regard, G. Odasso writes:

> In the light of the risen Lord, the community of the baptized, as it sees in Jesus the paradigm of its own existence, so it can grasp in him the funda-mental values that characterize any authentic experience of the divine . . . Knowing how to recognize the more authentic dimensions of these val-ues, as well as understanding in a sapiential way what the New Testament

attests of the experience of Jesus in his relationship with the Father and in his mission to human beings...means...recognizing that all men are called to be participants in the transcendent event of the risen Lord.[19]

The apostolic church was quite conscious of living that relationship of salvation with God in the risen Christ in a privileged way as a community of faith. Indeed, it was familiar with the temptation experienced first by the people of Israel, conscious of having been the object of a special choice by the God of the covenant, namely the temptation of an exclusivist vision of its own situation vis-à-vis divine salvation, and consequently of forgetting its own universalizing vocation. The New Testament data on its stance toward the "pagans" are in fact complex and ambivalent.[20] With regard to its relationships to the people of Israel, on the other hand, while for decades, as emphasized earlier, the early church remained in communion with the Jewish people and continued to share its tradition, religious life, and worship, there came a moment of painful separation between mother and daughter religion. This is not the place for us to enter into the reasons that caused the break, whether they were of a human and cultural nature, or religious, or even of faith. It must be recognized, however, that there was in fact a growing alienation between Israel and what was by then being called not only the "way" of Jesus, but Christianity. The Acts of the Apostles recall that the disciples of Jesus were first called "Christians" (Acts 11:26) in Antioch. A current of mutual opposition between both communities of faith and religion had been developing gradually, as attested by a certain "anti-Judaism" that scholars recognize as already present in John's gospel, and in Matthew's as well.

Yet that is not the entire story, thank God. Our driving concern in this second half of the chapter is to show through the key New Testament texts that the paschal event of Jesus, far from isolating the early Christian church in the security of its privileged position, pushes it to discover the truly universal meaning of the Jesus Christ event, and consequently its effective and saving presence within human beings in other religious situations. As we will see further ahead, in the New Testament there are texts and statements that can be interpreted in an "exclusive" way, as if only members of the Christian community, baptized in his name, could attain divine salvation in Jesus Christ. Hence, it must be shown how such statements are understood: namely affirmatively, but not exclusively. It is also important to show how the New Testament texts are helpful for discovering the positive religious values present and at work in the religious life of the "others" and in the religious traditions to which they adhere.

What requires explanation is how the saving power of the paschal event of Jesus reaches the members of other religious traditions. What does the theology of the apostolic church as it is recorded in the New Testament have to offer about the meaning of other religious traditions for the salvation of their adherents?

---

19. G. Odasso, *Bibbia e religioni: Prospettive bibliche per la teologia delle religioni*, 315–16.
20. Cf. J. Dupont, *The Salvation of the Gentiles* (New York: Paulist Press, 1979).

THE LAW WRITTEN ON THE HEART

Paul's realism in chapter 1 of Romans about the universality of sin is well known. He declares that God's wrath will fall on the pagans because they have not recognized his ongoing revelation through the cosmos (Rom 1:18–32). It should be noted immediately, however, that the Jews incur the same condemnation and will fall under the same judgment, despite the extra gifts that they have received (Rom 2:1–11). In fact, Paul observes at the outset that all men are equally subject to the divine judgment, whatever their religious situation, and they will receive according to their works: "There will be anguish and distress for everyone who does evil, the Jew first and also the Greek, but glory and honor and peace for everyone who does good, the Jew first and also the Greek. For God shows no partiality" (Rom 2:9–11). Paul here takes up paradigmatically the great principle stated with particular intensity in Deuteronomy (cf. Deut 10:16–18), already mentioned a number of times.

The next passage, however, must be examined closely because, as G. Odasso notes, it includes statements that "open a particularly fruitful horizon for a theological reflection on the religions present on the earth. In particular, analysis of the text makes it clear that the Gentiles are in some manner reached by the reality of the new covenant, and therefore by the saving power of Christ's resurrection."[21] This is the Law engraved in the hearts of the Gentiles (Rom 2:14–16). Even though they have not received the biblical revelation, they can act according to the "Torah." They do so "naturally" (*phusei*), that is, spontaneously. They indeed show that they have the works of the Law written on their hearts (cf. Rom 2:15). That law written on the heart is comprised of love itself, the *agapè* of the New Testament. This is accordingly not to be understood in the sense of the "natural law," or of any sort of instinctive or innate sensitivity. On the contrary, this recalls the well-known text of Jeremiah 31:31–34, where the new covenant is announced: "I will put my law within them, and I will write it on their hearts" (Jer. 31:33). In this regard, Odasso explains: "Even the Gentiles, who do not have the Torah, if they act according to their deep yearning, in other words, if they lead a life fundamentally inspired by authentic mutual love, show that they have been reached by the divine promise of the new covenant, which has been fulfilled in Jesus, 'Messiah and Lord'" (p. 322). They are reached by the new covenant, by the mystery of salvation in Jesus Christ, and hence internally vivified in some fashion by the Spirit of God.

It is remarkable that the Apostle to the Gentiles applies to these same Gentiles the "circumcision of the heart" spoken of in Jeremiah 4:4 with regard to the Jews: "Circumcise yourselves to the Lord, apply circumcision to your hearts." Circumcision of the heart is synonymous with true conversion. Paul now applies it to the Gentiles who have the works of the law written on their hearts: "So, if those who are uncircumcised keep the requirements of the law, will not their uncircumcision be regarded as circumcision? . . . For a person is not a Jew who is

---

21. Odasso, *Bibbia e religioni*, 317; cf. 317–34, which is being cited here several times.

one outwardly, nor is true circumcision something external and physical. Rather, a person is a Jew who is one inwardly, and real circumcision is a matter of the heart — it is spiritual and not literal. Such a person receives praise not from others but from God" (Rom 2:26–29). The implication is clear: for the Apostle, the Gentiles "who observe the law" are reached in a mysterious manner by the saving grace manifested in Christ Jesus: even if they do not know it, they are "in the Spirit," albeit in an imperfect manner, precisely because it is not transfigured by faith in the risen Lord. Odasso highlights the consequences of Paul's statements in Romans 2:12–16 and 2:25–29 "for theological reflection on the religions."[22] First, from all that Paul says about the concrete situation of the religious life of the "pagans" and Gentiles, it is clear that they can attain saving faith, that is, without explicit faith in Jesus Christ, in whom the mystery of salvation has been achieved by God, at least through "a fundamental option vis-à-vis the Absolute." But that is not all. The religious life of the Gentiles cannot be reduced to some "natural religion." In this regard, he cites a passage from B. Stoeckle:

> It is not right to interpret the peculiarity of the extrabiblical religions vis-à-vis the biblical religion of the Old and New Testament, on the basis of the theoretical-abstract differentiation between natural and supernatural (in the traditional sense) knowledge of God. For creation has an original supernatural destination, inasmuch as it is "designed for Christ"; ... what the pagan religions that are turned to the cosmos are offering of humanly significant values ... is infinitely more than the influence of a "prime mover" indifferent to salvation: here the true grace of Christ, genuine supernatural communication of salvation, is profoundly expressed.[23]

Odasso further observes that in Paul and in the New Testament as a whole, there is a tension between the "yes to the religions" and the "no to the religions." Such a tension is noted in that same Letter to the Romans, between Romans 1:18–31, on the one hand, and Romans 2:12–17 and 25–29, on the other. But such tension is to be understood by keeping in view the fundamental perspective of the New Testament, which proclaims the definitively victorious character of the salvation that God has brought about with the death and resurrection of Christ (cf. Rom 5:12–21). And he rightly concludes his reflections on Romans 2, stating that the picture drawn by Paul makes clear the real possibility of the church engaging in dialogue with the religions. Such dialogue entails reciprocity:

> If the Spirit of Christ is present in the man who seeks the Lord, if the various religions with their way of acting and living, with their precepts and their doctrine, "often reflect a ray of that Truth which enlightens all men" (*Nostra Aetate* §2), it seems that Christians can find in the way in

---

22. Ibid., 329–34.

23. B. Stoeckle, "Die ausserbiblische Menschheit und die Welt-Religionen," in *Mysterium Salutis*, ed. J. Feiner and M. Löhrer (Einsiedeln: Benziger Verlag, 1967), 2:1069–70.

which adherents of other religions profess and live out their religious dimension, questions and experiences that point toward a more enlightened understanding and more genuine testimony to their own faith. (pp. 333–34)

THE UNKNOWN GOD

The preaching to the Gentiles attributed to Paul in Acts, first in Lystra (Acts 14:8–18) and then before the Areopagus in Athens (Acts 17:22–31), attests to the Apostle's attitude of openness to the Gentiles in terms of their "religiosity." In Lystra the Apostle recognized that the paralyzed man who was listening to him "had the faith to be healed," and he healed him (Acts 14:8–11). Speaking of the religion of the Greeks, now superseded by faith in Jesus Christ, he observed: "In past generations he [God] allowed all the nations to follow their own ways; yet he has not left himself without a witness in doing good — giving you rains from heaven and fruitful seasons, and filling you with food and your hearts with joy" (Acts 14:16–17). That all corresponds to God's revelation through the cosmos spoken of in the Letter to the Romans (Rom 1:18–32). The manifestation of God through "nature" is already divine revelation.

Paul's speech in Athens (Acts 17:22–31) is more positive in nature. Here Paul praises the religious spirit of the Greeks, and proclaims to them the "unknown God" whom they adore without knowing him. Whatever the problems raised about this passage — concerning, among other things, whether the speech is of Pauline or Lucan derivation[24] — the message surely seems to be that the religions of the nations are not devoid of their own value, but find in Jesus Christ the fulfillment of their aspirations. They constitute a positive preparation for Christian faith.

"Athenians, I see how extremely religious you are in every way. For as I went through the city and looked carefully at the objects of your worship, I found among them an altar with the inscription, 'To an unknown god.' What therefore you worship as unknown, this I proclaim to you" (Acts 17:22–23). Paul then speaks of the one and only God, who has made the world and all that it contains, who "gives to all mortals life and breath and all things," and "from one ancestor... made all nations to inhabit the whole earth, and... allotted the times of their existence and the boundaries of the places where they would live, so that they would search for God and perhaps grope for him and find him" (Acts 17:25–27). This passage connects with the teaching of Romans 1 about

---

24. Within the vast literature, the following may be mentioned: J. Dupont, "La rencontre entre Christianisme et Hellénisme dans le discours à l'Aréopage," in Commission Biblique Pontificale, *Foi et culture à la lumière de la Bible* (Leuman [Turin]: Elle Di Ci, 1981), 261–86; L. Legrand, "The Missionary Significance of the Areopagus Speech," in *God's Word among Men*, ed. G. Gispert-Sauch (Delhi: Vidyajyoti Institute of Religious Studies, 1974), 59–71; idem, "The Unknown God of Athens: Acts 17 and the Religion of the Gentiles," *Vidyajyoti* 45 (1981): 222–31; idem, "Aratos est-il aussi parmi les prophètes?" in *La Vie de la parole: De l'Ancien au Nouveau Testament: Etudes d'exégese et d'herméneutique bibliques offertes à Pierre Grelot* (Paris: Desclée, 1987), 241–58. In addition, Odasso, *Bibbia e religioni*, 335–55; Song, *Jesus in the Power of the Spirit*, 80–94.

God's self-revelation to all peoples through the cosmos, through which they can recognize him.

Here, however, Paul takes a further step, stating that God is close to every people: "indeed [*kai ghè*] he is not far from each one of us" (Acts 17:27). In confirmation of that statement, Paul refers to an expression suggested by the Greek prophet Ephimenedes (sixth century B.C.E.): "In him we live and move and have our being" and then cites another Greek writer, the poet Arato (third century B.C.E.), who had written: "For we too are his offspring" (Acts 17:28). Beyond any rhetorical device and any appeal to goodwill (*captatio benevolentiae*), this amounts to recognizing in the (Platonic and Stoic) Greek tradition a genuine "search for God." The fact that the dialogue breaks off when Paul speaks of the resurrection of Jesus (Acts 17:32) changes nothing: it does not mean that Paul's approach fails, because Luke adds: "some of them joined him and became believers, including Dionysius the Areopagite and a woman named Damaris, and others with them" (Acts 17:34). As limited as Paul's success may have been in Athens, the speech to the Areopagus begins a missionary strategy based on a positive approach to the religiosity of the Greeks. The perspective on the religion of the Gentiles in Acts 17 presents us a Greek world awaiting the "unknown God" and predisposed to meet him in its poet-theologians.[25]

According to Odasso, the speech in Athens is presented as the "paradigm" of preaching to the Gentiles, and in particular to the cultured stratum of society. The sentence, "What therefore you worship as unknown, this I proclaim to you" (Acts 17:23b), unquestionably has a positive perspective, and its exact function within the speech must be seen correctly. It represents the *propositio* of the speech, i.e., it contains the announcement of the theme that is to be developed in the *probatio*, which extends from v. 24 to v. 29. It is thus the key to the interpretation of the entire speech. The Gentiles worship in a situation of "not-knowing." Such "ignorance" has an essentially religious connotation. It indicates the absence of that "knowledge" which constitutes the experience of God proper to one who lives in the experience of resurrection. Odasso writes: "The church is the communion of the resurrection and revelation. It understands that outside of the light of revelation of the Risen One there is no share in that hope of the resurrection, which is, however, already operating salvifically in the world and in history through the power of the Spirit of him who has raised Jesus from the dead" (p. 347). In the religious depths of their being, human beings can open up to an encounter with the divine world in such an authentic way as to develop an experience of intense spiritual values. But that does not take away the fact that the Christian bears a light of revelation that is enkindled in the human heart only by acceptance of the gospel of God.

Understood in this manner, the speech in the Areopagus offers a contribution of unquestionable importance for the Christian understanding of the religions.

---

25. L. Legrand, "Jésus et l'Eglise primitive: Un éclairage biblique," *Spiritus* 138 (February 1995): 64–77; cf. 75–76.

First of all, the text makes it possible to comprehend the positive value of human religious experience. The "search" for God is already a gift of God. God reveals himself by being sought. Such seeking is not situated at the level of philosophy, but connotes an experience of faith. Moreover, as eminently noted by Karl Rahner,[26] the religious experience is lived within a religion, from which it may be conceptually distinct, but not separated in reality. The speech does not ignore the limits, or even the possible partial deviations, in the religious lives of others, and of the religions themselves; indeed, it views the religions in a perspective of incompleteness at an even deeper level, that is, at the level of faith in the risen Lord whom the church is charged with proclaiming. The church — which can never be identified with the Reign of God present in the world — is called to give witness to that presence of the Reign through the proclamation of the "gospel" of the risen Lord. It is also called to discern in the Spirit the gospel values, the seeds "of truth and grace" (*Ad Gentes* §9), present in the religious journey of humankind and in the religious traditions of peoples.

GOD SHOWS NO PARTIALITY

The Petrine cycle of the book of the Acts of the Apostles also reports an incident in which Peter — like Paul — had to learn to cross beyond the boundaries of his own religious tradition. It is the complex episode of Peter who is called to preach to the family of Cornelius, the centurion in Caesarea (Acts 10:1–11, 18). Like Paul, Peter had to run up against the culture and the religion of the people who were calling him to listen to him. Luke notes at the outset that Cornelius was "a devout man who feared God with all his household; he gave alms generously to the people and prayed constantly to God" (Acts 10:2). Such a laudable religious attitude on the part of a "centurion of the Italic Cohort" could not but raise the issue of the value of the religious life of the "pagans." However, the difference is not only of religion but of culture. Peter had to learn, contrary to his own tradition, that it is not up to the members of one ethnic or religious group to declare the customs of the "others" profane and unclean. It makes Peter understand the strange vision that he had before being sought by the centurion. "What God has made clean, you must not call profane" (Acts 10:15). Who decides which food is clean or profane? Is it a matter for tradition, community, or religious authority? Nothing of the sort. Rather it is up to God, the God who has created heaven and earth (cf. Gen 1:1). Peter must have slowly understood that the vision that he received from heaven was about the Roman centurion who was inviting him. And likewise, the animals that he was calling impure and profane, were they not connected with the Gentiles? How could he call the Gentiles profane when they are people whom God calls pure? Peter had to reflect at length during his journey. In any case, upon arriving at his host's, he declared, "You yourselves know that it is unlawful for a Jew to

---

26. K. Rahner, "Christianity and the Non-Christian Religions," in *Theological Investigations* (London: Darton, Longman & Todd, 1966), 5:115–34.

associate with or to visit a Gentile; but God has shown me that I should not call anyone profane or unclean" (Acts 10:28). Peter thus crossed over the border of his own Judaism and entered into the territory of God where all peoples are considered pure, including Cornelius, the Roman centurion and his family. Once the border had been crossed, Peter saw things from a different perspective. At the beginning of his speech to the family of Cornelius, he declared, "I truly understand that God shows no partiality, but in every nation anyone who fears him and does what is right is acceptable to him" (Acts 10:34–35). Luke deliberately makes explicit on Peter's lips the principle already stated in Deuteronomy (Deut 10:17), which, as already noted, Paul had used in the Letter to the Romans: "God shows no partiality" (Rom 2:11). Obviously, such a principle serves the apostolic church as its primary guide for going beyond any border built by humans and by their traditions, so as to enter into the territory of God, in his thinking by which all humans and people are equal, all equally created by him and intended for the same destiny. The various kinds of differences, whether ethnic, cultural, or religious, are of less weight than the origin and common destiny of all in God. What has precedence is the justice of a "God-fearing" man (Acts 10:22).

Obviously this episode, like those recalled earlier where Paul was the main character, helps us to value the journey that the entire apostolic church had to make — not without hard work — to open up to a positive attitude toward the religious life of the Gentiles and their religious traditions. C. S. Song comments as follows:

> No more those religious conditions of salvation stipulated by one's own religion! No more division of the world into the sacred and the profane, and no more separation of people into the clean and the unclean! As to God, there is only one God who cares for all people regardless of where they are from, who and what they are. "In the question of salvation," in short, "God does not unjustly prefer one nation to another." Should not much of Christian theology, and certainly most of missiology, have to be rewritten on the basis of this *theo*-logical reorientation experienced by Peter?[27]

In these stories — that of the Canaanite woman in the region of Tyre and Sidon, that of the speech to the Areopagus in Athens, finally that of the centurion Cornelius — the Gentiles became the occasion for Paul, for Peter, and for Jesus himself, to cross the borders of truth and salvation and enter the territory of God by whom all are created and saved in Jesus Christ. Once the border has been crossed they are constrained to recognize that God through his Spirit is present and at work everywhere in the world, outside of the community as well as within it.

---

27. Song, *Jesus in the Power of the Spirit*, 98.

GOD DESIRES EVERYONE TO BE SAVED

Everything that has been written thus far shows that in the thought of the Jesus of history and in the theology of the early apostolic church are found secure data on which to construct a positive assessment of the religious life of the Gentiles and pagans, and a theology open to the religious traditions to which they adhere. Such a positive attitude toward the "others," however, does not in any way require that the central affirmation of New Testament and Christian faith about the constitutive uniqueness of Jesus Christ as universal Savior of humankind be softened down. But even though that affirmation of faith is not called into question, it must be interpreted correctly, according to criteria of exegesis and history in the historic context of the apostolic church, as well as in the contemporary context. That is what remains to be shown.

The New Testament affirmation of the uniqueness of the man Christ as the "way" (Jn 14:6), the "one mediator" (1 Tim 2:5), and "only name" (Acts 4:12), in whom human beings can find salvation, should not be understood in a way that leads to an exclusivist theology of salvation. The affirmation is neither absolute nor relative; it should be integrated into the entirety of the biblical message and interpreted in context. In short, far from contradicting religious pluralism, faith in Jesus Christ requires acceptance and openness in dealing with it.

With great narrative skill, the evangelist Luke has shown the conflictive story within the Jewish religious community, which began with the ministry of Jesus and continued in the ministry of his disciples after his death and resurrection. Jesus' ministry was intended to revitalize the true spirit of the religion that Jesus shared with his people and to inspire a new vision of God's saving activity, not only in his own religious world, but in the outside religious world as well. In Peter's speech to the Sanhedrin, made up of priests, scribes, and elders, Luke has Peter say: "There is salvation in no one else, for there is no other name under heaven given among mortals by which we must be saved" (Acts 4:12). This proclamation by Peter, taken out of context, has become the *textus classicus* for those Christians who claim that unless one be converted to Christ and become a member of the Christian community, he or she cannot be saved. Is it not possible that such a claim contradicts what Jesus himself understood during his entire life and in his ministry? Does it not perhaps undervalue what the other religions have done for people who live outside the influence of Christianity? The problem lies in the fact that what Peter says in his speech to the Sanhedrin has been understood as a timeless truth detached from its historic context. In fact, however, the text is abused if it is used as a springboard for a negative judgment on the religions.[28]

It is likewise abused if it is brought in to help defend and support proselytizing activity by Christianity. As C. S. Song says in this connection:

---

28. Acts 4:12 cannot be isolated in Lucan theology from complementary texts, especially Acts 17:22–34, where Paul displays a very positive attitude toward Greek religiosity. See H. Flender, *St. Luke, Theologian of Redemptive History* (London: SPCK, 1967), on the complementary texts ("doublets") which are interpreted in tandem in Lucan theology and cannot be understood separately.

the fact of the matter is that Peter and the other apostles are engaged in neither interreligious dialogue nor Christian proselytism in this particular instance. What we have in this story is certain Jews speaking to other Jews. Here the addressees are Jews, and in [Acts] chapter 4 they are most specifically the Temple authorities. This immediate context of the text in question has to be borne clearly in mind if we are to understand what Peter meant by what he said.[29]

The context is inter-Judaic or intra-Judaic. It is about knowing "by what power" the disciples claimed to have performed such a miracle. Such power certainly does not belong to them; it belongs to God alone. This observation has important implications for anyone wishing to draw critical reflections on the nature of Christian faith and for an honest Christian appraisal of the other religious traditions. If the statement attributed to Peter by Luke in an internal Jewish setting is applied in a non-Jewish setting, the result is an interpretation that violates the biblical text. In the context of Acts 4, the "debate" is exclusively among Jews. It is not any sort of tension between Jews and Christians, but rather a tension between the Jewish religious establishment and the people. Hence, the text may not be abused in order to claim for Christianity absolute and exclusive access to divine salvation. In other words,

> The confrontation between the religious authorities and the apostles at the council is a confrontation between the religious establishment and the people outside it, between those who hold religious power and those under that power, between the rulers and the ruled, between the privileged class and the underprivileged class. This completely changes the focus of the story from the image of Jesus as the sole and only savior created by the Christian church to that of Jesus as friend of sinners and bringer of hope and future to the poor and the oppressed, an image that stands out distinctly in the Synoptic Gospels.[30]

C. S. Song concludes: If this is true, those Christians who use the "no-other-name" text to assert the supreme role of the Christian church in the salvation of humankind and those who reject it as too restricted and exclusive are both in error. Both have failed to understand the central focal point of the story. What emerges powerfully in Luke's account is an internal Jewish conflict that is at once political and religious. "By what power," asked the high priest, "or by what name did you do this?" (Acts 4:7). We must keep in mind the political nature of the religious confrontation between the apostles and the religious authority. For Peter and the other apostles, there is only one name in the entire Jewish nation, past, present, and future, that can perform healing miracles, restore the true spirit of the Jewish religion, and give hope to the suffering people. That name is Jesus. In the initial period after the death and resurrection of Jesus, the apostles still

---

29. Song, *Jesus in the Power of the Spirit,* 244.
30. Ibid., 245.

speak and act as members of the Jewish religious community, as Jesus himself had done during his life and ministry. They are not yet "Christians," in the sense of feeling that they are consciously members of a Christian church, detached from Judaism. They are followers of Jesus who have received from the Spirit the power to continue his ministry in the midst of their people. In short, in the Lucan story, Peter is telling the religious leaders within the Judaic setting that "there is salvation in no one else," that "there is no other name under heaven given" to us *Jews,* in which it is established that we can be saved (Acts 4:12). In his witness to the Sanhedrin, Peter has not invented a Christian "no-other-name" theology. Such a theology goes back to the Christian church well after the time of Jesus. Jesus himself would have disassociated himself from it, if understood absolutely and exclusively. He would not have liked to hear his name used against people of another faith; nor would he have liked to hear his name invoked against founders and believers of other religious faiths. In short, such a theology, often understood by the Christian churches in an exclusive and absolute sense, does not do justice to Jesus' ministry of the Reign of God, which recognized the positive value in God's eyes of the religious experience of others and of the religious traditions in which they lived their faith in the God of the Reign and of life.

It should not be concluded — erroneously — that the apostolic church did not affirm the constitutive uniqueness of Jesus Christ in the order of salvation. But it should be seen clearly where and in what terms that affirmation of faith was made by the apostolic church, in terms of different contexts and in any case avoiding any tendency to exclusivism. The First Letter to Timothy is a clear testimony of a mature affirmation by the apostolic church of the irreplaceable role of the risen Christ in the order of salvation for all humankind. The text recommends to the Christian community liturgical prayer "for everyone, for kings and all who are in high positions" (1 Tim 2:1–2). It continues: "This is right and is acceptable in the sight of God our Savior, who desires everyone to be saved and to come to the knowledge of the truth. For there is one God; there is also one mediator between God and humankind, Christ Jesus, himself human, who gave himself a ransom for all" (1 Tim 2:3–5).

Some observations should be made about the exact meaning of the "mediation" attributed by the apostolic faith to the risen Jesus, as it appears in that text. First of all, it is apparent that while the man Christ Jesus is called "mediator," the one who is "our Savior" remains the God who is beyond the risen Christ, as primary and ultimate source of the salvation of humankind. Jesus Christ does not replace the Father. Just as throughout his entire life and earthly ministry he was completely "related" to the Father, directed toward him and centered on him, so also his function as mediator, newly received from the Father in his resurrection, makes his bond with his Father one of total dependence and relationship. The universal "saving will" toward all humankind is attributed not to the risen Christ but to God. That universal divine will is the "absolute" element that constitutes the salvation of the world; it is the focal point for a correct understanding of the affirmation of faith in human salvation. Underlying that affirmation of universality is the basic principle, already affirmed in the Old Testament, of God's nonpartiality (Deut 10:17), and emphasized by Peter in his witness to the centurion Cornelius: "God has no favorites" (Acts 10:34) and by Paul in the Letter to the Romans: "God shows no partiality" (Rom 2:11). For both apostles that principle served as a foundation for their recognition of the operative presence of divine salvation beyond the boundaries of their own people and their own religion. The "mediation" of the risen Christ, highlighted in 1 Timothy, far from contradicting that affirmation, confirms it and assumes it.

In this regard, the text notes that the mediating function of the risen Christ is based on God's universal will of salvation. It is, so to speak, its concrete and visible expression, its sacrament: indeed, it represents the testimony given by God himself to human beings of the seriousness of his saving design. God efficaciously wills the salvation of all men. It is what shows through the relationship between the divine will and the mediation of Christ, as is indicated by the use of the preposition *gar:* God "desires everyone to be saved ... *For* there is only one God; there is also one mediator between God and humankind" (1 Tim 2:5). The constitutive uniqueness of Jesus Christ, universal mediator of salvation, does not nullify anything that is affirmed positively in the New Testament, with regard to the Jesus of history and the apostolic church, about the religious life and the religious traditions of others. Indeed it explains that the effectiveness of salvation, already operative within them, is due to the universal and effective presence of the risen Christ, become "transhistoric" through the paschal mystery of his death and resurrection. Any exclusivist interpretation of the mediation of Christ that would exclude and deny any positive value of other saving figures and of the world's other religious traditions would have no biblical or theological basis.

Similar observations would have to be made about other New Testament passages in which the constitutive uniqueness of Jesus Christ as universal mediator of salvation is affirmed. One such case is the passage where John's gospel has Jesus say: "I am the way, and the truth, and the life. No one comes to the Father except through me" (Jn 14:6). The mediation of Jesus Christ as "the way" to the Father does not mean that other religious traditions cannot offer their adherents "paths" of salvation through which the constitutive way of Jesus Christ might be operative, albeit in secret and imperfectly; nor that the founders and saving figures of other religious traditions cannot serve in an unconscious and incomplete way as "pointers" toward the salvation realized in him who is personally constituted by God as the only way to him. Christ's sole mediation does not stand in the way of the "participated mediations" — about which more will be said later — present and operative in other traditions, which derive their meaning and their saving power from Christ.

That is also why the "great commission" or the "universal mission" entrusted by the risen Christ to the incipient church is not to be understood in an exclusivist sense, as though anyone who has not heard the gospel of Jesus Christ and has not followed him would be beyond salvation. The gospel texts and those of Acts (Mt 12:18–20; Mk 16:15–18; Lk 24:47–49; Jn 20:21–23; Acts 1:8) do not understand it in that sense. It should be noted that the various texts emphasize different aspects of the mission entrusted to the disciples: in Luke it is about "giving witness" (*marturein*) (Lk 24:48; Acts 1:8); in John about "forgiving sins" (Jn 20:23); in the "conclusion of Mark" about "proclaiming the gospel (*kèrusein to euanggelion*) to every creature" (Mk 16:15). The next line reads: "The one who believes and is baptized will be saved; but the one who does not believe will be condemned" (Mk 16:16). It does not say that there is no salvation without baptism, but that there is none without faith. In Matthew, according to an exact translation of the text, it is about "making disciples (*mathèteuein*) among all nations, baptizing them [the disciples, not the nations]...[and] teaching them..." (Mt 28:19–20). A certain caution is called for in interpreting this text, at least in drawing theological conclusions about the specific need of baptism for all for salvation. What is absolutely required for salvation is faith, and such faith is understood as faith in the God of life and of the Reign of God; explicit faith in Jesus Christ is an extra gift from God. The former belongs to the *esse* of salvation; the latter to its *bene esse*. The former is at work in anticipation of the latter, toward which it remains constitutively directed. Otherwise, the gospel of Jesus Christ would not be, nor could it be, "good news" for all.

By way of conclusion it will suffice to make some important observations on how the biblical message should — and should not — be read and understood with regard to the world religions in the thought of the Jesus of history and of the early church.

A first observation is that we should refrain from a directly and exclusively "Christian" reading of the gospel, as if everything said and done by Jesus had to do solely with "Christians." Such a reading would seriously err out of a lack of historical perspective and would be guilty of anachronism. A clear case of such an exclusively Christian reading — one referred to earlier — is that of the sermon on the mount, and the beatitudes in particular. They are not to be understood solely as the charter of the Christian life which has nothing to do with others, but rather as the charter of the Reign of God, open to all, independently of their own religious obedience, and of which all can become truly members through faith and conversion to God.

A second and equally important observation has to do with the need to refrain from any reading that tends toward exclusivism where the biblical statements are made affirmatively, not exclusively. To say that the Christian church founded on Jesus has an irreplaceable function vis-à-vis the Reign of God and salvation in Christ does not mean that it has a monopoly on salvation and grace. To say that Jesus Christ is the only mediator between God and human beings does not necessarily lead to the conclusion that there are no saving values and seeds "of truth and grace" (*Ad Gentes* §9) outside of him, even possibly "participated mediations" connected to his mediation. Christian theology has often been guilty of interpreting in an exclusivist sense biblical claims made affirmatively, but not exclusively. The irreplaceable role of the church in salvation became, in the hands of theologians and even in official church teaching, the exclusion of any possibility of salvation outside of it: *Extra ecclesiam nulla salus*. Such an inflation of the true meaning of the affirmations of faith has done great harm to relations between Christians and the other religious traditions, and indeed to the Christian message itself.

A third observation has to do more directly with how to interpret the biblical data on the life and religious experience of others and on the value of their religious traditions. There is a tendency, present even today in theological discussion of the religions, to reduce a priori to the gifts of "nature," that is, to some "natural" knowledge of God innate in humans themselves and to an instinctive "natural law" imprinted on them, the "supernatural" gifts granted to them by the God of life, truth, and grace. An example mentioned earlier is that of the "law written on the hearts" of the "pagans" and the Gentiles, according to Paul's letter to the Romans. Such reductionism still continues to affect very negatively the assessment made of other religious traditions and of their significance in the divine plan for humankind. In a statement borrowed from G. Odasso, such a biased attitude prevents theology and theologians from recognizing the true nature of the religious traditions of the world as "gifts of God" to all peoples of the earth. In concluding his inquiry into the "biblical perspectives on the theology of the religions," he writes:

> That the religions are so many expressions of God's design is by now established, indeed because as can be seen from the perspective disclosed by the texts of the Old and New Testament, they are on earth *a gift of God to all peoples,* and therefore, a sign of the salvifically operative presence of Wisdom. Hence, the religions, as expressions of the divine design, are necessarily related to the resurrection of Christ, precisely because the resurrection represents the ultimate fulfillment of God's saving design. (Emphasis added)[31]

---

31. Odasso, *Bibbia e religioni,* 372.

Chapter Two

AT THE CROSSROADS
OF VATICAN II

A s WE SAID in the introduction to the book, at this point we are making a huge leap from the first century to the twentieth. We have indicated in a nutshell the development of the concrete attitudes toward other religious traditions and the theological assessment of them, with high and low points, that have typified most of the church's history. We now want to come closer to the present. As everyone knows, Vatican II has been the most important doctrinal event of the past century in the life of the Catholic Church. However, the council did not drop down from heaven without preparation and without noteworthy effort by theologians. The aim in this chapter is to situate this event that is providential for the future of the church in its historic context. To what extent was the council prepared by movements of exegetical, patristic, theological, and liturgical renewal, particularly with regard to other religions? What theology of the religions was being proposed by Catholic theologians during the decades preceding the council event? What is the exact significance of the assertion made by the council on the significance of the religious traditions? How is it to be interpreted and assessed in an objectively correct way? What has been the echo of the council's teaching on the church's official doctrine since the council event? More than thirty years after the council, what acceptance has that doctrine had in the real life of the church and in the theology of the religions that is being elaborated in recent years? These questions must be examined closely before we can turn to the current state of theological discussion on the matter, in the next chapter.

We have said, albeit rapidly, that for centuries the theological perspective on the religions had to do with the possibility of individual salvation of people who have not heard or received the Christian message. During the period under examination here the picture is enlarged into a consideration of the religions themselves as they relate to Christianity. In the next chapter, it will be noted that in theological consideration of the religions, a distinction into three main paradigms has by now become classic: exclusivism (or ecclesiocentrism), inclusivism (or Christocentrism), and so-called "pluralism" (or theocentrism). With regard to the preconciliar Catholic theology of the religions taken up in this chapter, it can calmly be said that almost all of it is covered by the umbrella of inclusivism. This does not mean that no Catholic theologian is endorsing the paradigm of exclusivism, more or less inspired by the "dialectical theology" of K. Barth, for whom other religions are nothing but idolatrous human attempts at self-justification, whereas only faith in Jesus Christ is able to save. But those who do are the rare exceptions that confirm the rule. Exclusivism, however, remains rather widespread among "evangelical" Protestant groups.

The vast majority of Catholic theologians at that time acknowledged a positive relationship between the other religions and Christianity. They wondered, as an ancient tradition had suggested, whether these religions could still be regarded — to use Eusebius's expression — as a "gospel preparation" (*praeparatio evangelica*) and, if so, in what sense? Far from being an obstacle to faith, could the religions be seen as something that could open people to God's revelation in Jesus Christ? Did they bear within themselves the expression of an innate desire of the human person to be united to God, and did they constitute, as it were, a "stepping stone" toward the Christian revelation — *anima naturaliter christiana*, in Tertullian's phrase? In short, did they have the same relationship to Christianity that nature has to the supernatural, by which nature is not destroyed but perfected (*gratia non destruit sed perficit naturam*)? The relationship of "potency" to "act"? Of aspiration to fulfillment? Of shadow to reality?

Others wondered, moreover, whether the religions did not themselves make a contribution — but what? — to the mystery of salvation of their members in Jesus Christ. Were those who were saved in Jesus Christ saved inside or outside of their religions? Despite them — or in some mysterious manner by virtue of them? What positive role do the other religions perform now — if they do so — within the mystery of the salvation of their adherents in Jesus Christ? Could they ultimately be called "means" or "ways" of salvation? And if so, in what sense? Was there "salvation without the gospel"?

These are powerful questions that began to occupy the attention of theologians during the precouncil period and would continue to interest them even afterwards, until an even broader perspective would open to them in more recent years, in what we have called the "perspective of religious pluralism." Solutions entailing the possibility of a positive relationship between the other religions and Christianity, and possibly a positive role of the religions in the mystery of the salvation of their adherents, were quite varied, however. At the cost of some simplification, the various positions may be grouped in two categories, representing in effect two contrasting perspectives.

On one side stood those for whom the various religions of humankind represented the innate desire of the human being to be united to the Divine, a desire present through various expressions in the diverse cultures and geographical areas of the world. In this perspective, Jesus Christ and Christianity denote in turn God's personal response to this universal human aspiration. Whereas all religions are simply varied expressions of *homo naturaliter religiosus* and hence of "natural religion," Christianity as divine response to the human search for God constitutes the only "supernatural religion." This first position is often called the "fulfillment theory." According to this theory, salvation in Jesus Christ reaches members of other religions as a divine response to the human religious aspirations expressed by every person through his or her own tradition; in themselves, such religious traditions do not play any role in this mystery of salvation.

According to the other position, by contrast, the various religions of humankind in themselves represent specific albeit initial interventions by God in the history of salvation. These divine interventions in history, however, are ordered to the decisive saving event in Jesus Christ. In that sense, they have played a positive role before the Christ event as *praeparatio evangelica;* they still retain a positive value in the order of salvation by virtue of the active presence in them, and in some way through them, of the saving mystery of Jesus Christ. This second theory may be designated, for want of a better expression, as the "theory of the presence of Christ in the religions" or of the "inclusive presence of Christ." The saving mystery is certainly unique. But all the other religious traditions are placed in relationship to that mystery by virtue of the divine saving design of which they form part; each in its own way is ordered to that mystery or is a providential preparation for it. Thus, no religion is purely natural. In every religion a divine intervention in the history of the nations can be found historically, and an existential presence of the mystery of salvation in Jesus Christ is recognizable. All religions are accordingly supernatural for more than one reason.

As is clear from the labels assigned to the two positions representative of preconciliar Catholic theology, the debate has shifted from the primarily ecclesiological question of salvation inside or outside the church to that of conscious or unconscious salvation in Jesus Christ in the real situation of people in their own religious tradition, that is, from a primarily ecclesiocentric viewpoint to a more distinctly Christocentric viewpoint. The immediate question is no longer what happens to those outside the "ark of salvation," i.e., the church, but how Jesus Christ and his mystery reach those who do not know him.

The chapter will be made up of three main parts. The first part tells of the presence in preconciliar theology of the "fulfillment" theory, and of that of the "inclusive presence of Christ." The second part examines the council doctrine on the value of the religious traditions. The third part follows the council doctrine in the postconciliar magisterium to examine its "reception" and subsequent developments.

PRE-VATICAN II THEOLOGY OF THE RELIGIONS

FULFILLMENT THEORY: THE BINARY DANIÉLOU–DE LUBAC

Jean Daniélou may be regarded as the first Western exponent of the "fulfillment theory." From the early 1940s into the 1970s he wrote extensively on the topic.[1]

---

1. Cf. J. Daniélou, *The Salvation of the Nations* (Notre Dame, Ind.: University of Notre Dame Press, 1962); *The Advent of Salvation* (New York: Paulist Press, 1962); *The Lord of History: Reflections on the Inner Meaning of History* (London: Longmans, Green, 1958); *Holy Pagans in the Old Testament*

The standpoint from which he looks at the religious traditions of the world is unquestionably that of God's design for the salvation of humankind in Jesus Christ as it is understood by Christian faith. In this context, Daniélou asks what Christianity may have to say about the religions that it has encountered in the past and that it continues to encounter ever more frequently in modern times. One leading thread of his thought is a theology of history as gradual manifestation of God to humankind. Salvation history properly speaking is limited, according to Daniélou, to the Judeo-Christian tradition: it starts with God's personal revelation to Israel through Abraham and Moses, runs through the whole history of the chosen people, and culminates in Jesus Christ, whose message of salvation has been entrusted to the church. Everything that precedes God's personal manifestation in history, even though already inscribed in God's one design for humankind, may be defined at best as a "prehistory" of salvation. The term "prehistory" is also applicable to any religious experience that can be found today outside the Judeo-Christian tradition, in the religions of the world. What then is the exact significance and value of the religions of the world? In what sense do they represent a "preparation for the gospel"?

Daniélou draws a sharp distinction between nature and the supernatural, or equivalently, between religion and revelation. "Non-Christian" religions belong to the order of natural reason, Judeo-Christian revelation to that of supernatural faith. They are different orders. The "cosmic" covenant is equivalent to God's manifestation through nature, even though in the concrete (supernatural) order of reality it is already ordered to God's personal manifestation in history. The cosmic covenant manifests God's ongoing presence in creation and it is symbolized in the story in Genesis of Noah and the rainbow, sign of the "everlasting covenant between God and every living creature of all flesh that is on earth" (Gen 9:8–17; cf. v. 16).

It is this faithfulness of God in the course of nature that Paul had in mind when he wrote in the Letter to the Romans that through nature God had manifested himself to all human beings, as creator of all things (Rom 1:19–20). Paul added, as a sweeping statement, that human beings were to blame for not having recognized God in the things created by him (Rom 1:20–21). They fell victims to polytheism and idolatry. Daniélou sees described here the situation of those who find themselves in non-Christian religions. The knowledge of God accessible to them is that of the order of nature, whether it reaches them through the created world or through the voice of personal conscience. Insofar as they have recognized God as creator, they have acquired a valid natural knowledge of him; insofar, however, as they have not recognized their Creator, their minds have been darkened and have become godless. In the first case, they have known God, even though their knowledge has remained limited to the order of nature;

(London: Longmans, Green, 1957); *Gospel Message and Hellenistic Culture* (Philadelphia: Westminster Press, 1973); *The Faith Eternal and the Man of Today* (Chicago: Franciscan Herald, 1970).

in the opposite case, they have "exchanged the glory of the immortal God for images resembling a mortal human being..." (Rom 1:23).

The religions of the world, as we know them historically, are thus a mixture of truth and falsehood, of light and darkness, of upright conduct and evil ways. They belong to the order of "cosmic religion," representing what is proper to the "cosmic covenant." This covenant, albeit part of God's design for humankind and the world, serves only as the substratum for God's personal revelation in history. It represents the "prehistory" of salvation. There is a certain continuity between the cosmic and the historic covenant insofar as the former functions as the necessary basis for the latter; but God's free intervention in history inaugurates a new order, which produces a discontinuity even greater than the continuity.

No doubt some of those who lived under the regime of the cosmic covenant were "pleasing to God"; that much is proven by the "holy pagans" recorded by the Old Testament[2] whose faith is celebrated in the Letter to the Hebrews (Heb 11). The Bible does not say how many there were, but the Old Testament and Paul in Romans eloquently describe the evil customs into which the nations fell. Be that as it may, if there may be found in the religions of the world a "preparation for the gospel" it occurs at best as in the form of a "substratum" within nature of God's personal commitment to humankind in the history of Israel, and finally in the event of Jesus Christ, the summit of salvation history.

In any case, "cosmic" religions — a term used for all the religions in the world, except the three "monotheistic" religions: Judaism, Christianity, and Islam — are nothing but human elaborations of a knowledge of God obtained through the order of nature. As such, they were unable in the past, and are still unable today, to lead to saving faith, which can come only through God's gracious intervention in people's lives. In themselves, they have no saving power; at best they represent various expressions within different cultures of the aspiration of the human person for an Absolute Being. Indeed, in the realm of salvation history, they have become "doubly anachronistic," superseded as they have been first by Judaism, and then even more definitively by the Christ event and Christianity. They are "outmoded survivals" of a bygone period of history. "Theirs is a sin of persistence."[3] In short, they are "natural religions," as opposed to Christianity, the only "supernatural religion," which (contrary to Judaism) still retains its saving validity. Christianity is the universal means of salvation; it is also the normative way. If salvation is possible for "non-Christians" outside the church, that is always in any case a "limit situation" from which no consequence for a positive role of the "non-Christian" religions in the order of salvation may be deduced.

A quote from Daniélou himself may be useful for summarizing the matter. On the uniqueness of Christianity, he writes:

2. Cf. Daniélou, *Holy Pagans in the Old Testament.*
3. Cf. D. Veliath, *Theological Approaches and Understanding of Religions: Jean Daniélou and Raimundo Panikkar: A Study in Contrast* (Bangalore: Kristu Jyoti College, 1988), 76.

Christianity does not consist in the strivings of men after God, but in the power of God, accomplishing in man that which is beyond the power of man; human efforts are merely the response called forth by the divine initiative. This, then, is the second mark of the transcendence of Christianity.

Here we put our finger on the essential distinction, the specific element of Christianity, the ultimate reason of its unique transcendence: it is Jesus Christ, Son of God, our Savior. The religions of nature bear witness (and this is the measure of their real worth) to the natural tendency of man towards God: Christianity is God's approach towards man in Jesus Christ, taking possession of man to bring him to himself.[4]

The fulfillment theory proposed by Daniélou exercised a profound influence. As will be seen later, the "Daniélou tendency" has had a significant impact on the magisterium of the church, and it is still found in some post–Vatican II documents.

Henri de Lubac came to the theology of religions through studies comparing some "aspects of Buddhism" and Christianity. In those studies, not without sympathy but with great lucidity and with no complacency, he pointed to two apparently irreconcilable conceptions of the path of the human person toward liberation within two different worldviews.[5] Early in his career, de Lubac had published works on the mystery of the supernatural — first a historic study of tradition, and then a systematic monograph.[6] These studies had prepared him for comparing Christianity and the other religions and to highlight the singularity and uniqueness of the former over the latter, both in terms of doctrine and mysticism.

As early as his classic study, *Catholicism,* de Lubac had written of the "absolute newness" that Christianity represented in the religious history of humankind:

> Christianity brought into the world something absolutely new. Its concept of salvation is not only original in relation to that of the religions that surrounded its birth; it constitutes a unique event in the religious history of humankind... In this universal concert of religions Christianity alone affirms, at once and indissolubly, a transcendent destiny of the human person and for the whole of humankind a common destiny. For this destiny the entire history of the world is a preparation. From the first creation down to the final consummation... a unique divine project is being fulfilled.[7]

As was already the case with Daniélou, so for de Lubac the relationship between the world religions and Christianity follows the structure that distinguishes — without separating them — nature and the supernatural. The

---

4. Daniélou, *The Lord of History,* 115–16, 118–19.

5. H. de Lubac, *Aspects du Bouddhisme,* 2 vols. (Paris: Seuil, 1951–55); idem, *La rencontre du Bouddhisme et de l'Occident* (Paris: Aubier, 1952).

6. H. de Lubac, *Surnaturel: Etudes historiques* (Paris: Aubier, 1946); idem, *The Mystery of the Supernatural* (London: G. Chapman, 1967).

7. H. de Lubac, *Catholicisme: Les aspects sociaux du dogme* (Paris: Le Cerf, 1952), 107–10.

supernatural, while absolutely gratuitous on God's part, satisfies the natural desire of the human person to be united with the Divine. Both are intimately united in Jesus Christ. In him and through him, the supernatural does not replace nature, but informs it and transforms it. The same is true of the relationship between the world religions and Christianity. Nor is there here competition between one and the others. As incarnation of God's grace in Jesus Christ, Christianity is *the* supernatural religion. It does not thereby follow that the other religions are without any truth and goodness: indeed grace "does not destroy nature." Nevertheless, just as human nature is both created and sinful, the world religions simultaneously contain "seeds of the Word" and spurious elements, traces of God and traces of sin. Without competing with them, Christianity unveils their positive values; by assuming them, it purifies and transforms them.[8]

The relationship between Christianity and the world religions and in particular the way in which salvation in Jesus Christ reaches "non-Christians" are set forth in a short chapter in his book *Paradoxe et mystère de l'Eglise.*[9] According to the "fulfillment theory" that de Lubac makes his own, the mystery of Christ reaches the members of other religious traditions as the divine response to the human aspiration for union with the Divine, but the religious traditions in themselves do not play any role in this mystery of salvation. De Lubac explains that to attribute to them a positive saving role would amount to placing them in competition with Christianity, thereby obscuring the uniqueness of the latter. Citing Pierre Teilhard de Chardin, he observes that the divine design cannot but be an ordered design: it must have an "axis," a single pole. This pole is Christianity, the only way of salvation. To attribute to other traditions a positive role in the mystery of the salvation of their members would in fact mean making them parallel ways of salvation, thereby destroying the unity of the divine design (pp. 148–49). De Lubac writes:

> If there exist objectively several ways of salvation which run as it were parallel, we are faced with a scattering, no longer with a spiritual convergence. What is then unduly called a "divine plan" lacks unity. There ought to be a single axis ... If, in accordance with the design of God, we care for the salvation of humankind, if we believe in the reality of its history and aspire

---

8. As early as *Le fondement théologique des missions* (Paris: Seuil, 1946), de Lubac wrote: "In the many diverse religions ... a similar trend emerges, a similar yearning is expressed which, under the divine light, we are able to discern. Borrowing the language of the Bible and the fathers of the church, we may say that every soul is naturally Christian. Not in the sense that it would already possess an equivalent or, as it were, a first 'stage' of Christianity, but because in the depth of that soul the image of God is shining, or rather, because the soul itself is that image; and, longing as it is to be reunited with its Model, it can be so united only through Christ. If Christianity is destined to be the religion of the world, if, being truly supernatural, it transcends all human endeavor, it must also gather in itself the human longing of the whole world" (71–72). And he added in a note: "Christianity does not come to add something to the human religions, except as the solution adds to the problem, or the goal to the race ... It comes to straighten out [the human religious endeavor], to purify it, to transform it so that it may reach its goal. Christianity is the religion that effectively unites man to God" (n. 1).

9. H. de Lubac, *Paradoxe et mystère de l'Eglise* (Paris: Aubier-Montaigne, 1967). Cf. the chapter entitled "Les religions humaines d'apres les Pères," 120–63.

to unity, we cannot escape looking for an axis and a drawing and unifying force which is the Spirit of the Lord that animates the Church.

In response to de Lubac we may nevertheless observe that if the unity of the divine design indeed calls for a single pole, that is not primarily — according to Teilhard de Chardin himself — Christianity as such or the church, but Jesus Christ. The Teilhardian conception is unequivocally Christocentric: the church is the portion of the world that is "reflexively Christified,"[10] while the eschatological fulfillment of the Reign of God will consist in the universal Christification of all things.[11] A single citation will suffice to show that Teilhard regards a Christified universe as the end point of cosmic evolution. He writes:

> Christ . . . is the alpha and omega, the principle and the end, the foundation stone and the keystone, the Plenitude and the Plenifier. He is the one who consummates all things and gives them their consistence. It is towards him and through him, the inner life and light of the world, that the universal convergence of all created spirit is effected in sweat and tears. He is the single center, precious and consistent, who glitters at the summit that is to crown the world.[12]

It may be doubted whether attributing to other religious traditions a positive role in the salvation of their adherents necessarily pits them against Christ and the religion founded by him: could there not exist various nonparallel modalities of mediation of the mystery of salvation, all in relation to the mystery of Jesus Christ? In any case, it is certain that for the fulfillment theory there is no salvation without the gospel, nor anything like an "anonymous Christianity," which is discussed below. It is also true that the "fulfillment theory" model proposed by de Lubac has exercised a significant influence on theology and on the magisterium of the church. There will be occasion further ahead to find some expressions that he used about the other religions right in the documents of Vatican II.

THE INCLUSIVE PRESENCE OF CHRIST: THE DIVERGENCE BETWEEN RAHNER AND PANIKKAR

The distance between the "fulfillment theory" and the theory of the "presence of the mystery of Christ" in other religious traditions is indeed substantial. The former is built on dichotomies that are understood to be insuperable, such as that between the human and the divine, the impersonal and the personal, the pretension of human self-liberation and the salvation granted by God. The latter, while distinguishing these contrasting elements, refuses to separate nature from grace. Its aim is to transcend the dichotomies between the human pursuit of self-transcendence and God's effort to meet us. Like the "fulfillment theory," that of

---

10. Cf. P. Teilhard de Chardin, *Comment je vois* (1948), n. 24, cited by de Lubac, *Paradoxe et mystère de l'Eglise*, 145.

11. Cf. U. King, *Towards a New Mysticism: Teilhard de Chardin and Eastern Religions* (New York: Seabury Press, 1980).

12. P. Teilhard de Chardin, *Science and Christ* (New York: Harper and Row, 1965), 34–35.

"the inclusive presence of Christ" was worked out in the years just leading up to or surrounding Vatican Council II. It succeeded in looking at other religious traditions with greater openness, seeing in them the operative presence of the mystery of Jesus Christ, the universal Savior. According to this theory, members of those traditions are saved in Christ, not despite their religious allegiance and their sincere practice of their traditions, but through that allegiance and practice. There is then salvation without the gospel, although it is not a salvation without Christ or apart from him. The operative presence of the mystery of Jesus Christ in the other religious traditions is certainly hidden and remains unknown to their adherents, but it is not thereby any less real. There are, however, distinctions to be made between the advocates of the so-called "theory of the inclusive presence of Christ," each of whom has his own way of understanding that presence.

It is the hidden and unknown operative presence of the mystery of Christ in other religious traditions that Karl Rahner has designated by the controversial term "anonymous Christianity."[13] Rahner's theory is based on his theological anthropology, that is, on a philosophico-theological analysis of humankind in the concrete historical condition in which it is created by God and destined for union with God. The "supernatural existential" inherent in the concrete historical human person is not to be identified with an "obediential potency" or a "natural desire" for the vision of God inherent in human nature as such, metaphysically considered. In the concrete, supernatural order of reality, we carry within ourselves more than a mere passive potency for self-transcendence in God. We are concretely and actively oriented toward the realization of such a self-transcendence. The "supernatural existential" is the fundamental structure, built into us by God's free initiative of grace, that spurs our intentional activity toward him. It is the "transcendental experience" of God inherent in every activity of the human person, destined to become historically concrete in the "categorical" or "thematic" order. It achieves a certain concreteness in the religious traditions of humankind in which is embodied an inchoate "categorical" mediation of supernaturally elevated transcendentality.

This is where the Christian mystery at once finds its roots in the human person and its specific role. The human person is both the event and the locus of God's self-communication in Jesus Christ. In him God has accomplished historically and definitively his self-gift to humankind, in grace and forgiveness. The human person does not have the initiative in searching for God; God's self-gift in Jesus Christ is the source of our search for him. Slightly modifying Blaise Pascal's celebrated phrase, one could say: "You would not seek me, *unless I had first found you.*" From the vantage point of Christian revelation, salvation history,

---

13. The theme has been formulated by K. Rahner in various essays contained in the *Schriften zur Theologie*, 16 vols. (Einsiedeln: Benziger Verlag, 1961–84). English edition in *Theological Investigations*, 21 vols. (London: Darton, Longman & Todd, 1961–88). It has been reformulated in a more synthetic way in *Foundations of Christian Faith: An Introduction to the Idea of Christianity* (London: Darton, Longman & Todd, 1978).

which culminates in Jesus Christ, is coextensive with world history.[14] Through-out that history, each person experiences God's offer of grace to which one must open oneself in free acceptance. Whether this is thematically apprehended by the person's awareness or not, the offer and gift of grace always take place concretely and existentially in Jesus Christ. Thus, human beings are awaiting in anticipa-tion, existentially, the mystery of salvation. But outside the Christian revelation the experience of God's offer of grace in Jesus Christ remains veiled. While its thematization may in various forms already be partially present in the concrete reality of the religious traditions of humankind, it remains there unfinished and ambiguous. Its "anonymity" can only be lifted by the Christian message, which communicates explicit knowledge of Jesus Christ. Rahner writes:

> There is an implicit and anonymous Christianity... an anonymous and yet real relationship between the individual person and the concrete his-tory of salvation, including Jesus Christ, in someone who has not yet had the whole, concrete, historical, explicit and reflexive experience in word and sacrament of this reality of salvation history. Such a person has this real and existentiell [*sic*] relationship merely implicitly in obedience to his orientation in grace towards the God of absolute, historical pres-ence and self-communication. He exercises this obedience by accepting his own existence without reservation... Alongside this there is the fullness of Christianity which has become conscious of itself explicitly in faith and in hearing the word of the Gospel, in the Church's profession of faith, in sacrament, and in living an explicit Christian life which knows that it is related to Jesus of Nazareth.[15]

Anonymous Christianity, Rahner explains, is lived by members of other reli-gious traditions in the sincere practice of their own traditions. Christian salvation reaches out to them, anonymously, through these traditions. This affirmation is based on the social character of a person's religious life, which is insepara-ble from the religious tradition and community in which it is lived.[16] Thus we must acknowledge in these traditions "supernatural elements" arising out of grace (pp. 121, 130). As long as the obligation to adhere to Christ as Savior is not im-posed on the personal conscience of a given individual by God's offer of faith in Jesus Christ, the mediation of the saving mystery through the individual's re-ligious tradition and in its sincere practice remains effective. To such a person the gospel has still not been "promulgated." One can, however, open oneself to God's self-gift in Jesus Christ, unknowingly, within one's religious tradition. The anonymous Christian is a Christian unawares. The difference between such a

---

14. K. Rahner, "History of the World and Salvation History," in *Theological Investigations*, 5:97–114.

15. Rahner, *Foundations of Christian Faith*, 306.

16. K. Rahner, "Christianity and the Non-Christian Religions," in *Theological Investigations*, 5:128–29.

person and an explicit Christian is partly one of subjective awareness (absent in the one, present in the other) of "being a Christian."

A question has been raised in this regard, however. Is the difference between the anonymous Christian and the explicit Christian only a matter of the reflexive awareness — absent in the one case and present in the other — of being a Christian? And does the passage from anonymous to explicit Christianity, when it occurs, simply entail coming to a formal awareness of being what one has always been without knowing it? Is there no difference in the way in which the saving mystery of Jesus Christ is mediated — no new regime of mediation? An awareness of being a Christian is certainly part of the mediation of the mystery of salvation proper to Christianity. But can that mediation be reduced to such awareness? Does not that mediation necessarily entail an acceptance of the word of the gospel, the sacramental life of the church, and a profession of faith in the ecclesial communion?

If some of Rahner's writings seem to leave some doubt on the matter, *The Foundations of Christian Faith,* cited earlier, eliminates all possible ambiguity. Anonymous Christianity and explicit Christianity entail distinct regimes of salvation and distinct modalities of mediation of the mystery of Jesus Christ. Such mediation in explicit Christianity implies becoming "conscious of itself explicitly in faith and in hearing the word of the gospel, in the church's profession of faith, in sacrament, and in living an explicit Christian life which knows that it is related to Jesus of Nazareth." Thus anonymous Christianity remains a fragmentary, incomplete, radically deficient reality. It harbors dynamics that impel it to become part of explicit Christianity.[17] Nevertheless, the same mystery of salvation is present on both sides, through different mediations. It is the mystery of Jesus Christ, whose operative presence is concealed and unconscious on one side, and reflexive and conscious on the other.

What, then, does "anonymous Christianity" mean? The expression refers directly to the universal presence of the mystery of Jesus Christ, rather than of "Christianity," in the sense of the Christian community where the Christian faith is explicitly professed. "Anonymous Christianity" means that salvation in Jesus Christ is available to human persons in whatever historical situation they may find themselves, insofar as in a hidden way they open themselves to God's self-communication which culminates in the Christ event. "Anonymous Christianity" likewise means that that mystery of salvation reaches out to them not by a mere invisible action of the risen Lord but indeed mysteriously through a mediation by the religious tradition to which they belong. Thus there is an anonymous or implicit Christianity, and there is an explicit Christianity. Despite the distance between them, both really bring about contact with the Christic mystery of salvation.

Raimon Panikkar's first book on the theology of the religions was entitled *The*

---

17. K. Rahner, "Anonymous Christians," in *Theological Investigations,* 6:390–98.

Unknown Christ of Hinduism.[18] It is to that book, it may be said, that the theory of the "presence of Christ" in the religious traditions owes its name. Speaking not of religious traditions in general but specifically of Hinduism, Panikkar wrote that "There is a living presence of Christ in Hinduism" (p. ix). This presence resides not only in the private and subjective life of religiously minded and sincere Hindus but in Hinduism as an objective and social religious phenomenon. With this affirmation, Panikkar expressed from the outset his firm stand in favor of a theory which would go beyond any form of "fulfillment theory," as the term has been understood in the preceding pages dealing with Danièlou and de Lubac. Panikkar says, "Christ is *not only* at the end but also at the beginning . . . Christ is not only the ontological goal of Hinduism but also its true inspirer, and his grace is the leading, though hidden, force pushing it towards its full disclosure" (p. x). Christ, the only source of every authentic religious experience, is the "ontological meeting-point" between Hinduism and Christianity. For indeed, he "does not belong to Christianity, he only belongs to God. It is Christianity and Hinduism as well that belong to Christ, though in two different levels" (pp. 20–21).

Hinduism, then, has a place in the Christian economy of salvation. In order to determine this place, Panikkar develops a "peculiar dialectic" of Hinduism and Christianity: "Hinduism is the starting-point of a religion that culminates in Christianity"; it is "Christianity in potency"; it already contains "the symbolism of the Christian reality" (pp. 58–60). This, however, does not mean that a mere "natural prolongation" will eventually lead from one to the other or that the dialectic involved is similar to the relationship between the old and the new covenants. For although Hinduism and Christianity both move in the same direction, the transition from one to the other implies a conversion, "a passage," a mystery of death and life. Hinduism must descend "into the living waters of baptism in order to rise again transformed." At the same time, it will not arise "as *another thing,* another religion"; rather it will be "a better *form* of Hinduism," for "the Christian mystery of resurrection is not an alienation" (pp. 60–61). Since Christ has been at work in anticipation in Hinduism, the task of Christian revelation consists at least partly of "the unveiling of reality." "The Christian attitude is not ultimately one of bringing Christ in, but of bringing him forth, of *discovering* Christ" (p. 45).

For Panikkar the mystery of Jesus Christ is therefore present in a hidden way, perceptible to Christian faith alone, in the religious traditions and in Hinduism in particular. The two modes of active presence of that mystery in Christianity and elsewhere are not, perhaps, as clearly distinguished as might be desirable. Panikkar writes: "We are not self-sufficient monads, but fragments of the same, unique religion, though the level of the waters may be, and is, different"; we must "dis-cover" our unity and, "because we are the same," "discard [the] veil of *maya*" that separates us (pp. 21–22). Expressing himself this way, however, seems

---

18. R. Panikkar, *The Unknown Christ of Hinduism* (London: Darton, Longman & Todd, 1964).

to expose him to the main criticism that was formulated — unduly — against Rahner's "anonymous Christianity." Can the distinction between Christianity and Hinduism be reduced to a "veil" of *māyā* (ignorance) or to mere presence or absence of awareness?

In any case, in this work the Christ whose hidden presence is discovered in Hinduism seems clearly to be the Christ of faith understood by the Christian tradition as personally identical to the pre-Easter Jesus, transformed in his human existence by the mystery of his resurrection. However, the situation seems to change with some of Panikkar's more recent writings.[19]

In 1981, *The Unknown Christ of Hinduism* appeared in a new revised and expanded edition in English. Even the title of the work was expanded, to become *The Unknown Christ of Hinduism: Towards an Ecumenical Christophany*. In a lengthy introduction, the author explains that, while he still regards the basic intuition of the book in its first edition as valid, he now sees it in a new light. He now describes his general theme as follows: "I speak neither of a principle unknown to Hinduism, nor of a dimension of the Divine unknown to Christianity, but of the unknown *reality*, which Christians call Christ, discovered in the heart of Hinduism, not as a stranger to it, but as its principle of life."[20] He continues: "The Christ of whom this book speaks is the living and loving reality of the truly believing Christian in whatever form the person may formulate or conceptualize this reality" (p. 22).

What, then, does Christ represent? Panikkar explains that, for him, Christ is the most powerful symbol — but not a symbol limited to the historical Jesus — of the full human, divine, and cosmic reality which he calls the Mystery (pp. 23, 26–27). The symbol can have other names: for example, Rāma, Kṛṣṇa, Iśvara, or Puruṣa (p. 27). Christians call him "Christ" because it is in and through Jesus that they themselves have arrived at faith in the decisive reality. Each name, however, expresses the indivisible mystery (p. 29), each by representing an unknown dimension of Christ (p. 30).

A new question arises here: How are we to conceive the relation of the "reality" or "mystery" — the Christ symbol — to the historical Jesus? It is on this point that Panikkar's thinking seems to have evolved, not without consequences: it may indeed be asked whether a distinction has now been introduced between the Christ mystery and the historical Jesus that no longer seems to give adequate account of the Christian assertion that Jesus *is* the Christ. It would seem, in fact, that what Panikkar really thinks on the subject appears more clearly in

---

19. Especially in the revised and enlarged edition of *The Unknown Christ of Hinduism*, entitled *The Unknown Christ of Hinduism: Towards an Ecumenical Christophany* (London: Darton, Longman & Todd, 1981); also *The Intrareligious Dialogue* (New York: Paulist Press, 1978); idem, *Salvation in Christ: Concreteness and Universality: The Supername* (Santa Barbara, Calif., 1972). In "A Christophany for Our Times" (*Theology Digest* 39, no. 1 [1992]: 3–21), Panikkar rejects the accusation, made against him by some theologians, of distinguishing a universal Christ from the Jesus of history. The clarifications made in that article notwithstanding, there remain some ambiguous formulations.

20. R. Panikkar, *The Unknown Christ of Hinduism: Towards an Ecumenical Christophany*, 19–20.

The Intrareligious Dialogue published in English before the new edition of *The Unknown Christ of Hinduism*.

Panikkar introduces here a distinction between faith and belief. Faith, he explains, is the basic religious experience of the human person, and is a constitutive element of the person. Belief, by contrast, is the particular expression adopted by this fundamental human attitude in any given tradition. The content of faith, which he calls "the Mystery," is the lived relationship to a transcendence which seizes the human being. It is common to all religions. Panikkar calls this mystery "cosmotheandric reality," to denote a transcendence experienced by the human being in the cosmos. The content of beliefs, on the other hand, consists of the various religious myths in which faith takes concrete expression. In Christianity we have the "Jesus-myth"; other traditions offer other myths. All of these myths have equal value. Christianity gives the Mystery the name of Christ, but it can assume other names. While the various religious traditions differ on the level of beliefs, they are all seen to coincide on that of faith. Intrareligious and interreligious dialogue cannot require a bracketing (*epochè*) of faith, but it can demand a bracketing of beliefs — indeed, their transcending. Panikkar hopes for a cross-fertilization of the beliefs of the various traditions.

If this rapid description gives a faithful account of Panikkar's thought, which is undoubtedly complex, the place held in Christian faith by the Jesus of history seems to become problematic. For the first Christians, as the apostolic kerygma testifies (Acts 2:36), the historical Jesus was personally identical to the Christ of faith. He had become the Christ in his being raised by the Father. He was also the very mystery (Rom 16:25; Eph 3:4; Col 2:2; 4:3; 1 Tim 3:16) preached by Paul. Thus Jesus himself belongs to the actual object of faith. He is inseparable from Christ, on whom he bestows historical concretion.

Panikkar, on the contrary, makes a distinction between the Mystery and the Jesus-myth — that is, the Christ of faith and the Jesus of history — whom he distinguishes as objects of faith and belief, respectively. But is a reduction of the Jesus-myth to an object of belief as distinct from faith compatible with the Christian profession of faith in the person from Nazareth? And is not the content of faith consequently reduced to a neutral relationship to a transcendence with no concrete object? Panikkar notes specifically that only the Christian is *aware* that Jesus is the "way." This is perfectly clear. But must it not be added that Jesus-the-Christ is in some real sense the Way for all, even for those who remain unaware of the fact? Must we not maintain that it is indeed the indissoluble mystery of Jesus-the-Christ that is present both in Christianity and in the other religions? That in and through that mystery not only Christians but others too encounter and receive the mystery of salvation? Such is, in any case, the way in which the theory of the "presence of Christ" in other religious traditions is commonly understood. It can thus be understood why as a subtitle to our treatment we took note of a "Divergence between Rahner and Panikkar." The mystery of Christ, which is said to have a universal presence, in Christianity and in the other religious traditions, is that of the indivisible person of the Jesus of history who has become the Christ through his resurrection by God.[21]

Our study — albeit rapid and with no pretense at being exhaustive — of the new perspectives and advances in the theology of religions in the years surrounding Vatican II comes thus to a close. From such a study there result two significant lines of thought which were operative at the time of the council and were to influence its deliberations on the issue of the religions. Both views have in common that they see the other religions as oriented to the Christ event in the history of salvation: in this sense both could be called "fulfillment theories," but with a difference, which amounts to a sharp contrast. For while the first holds on to the dialectic of nature–supernatural, human search–divine gift, the other overcomes such dichotomies to visualize the unfolding of God's saving history as a process entailing diverse modalities of God's revelation and personal involvement in human history. While for the former, the "pre-Christian religions" lose their propaedeutic value with the coming of the Christ event, for the latter, their positive role in the order of salvation remains in place by virtue of their organic link to the all-embracing mystery of Christ, at least until the "promulgation" of the gospel understood as to individuals. The task of the second section of this chapter will be to examine how the two currents present among the theologians of the council period influenced the council's discussion of the topic and how successfully they did so.

VATICAN II: A WATERSHED?

Could Vatican II, which held its sessions in the midst of this theological debate, declare itself in favor of one of these two opinions? That would be unlikely a priori for more than one reason. First, the council's perspective was pastoral rather than doctrinal. With regard to the other religions, the council's aim was to foster new attitudes of mutual understanding, esteem, dialogue, and cooperation between them and Christianity. To foster such attitudes it did not seem necessary to opt for a particular position in the debate on the theology of religions among Catholic theologians at that time. The council quite deliberately had no intention of making such a choice. To which must be added the fact that the council fathers, coming from vastly different theological backgrounds, would have been strongly divided on the properly theological issues. The intention, on the contrary, was to rally the highest possible majority on the council floor in favor of a change of attitude of Christians and the church toward the members of other religions. Such an aim could not be put in jeopardy by entering into intricate theological discussions.

It is, moreover, important to situate Vatican II in the conciliar history of the church. The Council of Florence (1442) had assumed the more rigid understanding of the axiom *Extra ecclesiam nulla salus*. A century later (1547) the Council of Trent, with its doctrine of "baptism of desire," had solemnly affirmed the

---

21. Further precisions on other recent developments in Panikkar's theology of religions are left for subsequent chapters.

possibility of salvation for those who were outside the church. Later church documents reaffirmed — though not without a marked caution — such a *possibility*. But over the centuries hardly ever did church documents — whether conciliar or otherwise — take a position on religions as such, let alone in any positive manner. Vatican II was to be the first in the conciliar history of the church to speak positively, albeit guardedly, about the other religions.

This is not the place to explain the genesis of the council documents on the matter. Suffice it to say that initially the council had only intended to append to the Decree on Ecumenism a statement which would help create a new climate in the tense relations between Christians and Jews. Because of the request made by some bishops from predominantly non-Christian areas, the scope of the document was broadened to include other religions besides Judaism. The creation by Pope Paul VI of the Secretariat for Non-Christians in 1964; the publication in the same year of the encyclical *Ecclesiam Suam* on dialogue (including dialogue with non-Christians); the pope's visit to India, likewise in 1964, and his meeting there with leaders of non-Christian religions whom the pope addressed with great humanity and warmth: all these gestures were for the council an incentive to lift its gaze beyond the narrow confines of the Western world and to reflect "on the Church's relations with non-Christian religions" (title of the declaration *Nostra Aetate*) in terms not only of matters related to Judaism but also of religions the world over. So it was that the scope of the declaration *Nostra Aetate* and the constitution *Lumen Gentium* came to include other religions besides Judaism.

The two documents take up the church's relations with the other religions from opposite directions. *Lumen Gentium* §16 starts talking directly of the different ways in which members of non-Christian religions are "oriented to" (*ordinantur*) the church: first come the Jews, with whom the church entertains the closest ties; then the Muslims, who "profess to hold the faith of Abraham"; there follow those who "in shadows and images seek the unknown God since he gives to all human beings life and breath and all things" (*Lumen Gentium* §16). *Nostra Aetate* takes the opposite course: first, human religiosity in general (present in "traditional religions"); then the religions "connected with the progress of culture," such as Hinduism, Buddhism, and others (§2); then Islam (§3); and finally the Jewish religion (§4), to which the longest section of the document is devoted. At each level the declaration shows the close links and the deep ties existing between the church and the various groups in question. They are very different from one another. While the three religions which trace their roots to the faith of Abraham have their origins in a single family, it is with Israel that the church has the closest ties and entertains the deepest relations, having received the Old Testament revelation "by way of that people" with whom God established a special covenant. In *Nostra Aetate,* however, the council's intention is not to show a graded "orientation" of members of other religions toward the church; it rather consists in exhorting everyone to overcome divisions and to foster friendly relations (*Nostra Aetate* §5). Such relations should be based on what all people, their specific allegiances notwithstanding, "have in common, [which] tends to promote fellowship among them" (§1). The nondoctrinal, concrete, and pastoral intent of the document is thus clear.

This is not to say that the council's thinking on the issue of the religions is purely pragmatic and devoid of any doctrinal significance. For the council was bound to establish its open pastoral approach on some doctrinal foundation. The ancient prejudices and negative assessments of the past had to be knocked down, and that could be done only by pointing to the positive values and divine gifts of the other religions. The council, therefore, could not be satisfied to speak about the orientation of non-Christian *individuals* to the church; it had to speak — and did so in a positive manner for the first time in conciliar history — about a relationship of the church to non-Christian religions as such. How far did the council go in recognizing positive values in the religious traditions themselves? What significance — if any — did it assign to them in God's design for the salvation of humankind? How did it conceive the relationship of Christianity to other religions: with the benefits going only to the latter, or as a two-way and mutually beneficial interaction?

POSITIVE VALUES CONTAINED
IN RELIGIOUS TRADITIONS

In assessing the council's teaching on the question of "non-Christians" and their religions, two questions must be clearly distinguished. One has to do with the individual salvation of persons belonging to the other religious traditions; the other, with the significance which these traditions may have in God's design for humankind and the role they ultimately play in the salvation of their members.

The first question is not new. As already noted, the possibility of salvation outside the church had been recognized by the church tradition long before Vatican II. If the council introduces anything new on this point, it must be seen in the optimism with which it views the world at large, as is best exemplified by the pastoral constitution *Gaudium et Spes*. What in previous church documents was affirmed — firmly but cautiously — as a *possibility* based on God's infinite mercy and in any event to be left to his judgment is now being taught by the council with unprecedented assurance: in ways known to him, God can lead those who, through no fault of their own, are ignorant of the gospel to that faith without which it is impossible to please him (Heb 11:6) (*Ad Gentes* §7). Nor does the council stop with simply stating the fact by itself. It proceeds further to explain how this concretely happens, that is, through the universal working of the Spirit of God. The clearest text in this regard is found in *Gaudium et Spes* where the council states: "Christ died for all (cf. Rom 8:32), and since all human beings are in fact called to one and the same destiny, which is divine, we must hold (*tenere debemus*) that the Holy Spirit offers to all the possibility of being associated, in a way known to God, with the Paschal Mystery" (§22).

The second question is the more important, and also more complex. To decide whether the council's outlook goes beyond the "fulfillment theory" to the point of positing a permanent role for the religious traditions in the order of salvation, we must turn our attention to what in the texts has to do not only with the salvation of individual "non-Christians" but with the positive values enshrined in the religious traditions to which they belong and in which they live their religious life. The main texts under consideration belong (in the order of publication by the council) to the constitution *Lumen Gentium* (§§16–17), the declaration *Nostra Aetate* (§2), and the decree *Ad Gentes* (§§3, 9, 11). In each of these the council develops three themes: (1) the salvation of people outside the church, (2) the authentic values found in "non-Christians" and in their religious traditions, and (3) the church's appreciation of these values and the consequent attitude which it takes toward the religious traditions and their members.

　　Lumen Gentium §16 affirms that God's assistance for salvation is available not only to people in different religious situations but also to those who, "without any fault of theirs, have not yet arrived at an explicit knowledge of God and who, not without grace, strive to lead a good life." The text goes on to say: "Whatever goodness or truth is found among them is considered by the church as a 'preparation for the Gospel,' a gift from him who enlightens all human beings that they may finally have life." Let us note immediately that the references to John 1:4 and 1:17, and especially to John 1:9 — to which we will often have to turn further on — remain implicit in the text. In the first part of this passage a positive value is attributed to the dispositions of individual people, not to any religious or other groups to which they belong. The text goes on to state that the church's mission consists of announcing the gospel of salvation for all in Jesus Christ and adds, "By her activity whatever good is found sown in the minds and hearts of human beings, or *in the rites and customs proper to various peoples*, is not only saved from destruction, but is also healed, ennobled, and brought to perfection, for the glory of God, the confusion of the devil, and the happiness of human persons" (*Lumen Gentium* §17, emphasis added). It will be noted how easily the council passes from the affirmation of rightful dispositions in people to that of the positive values enshrined in their religious traditions and cultures.

　　The same combination of subjective dispositions and objective values is found in *Ad Gentes* §3 and §9: "[The] universal design of God to save the human race is not achieved only in secret, as it were, in the hearts of people; nor merely through the undertakings, including religious ones (*incepta, etiam religiosa*), by which they seek God in many ways." Here too the "religious undertakings" seem to refer to objective elements belonging to the religious traditions. Such "undertakings" (*incepta*), however, "need to be enlightened and healed, even though, in the merciful design of the provident God, they may sometimes be taken as leading the way (*paedagogia*) to the true God and as a preparation for the Gospel" (§3). The same doctrine recurs once more in *Ad Gentes* §9: the council explains that the church's missionary activity purifies, raises, and brings to perfection in Christ "whatever truth and grace (*quidquid veritatis et gratiae*) is already found among the nations as a sort of secret presence of God." Likewise, "whatever good is found sown in the hearts and minds of human beings, or in the rites and cultures proper to various peoples, is not only saved from destruction but is also healed, ennobled and brought to perfection, for the glory of God, the confusion of the devil and the happiness of the human person" (§9). From the recognition of some goodness in the "non-Christian" world, *Ad Gentes* §11 draws conclusions about how the Christian mission must operate: "with joy and reverence they must discover the seeds of the Word hidden" in these national and religious traditions, and through a sincere dialogue discover "what treasures the bountiful God has distributed among the nations."

Nostra Aetate places the meeting of the church with the world religions in the broader context of the common origin and destiny of all people and the effort, common to all religious traditions, to answer the ultimate questions that beset the human spirit (§1). The declaration's general assessment of religions and the attitude that the church should consequently assume toward them is expressed by the Declaration as follows:

> The Catholic Church rejects nothing of what is true and holy in these religions. With sincere respect she looks on *those ways of conduct and life, those precepts and teachings* which, though differing on many points from what she herself holds and teaches, yet not rarely reflect a ray of that Truth (*radium illius Veritatis*) which enlightens all human beings. But she proclaims and must ever proclaim, "the way, the truth and the life "[Jn 14:6], in whom human beings find the fullness of religious life, and in whom God has reconciled all things to himself [cf. 2 Cor 5:18f].
>
> And so the Church has this exhortation for her children: prudently and lovingly, through dialogue (*colloquia*) and collaboration with the followers of other religions, and in witness to the Christian faith and life, acknowledge, preserve and promote the spiritual and moral good, as well as the socio-cultural values found among them. (§2) (emphasis added)

It may be noted that the existence of authentic values in the religious traditions themselves is expressed here more forcefully than in the previous texts: it is explicitly a matter of "ways of conduct and life ... precepts and teachings which ... not rarely reflect a ray of that Truth which enlightens all human beings." Although no explicit reference is made to John 1:9, the allusion is unmistakable, clearer indeed than it was in *Lumen Gentium* §16, cited above. The text of John 1:9, as will be seen further ahead, is of primordial importance for a theology of the religions. Unfortunately, the council kept the citation implicit and did not consider its possible consequences. Even so, according to the council it is the incomplete but real presence of "that Truth" in the other religions that is to guide the church's attitude of respect toward them and its wish to promote their spiritual and cultural values, while its mission also requires of it that it proclaim the "fullness of religious life" in Jesus Christ.

The council's doctrinal assessment of religions consists primarily of descriptive statements, in which various expressions are taken from the early tradition, without, however, their exact meaning in the council's mind being clearly defined. For example, it is never said how the "seeds of the Word" are to be understood.

Is this the *logos spermatikos* of Stoic philosophy, that is, an impersonal principle of order in the cosmos or of "natural" reason; or it is the personal Logos of the Prologue to John, who was in God eternally and has sown his seeds among human beings throughout the entire history of humankind, being "the light that enlightens every human being" (cf. Jn 1:9)? As will be seen later, the differences in the understanding of the "seeds of the Word" lead to very different theologies of the religions. The council has left us in doubt about its true intentions on the matter. While the general assessment of the religions sounds rather positive, it still suffers from a certain vagueness.

TOWARD A BALANCED CRITICAL APPRAISAL

The council's doctrine on other religions has met with divergent interpretations, ranging from the resolutely reductionist to the blatantly maximalist. Some interpreters reduce the positive values contained in the other traditions to goods of "nature." Thus in their eyes, the council affirmed nothing more than a "natural" knowledge of God attainable by "non-Christians" in the way Paul in Romans 1 affirms the possibility of such knowledge through creation. Others, by contrast, taking advantage of the council's most forceful expressions, claim that the "preparation for the gospel" contained in the religions is not reduced to a natural substrate. They think rather that the council was considering the other religions to be "ways," "paths," or "means" of salvation for their adherents. Between these two interpretations — both mistaken, one by a lack and the other by exaggeration — what should be the correct interpretation of the doctrinal import of the council? It seems that it should be found in between them.

It may be asked whether the council simply followed the "fulfillment theory" in its classical form or, on the contrary, whether it made its own the theory of the "presence of Christ's saving mystery" in the religious traditions. Thus formulated, the question does not allow for a simple answer one way or the other. On the one hand, it is true that much of the terminology describing the church's attitude toward other religions repeats terms familiar to the fulfillment theory: to assume and to save, to heal and to restore, to ennoble and to bring to perfection. On the other hand, the elements of "truth and grace" (*Ad Gentes* §9) — an expression, we have already noted, borrowed from an essay written by Karl Rahner shortly before the council[22] — found "as a sort of secret presence of God" (*Ad Gentes* §9) within these very traditions (in their teachings, their rites, their ways of life; or in their creeds, cults, and codes of behavior) strongly incline in the opposite direction.

For Paul F. Knitter, while "Vatican II forms a watershed in Roman Catholic attitudes toward other faiths," there still remains "a residual ambiguity in its understanding of just how effective the truth and grace within the religions are."[23] According to him, the ambiguity "stems from the tension between God's salvific

---

22. K. Rahner, "Christianity and the Non-Christian Religions," in *Theological Investigations*, 5:115–34.

23. P. F. Knitter, *No Other Name? A Critical Survey of Christian Attitudes toward the World Religions* (Maryknoll, N.Y.: Orbis Books, 1985), 124.

will and the necessity of the church that is evident throughout the history of Catholic thought" (ibid.). This dilemma must be examined later when we discuss how the "necessity" of the church affirmed by the council is to be understood. Meanwhile, we may be content to answer that for many Catholic theologians the "necessity" of the church need not a priori rule out any saving value for other religions.

A balanced appraisal of the council's doctrine on religions has to be at once positive and critical. In Karl Rahner's view, the council's main achievement consists of having looked beyond the question of the salvation of individual non-Christians to a positive relationship of the church with the religions as such. However, while supernatural salvation in God's actual self-gift to all individual people is looked upon with great optimism by the council, equal optimism is not explicitly professed in connection with the religions. In this regard, "the essential problem for the theologian has been left open"; "the declaration leaves the properly theological quality of non-Christian religions undefined." Do "non-Christians" attain salvation outside of or within the life of their religions as such? Are such religions salvific in some manner or not? The question is not explicitly answered.[24] Although much of what the council affirms suggests a positive answer, the conclusion is not certain.

Other limitations of the council's doctrine on religions have been pointed out, one of which seems especially relevant. H. Maurier speaks of the strongly "ecclesiocentric" perspective of the conciliar teaching in general, and of *Nostra Aetate* in particular. The church seems to recognize as positive and good only those things in the other religions that are found in it superabundantly. Must the "rays" of truth present in them necessarily be related to the fullness of them possessed by the church? Or would the declaration be prepared to acknowledge in the other religions the presence of rays of truth not found in the church? The church's way of thinking remains "egocentric," that is, "ecclesiocentric."[25] Such a perspective easily leads to the "fulfillment theory," according to which, inasmuch as they represent the search of the human person for God, the other religions become obsolete by the very fact of reaching their fulfillment in Christianity (p. 135). It must be asked, however, whether the dialogue with the other religions which the council meant to foster does not presuppose the recognition in them of authentic human values not equally possessed by Christianity. Only then will dialogue be viable and meaningful. Indeed, by definition, dialogue is a two-way street in which there is give-and-take. Does the Vatican II church present itself as inclined to receive anything from other religions (pp. 139–43)? The effect of Vatican II's ecclesiocentric angle of vision, it may be noted, is that the religions are never considered by themselves in their specificity and their own consistence, in their own self-understanding and their value by themselves, independently of their relationship to the church as understood by the church itself.

---

24. K. Rahner, "On the Importance of the Non-Christian Religions for Salvation," in *Theological Investigations*, 18:288–95.

25. H. Maurier, "Lecture de la Déclaration par un missionaire d'Afrique," in *Les relations de l'Eglise avec les religions non-chrétiennes*, ed. A.-M. Henry (Paris: Cerf, 1966), 119–60, cf. 133–34.

We have elsewhere considered the "ecclesiocentric" viewpoint of the council's theology of the other religious traditions, as the probable reason for its limitations and silences. We wrote:

> The very title of the Declaration *Nostra Aetate* — "On the Relations of the Church with non-Christian Religions" — demonstrates this. The question posed here is not directly that of the vertical relationship of humanity's religious traditions with the mystery of Jesus Christ. It is the question of the horizontal relationship of these same traditions with Christianity or the Church. The first question could have contributed to the acknowledgment of a hidden presence of the mystery of Christ in these same traditions, and of a certain mediation of this same mystery through them. The second question, of course, did not naturally lead in this direction. Is not this the reason why, despite the council's assertion of the presence of values and positive elements in these religious traditions, it does not explicitly venture in the direction of an acknowledgment of these same traditions as legitimate paths of salvation for their members, although necessarily in relation to the mystery of Christ?[26]

Alongside the silences and limits of Vatican II's teaching on the religions, we may mention a certain disillusionment and dissatisfaction that can be felt upon rereading some council texts almost forty years later. It is true that the council must be situated in the context of its time; but it is likewise true that it should be possible to "receive" it today. We have already mentioned the need for a "purification of theological language" on the religions in the contemporary context of interreligious dialogue. It cannot be denied that certain expressions adopted by the council sound bad in this new context. To take a clear example, the Declaration *Dignitatis Humanae* on religious liberty speaks of "this one true religion which subsists (*subsistere*) in the Catholic church" (§1). The meaning is that the Christian religion is "the one true religion" which is completely present in the Catholic Church, while present imperfectly in the other Christian churches. In the contemporary context in which the presence of elements "of truth and grace" — affirmed by the council (*Ad Gentes* §9) — is ever more recognized theologically, it may be asked whether it was a good idea to use a hackneyed expression from the apologetics of the past (the now obsolete theological tract *De vera religione*) in the council text. Would it have not been possible to speak of the fullness of revelation and of the means of salvation present in Christianity in such a way as to take into account that divine truth and goods of salvation are in some way present also outside Christianity? Obviously, the council did not yet have the sensitivity that postconciliar theology has fortunately developed toward the "others" and their traditions.

---

26. J. Dupuis, *Jesus Christ at the Encounter of World Religions* (Maryknoll, N.Y.: Orbis Books, 1991), 98.

THE POSTCONCILIAR MAGISTERIUM

A certain ambiguity remains in the conciliar doctrine. Our task is now to inquire whether the church's postconciliar teaching authority has shed any more light on the council's teaching. In particular, has any further step been taken toward a positive appraisal of the religions themselves? Has a too narrowly church-centered perspective perhaps given way to a broader outlook, allowing for a clearer recognition of the role of religions in God's saving design for humankind? These and other related questions must be kept in mind while reviewing official church teaching on religions during the more than thirty years that separate us from the council. Only key texts with significant doctrinal content will be considered here.

THE PONTIFICATE OF PAUL VI

The encyclical *Ecclesiam Suam* was published by Paul VI between the second and third sessions of Vatican II (August 6, 1964). It marks the appearance of "dialogue" (here called *colloquium*) on the program of the church renewal intended by the council. The pope explains that the history of salvation is that of a continuous dialogue of God with humankind; the church's role is to prolong that dialogue. The church, then, finds itself in a privileged situation to enter into dialogue with the entire world on four levels. Drawing concentric circles and starting from the one most remote, the pope distinguishes in succession, the church's dialogue with the entire world; with the members of other religions; with the other Christian churches; and finally, in the innermost circle, dialogue within the church. The second circle is "composed essentially of those who worship the one sovereign God whom we, too, adore," and includes not only Jews and Muslims but the faithful of the great African and Asian religions. The pope is very cautious in establishing the foundation and conditions of such interreligious dialogue on doctrinal grounds. He writes:

> It is obvious that we cannot agree with various aspects of these religions and that we cannot overlook differences or be unconcerned with them, as if all religions had, each in its own way, the same value, which would dispense those who follow them from the need of inquiring whether God has revealed a way free from all error and certain, by which he desires to make himself known, loved and served. Indeed, honesty compels us to declare openly what we believe, namely that there is one true religion, the Christian religion, and that we hope that all who seek God and adore him, will come to acknowledge this.[27]

Nevertheless, the pope states: "We do acknowledge with respect the spiritual and moral values of various non-Christian religions, for we desire to join with them in promoting and defending common ideals ... On these great ideals that

---

27. *AAS* 56 (1964): 655; J. Neuner and J. Dupuis, eds., *The Christian Faith in the Documents of the Catholic Church* (2001), n. 1029.

we share with them we can have dialogue, and we shall not fail to offer opportunities for it whenever, in genuine mutual respect, our offer would be received with good will" (ibid.). Respect for the moral and spiritual values of other religions notwithstanding, the exclusiveness of Christianity as the "one true religion" stands out unequivocally, as it will also stand out in the council itself in 1965 (cf. *Dignitatis Humanae* §1 cited above). The refinements and nuances made by the council on the religions did not soften the papal (and conciliar) affirmation of Christianity's exclusive claims.

An important occasion for reaffirming those claims occurred with the apostolic exhortation *Evangelii Nuntiandi*, following upon the 1974 synod of bishops on the evangelization of the modern world. Among other themes bearing on evangelization, the synod had touched on interreligious dialogue and, in view of this, on a Christian evaluation of non-Christian religions which would serve as its necessary foundation. It must be said honestly that the apostolic exhortation *Evangelii Nuntiandi* of Pope Paul VI (December 8, 1975) presents a rather negative assessment of them. After duly recalling the church's esteem for non-Christian religions professed by the council documents, the pope expresses himself as follows:

> Even in the face of the highest forms of natural religions, the Church thinks that . . . the religion of Jesus which she proclaims through evangelization truly puts human beings in contact with the plan of God, with his living presence and his action. It does enable them to meet the mystery of the Fatherhood of God that bends over towards humanity. In other words, through our religion an authentic and living relationship with God is truly established, such as other religions cannot bring about even though they have, as it were, their arms stretched out towards heaven.[28]

The image of the "arms stretched out towards heaven," as against God's "bending over towards humanity" in Jesus Christ in response to human aspirations; the distinction between the "highest forms of natural religions" and the religion of Jesus, through which alone an "authentic and living relationship with God is truly established" — all make it plain that the pope is here taking up the "fulfillment theory" in its classical form. The more insightful elements of the council are here disappearing from view. Paul VI, who with the programmatic encyclical *Ecclesiam Suam* had become the "pope of dialogue," in *Evangelii Nuntiandi* says nothing about interreligious dialogue.

THE PONTIFICATE OF JOHN PAUL II

As the foundation for a Christian understanding of the church's relationship to world religions, *Nostra Aetate* had laid a double commonality existing between all persons and peoples: their common origin from God, on the one hand; their common destiny in God according to God's design of salvation for humankind,

---

28. Text in *AAS* 68 (1976): 41–42; Neuner and Dupuis, eds., *The Christian Faith in the Documents of the Catholic Church*, n. 1036.

on the other (§1). Such a design, as the council suggested, was accomplished by God in Jesus Christ. No mention, however, was made in this connection of the universal presence and action of the Spirit of God among human beings through the ages. It may be said that the singular contribution of Pope John Paul II to a "theology of religions" consists of the emphasis with which he affirms the operative presence of the Spirit of God in the religious life of non-Christians and the religious traditions to which they belong. Already in his first encyclical letter, *Redemptor Hominis* (March 4, 1979), the pope saw in the "firm belief" of "non-Christians" an "effect of the Spirit of truth," and he asked: "Does it not sometimes happen that the firm belief of the followers of the non-Christian religions — a belief that is also an effect of the Spirit of truth operating outside the visible confines of the Mystical Body — can make Christians ashamed at often being themselves so disposed to doubt concerning the truths revealed by God and proclaimed by the Church?" (§6).[29]

The missionary attitude, therefore, always begins with a feeling of deep esteem for "what is in the human being" (Jn 2:25), for what one has worked out in the depths of one's spirit concerning the most profound and important problems. It is a question of respecting everything that has been brought about in one by the Spirit, who "blows where he wills" (Jn 3:8). John 3:8 is a quotation which recurs often from the pope's pen. Another is Romans 8:26, where Paul speaks of the Holy Spirit who prays in us. The pope applies Paul's words to every authentic prayer, whether of Christians or otherwise:

> Even when, for some, he is the great Unknown, he nevertheless remains always in reality the same living God. We trust that wherever the human spirit opens itself in prayer to this Unknown God, an echo will be heard of the same Spirit who, knowing the limits and weakness of the human person, himself prays in us and on our behalf, "expressing our plea in a way that could never be put into words" (Rom 8:26). The intercession of the Spirit of God who prays in us and for us is the fruit of the mystery of the redemption of Christ, in which the all-embracing love of the Father has been shown to the world.[30]

Through these texts the same teaching is gradually emerging: the Holy Spirit is present and active in the world, in the members of other religions, and in the religious traditions themselves. Authentic prayer (even if addressed to an Unknown God), human values and virtues, the treasures of wisdom hidden in the religious traditions, and true dialogue and authentic encounter among their members — these are so many fruits of the active presence of the Spirit.

---

29. Text in *AAS* 71 (1979): 257–347; Neuner and Dupuis, eds., *The Christian Faith in the Documents of the Catholic Church*, n. 1037.

30. Message of John Paul II to the inhabitants of Asia (Manila, February 21, 1981), n. 4. Text in *AAS* 73 (1981): 391–98; Neuner and Dupuis, eds., *The Christian Faith in the Documents of the Catholic Church*, n. 1040.

We cannot fail to mention the important address given by Pope John Paul II to the members of the Roman curia on December 22, 1986, after the World Day of Prayer for Peace, which had been held at Assisi two months earlier (October 17, 1986).[31] The address spoke of a "mystery of unity" — based on the unity of humankind in creation and redemption — which unites all people, however distinct may be the circumstances of their lives: "The differences are a less important element, when confronted with the unity which is radical, fundamental and decisive" (§3). On one point, however, just as in the documents recalled above, the pope spoke more clearly than any of the council documents: on the active presence of the Holy Spirit in the religious life of the members of other religious traditions. Indeed, the pope observes that at Assisi there had been a "wonderful manifestation of that unity which binds us together beyond the differences and divisions which are known to all." He explains it as follows:

> Every authentic prayer is under the influence of the Spirit "who intercedes insistently for us . . . because we do not even know how to pray as we ought," but he prays in us "with unutterable groanings," and "the One who searches the hearts knows what are the desires of the Spirit" (cf. Rom 8:26–27). We can indeed maintain that every authentic prayer is called forth by the Holy Spirit, who is mysteriously present in the heart of every person. (§11)

The most explicit text on the economy of the Spirit is, however, to be found in the encyclical on the Holy Spirit, *Dominum et Vivificantem* (May 18, 1986), where the pope explicitly mentions the universal activity of the Holy Spirit before the time of the Christian dispensation — "from the beginning, throughout the world" — and today after the Christ event "outside the visible body of the Church." Before the time of the Christian dispensation, the activity of the Spirit, by virtue of the divine plan of salvation, was ordered to Christ. Outside the church today, it results from the saving event accomplished in him. Thus the pope explains the Christological content and pneumatological dimension of divine grace (§53).[32]

The theme of the universal presence and activity of the Spirit recurs once more in the encyclical letter *Redemptoris Missio* (December 7, 1990).[33] The text states with great clarity that the presence of the Spirit affects not only individual persons but the religious traditions themselves. It says:

> The Spirit manifests himself in a special way in the Church and her members. Nevertheless, his presence and activity are universal, limited neither by space nor time . . . The Spirit . . . is at the very source of the human person's

31. The texts on the Day of Prayer have been published by the pontifical commission "Justitia et Pax," in *Assise: Journée mondiale de prière pour la paix (27 octobre 1986)* (Città del Vaticano, 1987). The text of the pope's address is found on pp. 147–55. It is also found in *Bulletin* (Secretariat for Non-Christians) 64, no. 2 (1987): 54–62.

32. Text in *AAS* 78 (1986): 809–900; Neuner and Dupuis, eds., *The Christian Faith in the Documents of the Catholic Church*, n. 1048.

33. Text in *AAS* 83 (1991): 249–340.

existential and religious questioning which is occasioned not only by contingent situations but by the very structure of its being. The Spirit's presence and activity affect not only individuals but also society and history, peoples, cultures and religions. (§28)

But if the question is asked whether the recognition of the active presence of the Spirit of God not only in the members of other religious traditions but in the traditions themselves influences positively the encyclical's approach to the significance and value of those traditions, the answer is quite inconclusive. All that the encyclical ventures to say on the matter is captured in two sentences. On the one hand, it affirms that salvation in Christ is accessible to those who are outside the church "by virtue of a grace which, while having a mysterious relationship to the Church, does not make them formally part of the Church but enlightens them in a way which is accommodated to their spiritual and material situation" (§10). On the other hand, while stressing "Christ's one, universal mediation," the document recognizes the possibility in the order of salvation of "various kinds of participated forms of mediation," saying, "Although participated forms of mediation of different kinds and degrees are not excluded, they acquire meaning and value *only* from Christ's own mediation, and they cannot be understood as parallel or complementary to his" (§5). It is not explicitly stated whether among the "participated mediations" contemplated in this text are included, for the benefit of members of the other religions, the traditions to which they belong. We will return to this issue later.

Indeed, despite the repeated affirmation that the Spirit of God is present in the religious traditions, in some recent pronouncements Pope John Paul II takes up the "fulfillment theory" in a way that is reminiscent of Paul VI's assessment of "non-Christian" religions in *Evangelii Nuntiandi* (§53). Thus, in the apostolic letter *Tertio Millennio Adveniente* (November 10, 1994), the pope writes:

> Jesus does not...merely speak "in the name of God" like the prophets, but he is God himself speaking in his eternal Word made flesh. Here we touch upon *the essential point by which Christianity differs from all the other religions*, by which *the human search for God* has been expressed from earliest times. Christianity has its starting-point in the incarnation of the Word. Here, it is not simply a case of a human search for God, but of God who comes in person to speak to human beings of himself and to show them the path by which he may be reached... *The Incarnate Word is thus the fulfillment of the yearning present in all the religions of humankind*: this fulfillment is brought about by God himself and transcends all human expectations. It is the mystery of grace. In Christ, religion is no longer a "blind search for God" (cf. Acts 17:27) but the *response of faith* to God who reveals himself... *Christ is thus the fulfillment of the yearning of all the world's religions and, as such, he is their sole and definitive completion.* (§6)[34]

---

34. Text in *AAS* 87 (1995): 8–9.

This text visualizes the fulfillment of the other religions in Jesus Christ and Christianity in terms of God's self-communication in his Son incarnate in response to the universal human search for God expressed in the religious traditions — in other words, in terms of divine revelation and grace meeting the natural religious aspiration of humankind. The "fulfillment theory" in its classic form is thus reproduced. This seems to leave no room for recognizing in the other religious traditions themselves a first divine initiative toward human beings, no matter how incomplete, and for attributing to the religious traditions a positive role in the mystery of salvation of their followers. The Christian "way" is the only one on which "God may be reached."

We come closest to an affirmation of a positive role of the traditions in a document jointly published by the Pontifical Council for Interreligious Dialogue and the Congregation for the Evangelization of Peoples, entitled "Dialogue and Proclamation: Reflections and Orientations on Interreligious Dialogue and the Proclamation of the Gospel of Jesus Christ" (May 19, 1991).[35] The section titled "A Christian Approach to Religious Traditions" (§§14–32) — a first among documents of the church's magisterium on the subject of members of other religions and their traditions — contains an important paragraph which, with regard to the role played by religious traditions in salvation in Jesus Christ, goes beyond anything said previously in church documents:

> From this "mystery of unity" it follows that all men and women who are saved, share, though differently, in the same mystery of salvation in Jesus Christ through his Spirit. Christians know this through their faith, while others remain unaware that Jesus Christ is the source of their salvation. The mystery of salvation reaches out to them, in a way known to God, through the invisible action of the Spirit of Christ. Concretely, it will be *in the sincere practice of what is good in their own religious tradition* and by following the dictates of their conscience that the members of other religions respond positively to God's invitation and receive salvation in Jesus Christ, even while they do not recognize or acknowledge him as their Savior (cf. *Ad Gentes* §§3, 9, 11). (§29) (emphasis added)[36]

Undoubtedly, the statement is a guarded one — not without reason, considering the circumstances and the context in which it was written.[37] Nevertheless, a door seems to be timidly opened here, for the first time, for the recognition on the part of the church authority of a "participated mediation" of religious traditions in the salvation of their members. With such a statement we seem to

35. Text in *Bulletin* no. 77: 26, no. 2 (1991): 210–50.

36. In *Bulletin*, ibid., 223; Neuner and Dupuis, eds., *The Christian Faith in the Documents of the Catholic Church*, n. 1059.

37. For a critical study and an account of the genesis of this document, in addition to a theological comparison between the encyclical *Redemptoris Missio* and *Dialogue and Proclamation*, cf. J. Dupuis, "A Theological Commentary: Dialogue and Proclamation," in *Redemption and Dialogue*, ed. W. R. Burrows (Maryknoll, N.Y.: Orbis Books, 1993), 119–58; idem, "Dialogue and Proclamation in Two Recent Documents," *Bulletin* no. 80: 27, no. 2 (1992): 165–72.

be definitely moving from the "fulfillment theory" to that of an active presence of the mystery of Jesus Christ in the traditions themselves.[38]

OUR OVERVIEW OF VATICAN II and of the postconciliar magisterium has presumably succeeded in showing that church doctrine is neither monolithic nor of one piece. From one document to another, different implications and shades of meaning as well as different perspectives may be found, somewhat at odds with one another. Recent official teaching on the matter has had ups and downs, ambiguities and fluctuations. It would thus be wrong to insist on affirming the continuous existence of a single theological viewpoint in the recent magisterium on the religions. Rather it must be recognized that there are in it different stances which leave the door open to varied further developments. It is not always easy to decide the precise meaning or import of this or that statement or affirmation. In any case, from the quick survey above it seems possible to draw the following conclusions.

The relevant texts of the council, without wishing to take sides on disputed doctrinal issues, display a certain openness toward the other religious traditions which, while remaining limited, is without precedent in previous official documents of the church. While never formally recognizing in the other religious traditions channels of salvation for their members, the council seems to incline in that direction by implication when it acknowledges the existence in those traditions not merely of positive human values but also of elements of "truth and grace" "through a hidden presence of God in the midst of the peoples" (*Ad Gentes* §9).

As for the postconciliar magisterium, it is marked by a certain ambiguity. While Paul VI seems clearly to hold on to the fulfillment theory as traditionally understood before the council, John Paul II, principally with his emphasis on the universal active presence of the Spirit of God in the religious traditions themselves, is more positive and shows a greater disposition toward a broader perspective, without, however, clearly going beyond the preconciliar understanding of fulfillment. Only one official document from the Vatican allows it to be prudently affirmed that God's grace and salvation in Jesus Christ reach the members of the other religious traditions within them and through the "practice" of them.

This is as far as the official doctrine enables us to reach, but no further. The task of the next chapter will be to show that the theological debate which has continued, principally since the time of the council, among Christians at large, is in effect much broader and more variegated than has been accounted for so far, including as it does some extreme positions. Hence, the entire spectrum of opinions held in the theological debate now taking place must be examined.

---

38. The document of the International Theological Commission entitled "Le Christianisme et les religions" (1997) is not taken up in this chapter, because it does not form part of the church's magisterium. It will occasionally be mentioned in subsequent chapters. The text has been published in French under the title *Le Christianisme et les religions* (Paris: Centurion-Cerf, 1997). An English translation is found in *Origins* 27 (1997–98): 149–66.

Chapter Three

CHRISTIANITY
AND THE RELIGIONS
IN RECENT THEOLOGY

ATICAN II CONSIDERED "the relations of the Church with non-Christian religions" within clearly defined parameters. The church indeed wished to foster mutual esteem and cooperation, but within the limits imposed by its self-identity and its understanding of its own mission. Many nonnegotiable elements were presupposed in the discussion: the "uniqueness" of Jesus Christ in whom alone humankind could find salvation, the irreplaceable role of the church as the universal sacrament of salvation in Jesus Christ. Within the limits imposed by these basic elements of traditional Christian faith, the space for negotiating different theological evaluations of religions seemed somewhat restricted. The rigid interpretation of the ancient adage "Outside the church no salvation" being clearly excluded (as Pius XII had reminded in 1949), there seemed to remain two ways — those in fact suggested by Catholic theology at the time of the council, which have been reviewed in the previous chapter. The council did not formally adopt either one or the other. While it seemed to incline to the more positive vision, it nevertheless left the theological debate open.

The theological debate had, in fact, for some time taken on much broader dimensions than the council ever could or would consider. This is evident if, looking beyond the positions then widely held by Catholic theologians, we visualize the whole range of opinions held earlier by theologians of various Christian traditions, between the two extremes, with Karl Barth's "dialectical theology," on one side, and the liberal views with which he was in conflict, on the other. Nor has the breadth of that range narrowed in recent years; rather it has widened as the discussion has developed. Today the debate on the theology of religions stands in a preeminent place on the theological agenda, as proven by the ceaseless outpouring of literature on the subject.

It is this debate, as it stands today, that we intend to review in this chapter. We intend to identify the main "paradigms" that have dominated the effort to construct a theology of religions — and of religious pluralism; in other words, to determine the fundamental perspective, the principle of intelligibility, according to which the various theories are being proposed as to how the various religious traditions — Christianity included — relate to each other.

Before entering into the matter, some precisions are in order with regard to terminology. The term "paradigm" is being used intentionally as opposed to "model," which is also being used in these pages. The distinction is important. Briefly, the following may be said. "Models" are descriptive; they call attention to aspects of some reality without claiming to define it adequately or distinctly. Consequently, the various models do not exclude one another; rather, they must be viewed as complementing each other and need to be combined in order to yield a comprehensive view of the reality concerned. The opposite is the case where "paradigms" are concerned. In this instance, principles of understanding, overall keys for interpreting reality, are involved; because they are opposed to each other, they are mutually exclusive. It is impossible to sustain simultaneously a Ptolemaic and a Copernican worldview! (The comparison is relevant as will be seen further on.) Hence the need, if one paradigm is judged to be unusable, to abandon it and to "shift" to another. In our present case, it will be important to keep in mind the contradiction intended between each couple of paradigms and the disavowal entailed in every "paradigm shift" of everything that has preceded it.

Many recent authors use a tripartite division of opinions. They distinguish three fundamental perspectives — ecclesiocentric, Christocentric, and theocentric — and in parallel with these, three basic positions, respectively designated exclusivism, inclusivism, and "pluralism."[1] These distinctions correspond to a twofold paradigm shift. It must be added that further discussions on the subject have caused more recent categories to arise. As will be seen later, they do not represent new paradigm shifts in the sense defined above, but only suggest new models for assessing the respective value of different religions. These more recent developments and the new categories of opinions that they have produced will have to be assessed.

The task in this chapter will thus be to explain the pressures under which the theology of religions has undergone a double paradigm shift, from ecclesiocentrism to Christocentrism, and from Christocentrism to theocentrism. It will likewise have to show how more recent debates have resulted in the addition of new models for evaluating the different religions. In this manner, it will become apparent that the Christological question, which originally stood at the center of the entire discussion of the theology of religions, is tending in the minds of many — rightly or wrongly — to be progressively marginalized. This tendency therefore needs to be discussed, and it must be shown that from a Christian standpoint, the Christological question still must stand at the center of the debate. Finally, a workable model must be sought for a synthetic theology of religions that is both Christian and open.

---

1. A. Race, *Christians and Religious Pluralism: Patterns in the Christian Theology of Religions* (London: SCM Press, 1983); H. Coward, *Pluralism: Challenge to World Religions* (Maryknoll, N.Y.: Orbis Books, 1985).

PARADIGM SHIFTS

FROM ECCLESIOCENTRISM
TO CHRISTOCENTRISM

The first paradigm shift can be treated rapidly. We have already recalled the negative Barthian verdict on religion in general, and implicitly on religions. Karl Barth's disciples, such as H. Kraemer,[2] applied "dialectical theology" to the religions they encountered in missionary situations. Since salvation could be obtained only through faith in Jesus Christ professed in the church, "non-Christian" religions were at best futile human attempts at self-justification. Karl Barth was not, however, alone in reacting vehemently against the liberal views that had been put forward by historians of religion, such as Ernst Troeltsch and Arnold Toynbee.[3] Others did likewise, for instance, Emil Brunner, who, notwithstanding differences, is on this point very close to Barth.[4]

Nor must it be thought that the exclusivist stand of Protestant neoorthodoxy has become altogether a thing of the past. It survives to some extent in evangelical circles, even today, as evidenced in recent works, such as those of H. A. Netland,[5] A. D. Clarke–B. M. Winter,[6] and, on a more institutional level, the "Lausanne Covenant," issued by the International Congress on World Evangelism (1974), and the "Manila Manifesto," published by the same organization in 1989. The "Manila Manifesto" states that there is "no warrant for saying that salvation can be found outside Christ or apart from an explicit acceptance of his work through faith."[7] Quite similar positions can likewise be found even today among Catholic authors. One example is H. van Straelen, who wrote in a recent book, "The church has always taught that in order to obtain salvation, man must accept the gospel message, reject false gods, and turn to the living God of Abraham, Isaac, and Jacob, as he has revealed himself in Jesus."[8] This is tantamount to saying that explicit faith in Jesus Christ is necessary in order to be saved. Such statements recall the exclusivist paradigm, explicitly rejected by the church's magisterium as found in the 1949 letter of the Holy Office under Pius XII.[9]

---

2. Cf. H. Kraemer, *The Christian Message in a Non-Christian World* (London: Edinburgh House, 1947); idem, *Why Christianity of All Religions?* (London: Lutterworth, 1962).

3. E. Troeltsch, *The Absoluteness of Christianity and the History of Religions* (Richmond: John Knox Press, 1971); A. Toynbee, *Christianity among the Religions of the World* (New York: Scribner's, 1957).

4. E. Brunner, *Offenbarung und Vernunft: Die Lehre von den christlichen Glaubenserkenntnis* (Zürich and Stuttgart: Zwingli Verlag, 1961).

5. H. A. Netland, *Dissonant Voices: Religious Pluralism and the Question of Truth* (Grand Rapids, Mich.: Eerdmans, 1991).

6. A. D. Clarke and B. M. Winter, eds., *One God, One Lord: Christianity in a World of Religious Pluralism* (Grand Rapids, Mich: Baker, 1992).

7. Cf. E. L. Stockwell, "One Perspective on Lausanne II in Manila," July 11–20, 1989, manuscript, n. 3.

8. H. van Straelen, *L'Eglise et les religions non-chrétiennes au seuil du XXIe siècle* (Paris: Beauchesne, 1994), 281. The author previously had written *Ouverture à l'autre, laquelle?* (Paris: Beauchesne, 1982).

9. H. Denzinger, *Enchiridion symbolorum, definitionum et declarationum de rebus fidei et morum,* nos. 3866–72; J. Neuner and J. Dupuis, eds., *The Christian Faith in the Doctrinal Documents of the Catholic Church,* nos. 854–57.

The paradigm shift from ecclesiocentrism to Christocentrism represents, in fact, a significant reversal, with weighty consequences, not merely for a theology of religions (inclusivism versus exclusivism) but for theology as a whole. It implies a radical "decentering" of the church, which now finds itself "recentered" on the mystery of Jesus Christ. He, indeed, not the church, stands at the center of the Christian mystery; the church, by contrast, is a derived, related mystery, which finds in him its raison d'être. Such a decentering of the church and its consequent recentering on Jesus Christ are absolutely necessary if theology wants to avoid maximalist ecclesiological tendencies, of which the axiom "Outside the church no salvation" represents an extreme example. A narrow ecclesiocentric approach must be replaced by a broader Christocentric perspective.

For the theology of religions, the paradigm shift from exclusivism to inclusivism implies a clear-cut distinction between the role of Jesus Christ and that of the church in the order of salvation. They are not, and can never be, placed on the same level. For the New Testament, Jesus Christ alone is the "mediator" between God and human beings (cf. 1 Tim 2:5; Heb 8:6; 9:15; 12:24). Whatever role may have to be attributed to the church in the order of salvation, it can never be placed on a par with that of Jesus Christ; nor can the same necessity ever be attributed to it. This demonstrates the need to transcend an overly narrow ecclesiocentric outlook. A theology of religions cannot be built on an ecclesiological emphasis that would falsify perspectives. The church, as a derived mystery and utterly relative to the mystery of Christ, cannot be the yardstick by which the salvation of others is measured. What role is to be assigned to it in relation to the religions and their members, in a decentered perspective, is a question to which we must return later.

FROM CHRISTOCENTRISM
TO THEOCENTRISM

In the recent discussion on the theology of religions, there are, however, many writers who have argued for and promoted a second, even more radical, paradigm shift. To inclusivist Christocentrism is being opposed a theocentric perspective, also called "pluralism." The significance of the term and the paradigm shift involved must be clearly perceived. Any paradigm shift involves rejecting the previous paradigm; in this case, that of the centrality of Jesus Christ in the order of salvation, as traditionally conceived by Christian faith. These authors wish to abandon not only the view that places the church at the center of the theological perspective but even that which situates there the mystery of Jesus Christ. In the new perspective, in the center stands God and God alone. The term "pluralism" refers to the replacement of the single universal and constitutive mediation of Jesus Christ with many "ways" or saving figures leading to God-the-Center. The various religions, Christianity included, represent so many ways leading to God, each of which, differences notwithstanding, has equal validity and value. The main lines of the reasoning are as follows.

If Christianity sincerely seeks a dialogue with the other religious traditions —

a dialogue that it can seek only on a footing of equality — it must first of all renounce any claim to uniqueness for the person and work of Jesus Christ as a universal "constitutive" element of salvation. To be sure, this position is open to various interpretations. According to some, while not being "constitutive" of salvation in the sense that universal salvation depends on his person and work, Jesus Christ nevertheless remains "normative" as the most perfect symbol and even ideal model of human-divine relations. For others he is neither "constitutive" nor "normative." Examples of those who hold to the idea of Jesus as "normative" would include E. Troeltsch and P. Tillich,[10] and "process" theologians like J. B. Cobb and S. M. Ogden.[11] For others Jesus is neither "constitutive" nor "normative." The primary exponent of this extreme position is undoubtedly John Hick.

Hick's position is so representative of a theological pluralism understood in the radical sense that it is worth pausing a moment to consider it.[12] Hick advocates a "Copernican revolution" in Christology, a revolution that must specifically consist of a shift in paradigm, a movement from the traditional Christocentric perspective to a new theocentric perspective. The expression "Copernican revolution" originally designated the passage from one system for explaining the cosmos, now antiquated and overthrown, to another system that actually corresponds to reality. This passage took place when the Ptolemaic system was replaced by that of Copernicus. Having believed for centuries that the sun revolves around the earth, we finally discovered, with Galileo and Copernicus, that the earth actually revolves around the sun. Likewise, having believed for centuries that the other religious traditions revolved around Christianity, today we must acknowledge that the center around which all religious traditions revolve (including Christianity) is actually God. Such a paradigm shift necessarily entails the abandonment of any claim to a unique meaning not only for Christianity but for Jesus Christ himself.

Hick does not ignore theological writings representing the middle position between exclusivism and "pluralism," that of inclusivism, in the manner of Karl Rahner, for example. Still, for Hick, all the efforts of an impressive number of recent (especially Catholic) theologians to endow the theology of religions with an inclusive, open Christocentrism capable of combining, on the one hand, the "constitutive" sense of the Jesus Christ event for the salvation of humanity, with, on the other hand, the value of other religious traditions as representing interventions of God in the history of human cultures, and vehicles for "elements of grace" and salvation for their members — all of these efforts may be set aside as

---

10. E. Troeltsch, *The Absoluteness of Christianity and the History of Religions;* P. Tillich, *Systematic Theology,* vols. 2–3 (Chicago: University of Chicago Press, 1957–63); idem, *Christianity and the Encounter of World Religions* (New York: Columbia University Press, 1963).

11. Cf. J. B. Cobb, *Christ in a Pluralistic Age* (Philadelphia: Westminster Press, 1975); idem, *Beyond Dialogue: Toward a Mutual Transformation of Christianity and Buddhism* (Philadelphia: Fortress Press, 1982). Cf. also S. M. Ogden, *Christ without Myth* (New York: Harper and Brothers, 1963); idem, *Is There Only One True Religion or Are There Many?* (Dallas: Southern Methodist University Press, 1992).

12. Cf. especially J. Hick, *God and the Universe of Faiths: Essays in the Philosophy of Religion* (London: Macmillan, 1973); idem, *God Has Many Names: Britain's New Religious Pluralism* (London: Macmillan, 1980); idem, *Problems of Religious Pluralism* (London: Macmillan, 1985).

unworthy of serious consideration. Indeed, they are comparable to the "epicycles" concocted by ancient science in its vain attempt to force certain recalcitrant phenomena into the Ptolemaic system, until the latter finally collapsed with all its epicycles, making room for the Copernican revolution. Likewise, the Copernican revolution in Christology, which Hick is determined to promote, rejects all inclusive Christologies as if they were useless, antiquated epicycles. The only valid surviving theology of religions will now be that of a theocentric pluralism, which accounts for all the phenomena, transcends any Christian claim to a privileged, universal role for Jesus Christ, and at last establishes interreligious dialogue on a genuinely equal footing.

It may further be noted that Hick's thinking has fostered an actual school of thought that vaunts a somewhat militant attitude, as attested by its slogans. Besides the paradigm shift of the Copernican revolution, one hears talk of "crossing the Rubicon." "Crossing the Rubicon" obviously signifies irrevocably recognizing the equal meaning and value of the various religions and waiving any claim not only to exclusivity but also to normativity for Christianity or Jesus Christ.[13] If there is any universality in Jesus Christ, it can only be that of the attraction his message might have in terms of the aspirations of men and women in general. Of course, other salvific figures could exert the same kind of attraction.

FURTHER MODELS AND BEYOND

REGNOCENTRISM AND SOTERIOCENTRISM

One of the main objections raised against the theocentric paradigm has to do with its uncritical assumption of a concept of the Absolute Reality akin to the monotheistic and prophetic religions of the Western Hemisphere, but completely alien to the mystical traditions of the East. A preconceived idea of God is being imposed on all religions in an attempt to show how even in their differences they converge on the same Divine Center. Such objections have forced those advocating theocentric pluralism to propose further models which, however, simply amount to new variations on the same paradigm.

Hick now proposes the model of "Reality-Centeredness."[14] This means that all religions are oriented in different ways toward that which they view as the Central Reality or Divine Absolute. Sharing in this universal search, all religious traditions have, in their differences, equal value: none has precedence over the others or has the privilege of a special divine revelation. "Ultimate Reality" refers

13. Cf. L. Swidler, ed., *Toward a Universal Theology of Religion* (Maryknoll, N.Y.: Orbis Books, 1987); especially P. F. Knitter, "Hans Küng's Theological Rubicon," 224–30. Cf. also J. Hick and P. F. Knitter, eds., *The Myth of Christian Uniqueness: Towards a Pluralistic Theology of Religions* (Maryknoll, N.Y.: Orbis Books, 1987).

14. Cf. J. Hick, *An Interpretation of Religious Responses to the Transcendent* (New Haven and London: Yale University Press, 1989). For a more accessible presentation of the theory, cf. J. Hick, *The Rainbow of Faiths* (London: SCM Press, 1995).

to the fact that ultimately the Divine can be considered neither personal (as in theistic traditions) nor impersonal (as in nontheistic traditions). The notion of "myth," used earlier with reference to Christology, is also applied to the idea of the Divine Ultimate, regardless of the form under which it comes to be known in the different religions: the Hindu *Brahman*, the *Allah* of Islam, the *Yahweh* of Judaism, the *Abbà* of Christianity.[15] To speak of "Our Father who is in heaven" means referring, in the Christian mythical key, to that which is "the Real."

Hick, therefore, now denies any real correspondence between human knowledge and the divine reality; religious language has but a perfunctory function to play. Of the Real *an sich* we really know nothing; our consciousness can only gain access to phenomena. What matters, however, is that all religions — whichever be their characteristic idiom — have the potential to spur people to go out of themselves in search of the supreme Reality which nourishes love and compassion. Applied to God, the notion of "myth" puts the theocentric model off-center, opening the way to "Reality-centeredness." In the soteriological key, all religions have the power to transform people from their self-centeredness to "Reality-centeredness." But all religious traditions, theistic or otherwise, must be subjected to a process of "demythization"; it will then be seen that none has or can claim a privileged access to "Reality."

Faced with the objections leveled at the theocentric paradigm, Paul Knitter has reacted in a more practical and concrete way. He now proposes that the theocentric model be replaced by what he calls "regnocentrism" or "soteriocentrism."[16] Knitter observes that all religions propose a message of salvation or human liberation. Regardless of the ways in which that aim is conceived and pursued, all religions share the same potential of becoming ways of salvation for their followers. The criterion for assessing them is the extent to which, rather than being sources of enslavement and oppression, they actually contribute to the liberation of people. In specifically Christian language, this will mean that all religions are destined to be visible signs of the presence in the world of the Reign of God, but understood in a limited horizontal way; all can and ought to contribute, from different angles, to the growth of God's Reign among persons and peoples.

More recently, Knitter has further developed the liberation model. He now unites closely the double concern for a liberation praxis and interreligious dialogue.[17] The *sòtèria* he advocates calls for the global responsibility and shared commitment of the different religious traditions for "eco-human well-being." The theology of religions is no longer centered on the Christ event but on the Reign of God, which is built up through history and is destined to reach its

15. Hick, *An Interpretation of Religious Responses*, 343–61.

16. P. F. Knitter, "Towards a Liberation Theology of Religions," in *The Myth of Christian Uniqueness*, ed. Hick and Knitter, 178–200; idem, "Interreligious Dialogue: What? Why? How?" in L. Swidler et al., *Death or Dialogue? From the Age of Monologue to the Age of Dialogue* (London: SCM Press, 1990), 19–44.

17. Cf. P. F. Knitter, *One Earth, Many Religions: Multifaith Dialogue and Global Responsibility* (Maryknoll, N.Y.: Orbis Books, 1995); idem, "Toward a Liberative Interreligious Dialogue," *Cross Currents* 45, no. 4 (1995): 451–68.

fulfillment in the eschatological age. Attention is no longer on the past but on the future; God and his Reign are the goal of history toward which religions, Christianity included, are all heading together as to their common destiny.

The Reign of God model is understood by Knitter as a new version of the theocentric model. It has the merit of affirming that the followers of other religious traditions are already members of the Reign of God in history, and that together with Christians they are destined to aid in the growth of the Reign toward its eschatological fullness; we must return to these matters later. However, quite apart from the fact that such a model continues to refer to a concept of God proper to the monotheistic religions, for traditional Christian faith it does not and cannot represent a paradigm shift from the Christological paradigm. To claim otherwise would mean forgetting that the Reign of God has broken into history in Jesus Christ and the Christ event; that it is through the action of the risen Christ that the members of the various religious traditions share in the Reign of God historically present; and finally, that the eschatological Reign to which the members of all religious traditions are summoned together is that Reign which the Lord Jesus Christ will hand over to his Father at the end (see 1 Cor 15:28). As theocentrism and Christocentrism do not constitute different paradigms, so neither do regnocentrism and Christocentrism; on the contrary, they are inseparable aspects of the same reality.

LOGOCENTRISM AND PNEUMATOCENTRISM

Among models which are being proposed today as possible substitutes for the Christocentric model, reference must also be made to the universal active presence in the world and history of the Word of God, on the one hand, and of the Spirit of God, on the other. In these models, the *Logos* and the *Pneuma*,[18] the divine "Word and Spirit" of God — whom St. Irenaeus saw as the "two hands of God," jointly carrying out his work (*Adv. Haer.* IV, 7, 4) — tend to be severed from the Christ event, to be viewed as autonomous and independent agents, transcending the historical and the particular, whose distinct and separate action constitutes two economies of divine salvation, alternative to that which is in Jesus Christ.

With regard to the Word of God (*Logos*), it is remarked that the revealed message itself witnesses to his universal action through world history; the post-biblical tradition of the early apologists does likewise. The conclusion is being drawn that in every event and circumstance, it is the Word of God who saves, not precisely the Word-of-God-made-flesh, that is, Jesus Christ. Along these lines A. Pieris writes, "He who reveals, who saves and transforms is the Word himself." "The Christ" is a title; a title does not save. As for Jesus, he is "he in whom Christians recognize the Word, as seen, heard and touched by human senses."[19]

---

18. Y. Congar, *The Word and the Spirit* (London: G. Chapman, 1986).

19. A. Pieris, "Inculturation in Asia: A Theological Reflection on an Experience," in *Jahrbuch für kontextuelle Theologien* (Frankfurt: Verlag für interkulturelle Kommunikation, Missionswissenschaftliches Institut Missio, 1994), 60.

In equivalent words, it can be said that it is the Word as such that saves, whereas Jesus is only he in whom the Word is recognized by Christians. Along these same lines, C. Molari asks: "When it is said, 'There is salvation in no one else' (Acts 4:12)...the problem lies in establishing what is meant by the 'Name' invoked in whom resides the saving power; the symbol name (Jesus) or the ineffable divine name of the God who is revealed in Jesus, and therefore the inexpressible power of the eternal Word that resounds in Jesus."[20] He responds that in every divine manifestation it is always the Word of God who brings revelation and salvation. Likewise, in the case of Jesus. The titles "only-begotten" or "Son" may be applied to him insofar as he is "constituted Messiah through his fidelity to the Father's will and through the revelation that God has effected in him" (p. 44). Here as well it seems that the Word who saves as such is being separated from the Jesus in whom we Christians encounter him. Thus a logocentric model is being built in which the Word and the man Jesus seem to be separate. And the door is opened to two economies of salvation, one through the Word of God encountered in Jesus Christ for Christians, and the other through the Word as such for the "others."

Certainly, following John's Prologue, a universal presence of the Logos before his incarnation in Jesus Christ (Jn 1:1–4) must be affirmed. He is the "true Light that enlightens every human being" (Jn 1:9). This anticipated presence and action of the Logos do not, however, prevent the New Testament from seeing in the Word incarnate, of whom the Prologue of the Johannine Gospel also speaks (1:14), that is, in Jesus Christ, the universal Savior of humankind (cf. Lk 2:11; Jn 4:42; Phil 3:20; Eph 5:23; 2 Tim 1:10; Titus 1:4; 2:13; 3:6, etc.). Christianity has traditionally understood this to mean that the anticipated action of the Word of God is related to the event of Jesus Christ in which God's plan for humankind comes to a climax. The Word-to-be-incarnate and the Word incarnate are a single indivisible reality. Logocentrism and Christocentrism are not mutually opposed; they refer back and forth to one another in a single divine economy of salvation which unfolds in history, and at the center of which stands the event of Jesus Christ, incarnate Word.

Similar remarks may be made when the universal economy of the Spirit of God tends to be viewed as independent from the historical event of Jesus Christ. In this instance, it has been suggested that in order to avoid the blind alley to which a narrowly Christocentric perspective necessarily leads, there is need for a new theology of religions built on a pneumatocentric model. In this direction P. F. Knitter writes: "A pneumatological theology of religions could dislodge the Christian debate from its confining categories of 'inclusivism' or 'exclusivism' or 'pluralism,'"[21] in accordance with the opposite Christological positions. It is then observed that unlike the economy of the Christ event, which is unavoidably lim-

---

20. C. Molari, "Introduzione," in *L'unicità cristiana: Un mito? Per una teologia pluralista delle religioni,* ed. J. Hick and P. F. Knitter (Assisi: Cittadella, 1994), 35–36.
21. P. F. Knitter, "A New Pentecost?" *Current Dialogue* 19, no. 1 (1991): 35.

ited by the particularity of history, the economy of the Spirit knows no bounds of space and time. Free of all constraints, the Spirit "blows where he wills" (see Jn 3:8). The Spirit of God has been universally present throughout human history and remains active today outside the boundaries of the Christian fold. He it is who "inspires" in people belonging to other religious traditions the obedience of saving faith, and in the traditions themselves a word spoken by God to their adherents. Indeed, could it not be thought that, whereas Christians obtain salvation through the economy of God's Son incarnate in Jesus Christ, others receive it through the immediate autonomous action of the Spirit of God? The personal distinction between God's two "hands" is warrant for the two distinct channels through which God's saving presence reaches out to people in distinct economies of salvation. Indeed, P. F. Knitter writes, "The Reign of God, as it may be taking shape under the breath of the Spirit, can be seen as 'an all-comprehensive phenomenon of grace'; that is, an economy of grace genuinely different from the one made known through the Word incarnate in Jesus."[22] In short, the Holy Spirit being God's necessary "point of entry" in the life of human beings and of peoples, his immediate action — which bypasses the punctual event of Jesus Christ — opens the way for a different model of the Christian theology of the religions, a model no longer Christocentric but pneumatocentric.

That the Holy Spirit is God's "point of entry" wherever and whenever God reveals and communicates himself to people is certain. Indeed, it is so by virtue of the necessary correspondence which exists between the mystery of the Triune God in itself and that of God's manifestation in the world. The immanent presence of the Holy Spirit is always and in all circumstances the reality of God's saving grace. However, can a model centered on the Spirit be separated from the Christological model? It does not seem to be so. The universal action of the Spirit throughout human history must be clearly affirmed, both before and after the historical Jesus Christ event. But Christian faith holds that the action of the Spirit and that of Jesus Christ, though distinct, are nevertheless complementary and inseparable. Pneumatocentrism and Christocentrism cannot, therefore, be construed as two distinct economies of salvation, one parallel to the other. They constitute two inseparable aspects, or complementary elements, within a single economy of salvation.

If, then, the Spirit is present and active in history before the Jesus Christ event, he is so in view of, and in relation to, the historical event which stands at the center of the history of salvation. The specific function of the Spirit consists of allowing persons to become sharers, before or after the event, in the paschal mystery of Jesus Christ's death and resurrection (*Gaudium et Spes* §22). Thus, through the power of the Spirit, the Jesus Christ event is being actuated through all times; it is present and active in every generation. In all cases the immediate influence of the Spirit gives expression to the operative presence of

---

22. P. F. Knitter, *Jesus and the Other Names: Christian Mission and Global Responsibility* (Maryknoll, N.Y.: Orbis Books, 1996), 113.

God's saving action which has come to a climax in Jesus Christ. Christocentrism and pneumatology are combined in a single economy of salvation.

BEYOND WESTERN CATEGORIES

The preceding discussion will have shown that for the most part the recent debate on the theology of religions has been dominated by three mutually incompatible perspectives. The argument has evolved around the possibility or the need for changing paradigms from narrow ecclesiocentrism to Christocentrism, and then to theocentrism. Other models, as has been seen, are simply substitutes for the theocentric or pluralistic paradigm. However, it is being asserted today by a sizable number of theologians that the categories within which the debate is thus being framed betray a Western way of thinking which can yield no satisfactory answer to the problem. The main misgiving is that the problematic of shifting paradigms, around which the discussion revolves, implies an either-or (*aut-aut*) mode of contradiction that is not very congenial to the Eastern mindset, which rather thinks in terms of both-and (*et-et*). If we hope to build a theology of religions founded not on mutual contradictions and confrontation but on harmony, convergence, and unity, the current problematic must be abandoned.

The implication seems to be that the theocentric paradigm itself, in its opposition to the Christocentric, has become inappropriate; in short, that discussion on the pros and cons of uniqueness must be abandoned. Only then will we be in a position to discover the specificity and singularity of each religious tradition, as well as the positive significance of their multiplicity. Religious pluralism, it is being suggested, is rooted in the depth of the Divine Mystery itself and in the manifold way in which human cultures have responded to it. Far from being a hindrance that must be overcome, or a fact of life that we must be resigned to tolerating, religious pluralism is to be gratefully welcomed as a sign of the superabundant riches of the Divine Mystery which overflows to humankind and as an outstanding opportunity for mutual enrichment, "cross-fertilization," and "transformation" of the traditions themselves.[23]

A considerable number of authors, particularly from the Asian continent, have denounced recently the inadequacies of the problematic at work in the Christocentric, or even in the so-called pluralistic, paradigm. Some examples may be mentioned.

Aloysius Pieris writes: "I have found myself gradually appropriating a trend in Asia, which adopts a paradigm wherein the three categories mentioned above [of exclusivism, inclusivism, and pluralism] do not make sense."[24] For Felix Wilfred, the issue of "uniqueness" betrays a Western problematic. He writes:

---

23. Cf. R. Panikkar, *The Intrareligious Dialogue* (New York: Paulist Press, 1978); J. B. Cobb, *Beyond Dialogue: Toward a Mutual Transformation of Christianity and Buddhism* (Philadelphia: Fortress Press, 1982)

24. A. Pieris, "An Asian Paradigm: Interreligious Dialogue and the Theology of Religions," *The Month* 26 (1993): 130.

The debate around the issue is mainly a debate of Western factions — the dogmatic, and the reactionary liberals who try to relativize the claim of uniqueness. This language ... has its presuppositions and epistemological background, and it is not clear that [it] could be extrapolated to other cultural areas ... Seen from the Indian perspective, tradition and frame of reference, the need to use the language of uniqueness does not arise.[25]

A view of religious pluralism which seeks to transcend conflicting claims to uniqueness on the part of Christianity and other religious traditions finds a favorable echo in recent Asian assemblies on the theology of religions. An example is the statement issued by the Thirteenth Annual Meeting of the Indian Theological Association (December 28–31, 1989), under the title "Towards an Indian Christian Theology of Religious Pluralism."[26] The statement points to the limitations of the categories currently used in the debate on the theology of religions; these betray "theoretical approaches to the faith of other people," issuing "from a mono-religio-cultural society and a mere academic and speculative point of view" (§4). "We would rather approach the issue from a different perspective," that, namely, of a live encounter and dialogue. In such an approach, Christ remains for us "constitutionally the Way to the Father" (§28). However, while we continue to approach the problem "from our own faith perspective" (§9), we also "understand the purpose and meaning of the wonderful religious variety around us and its role and function in the attainment of salvation" (§8).

Several voices in the Western world have responded positively to the new perspective advocated by Eastern theologians. M. Barnes argues that an escape must be negotiated from the rigid patterning of the threefold paradigm. The answer is not to be found in shifting from a Christocentric to a theocentric position. It lies beyond pluralism. Under the influence of interfaith encounter, the theology of religions is in fact shifting "from a pluralist to a post-modern mode."[27] This requires that theologians learn to be "systematic without being systemic." While holding on to their religious identity, they must engage in a "theology *of* dialogue," not merely build a "theology *for* dialogue."[28] "The first demand of such a theology is to accept that all dialogue is established precisely in asymmetry, that is to say by the difference between the partners. Community or communality has yet to be established: this is the phenomenon which governs all faith encounters."[29]

---

25. Cf. F. Wilfred, "Some Tentative Reflections on the Language of Christian Uniqueness: An Indian Perspective," in Pontifical Council for Interreligious Dialogue, *Bulletin* 85–86, nos. 1–2 (1994): 57.

26. Cf. K. Pathil, ed., *Religious Pluralism: An Indian Christian Perspective* (Delhi: ISPCK, 1991), 338–49.

27. Cf. M. Barnes, "Theology of Religions in a Post-modern World," *The Month* 28 (1994): 270–74; 325–30. Also cf. idem, *Christian Identity and Religious Pluralism: Religions in Conversation* (Nashville: Abingdon Press, 1989).

28. Cf. D. Tracy, *Dialogue with the Other: The Interreligious Dialogue* (Louvain: Peeters Press, 1990).

29. Cf. Barnes, "Theology of Religions in a Post-modern World," 273.

Other authors concur in saying that the dilemma between inclusivism and pluralism, or, equivalently, between Christocentrism and theocentrism, must be transcended. J. A. DiNoia notes that both inclusivists and pluralists minimize the differences of the others and hence the import of the interreligious conversation.[30] The order of the day is not a "theology *for* dialogue" but a "theology *in* dialogue" (p. 111). On the one hand, interreligious conversations must not "serve the purpose of disclosing Christian-like virtualities" in the doctrines of other religious communities, as the inclusivist thesis is prone to do, but should "entertain such doctrines as self-consistent alternative teachings about that upon which human life should be focused" (p. 138). On the other hand, the pluralistic accounts of religious systems also appear to "attenuate the significance of religious differences in the course of trying to account for them" (p. 152). The way out of the "current impasse" in the theology of religions consists in recognizing squarely that distinct religious communities actually propose distinct aims for human life, as well as the legitimacy of such claims from the point of view of their faith (pp. 163–65). That Christian theology interprets other aims in terms of its own understanding is normal and legitimate; but so too is the reverse. Nor must one interpretation become exclusivist of the other at any time.

In such a situation, one recent author, James Fredericks, hopes for a temporary moratorium on any effort to construct a "theology of religions." What is actually needed today is a "comparative study of religions."[31] He bases his opinion on the fact that all three of the main paradigms (exclusivism, inclusivism, and pluralism) around which the discussion of the theology of religions has taken place are flawed insofar as they have been unable to recognize and take seriously the specific difference and the inner consistency proper to the various religious traditions. The validity of a Christian theology of religions is to be appraised in terms of a twofold criterion: its faithfulness to Christian tradition on the one hand, and on the other its ability to prompt Christians to have positive and fruitful relations with the "others." In his view all three of the classic paradigms have failed in terms of one or both of the criteria. This is why the pretense of constructing a formal theology of the religions ought to be abandoned. He writes:

> At this time in the history of Christianity, as Christian believers look beyond their own faith into a world of immense religious diversity, a completely satisfactory account of the meaning of non-Christian religions is no longer possible. Our survey of the debate over the theology of religions amply supports this conclusion. None of the three basic candidates for a theology of religions meets the standards set by the two criteria we have been discussing. This being the case, the question of a theology of religions should be put aside for the time being. (pp. 165–66)

---

30. Cf. J. A. DiNoia, *The Diversity of Religions: A Christian Perspective* (Washington, D.C.: Catholic University of America Press, 1992), 127.

31. J. L. Fredericks, *Faith among Faiths: Christian Theology and Non-Christian Religions* (New York and Mahwah, N.J.: Paulist Press, 1999).

We could listen to further voices, not all of them in agreement with one another. Yet it is well to note that despite diverse views on what course should be taken to overcome the contradictory claims of inclusivism and pluralism, there seems to be emerging a certain consensus on the need to avoid both "absolutism" and "relativism" wherever found. Plurality needs to be taken seriously and to be welcomed, not merely as a matter of fact but in principle. Its place in God's plan of salvation for humankind must be stressed. It must also be shown that commitment to one's faith is compatible with openness to that of others; that the affirmation of one's religious identity grows, not from confrontation with other identities, but in encounter with them. A theology of religions must ultimately be a theology of the plurality of religious traditions, or religious pluralism. Which model such a theology may follow in order to be truly Christian remains to be shown.

TOWARD A MODEL OF INCLUSIVE PLURALISM

THE CHRISTOLOGICAL QUESTION

From the foregoing it is clear that at the heart of the paradigm shifts analyzed so far is the Christological question. Involved in the first paradigm shift from ecclesiocentrism to Christocentrism is the centrality that the Christian church attributes to Jesus Christ in relation to the role of the church itself (which in relation to Jesus Christ is a derived mystery); in the second shift from Christocentrism to theocentrism what is at stake is the universal constitutive mediation that Christian faith has traditionally assigned to him in God's plan of salvation for humankind.

At stake, therefore, is the universal significance and constitutive role which Christianity attributes to Jesus Christ. According to the pluralists, having faith in Jesus Christ means that one has encountered God's self-gift in the human person Jesus of Nazareth; it does not mean, however, that this historical person represents the constitutive way for all human beings, regardless of the circumstances of place and time. In other words, faith in Jesus Christ means believing that I, as a Christian, can be saved through him; not, however, that he is the Savior of the world. Jesus is the way for Christians, but the existence of other ways means that he is not necessary for the others.

Viewed in this fashion, the theocentric paradigm shift revolves entirely around the Christological problem. Its adoption or disavowal primarily depends on acceptance or rejection of a "revisionist" Christology which departs substantially from that of mainstream Christianity. It is no coincidence that the exponents of the theocentric perspective base their advocacy of such a paradigm shift on a Christology "revised" or "reinterpreted" in the context of religious pluralism.[32] To

---

32. Cf. J. Hick, ed., *The Myth of God Incarnate* (London: SCM Press, 1977); *The Metaphor of God Incarnate* (Louisville: Westminster/John Knox Press, 1993).

them such a revisionist Christology seems necessary for several reasons, including: (1) a newly acquired historical consciousness; (2) the inseparability of content and context in any human experience; (3) the relativity of every experience of the Divine Mystery, which in itself remains beyond all telling and is inexhaustible; (4) the particularity and contingency of the historical event Jesus of Nazareth; (5) the "theocentric" outlook of Jesus himself as opposed to the Christocentric approach of the apostolic church; (6) the total discontinuity between Jesus' own self-understanding and the kerygmatic proclamation of him; (7) the "mythical" or "metaphorical" language of the late New Testament Christology and its continuations in postbiblical tradition; and so forth.[33]

Fundamentally, the question which is being asked is whether in the present context of dialogue the unequivocal witness of the New Testament — which is not being denied — to the universal significance of Jesus Christ need not be reexamined and reinterpreted. Does that witness belong to the substance of the message, or is it due to the cultural idiom in which the experience of the early Christians has been expressed and to the circumstances in which the experience itself was made? In the light of what we know today about the other religious traditions and their followers, is it still possible to make the salvation of all human beings depend on the particular historical individual Jesus of Nazareth, about whom often they have not heard or whom otherwise they have not been in a position to recognize? More radically, what authority as a "norm of faith" does the New Testament witness still retain, once it is confronted with our present experience of dialogue? Some of these questions will claim our attention later.

Meanwhile, two observations should be made on the Christological debate in the context of the theology of religions. The first is that the assumption made by a growing number of theologians that a Christocentric perspective is no longer tenable calls for some clarifications. Are Christocentrism and theocentrism really at odds, as is being claimed, as two contradictory paradigms? To say so is already in itself a theological and Christological option. The Christocentrism of Christian tradition is not, in fact, opposed to theocentrism. It never places Jesus Christ in the place of God; it merely affirms that God has placed him at the center of his saving plan for humankind, not as the end but as the way, not as the goal of every human quest for God but as the universal "mediator" (cf. 1 Tim 2:5) of God's saving action toward people. Christian theology is not faced with the dilemma of being either Christocentric or theocentric; it is theocentric by being Christocentric and vice versa. This amounts to saying that Jesus Christ is the "medium" (*le milieu*) of God's encounter with human beings. The man Jesus unquestionably belongs to the order of signs and symbols; but in him who has been constituted "Lord and Christ" (Acts 2:36), God's saving action reaches out to people in various ways, knowingly to some and to others unknowingly.

---

33. I have tried to resolve some of these questions by highlighting the continuity-in-discontinuity between the different levels of the development of the church's Christological faith. Cf. J. Dupuis, *Who Do You Say That I Am? Introduction to Christology* (Maryknoll, N.Y.: Orbis Books, 1994), 57–110.

The second observation has to do with the kind of Christology that underlies the Christocentric and the theocentric paradigms. All recent and contemporary Christologies get their bearings "from below," that is, starting out from the human Jesus and his historic event, rather than "from above," that is, from his personal identity as the "only-begotten" preexisting Son of God — as used to be done in the past. But even starting "from below," Christological reflection must let itself be brought through the dynamism of faith itself toward a "high" Christology. Some Christologists, however, refuse this ontological ascent, and therefore remain on the level of a "low" Christology. Using this distinction between "high" and "low" Christology, it is clear that the inclusivist or Christocentric model of a theology of religions is consonant with a "high" Christology in which the personal identity of Jesus Christ as the "only-begotten" Son of God is unambiguously recognized; by contrast, the pluralist or theocentric model postulates a "low" Christology which questions and ultimately denies such ontological affirmations about Jesus Christ. The Christian tradition amply attests, however, that the only adequate foundation on which the singular uniqueness of Jesus Christ can be based is his personal identity as the Son of God made man, as God's incarnate Word. No other Christology can ultimately provide a persuasive account of Christ's universal mediatorship in the order of salvation. The kind of logic by which the pluralist theologians reject the uniqueness and saving universality of Christ thus becomes intelligible.

Concretely, then, the choice between a Christocentric and a theocentric paradigm in the theology of religions depends on the option between a "high," ontological Christology and a "low" Christology, deliberately anchored at the "functional" level. Such a choice has weighty consequences. The price that traditional Christian faith finds itself paying in terms of the mystery of the person and work of Jesus Christ is considerable. It is not surprising that some recent authors not only have rejected the option set up by the pluralists between two paradigms but have shown their position to be in fact untenable.[34] A book by Gavin D'Costa, entitled *Theology and Religious Pluralism*,[35] deserves special mention in this regard. The author recalls two basic axioms of traditional Christian faith: the universal salvific will of God (1 Tim 2:4) and the necessity of the mediation of Jesus Christ (cf. 1 Tim 2:5). D'Costa shows that contrasting attitudes toward these two axioms account for the three basic positions of exclusivism, inclusivism, and pluralism. While exclusivism relies on the second axiom and neglects the first, and pluralism relies on the first to the detriment of the second, inclusivism alone succeeds in accounting for and holding both at once. A unilateral emphasis on one of the two crucial axioms that ought to govern a Christian theology of religions leads to theological positions that are unsustainable.

What remains according to the author is the model of inclusivism. He shows that only the inclusivist position is in a condition to assume and harmonize the

---

34. Cf. G. D'Costa, ed., *Christian Uniqueness Reconsidered: The Myth of a Pluralistic Theology of Religions* (Maryknoll, N.Y.: Orbis Books, 1990).

35. Cf. G. D'Costa, *Theology and Religious Pluralism: The Challenge of Other Religions* (London: Basil Blackwell, 1986).

two traditional axioms of Christian faith that remain obligatory for any Christian theology of religions. On the one side, in inclusivism Jesus Christ is clearly asserted to be God's decisive revelation and constitutive Savior. On the other side, the door is opened to a sincere acknowledgment of divine manifestations in the history of humanity in various cultures and of efficacious "elements of grace" to be found in other religious traditions: elements that are of saving value for their members. Revealed in a decisive manner in Jesus Christ, God (and the mystery of salvation) is nonetheless present and at work in other religious traditions. How this takes place will be clarified further ahead.

A TRINITARIAN CHRISTOLOGY AS INTERPRETATIVE KEY

From what has been said thus far, it is clear that a theology of religious pluralism must be situated beyond both the inclusivist and the "pluralist" paradigms, understood to be mutually contradictory. It must be shown that, whereas inclusive Christocentrism is nonnegotiable for Christian theology, it can be combined with a true theocentric pluralism, both aspects being complementary in a single reality. We are accordingly seeking an "inclusive pluralism" (or "pluralist inclusivism") model of the theology of religions.

A Christian theology of religious pluralism must be one based on the interaction of the Christian faith with the other living faiths, and in that sense it must be an interfaith theology. The need for dialogue as a foundation for a theology of the religions may perhaps be at least partly clarified by a consideration of the situation of dialogue that characterizes mutual relations between the various churches and Christian communities in the field of Christian ecumenism. The recognition of the imperfect ecclesiality of non-Catholic churches and Christian communities has opened the way for a new problematic in the search for Christian unity: unity by "returning" to the one true church of Christ of all individual Christians and Christian bodies who had gone astray or found themselves separated from that true church has given way to a "global ecumenism" which seeks the "recomposition" of organic unity between churches and ecclesial communities, within which the mystery of the one church willed by Christ is present and operative in different ways and degrees.

Similarly, while making allowance for differences, the "ecumenical ecumenism" of the relationship between Christianity and the other religions can no longer be viewed in terms of contradiction and opposition between realization here and "stepping-stones" there, much less between "absoluteness" on one side and mere potentiality on the other, or between a monopoly of truth and grace on one side and a complete void of such gifts on the other. The "one-true-religion" thesis has therefore now been superseded, as was noted earlier in connection with Vatican II. From now on the relationship between Christianity and the other religions must be thought of in terms of the relational interdependence, within the organic whole of universal reality, between diverse modalities of encounter of human existence with the Divine Mystery. The Catholic Church will no doubt continue to hold that the mystery of the church willed by Jesus Christ "subsists" (*subsistit*) (cf. *Lumen Gentium* §8) in it, while it "exists" in incomplete measure in other churches. Similarly, the Christian faith will continue to imply a "fullness" of divine manifestation and revelation in Jesus Christ not realized elsewhere with the same fullness of sacramentality. Nevertheless, in both cases, the realities involved will have to be viewed as mutually related and interdependent, constituting together the complete whole of human-divine relationships. It is in this direction that a Christian theology of religious pluralism must seek to overcome the dilemma between Christocentric inclusivism and theocentric pluralism, understood as mutually contradictory paradigms.

As we search for a model that would overcome this dilemma, we need to remember, as has been pointed out earlier, that the dichotomy referred to has been gratuitously and wrongly construed. Models which in themselves ought to have been seen as mutually complementary have in effect been made into contradictory paradigms. We have noted above that in Christian theology, Christocentrism, if correctly understood, must not be viewed as contradicting theocentrism; on the contrary, it presupposes it and calls for it. The same is true where the various binaries discussed above are concerned: Christocentrism and soteriocentrism, Christocentrism and regnocentrism, Christology and Jesuology, Christology and Logology, Christology and pneumatology. All members of these binary pairs are and ought to be viewed as interrelated aspects and complementary elements of the indivisible, whole, and entire reality; they can only wrongly be set in opposition to one another.

The integral model we are searching for in view of a Christian interpretation of religious pluralism can best be expressed in terms of a *Trinitarian Christology*. Such a Christology will place in full relief the interpersonal relationships between Jesus and the God whom he calls Father (*Abbà*), on the one side, and between Jesus and the Spirit whom he will send, on the other. These relationships are intrinsic to the mystery of the person and work of Jesus. Christology ought to be imbued with these intra-Trinitarian relationships, but this requirement is all the more urgent in the context of a theology of religious pluralism. Indeed, it may be thought that the mistaken development of Christocentrism into a closed and restrictive paradigm, incompatible with theocentrism, when it occurred, was caused by failure to pay adequate attention to the interpersonal dimension of Christology. As I have written elsewhere:

> Christology has often sinned by impersonalism. To remedy such a shortcoming, the personal and trinitarian dimension of the mystery must be present everywhere. A Christology of the God-man is an abstraction; the only Christology that is real is that of the Son-of-God-made-man-in-history. The personal intra-trinitarian relations must, therefore, be shown to inform every aspect of the Christological mystery.[36]

---

36. Dupuis, *Who Do You Say That I Am?*, 36.

What, then, would be the implications of a Trinitarian Christology for a theology of religious pluralism? On the divine side, it will be necessary to show clearly that Jesus Christ must never be thought to replace the Father. As Jesus himself was entirely "God-centered," so must the faith-interpretation proposed of him — the Christ — by the Christian kerygma remain at all times. The Gospel according to John calls Jesus "the way, and the truth, and the life" (Jn 14:6) — never the goal or the end; the same gospel makes it clear that the goal of human existence — and of history — is the unfathomable mystery of God, whom no human being has ever seen but who has been "made known" to us by his incarnate Son (Jn 1:18). The unique closeness that exists between God and Jesus by virtue of the mystery of the incarnation may never be forgotten, but neither can the unbridgeable distance that remains between the Father and Jesus in his human existence. In this sense, the theocentric paradigm advocated by pluralists in the present debate on the theology of religions touches an essential aspect of the mystery, which, however, it conceives one-sidedly and which should be stated correctly: God, and God alone, is the "absolute" mystery and as such is at the source, at the heart, and at the center, of all reality; the human reality of Jesus by contrast is created, and as such is finite and contingent. While it is true that Jesus the man is uniquely the Son of God, it is equally true that God (the Father) stands beyond Jesus. When he is said to be at the center of the Christian mystery, this is not to be understood in an "absolute" sense but in the order of the economy of God's freely entertained dealings with humankind in history.

The pneumatological aspect of the mystery of Jesus Christ needs to be high-lighted, even more than the Godward orientation of his person and work. A Trinitarian Christology will have to express clearly Jesus' relatedness to the Spirit. This too is a requirement to which Christology ought to be attentive in every circumstance. In the past the Western tradition has often lacked an adequate for-mulation of a *Spirit-Christology* that would show the influence of the Holy Spirit throughout the earthly life of Jesus, from his conception through the power of the Spirit (cf. Lk 1:35) to his resurrection at the hands of God by the power of the same Spirit (cf. Rom 8:11). A Christology of the Spirit would, furthermore, extend beyond the resurrection to illustrate the relationship between the action of the risen Lord and the work of the Holy Spirit. While an "integral Christol-ogy" requires this Spirit-component in all situations, the same requirement can be seen to be even more necessary for the sake of developing a Christian theology of religious pluralism. In such a theology the universal presence and action of the Spirit in human history and in the world will not only need to be affirmed; they will also have to serve as guiding threads and principles.

We have recalled earlier that Christology and pneumatology cannot be inter-preted as two distinct and separate economies of God's personal dealings with humankind; nevertheless, the "personal distinction" between the Word and the Spirit as well as the specific influence of each in all divine-human relationships, individual and collective, serve as a hermeneutical key for the real differentiation and plurality obtaining in the concrete realization of the divine-human relationships in diverse situations and circumstances. The message of the Christian tradition entails such a differentiation when it holds together two affirmations which at first sight would appear contradictory: namely, that, on the one hand, before the resurrection "the Spirit had not been given as yet, because Jesus was not yet glorified" (Jn 7:39), and, on the other, "without doubt, the Holy Spirit was at work in the world before Christ was glorified" (*Ad Gentes* §4). While it is true that "the Spirit is the Spirit of Christ and where the Spirit of Christ is, there is Christ,"[37] the reverse is also true: Christology does not exist without pneumatology; it cannot be allowed to develop into a "Christomonism."

The distinct stress laid by the Eastern and the Western traditions on the role of the Spirit, on the one side, and on the centrality of the Christ event, on the other, is well known and need not be elaborated here.[38] The reproach of "Christomonism" — which has often been brought by Eastern Christianity against the Western tradition — has had the happy result of developing in recent Western theology a new insistence on the role of the Spirit in the divine economy of salvation,[39] not least in Christology proper. This is the origin of the Spirit-Christology which today is developing fast in the West. A well-balanced theological account of the relationship between Christology and pneumatology must combine various elements: on the one hand, the roles of both the Son and the Spirit may not be confused but must remain distinct, even as their hypostatic identities are distinct; on the other hand, there exists between both a "relationship of order" which, without implying any subordinationism of one to the other, translates into the divine economy the order of eternal relations of hypostatic origination in the intrinsic mystery of the Godhead.

Thus, while the functions of the Son and the Spirit need to be kept clearly distinct, there is between them no dichotomy but total complementarity in a single divine economy of salvation: only the Son became man, but the fruit of his redemptive incarnation is the outpouring of the Spirit symbolized at Pentecost. The Christ event is at the center of the historical unfolding of the divine economy, but the punctual event of Jesus Christ is actuated and becomes operative throughout time and space in the work of the Spirit. Several Eastern theologians have laid stress recently on the interrelatedness and complementarity of the "missions" of the Son and of the Spirit in the one divine economy. N. A. Nissiotis has written:

> The salvific event of Christ and Pentecost can neither be confused nor separated. They imply one another; they are as it were the two hands of the Father's love. Their respective roles are equally essential and necessary, and,

---

37. Cf. J. B. Cobb, "The Christian Reason for Being Progressive," *Theology Today* 51, no. 4 (1995): 560.

38. For a brief exposition of this diversity, cf. J. Dupuis, "Western Christocentrism and Eastern Pneumatology," in idem, *Jesus Christ and His Spirit* (Bangalore: Theological Publications in India, 1977), 21–31.

39. Y. Congar, *I Believe in the Holy Spirit*, 3 vols. (London: G. Chapman, 1983); idem, *The Word and the Spirit* (London: G. Chapman, 1986).

on this very account distinct... Pentecost does not inaugurate a religion of the Spirit; it initiates the dispensation throughout space and time of the fruits of the incarnation.[40]

It follows that a theology of religious pluralism elaborated on the foundation of the Trinitarian economy will have to combine and to hold in constructive tension the central character of the punctual historical event of Jesus Christ and the universal action and dynamic influence of the Spirit of God. It will thus be able to account for God's self-manifestation and self-gift in human cultures and religious traditions outside the orbit of influence of the Christian message without, for that matter, construing Christology and pneumatology into two distinct economies of divine-human relationships for Christians and for the members of other traditions, respectively.

What terminology will best be adapted to refer to a Christian theology of religious pluralism built upon the hermeneutical key of Trinitarian Christology and Spirit-Christology? In the previously cited effort to transcend the dilemma between Christocentrism and theocentrism conceived as contradictory paradigms, M. Barnes views a Trinity-centered theology, and in particular a Spirit-Christology, as the road that can lead beyond a particularist exclusivism toward a "pluralistic inclusivism" capable of accounting within the perspective of Christian faith for a plurality of religions not only in fact but also in principle. He writes, for instance:

> A Spirit-centered theory of the interpenetration of traditions can help us to solve the loyalty-openness dilemma. Instead of asking how other religions are related to Christ, and raising the inevitable conundrum of his "latent," "unknown" or "hidden" presence, we look to the way the Spirit of Christ is active, in all religions, in revealing the mystery of Christ — the mystery of what Christ is doing in the world.[41]

Whatever terminology may be used to refer to the Trinitarian pneumato-Christological model, what matters is that it be capable of leading the Christian faith-commitment beyond the suspicion of claiming for itself, if not exclusivity, at least the obligatory reference point binding on all people vis-à-vis the divine-human relationships. The historical centrality of the Christ event cannot be allowed to obscure the Trinitarian rhythm of the divine economy, with its distinct and correlated functions.

THE TASK AHEAD is that of showing how the affirmation of Christian identity is compatible with a genuine recognition of the identity of the other faith-communities as constituting different aspects of the self-revelation of the Absolute Mystery, though related to the Christ event, in a single but complex and

---

40. N. A. Nissiotis, "Pneumatologie orthodoxe," in F. J. Leenhardt et al., *Le Saint-Esprit* (Geneva: Labor et Fides, 1963), 93.
41. M. Barnes, *Christian Identity and Religious Pluralism*, 143.

articulated divine economy. If the perspective to which the model of a Trinitarian Christology leads should be expressed in the parameters of the models that have become familiar in the theology of the religions, the most appropriate term, as already indicated above, seems to be that of "inclusive pluralism" or "pluralistic inclusivism"; this term holds together the universal constitutive character of the Christ event in the order of salvation and the saving significance of the religious traditions in a plurality of principle of the religious traditions within the one manifold plan of God for humankind.

Chapter Four

THE GOD OF THE COVENANT
AND THE RELIGIONS

C ENTRAL TO THE CHRISTIAN VIEW of God's dealings with humankind is a
historical perspective capable of accounting at once for a variety of divine
self-manifestations and the unity of a divinely preordained plan. God's design
for humankind is neither monolithic nor piecemeal, but singular and complex at
the same time. It is one and universal, given God's will to communicate with the
entire human race, irrespective of the historical situations and circumstances in
which men and women find themselves; and it is manifold and variegated in the
concrete forms that the divine unitary design assumes as it unfolds historically.

While the concept of salvation history is of relatively recent coinage, a
salvation-history perspective is deeply rooted in biblical revelation, ancient as
well as new. "Salvation history" operates as an important hermeneutical key for
Christianity's self-understanding and for understanding how it situates itself in
relation to world history in general and to the history of the religions in particular.

The intention of this chapter is to show that the Christian view of salvation
history allows for a more positive appraisal of other religious traditions than has
often been thought. Often enough these traditions have at best been considered
as provisional "stepping-stones" for "things to come"; perhaps useful stepping
stones, yet by their very nature transitory and in any event rendered obsolete and
abrogated by the advent of the reality to which they pointed or of which they
were "partial anticipations." The question here is whether the salvation-history
theological framework makes it possible to attribute to the religious traditions of
the world more than a transient character (whatever might have been their saving
significance for their members) in God's design for humankind: that is, whether
it allows us to assign to them a lasting role and a specific meaning in the overall
mystery of divine-human relations.

More clearly still: Is the relationship between God's dealings with the "Gentiles" through history, on the one side, and God's self-manifestation in biblical
history, on the other, one of mere replacement of shadow with reality? Or, on
the contrary, is there, in the divine plan, a mutual interaction between distinct
elements which, while not representing the reality in the same way, belong nevertheless inseparably together? Can salvation history accommodate not only the
idea of a "propaedeutic value" for world religions, but even the idea that in well-
determined conditions, they may be — eventually — acknowledged to have a

certain saving relevance: even to the point of recognizing an abiding meaning for the plurality of world religious traditions in accordance with God's universal saving design for humankind?

These and other questions will be answered by having recourse to Trinitarian Christology, which, we have suggested, constitutes a possible comprehensive model for a Christian theology of religious pluralism. Where the dimensions of salvation history are concerned, the Trinitarian model will make it possible to lay stress on the universal presence and activity of the "Word of God" and of the "Spirit of God" throughout human history as "medium" (*le milieu*) of God's personal dealings with human beings independent of their concrete situation in history. The connection of the action of the Word and of the Spirit to the particularized historical event of Jesus Christ will not thereby be overlooked or forgotten. The Trinitarian Christological model will likewise shed light on the meaning of the various covenants which according to the Christian tradition God has struck with humankind at various times; these need to be viewed as distinct but — equally important — as interrelated and inseparable. In the light of the model proposed here, a positive answer will be suggested to the vexing question of the abiding efficacy of "pre-Christian" covenants. Such lasting efficacy, as will be seen, is due to the interrelatedness between the distinct modalities of God's self-communication to persons and peoples within the overall history of God's dealings with humankind.

Central to the worldview of Judaism and Christianity is a "linear" concept of history in which divine interventions and human freedom encounter one another. It is indeed a hermeneutical key for events experienced by the people. History is made up of past, present, and future, all with a direction assigned by a provident God. The past continues and lives in the present that it has brought forth; in the present the future already exists in hope. In both Judaism and Christianity, a prototypical event of salvation stands at the midpoint of the linear trajectory, imprinting direction and movement on the entire process, both past and future. But there is a difference.

For the Hebrew people, the prototype standing at the midpoint of history is the Exodus-event in its complex reality, comprising God's revelation to Moses, liberation from Egypt, the crossing of the desert, the covenant and the Law on Mount Sinai. For the apostolic church and the Christian movement, the Christ event, with Jesus' tragic human career culminating in the showdown of his death and the vindication of his resurrection, becomes the focal point, informing the entire trajectory in both directions with new meaning and direction. History comes to be seen as possessed of unique meaningfulness because at its heart stands the incomparable, prototypical event of Jesus Christ.

Theologians writing on "salvation history" in recent years are substantially agreed on the exemplary meaning of the historical event of Jesus Christ, even while they hold distinct views on how to connect what has already happened through the paschal mystery of Christ's death and resurrection to what remains to be accomplished in his second coming by way of fulfillment. The abiding tension between the "already" and the "not-yet" is visualized differently by various authors. While Oscar Cullmann quite clearly places the focal point in what has already been achieved through the death/resurrection of Jesus Christ,[1] others, like Jürgen Moltmann, definitely lay the stress on the "eschatological remainder": the paschal mystery of Jesus Christ is the proleptic model for what remains in store until the eschatological fulfillment.[2] In a somewhat similar fashion, Wolfhart Pannenberg looks at the resurrection of Jesus Christ as the proleptic presence and anticipation in the glorified humanity of the eschatological transformation of world and history which is to take place at the eschaton.[3]

Such divergences will bear on questions under discussion in this chapter, in particular when the question of the abiding value of the Mosaic covenant is raised and the context of the Jewish-Christian dialogue evoked. The case of the Mosaic covenant will stand out as exemplary, and the question will be asked whether lasting, theological value should not be affirmed as well of other covenants struck by God with peoples throughout the historical unfolding of his saving design for humankind. This chapter therefore falls into two main parts, dealing with the extent of God's saving plan in human history and with the various covenants comprising it.

THE UNIVERSAL HISTORY OF SALVATION

BEYOND THE JUDEO-CHRISTIAN TRADITION

The first question to be asked is that of how far salvation history reaches into the overall history of the world. Does "salvation history" coincide with "profane history"? And if they differ, must it nevertheless be said that salvation history is coextensive with the history of the world, namely that it begins with its creation and goes all the way to its end?

Every attempt to situate the beginning of salvation history in the call of Abraham, and thereby to reduce its range to the "sacred history" (*histoire sainte*) that begins at that point, must be firmly resisted. Such an attempt always betrays an a priori tendency to discount any personal engagement of God in the events of humankind prior to and outside the tradition that issued from the call of the biblical patriarch. It calls to mind Karl Barth's professed a priori certitude that "other religions are just unbelief." From the assumption that religion and religions are simply vain human attempts at self-justification, it seemed to follow logically that salvation history could only start with the story of Abraham, the "father

---

1. Oscar Cullmann, *Christ and Time: The Christian Concept of Time and History* (London: SCM Press, 1952); idem, *Salvation in History* (London: SCM Press, 1967).
2. Jürgen Moltmann, *The Way of Jesus Christ: Christology in Messianic Dimensions* (London: SCM Press, 1990).
3. Wolfhart Pannenberg, *Revelation as History* (London: Macmillan, 1969); idem, *Systematic Theology*, vol. 2 (Edinburgh: T. & T. Clark, 1994).

of all who believe" (Rom 4:11), and had to be confined to the spiritual lineage deriving from his faith.

More recent theologians have proposed answers to the question of the extent of salvation history which, while being less negative, nevertheless remain unduly restrictive. Jean Daniélou is a case in point. In his view "cosmic religion," rather than being part of salvation history, constitutes a "prehistory" of salvation based upon a natural knowledge granted by God through the order of creation. Daniélou logically concludes that the religious traditions of humankind outside the Abrahamic-Mosaic stream of tradition could only represent natural human aspirations toward God, without involving any personal engagement of God toward peoples.[4] The opinion of Hans Urs von Balthasar comes very close to Daniélou. Only the Hebrew and the Christian religions, flowing from the faith of Abraham, qualify for being called "religions of revelation" and, hence, belong to salvation history proper; for only they represent God's search for and turning to humankind in word and history, in love and self-gift.[5] Other religions are of a natural character.

Against all reduction of the history of salvation-revelation to the Judeo-Christian tradition, it must be affirmed that salvation history coincides and is coextensive with the history of the world. It consists of human and world history itself, seen with the eyes of faith as a "dialogue of salvation" freely initiated by God with humankind from creation itself and pursued through the centuries until the fulfillment of God's Reign in the eschaton.

Likewise to be rejected is the idea of a "prehistory" in which salvation and revelation would be disconnected from one another. Such a concept has given rise to two different views of salvation history, both unduly truncated. According to the first, prehistory implied some (natural) "revelation" of God through created reality but remained impervious to salvation; for the other, divine "salvation" was possible for individual persons during the prehistory of salvation, but divine self-manifestation or (supernatural) "revelation" remained hidden in the future until God's revelation to Abraham.

Although each has a different viewpoint, it must be affirmed that world history and salvation history coincide and are coextensive; moreover, since human history is, from the start and throughout, the story of God-with-humankind, it must likewise be said to imply from the outset and at all times both divine self-revelation and salvation.[6] The New Testament's unambiguous assertion that God "wills [*thelei*] all human beings to be saved" (1 Tim 2:4) supposes no less. Nor can God's universal saving will be reduced to some kind of conditional and ineffective wish or velleity; this divine will is subject to no condition other than each human person's free acceptance of God's gratuitous self-manifestation and

---

4. Jean Daniélou, *The Salvation of the Nations* (Notre Dame, Ind.: University of Notre Dame Press, 1962).

5. Hans Urs von Balthasar, *A Theology of History* (London: Sheed and Ward, 1964).

6. Karl Rahner, "History of the World and Salvation History," in *Theological Investigations*, 5:97–114; idem, "Profane History and Salvation History," in *Theological Investigations*, 21:3–15.

self-bestowal. It is part of Christian tradition to assert that humankind has been at once and from the outset created and called by God to share in the divine life. The only concrete order in which humankind ever found itself in history is the "supernatural order" entailing God's offer of self-communication through grace. Such an order of world and history always brings with it — one way or another — a divine self-manifestation and the offer of salvation.

From the universality of this concrete human condition, it follows that there is a single unique history of salvation, of revelation, and of the offer of faith, that coexists with the world history. Karl Rahner writes very clearly, "As God's real self-communication in grace...the history of salvation and revelation is coexistent and coextensive with the history of the world and of the human spirit, and hence also with the history of religion."[7]

The universally present history of salvation must therefore be concretely embodied in the history of people. This happens in the history of religion in general and in particular in the historical religions of humankind. These may serve as historical mediations for the supernatural experience of God as divine revelation and thus "stir up" salvation in a positive manner. They may, therefore, be considered as willed by God insofar as they give concrete shape to the divine offer of grace universally present and operative throughout human history. In the religious traditions of the world, God's offer to people in revelation-salvation takes on an initial concrete shape.

Such a concrete shape is clearly embodied in the Jewish and Christian traditions. Here an explicit awareness and a recognition of historic events as constituent divine interventions come into play; divine intervention is guaranteed by a "word of God" by which such events are interpreted as saving events through a prophetic charism. Such a concrete form should not, however, be reduced a priori to these traditions. Other traditions may indeed contain prophetic words that interpret historic events as divine interventions in the history of peoples.

THE SAVING HISTORIES OF PEOPLES

Indeed, Jewish-Christian biblical revelation itself attests to saving acts performed by God on behalf of the peoples, even on behalf of the enemies of the "chosen people." Deuteronomy 2 states that Yahweh assigns a promised land to other peoples as well, and the prophet Amos guarantees that God also leads other peoples to exoduses of liberation (Am 9:7). The prophet Isaiah presses his vision even further. He dares to affirm that even for the Egyptians — historic enemies of the Jews and their oppressors — there will be a savior sent by Yahweh himself (Isa 19:22–25). Indeed it is startling that the Egyptians are here designated by God as "my people" (Isa 19:25)! These texts, admittedly few, make it possible to understand that God acts salvifically even toward other peoples. These historically tangible saving actions are analogous to those performed by God according

---

7. Karl Rahner, *Foundations of Christian Faith: An Introduction to the Idea of Christianity* (London: Darton, Longman & Todd, 1978), 153.

to the Old Testament witness, on behalf of Israel, even though the Christian tradition attributes to the history of the latter the unique particularity of being the immediate historic prologue to God's decisive saving intervention in the Christ event. God's *mirabilia* on behalf of human beings are not limited to Israel; they extend to other peoples as well.

This last observation suggests caution against drawing too neat a line of demarcation between what theology is wont to consider as belonging to "general" salvation history, on the one hand (religions in general), and to "special" salvation history, on the other (the Judeo-Christian tradition). Such a scheme easily leads to the idea that the "pre-Christian" religions, which belong to the "general" history of salvation, have been overcome and cast off, and have become obsolete or even "illegitimate."[8]

It must indeed be asked whether the history of other peoples cannot play for them, in the order of salvation, a role "analogous" to that played for the Hebrew people by the history of Israel, in the sense of comprising historical events whose divine salvific significance is guaranteed by a prophetic word. Could not what is called "special" salvation history be extended beyond the boundaries of the Hebrew-Christian tradition? Might not the story of each people contain traces of God's loving deeds on its behalf, constituting it as one of God's peoples and enlivening it with God's own life?

The Asian bishops followed this line of thought when they saw the great religious traditions of their peoples as "significant and positive elements in the economy of God's design of salvation" and asked: "How can we not acknowledge that God has drawn our peoples to himself through them?"[9] This would mean that God's saving and revealing action is present in the midst of such peoples through their history. In this regard A. Russo writes:

> There is not just one exodus, just one covenant, or just one promised land. Every people has its own road to liberation and development, with different bottlenecks, setbacks, twists, landing places. In the event of Israel everyone can read the true face of God, who makes himself neighbor to all and in whose heart is the fate of humankind. The many historic journeys of peoples are thus integrated without being lost, into the single history of salvation intended for all humankind. On the other hand, the special feature of the biblical events does not diminish the real consistency of the events narrated, but confers on them a significance that is both historic and emblematic. A universal history, if it wishes to avoid being reduced to a rhetorical abstraction, cannot ignore the multiplicity of particular histories.

---

8. Cf. Adolf Darlap, "Fundamentale Theologie der Heilsgeschichte," in *Mysterium Salutis,* ed. J. Feiner and M. Löhrer (Einsiedeln: Benziger Verlag, 1967), 1:143–47.

9. "Evangelisation in Modern Day Asia (Taipei, April 22–27, 1974)," Declaration of the First Plenary Assembly of FABC, in *For All the Peoples of Asia: Federation of Asian Bishops' Conferences Documents from 1970 to 1991,* ed. G. Rosales and C. G. Arevalo (Maryknoll, N.Y.: Orbis Books, 1992), 14.

He goes on to say:

> We can say that salvation history, although it is essentially one, is multiplied and refracted in as many ways as the histories of the peoples. For every people has its own history, different from others, and at work in every history is the healing and liberating grace of God, who carries out his unique design on behalf of all humankind over countless different roads.[10]

The widespread distinction between "general" and "special" salvation history thus seems to be somewhat deceptive and should not be rigidly assumed: the "extrabiblical" religious traditions cannot be excluded a priori from belonging to "special" salvation history. Making them part of it implies that there are events in the history of peoples that through a prophetic charism are interpreted as divine intervention. Such a presence would have to be verified concretely through a thorough, positive study of the various traditions. In any case, it cannot be denied that such traditions contain narratives of "events" whose existence is attributed to a divine intervention in the history of a people. Further on, it will be seen that the basis for such divine interventions in their history, according to the biblical revelation, consists in a "covenant" relationship between God and the peoples.

Assessing the presence of such divine interventions in the history of the peoples would entail setting aside an overly rigid distinction between "myth" and "history," by which the other religious traditions would be made up solely of "myth" whereas the "historic" would be the sole preserve of the Judeo-Christian tradition. In such a rigid way of seeing things, myth comes to be regarded as "tales" with no truth credentials, and the only events that can make any claim to truth are those that can be historically verified. However, such a negative conception of myth has been abandoned for a long time now.[11] "Myth" is not something that is not historically true; rather it refers back to that "primordial" time of which historic events are regarded as concrete embodiments. Eliade defines myth by saying that it "narrates a sacred history; it tells of events that took place in the primordial time." For his part, Bede Griffiths writes: "A myth is a symbolic story which expresses in symbolic forms which rise from the depths of the unconscious, man's understanding of God and the mystery of existence. Myths are of infinite value and importance... God revealed himself from the earliest times in the form of myth."[12] Extrabiblical "tales" cannot be separated from those in the Bible as mythical stories opposed to historical accounts. Such a dichotomy does not accord with the way things are.

It is true that the extrabiblical religions are extensively rooted in myth — Hinduism is a case in point. But such founding myths can be bearers of a di-

---

10. A. Russo, "La funzione d'Israele e la legittimità delle altre religioni," *Rassegna di Teologia* 40, no. 1 (1999): 109, 118.

11. Cf. among others, Mircea Eliade, *Cosmos and History: The Myth of the Eternal Return* (New York: Harper and Row, 1959); idem, *Aspects du mythe* (Paris: Gallimard, 1963); Ernst Cassirer, *Language and Myth* (New York: Dover, 1946); idem, *Symbol, Myth, and Culture* (New Haven: Yale University Press, 1979).

12. Bede Griffiths, *The Cosmic Revelation* (Bangalore: Asian Trading Corporation, 1985), 115.

vine message. The creation account in the book of Genesis is a myth whereby the mystery of the creation of human beings and of their communion with God is revealed. Noah is himself a "mythic" figure or "legendary" personage, and the story of God's covenant with him has a mythical character; however, as will be seen below, it communicates the truth of a covenant relationship of all peoples with God. Not even the stories of Abraham and Moses are without a certain mythical background; and yet they are the symbol by antonomasia of God's action in the history of the Israelite people and they constitute the cornerstone of the Hebrew conception of revelation as personal intervention by God in history. "Hebrew understanding emerged from the mythological background."[13] Through the interpretative charism of the great prophets, Israel decisively moved away from a mythological conception and approached a historic conception. This movement was later accentuated in the Christian vision, in which the Christ event occupies the midpoint of history.

The gradual evolution from a mythical conception to a historic conception in the passage from extrabiblical tradition to the Judeo-Christian tradition should not obscure the fact that "cosmic" religion already communicates a relationship of God with the peoples, expressed through the mediation of history and legend. And the revelatory function of myth in extrabiblical religion has not vanished with the advent of historic consciousness.

GOD'S COVENANTS WITH THE PEOPLES

COVENANTS NEVER REVOKED

In the biblical account, God's dealings with humankind are punctuated by covenants. The significance of the biblical term "covenant" (*berith*) when it refers to God's way of dealing with human beings need not be explained here. Let it suffice to recall that a covenant always represents a gratuitous initiative on the part of God, who freely enters into a personal relationship with human beings without any merit on their part. A "covenant" is a pact of friendship unilaterally initiated by the divine partner which, however, calls on the human partner for commitment and fidelity in response to God's gracious love; even human infidelity does not annul divine faithfulness.

Regarding the use in the biblical tradition of the covenant terminology with reference to God's dealings with human beings, we note the following: the term "covenant" is not found in the Genesis narrative of creation (Gen 1–2); however, outside of Genesis there are hints that creation is viewed as a cosmic "covenant" (cf. Jer 33:20–26).[14] In Genesis the term "covenant" initially has to do with the "everlasting covenant" struck by God with Noah (Gen 9:1–17); it recurs in the Abraham cycle (Gen 17:1–14). The covenant with Moses is dealt with at length in Exodus 19–24. A "new covenant" is foretold by Jeremiah 31:31–34, which the

---

13. Ibid., 121; cf. 109–31.
14. Cf. R. Murray, *The Cosmic Covenant* (London: Sheed and Ward, 1992).

Christian New Testament will see realized in the Christ event, more precisely in the paschal mystery of the death and resurrection of Jesus (Mt 26:28–29; Lk 22:20; 1 Cor 11:25).

Christian tradition has often conceived of four covenants made between God and humankind. A famous text of St. Irenaeus in *Adversus Haereses* states it clearly:

> Four covenants were given to the human race: one, prior to the deluge, under Adam; the second, that after the deluge, under Noah; the third, the giving of the Law, under Moses; the fourth, that which renovates the human being, and sums up all things in itself by means of the Gospel, raising and bearing human beings upon its wings into the heavenly kingdom.[15]

Questions of interpretation that have been raised with regard to the covenant with Noah need to be answered: What is the theological significance of that covenant? Is it understood to continue after the Christ event? To start with the second question, the context in which Irenaeus distinguishes four covenants gives us a clue for an answer. Irenaeus finds a symbolic meaning in the number four and he accordingly lists distinct, fourfold realities: "Such as was the course followed by the Son of God, so was also the form of the living creatures; and such as was the form of the living creatures, so was also the character of the gospel. For the living creatures are quatriform, and the gospel is quatriform, as is also the course followed by the Lord" (*Adv. Haer.* III, 11, 8). In other words, the Word of God has spoken in four different ways: to the patriarchs before Moses through his divinity; under the Law through a priestly ministry; thereafter, in his incarnation through his humanity; finally, as risen Lord, through the gift of the Spirit. Similarly, the gospel is fourfold: Matthew, Luke, Mark, and John. Four are likewise the covenants struck by God with humankind: in Adam, in Noah, in Abraham and Moses, and in Jesus Christ. Nothing in the succession of the four divine covenants suggests that one abolishes those preceding, any more than one form of the fourfold gospel replaces the other forms. All the covenants hold together just as the four gospels do.

According to Irenaeus, the covenants stand to each other as so many ways of divine engagement with humankind through the Logos. They are *Logophanies* through which the divine Logos "rehearses," as it were, his breaking into human history through the incarnation in Jesus Christ. As such, they relate to each other, not as the old that has become obsolete in the advent of the new which replaces it, but as the germ that already contains in promise the fullness of the plant which will issue from it.

Let us turn to the significance of the covenant with Noah: there is no question here — as has too often been supposed — of a mere manifestation of God through the phenomena of nature and the constancy of their recurrence. In the

---

15. Irenaeus, *Adv. Haer.* III, 11, 8.

case of the covenant in creation, the Genesis account testifies to God's familiarity with Adam and thus to a personal relationship between the Creator and
humankind. Similarly, the intimate relationship between God and Noah is emphasized in the inspired text (Gen 9:1–17). It had already been said that "Noah
found favor in the sight of God" (Gen 6:8) and that he "walked with God" (Gen
6:9). Likewise emphasized is the universality of the "everlasting covenant" (Gen
9:16) struck by God with Noah and his descendants; these elements in the story
symbolize a personal commitment of God toward the nations, that is, the universality of the divine intervention in the history of peoples, of which the religious
traditions of humanity are the privileged testimonies. The true character of the
covenant with Noah has been very well expressed as follows:

> How seriously God had thought of a regeneration is shown by the *covenant
> with Noah*. It constitutes the lasting foundation for the salvation of every
> human person. Its true significance is falsified if one sees in it — as a long
> tradition in Catholic theology has done — nothing beyond the setting up
> of a "natural" religion having nothing to do yet with a supernatural revela-
> tion. The particular characteristics recorded in the Scripture concerning the
> Noah covenant make it clear that there is question here of a true event of
> salvation, marked by grace... The entirety of the covenant with Noah ap-
> pears as an outline of the covenants with Abraham and Moses... Israel and
> the nations have thus a common base: they are in a state of covenantship
> with the true God and under the same salvific will of that one God.[16]

The covenant with Noah thus takes on a far-reaching significance for a theology of the religious traditions of peoples belonging to the "extrabiblical" tradition.
These peoples are also — and as we will see below, they remain — in a state of
covenantship with God. They too are covenant peoples and deserve to be called
"peoples of God."[17] The one God is the God of all peoples. In the same sense,
Bede Griffiths writes:

> This biblical perspective enables us to see this cosmic revelation and cosmic
> covenant as extending to all men and to all peoples. Every genuine religion
> stems from this cosmic covenant and is a way by which God reveals himself
> and offers himself to man for his salvation. In other words, they are ways
> of salvation willed by God.[18]

Turning to the covenant with Moses, it has been asked whether it has been
abolished with the coming of the "new covenant" established by God in Jesus
Christ. In a speech given in Mainz, Germany, in 1980, Pope John Paul II referred to "the people of God of the Old Covenant, which has never been revoked

---

16. Bernhard Stoeckle, "Die ausserbiblische Menschheit und die Weltreligionen," in *Mysterium
Salutis* 2:1053–54.
17. Cf. Walbert Bühlmann, *God's Chosen Peoples* (Maryknoll, N.Y.: Orbis Books, 1982).
18. B. Griffiths, "Erroneous Beliefs and Unauthorised Rites," *The Tablet* 227 (1973): 356.

(cf. Rom 11:29)."[19] The issue is whether with the coming of the Christ event and of the "new covenant" established in him, the "old covenant" with Israel has become obsolete and been abrogated, as the Christian tradition has often affirmed. How is the relationship between the Mosaic and Christic covenants to be understood? What light does the Hebrew-Christian dialogue cast on the subject? More particularly: Is God's grace-filled relation today with persons belonging to the Jewish people to be assigned to an enduring efficacy of the Mosaic covenant *or* to the new covenant established in Jesus Christ? Does the latter simply replace the former, henceforth rendered inoperative? Israel and Christianity obviously represent a singular case, owing to the unique relationship existing between the two religions; however, as will be suggested below, it may furnish — *mutatis mutandis* — an emblematic model for the relationship between Christianity and the other religions.

The question of the ongoing value of the Mosaic covenant is fraught with contentious historical evidence. The Council of Florence's Decree for the Copts (1442) declared that with the "promulgation of the gospel" the prescriptions of the Mosaic covenant are abolished. The document stated:

> [The Holy Roman Church] firmly believes, professes and teaches that the legal [statutes] of the Old Testament or Mosaic Law...were instituted to signify something to come, and therefore, although in that age they were fitting for divine worship, they have ceased with the advent of our Lord Jesus Christ, whom they signified. [With him] the sacraments of the New Testament have begun...After the promulgation of the Gospel (*post promulgatum evangelium*) they cannot be observed without the loss of eternal salvation.[20]

The document states unambiguously that "with the advent of our Lord Jesus Christ" the institutions derived from the old covenant have lost their efficacy. As signifying things to come, they were by nature transitory and, with the coming of the things signified, have become ineffective. The "promulgation of the gospel" referred to in this text raises many questions: When can it be said that the gospel has been "promulgated" and where? How does this promulgation take place, and under what conditions does it become effective? Must the promulgation of the gospel be viewed as having been realized for entire nations or groups of people at a certain point in time? Or must the case of each person be considered individually, so as to assess his or her position in relation to the gospel? According to Karl Rahner, the promulgation of the gospel can only be said to have reached individual persons when through the offer of divine faith the question of hav-

---

19. Text in *AAS* 73 (1981): 80.

20. Text in H. Denzinger, *Enchiridion symbolorum, definitionum et declarationum de rebus fidei et morum*, n. 1348; Neuner and Dupuis, eds., *The Christian Faith in the Documents of the Catholic Church*, n. 1003.

ing to respond positively to God's offer of salvation in Jesus Christ has been existentially raised for each one's personal conscience.[21]

What must retain our attention here, however, is the council's firm affirmation that the mystery of salvation accomplished in the Jesus Christ event — "with the advent of our Lord Jesus Christ" — has abolished the Mosaic covenant and the divine institutions that accompanied it. Certainly, the rejection of Jesus by "a part" of the Jewish people did raise in St. Paul's mind crucial problems with which he kept wrestling, especially in the Letter to the Romans (chaps. 9–11). Paul seems never to have found a decisive answer to these questions. What he proposed was that, the time of its infidelity notwithstanding, Israel would be saved at the end (Rom 11:25–26). However, one conviction remained firmly engraved in Paul's mind: Israel was and continued to be God's people; the covenant with Moses continued unceasingly, thanks to God's steadfast love and faithfulness. To the question, "Has God rejected his people?" he answered emphatically: "By no means" (Rom 11:1); and he explained: "The gifts and the call of God are irrevocable" (Rom 11:29). Israel unquestionably remained the people to whom "belong the sonship, the glory, the covenants, the giving of the Law, the worship, and the promises" (Rom 9:4).

St. Paul's questions continue to beset Christian theologians and Jewish scholars even today, in the context of the Jewish-Christian theological dialogue. In a recent book Norbert Lohfink[22] has taken a fresh look at the biblical evidence on the relationship between the "old" and the "new" covenants, especially in Jeremiah 31:31–34, Romans 9–11, and 2 Corinthians 3:14. The author shows that the New Testament data are more refined and more subtle than has been assumed by the long-standing Christian tradition about "two covenants," of which the "new" in Jesus Christ has abolished the "old" in Moses. We need only note the results of his research. The new covenant is no other than the first; it unveils the first by spreading abroad the splendor of the Lord which the first contained without revealing it fully. The fact is that in Jesus Christ the one covenant "has concentrated itself to eschatological radicalness" and so finds in him its "ultimate and most profound sense" (p. 81). And this leads the author to conclude: "I lean therefore to a 'one covenant' theory which however embraces Jews and Christians, whatever their differences in the one covenant, and that means Jews and Christians of today" (p. 84). But he adds: "From early Christian times, Jews and Christians have been on two ways. Because the two ways run their course within the one covenant which makes God's salvation present in the world, I think that one must speak of a 'twofold way of salvation'" (p. 84).

One should not speak, therefore, of one way which existed before Christ in Israel but which in the course of time bifurcated into two parallel ways, the

---

21. Karl Rahner, "Christianity and the Non-Christian Religions," in *Theological Investigations,* 5:115–34; idem, "Church, Churches, and Religions," in *Theological Investigations,* 10:30–49; at 47–49.

22. Norbert Lohfink, *The Covenant Never Revoked: Biblical Reflections on Christian-Jewish Dialogue* (New York: Paulist Press, 1991).

one destined by God for the Jewish people, and the other ordained by him for the Gentiles in Jesus Christ, the "Messiah of the pagans." Rather, one should speak properly of "one covenant, but a twofold way of salvation" for Jews and Christians (p. 84). What is entailed in the choice of the second formulation is the dynamic of the history of salvation, as Paul conceived it in Romans. God has but one plan of salvation, which embraces the Jews and the nations alike, even though that one plan unfolds "dramatically" in two times, and two different routes; their present historical divergence notwithstanding, these two times will ultimately converge — on a single path — even if only in the eschaton, at the end of time (pp. 84–85).

Regardless of the formula used, in the present context of Jewish-Christian dialogue two extreme positions must be avoided. These include, on one side, any theory of simple replacement in Jesus Christ of the promises and the covenant with Israel. Jesus' own claim to "have come not to abolish [the Law and the prophets] but to fulfill them" (Mt 5:17) prevents any replacement interpretation. On the other side, any semblance of dualism of parallel ways, which would destroy the unity of the divine plan of salvation for humankind which reaches its eschatological realization in Jesus Christ, must also be avoided. From a Christian standpoint, the middle-way position seems to be that of a single covenant and two interrelated ways within one organic plan of salvation. The divine plan of salvation has an organic unity, whose dynamism is manifested in history. This unfolding process contains various mutually related and complementary steps. For Christian faith the Christ event does not exist without Israel or making abstraction from it; conversely, Israel never was chosen by God except as that people from which Jesus of Nazareth would issue forth. Israel and Christianity belong together in salvation history under the span of the covenant. The covenant through which the Hebrew people obtained salvation in the past and continues to be saved even today is the same covenant through which Christians are called to salvation in Jesus Christ. There is no replacement by a "new" people of God of another people, henceforth declared "old," but rather an expansion to the ends of the world of the one people of God, of which the election of Israel and the covenant with Moses were and remain "the root and the source, the foundation and the promise."[23] As E. Zenger writes:

> We Christians believe, along with the New Testament, that the new cove-
> nant with God by which we can now live in his grace has been disclosed
> through the death and resurrection of Jesus. This is not another covenant
> replacing the one on Sinai. It is one and the same covenant of grace, in
> which the Jewish people and the peoples gathered in the church partic-
> ipate, in different ways of course. The covenant was established first of
> all with Israel, and only subsequently, "through Jesus Christ and together

---

23. Cf. J. Dupuis, "Alleanza e salvezza," *Rassegna di Teologia* 35, no. 2 (1994): 148–71. The last words are taken from the "Pastoral Orientations of the Commission of French Bishops for Relations with Judaism" (1973); text in *Documentation Catholique* 70 (1973): 419–22.

with his people was the church too brought in." The Jewish people and the church live like two entities, each with its own identity and both in a state of separation, which is not ignored, but which is set within the horizon of a common covenant, that which the Hebrew Bible, the so-called Old Testament, attests as given by God. The existence of the church is founded primarily not on the New Testament but on the Old. And if the church were to reject the Old Testament message it would renounce itself, as church of the new covenant.[24]

To the question of whether the Jews are saved today through God's covenant with Israel *or* through Jesus Christ in whom a "new" covenant has been realized, the answer is therefore that such a dichotomy is invalid: salvation comes to the Jews through the covenant made by God with Israel *and* brought to perfection in Jesus Christ. The covenant is still a way of salvation even today, but not independently of the Christ event.

The covenant with Moses thus still remains in place and has not been abrogated by the one in Jesus Christ. We noted that the case of Judaism and Christianity can serve as a catalyst for reorienting the relationship between Christianity and the other religions. What is true in the first case continues to be valid analogously in the second. Even the other religious traditions symbolized by the covenant with Noah retain, *mutatis mutandis*, a permanent value. As the Mosaic covenant has not been suppressed by the fact of having reached its fullness in Jesus Christ, so also the cosmic covenant made in Noah with the nations has not been cancelled by the fact that in the Christ event the goal that was set for it by God has been reached. That means that the other traditions still have saving value for their followers, but not unrelated to the Christ event. A. Russo expresses it well when he writes:

> Thanks to the Mosaic covenant . . . we acknowledge in the Jewish people . . . a dignity and a permanent function in the divine design. We ought to view in a similar manner those covenants that God has made with the other peoples of the earth, symbolically present in the Adam event, and more specifically in the story of Noah. If God's gifts are irrevocable, are not these extended to the other peoples also irrevocable? If we use this principle to validate the religion of the Jews, why not apply it also to the other covenants spoken of in scripture, rather than considering them, and only them, obsolete?[25]

THE TRINITARIAN STRUCTURE OF HISTORY

The model of a Trinitarian Christology proposed in the preceding chapter informs the entire process of God's self-manifestation in salvation-revelation,

---

24. Erich Zenger, *Il Primo Testamento: La bibbia ebraica e i cristiani* (Brescia: Queriniana, 1997), 133–35.

25. A. Russo, "La funzione d'Israele e la legittimità delle altre religioni," 116.

within history. In the Christian understanding of the historic unfolding of the single but holistic design of God for the salvation of humankind, the Christ event is the midpoint and the focal point. It is the pivot upon which the entire history of the dialogue between God and humanity turns, the principle of intelligibility of the divine plan concretized in the history of the world. It influences the entire process of history by way of a final cause, that is, as the end or the goal drawing to itself the entire evolutionary process: both "pre-Christian" and "post-Christian" history are being drawn by the Christ-Omega to himself.[26]

Yet the Christocentrism of salvation history must not be understood as a "Christomonism." The centrality of the Christ event does not obscure but rather supposes, calls forth, and enhances the universal operative presence of the "Word of God" and of the "Spirit of God" through salvation history and, specifically, in the religious traditions of humankind. Pope John Paul II rightly affirmed in the encyclical letter *Dominum et Vivificantem* on the Holy Spirit (1986) that in every historical situation, before the Christ event as well as after it and outside the Christian dispensation, "grace bears within itself both a Christological aspect and a pneumatological one" (§53).

According to the Old Testament biblical tradition, the divine Wisdom-Word (*ḥokhmāh-dābār*) and the Spirit (*rûᵃḥ*) serve as "mediums" for God's personal interventions in history, both in Israel and outside it. The "literary personification" of those divine "attributes" highlights the personal commitment of God to peoples which the revealed word intends to convey. The New Testament will later reveal the true "personhood" of the mediums of God's involvement in human history by progressively delving into the personal character of the Son (Logos-Wisdom) and of the Spirit. Henceforth, then, the Logos-Wisdom and the Spirit, who had already been operative in "pre-Christian" history, will be understood, by retrojection, as two distinct persons within the mystery of the Triune God: the Son who became incarnate in Jesus Christ, on the one hand, and the Spirit, on the other. The two divine persons had been present and operative in the pre-Christian dispensation without being formally recognized as persons.

The universal active presence of the divine Logos before the Christ event is clearly affirmed by the Prologue of the Gospel according to St. John: he was "the true light that enlightens every human being," coming into the world (Jn 1:9). The universal revelatory function of the Logos made him present to humankind throughout history from the beginning, even though that operative presence was to culminate in the coming in the flesh in Jesus Christ. With regard to the Spirit, his life-giving energy is present in human beings, in creation and re-creation. Pope John Paul II has highlighted his universal activity throughout human history in religious traditions as well as in individual persons.

What remains to be shown is how the universal action of the Word and the Spirit in the extrabiblical history of salvation combines theologically in a single

---

26. Karl Rahner, "Christology within an Evolutionary View of the World," in *Theological Investigations*, 5:157–92.

economy of salvation with the particularized historical event of Jesus Christ: that is, how Christocentrism, on the one hand, and Logocentrism and pneumatology, on the other, far from being mutually exclusive, need one another. On this point, Karl Rahner shows that the Christ event constitutes the goal or end of the anticipated action of the Logos-to-become-man and of the Spirit's universal working in the world before the incarnation. For this reason, the preincarnational action of the Logos is oriented toward the Christ event, just as the Spirit can rightly be called the "Spirit of Christ" from the beginning of salvation history. About the Spirit, Rahner therefore writes: "Since the universal efficacy of the Spirit is directed from the very beginning to the zenith of its historical mediation, which is the Christ event (or in other words, the final cause of the mediation of the Spirit to the world), it can be truly said that this Spirit is everywhere and from the very beginning the Spirit of Jesus Christ, the incarnate divine *Logos*."[27]

This amounts to saying that between the various components of the Trinitarian Christological salvation economy there exists a relationship of mutual conditioning by virtue of which no particular aspect can either be stressed to the detriment of the others or, on the contrary, played down in favor of them. The Christ event never stands in isolation from the working of the Logos and the Spirit, any more than these ever operate without relation to it.

In the last analysis, we here encounter the mystery of time and eternity as it affects God's dealings with humankind in history. While for our human discursive knowledge the historical unfolding of salvation is necessarily made up of beginning-middle-end, or of past-present-future, in God's eternal awareness and knowledge, all is continuous and coexisting, co-simultaneous, and interrelated.[28] Jesus Christ is the high point of God's personal involvement with humankind, eternally "preestablished," and, hence, in history the Christ event is the particularized "moment" in which God "becomes" God-of-peoples-in-a-fully-human-way. But since the incarnation of the Logos is eternally present in God's intention, its realization in time informs the age-long story of God's dealings with humankind.

The action of the Logos, the work of the Spirit, and the Christ event are thus inseparable aspects of a single economy of salvation. The fact that according to the Pauline tradition, human beings are "created in Jesus Christ" (Eph 2:10), who has primacy in the order of both creation and re-creation (Col 1:15–20; Eph 1:3–14), does not detract from, but demands the anticipated action of the Word-to-become-flesh (Jn 1:9) and the universal working of the Spirit: "Without doubt, the Holy Spirit was at work in the world before Christ was glorified," says Vatican II (*Ad Gentes* §4).

The structure of the self-revelation of the triune God, which follows that of the interpersonal relationships between the different persons in the inner mystery of God, must be kept in mind. The order of the persons coincides in both spheres

---

27. Karl Rahner, "Jesus Christ in the Non-Christian Religions," in *Theological Investigations*, 17:39–50; at 46.

28. Cf. Jean Mouroux, *Le mystère du temps: Approche théologique* (Paris: Aubier, 1962); Eberhardt Jüngel, *Gott als Geheimnis der Welt* (Tübingen: Mohr, 1977).

insofar as there is a necessary correspondence and correlation between the order of origin in the intra-divine self-communication of Father-Son-Sprit and the order of their self-communication to humankind in history: the "economic" Trinity prolongs the "immanent" Trinity, enabling it to overflow beyond itself toward history and into the world.[29] Or, inversely, the "immanent" Trinity is the a priori presupposition of the Trinitarian structure of the divine self-communication: from the Father, through the Son, in the Spirit. More simply, God, being a three-person communion, cannot but communicate God's self in this threefold manner: God gives God's self as God is!

The Trinitarian structure informs the various stages in which God's self-communication unfolds in salvation history. The same threefold character is also present and operative at all stages of its development. The Bible attests to this threefold structure with regard to creation: God created through his Word (Gen 1:3; Jdt 16:13–14; cf. Ps 33:9; 148:5; Jn 1:1–3) in the Spirit (Gen 1:2); the same threefold structure informs the history of Israel. It suffices to recall that God's interventions on behalf of his chosen people are generally performed through his Word; the Spirit of God takes possession of individuals to make them into instruments of God's action, and of prophets to give them the power to speak God's word.

In the Hebrew Bible no such clear indications can be found having to do with the covenant with Noah. Nevertheless, from the standpoint of Christian theology, that covenant — like the "extrabiblical religious traditions" — cannot but bear the stamp of the economic Trinity. As tradition has assiduously searched for and found "traces" of the Trinity (*vestigia trinitatis*) in creation, and more specifically in the spiritual activity of the human being, so we should search for and discover analogous traces outside the biblical tradition in the religious life of individuals and in their religious traditions. These traditions also in some manner re-echo in history the eternal uttering of the Word and the eternal "spiration" of the Spirit by the Father. If indeed God conceives and wills everything that is in the very act with which the Father utters the Word and "spirates" the Spirit, the same is all the more and necessarily true with regard to the covenant relationship with peoples in history. The fact that in the single order of the existing world, God has freely chosen to communicate personally with human beings means that all, in any situation in history — including extrabiblical traditions — find themselves, are included, and are, as it were, "caught up" in the Trinitarian structure of God's self-communication. As seen by Christian theology, God's cosmic covenant with humankind in Noah can only be stamped by a Trinitarian rhythm, like all of salvation history.

Salvation history is, in its entirety, the history of the origin of all things in God through his Word in the Spirit, and of their return to God through the Word in the Spirit. St. Paul said nothing less when he wrote: "for us there is one God, the Father, from whom (*ex hou*) are all things and for (*eis*) whom we

---

29. Karl Rahner, *The Trinity* (New York: Herder and Herder, 1970).

exist, and one Lord, Jesus Christ, through (*dia*) whom are all things and through (*dia*) whom we exist" (1 Cor 8:6) — a statement that the Letter to the Ephesians rounds out by adding that our journey from and to the Father through Jesus Christ is accomplished in (*en*) the Spirit (cf. Eph 2:18).

THE HOLY SPIRIT is at work at every stage of salvation history. In each of the covenants progressively made by God with. the human race, the Spirit is the immediate agent of the divine approach and engagement through human history. We could therefore say that the Holy Spirit presides over the divine destiny of humankind, in the sense that each divine covenant reaches humankind in the Spirit.

It is true that these considerations have meaning only within a Christian perspective; indeed, though not lacking grounds in scripture, they are based on a "high" ontological Trinitarian theology. However, from the standpoint of the Christian conception, such considerations have the merit of shedding light on the fact that the triune God brings extrabiblical religious humankind, collectively as well as individually, into a communion with Godself in grace and hope.

Chapter Five

"IN MANY AND VARIOUS WAYS"

"I N MANY AND VARIOUS WAYS God spoke of old to our fathers through the prophets; but in these last days he has spoken to us by the Son, whom he appointed the heir of all things, through whom also he created the world" (Heb 1:1–2). When the author of the Letter to the Hebrews wrote these words in his prologue, he surely did not look beyond the prophets of Israel for a word spoken "of old" by God to humankind. What the writer intended was to show that the event of Jesus Christ outdid immeasurably whatever God had said and done for Israel through its prophets. Nevertheless, his explicit reference to the fact that God had spoken in "many and various ways" and through the Son had "created the world" strikingly evokes what the Prologue of the Gospel according to John affirms of the Word, through whom "all things were made" (Jn 1:3) and who was "the true light that enlightens every human being" by coming into the world (Jn 1:9). The similarity between the two texts leads beyond the explicit reference made by Hebrews to the word spoken by God to Israel and encourages us to inquire about a divine revelation not confined to biblical history but extending to the entire history of salvation.

The last chapter ended up noting that God's covenant with Israel may serve, analogically, as a catalyst for a deeper perception of God's covenantal relationship with the nations. This observation leads to the further question of God's self-revelation to them. Is divine revelation coextensive with the history of salvation, which — as has been said — extends to all world history? No matter how "many and various" the ways in which God may have spoken, can it be thought that he did not "leave himself without witness" (Acts 14:17) at any time in history, not merely "in the things that have been made" (Rom 1:20) but also in speech and self-disclosure? How does God's speech to the nations relate to the Word which "in these last days he has spoken to us by the Son" (cf. Heb 1:2)? And how is the "only begotten Son" the one who "made him known" (Jn 1:18) if it is true that he had spoken and disclosed himself earlier in varied ways? Stated more clearly: How are we to understand that Jesus Christ is the "fullness" of divine revelation if it is true that God revealed himself through prophetic figures in various other religious traditions, both before and after him? Do the "sacred books" or "oral traditions" of other religions offer anything other than a human discourse about God or the Absolute? Do they in fact contain a "word spoken by God" to the

114

people of those religions and even to all humankind? If, moreover, Jesus Christ represents the "fullness" of divine revelation, has revelation come to a complete end with him? Or, on the contrary, can divine revelation in any way be conceived as an "ongoing process" both inside and outside Christianity that will reach its finality in the eschaton?

The questions raised here are only partially distinct from those examined in the previous chapter. We stressed then that God's self-manifestation in history takes place inseparably under the double form of words and deeds; it consists at once, necessarily, of revelation and salvation: God tells himself by giving himself; he shares himself by uttering himself. Hence to say that the whole of history is salvation history implicitly entails the universality of revelation.[1] Deeds and words, events and prophecy: both go hand in hand. Such, in any case, is the biblical understanding of salvation-revelation, which has been felicitously expressed by Vatican II's constitution *Dei Verbum,* which states: "This economy of revelation is realized by deeds and words, which are intrinsically bound up with each other. As a result the works performed by God in the history of salvation show forth and bear out the doctrine and realities signified by the words; the words, for their part, proclaim the works, and bring to light the mystery they contain. The most intimate truth which this revelation gives us about God and the salvation of man shines forth in Christ, who is himself both the mediator and the sum total of revelation" (*Dei Verbum* §2).

By virtue of the concomitance of the divine deeds and words, it seems theologically justified to search for divine speech in the nonbiblical religious traditions, even as it was thought necessary to include those traditions within the ambit of salvation history. God has spoken to the whole of humankind, because he has offered his salvation to all its members. Revelation is universal, even as is the offer of salvation.[2]

To say this is not to forget that the understanding of concepts such as "revelation," "salvation," and other cognate concepts differs vastly from one religious tradition to another — some points of contact notwithstanding. But it should not be forgotten either that the concept of revelation in recent Christian theology has undergone a clear shift of accent from revelation understood primarily as doctrine and communication of divine truths to revelation understood primarily as God's self-manifestation.[3] In a well-known book, Avery Dulles distinguishes five models of revelation, which are not to be seen as mutually exclusive, but rather as complementing and supporting one another.[4] Among these models, alongside that of revelation as doctrine, he considers those of revelation as "inner experience" and as "new awareness," both of them based on a divine inter-

---

1. Cf. Heinrich Fries, "Die Offenbarung," in *Mysterium Salutis,* ed. J. Feiner and M. Löhrer (Einsiedeln: Benziger Verlag, 1967), 1:117–238.
2. Cf. Gustave Thils, *Propos et problèmes de la théologie des religions non-chrétiennes* (Tournai: Casterman, 1966).
3. Gerald O'Collins, *Retrieving Fundamental Theology* (New York: Paulist Press, 1993).
4. Avery Dulles, *Models of Revelation* (Maryknoll, N.Y.: Orbis Books, 1992).

vention or aid. He moreover notes that these two models help discover the possibility of a divine revelation in other religious traditions, outside the Judeo-Christian tradition: This is true inasmuch as divine grace — which is universally offered — "discloses God as communicating himself and the human subject as tending toward transcendent self-fulfillment in union with God" (p. 100). "To the extent that any individual or community, empowered by God's presence, experiences itself as grounded in the divine, God's revelation may be found in it" (p. 107). He concludes: "The religions can be interpreted as expressions of a 'searching memory' which somehow anticipates God's culminating gift in Jesus Christ" (p. 182).

Nor should it be forgotten that, in its effort to transcend the dichotomy between inclusivism and pluralism, a valid theology of the religions must build on the recognition of the differences, without giving in to the illusory presumption of a "common essence" between the various religions and their underlying ideas. But due attention and respect for the differences do not do away with the right and duty for the Christian believer to interpret the data of other traditions from the vantage point of his or her own faith. For the Christian believer, writes Joseph A. DiNoia, "the existent with which all human beings are unconditionally engaged in all religious communities is the Triune God."[5] And "what else would a properly Christian theology of religions be competent to enunciate but appraisals of other religions framed in Christian terms?" (pp. 160–61).

What follows is, avowedly, a Christian evaluation, framed in Christian categories, of "divine revelation" in other religious traditions. According to such an evaluation, "an ineffable mystery, the center and ground of reality and human life, is in different forms and manners active among all peoples of the world and gives ultimate meaning to human existence and aspirations." It must be added, however, that "this mystery, which is called by different names, but which no name can adequately represent, is definitively disclosed and communicated in Jesus of Nazareth."[6] The "ultimate mystery," universally present yet never adequately comprehended, is, for the Christian, the "God and Father of Our Lord Jesus Christ" (2 Cor 1:3). A Christian theology of the "Word of God" in history must therefore be Trinitarian and Christological. It will search for the signs of God's action, for the "seeds of his Word," for the imprint of his Spirit in the foundational experiences and events upon which religious traditions have been built, and for traces of it in the sacred books and the oral traditions that constitute the official record and the living memory of those traditions. That is what is to be shown.

---

5. Cf. J. A. DiNoia, *The Diversity of Religions: A Christian Perspective* (Washington, D.C.: Catholic University of America Press, 1992), 136.

6. The citation is taken from the Declaration of the International Theological Conference on Evangelization and Dialogue in India (October 1971), n. 13; cf. J. Pathrapankal, ed., *Service and Salvation* (Bangalore: Theological Publications in India, 1974), 4.

THE GOD OF REVELATION

"ALL HAVE THE SAME GOD"

"Being is one — sages name it variously" (*Ṛg Veda*, I, 164, 46). In the context of the debate on the theology of religions, this Vedic verse is often quoted by upholders of the "pluralistic" thesis as a paradigmatic enunciation of their theological stand. "Being" (*sat*) is understood to stand for "God" or the Divine, whom pluralist theologians have substituted for Christ as the central point of reference for a viable theology of religious pluralism. Their understanding is that all religions represent diverse, historical manifestations of the one Divine Mystery and salvific ways tending toward the same mystery. The concept of God is intentionally kept sufficiently indeterminate to accommodate the various religious traditions in their manifold diversities; these are attributed to the distinct cultural areas in which the various traditions have originated. Thus their claim is that ultimately all religious traditions have the same indeterminate God as ultimate point of reference, no matter how different the names by which they call it and the concept they may form of it.[7] The Christian Father/Mother-God, the Jewish Yahweh, the Muslim Allah, the Hindu Brahman, the Buddhist Nirvāṇa, the Taoist Tao, and so on, are in short nothing but different terms with which the various traditions articulate a human experience of ultimate reality; the reality is the same and the experiences of equal value, notwithstanding the divergences which characterize them. All religious ways are equally salvific because they all tend to the same ultimate Reality.

Hence, the question of the Divine Mystery and of its many faces in the different religious traditions must be addressed. It poses many issues which need to be approached from the vantage point of a theology of religions that is both Christian and dialogical. Is the God of other religions the same as the God of Christians? This is a question which was often asked in Christian circles in the past and has not disappeared even today; it is heard — surprisingly — even with regard to Jews and Muslims. Before we proceed to an answer, some terminological clarifications are in order: Which God? Which "sameness"? Which religion?

The words of Blaise Pascal are well known: "The God of Abraham, the God of Isaac, the God of Jacob, not of philosophers and the wise (*savants*)...the God of Jesus Christ."[8] Pascal was referring to God's revelation to Moses: "I am the God of your father, the God of Abraham, the God of Isaac, and the God of Jacob" (Ex 3:6). He meant to distinguish the knowledge of God which we receive through the Judeo-Christian revelation from that limited knowledge which philosophy, even Christian philosophy, is able to reach; he did not mean to deny the personal identity of God in both cases. He deliberately stressed the limits of a philosophical apprehension of God as compared to the divine self-disclosure

---

7. Cf. the title of the book by John Hick, *God Has Many Names: Britain's New Religious Pluralism* (London: Macmillan, 1980); and his *God and the Universe of Faiths: Essays in the Philosophy of Religion* (London: Macmillan, 1973).

8. Blaise Pascal, "Le Mémorial," in *Oeuvres Complètes*, ed. L. Lafuma (Paris: Cerf, 1963), 618.

to Israel and in Jesus Christ. The divine identity must be clearly distinguished from the apprehension which human beings may have of it in different situations, through human reflection or divine revelation, in different religious traditions.

Equally to be kept in mind is the distinction made earlier between the "monotheistic" or "prophetic" religions, on the one hand, and the "mystical" religions of the East, on the other. Where the monotheistic religions are concerned, their common origin in the faith of Abraham guarantees the personal identity of the God worshiped by each. The continuity between the Yahweh of the Jewish religion and the "Father of Our Lord Jesus Christ" in Christianity can be historically substantiated, the differences between the Jewish scripture's concept of God and that of the Christian New Testament notwithstanding, as will be seen later. The same is true, though less widely recognized, where the personal identity between the Judeo-Christian God and that of the Qur'an and of Islam is concerned. Surely, the divergences in the concept of God will prove to be even greater in this case. Nevertheless, the Muslim God is that God in whom Abraham, the "father of all who believe" (Rom 4:11), placed his faith, and, after him, Israel and Christianity (Heb 11–12). Islam traces its historical origins to the faith of Abraham as truly as do Israel and Christianity.

The question is much more complex where the mystical religions of the East are concerned. This is the case for more than one reason — not least the luxuriant variety and enormous complexity of the data they offer and the distinct overall worldview (*Weltanschauung*) on which they are built. Nevertheless, the question must be asked theologically how the "Absolute Reality" which they affirm relates to the God of the monotheistic religions who, according to Christian faith, has been disclosed in a decisive manner in Jesus Christ.

Is it legitimate to think, from the standpoint of a Christian theology, that the Ultimate Reality to which those other religious traditions refer is, in spite of their vastly different mental constructs, the same which the monotheistic religions affirm as the God of Abraham, Isaac, and Jacob? Is there an "Ultimate Reality" common to all religious traditions, even if it is differently experienced and variously conceptualized by the various traditions? One Divine Mystery with many faces? And, if such is the case, can this "Ultimate Reality" be interpreted in terms of Christian Trinitarian theism, no matter how imperfectly apprehended? Or is it to be viewed as equally distant from all categories, theistic or otherwise?

The religious traditions offer a broad spectrum of contrasting positions, even of dichotomies of mutually contradictory terms: theism versus nontheism; monotheism versus polytheism; monism versus dualism; pantheism versus panentheism; personal God versus impersonal; and so forth. In this broad variety of standpoints, can there be a *reductio ad unum* in favor of a Christian Trinitarian theism? Is it theologically justified and practicable? If we speak of a universal hidden presence of the God of Jesus Christ in the "Ultimate Reality" appealed to by the other traditions, do we not unduly "absolutize" a particular "referent" as the only possible hermeneutical key to any religious experience whatsoever? And can any evidence be put forward to substantiate such a Christian interpretation?

"All have the same God," Walbert Bühlmann wrote,[9] and he understood it as the "God and Father of Our Lord Jesus Christ." This is a patently Christian theological stand which members of other traditions will not be prepared to make their own. Nor must they be asked to. Hindu *advaita* theology will continue to interpret reality in terms of nonduality (*advaita*) between Brahman and the self; the Buddhist interpretation will be in terms of "emptiness" (*śūnyatā*). For their part, Christians who, in continuity with the Jewish revelation and their own tradition, adhere to a *Trinitarian monotheism* cannot but think in terms of the universal presence and self-manifestation of the Triune God. For them the Divine Mystery with many faces is unequivocally the God and Father who disclosed his face for us in Jesus Christ.

THE "WHOLLY OTHER" AND THE "SELF OF THE SELF"

The three monotheistic religions are equally emphatic on the uniqueness of the God they worship. Reference can be made before all else to the *Shemá* of Israel: "Hear, O Israel: The Lord our God is one Lord" (Deut 6:4). The oneness of the God of Israel is further elaborated in Deutero-Isaiah: "I am the Lord, and there is no other; besides me there is no God" (Isa 45:5); "I, I am the Lord, and besides me there is no Savior" (Isa 43:11; cf. 43:8–13; 44:6–8, 24–28; 45:20–25; etc.). The same message is repeated in the Christian scripture: "Hear, O Israel: The Lord our God, the Lord is One; and you shall love the Lord your God with all your heart, and with all your soul, and with all your mind, and with all your strength" (Mk 12:29–30; see Mt 22:37–38); this is the first commandment. Christian monotheism claims to be in direct continuity with Israelite monotheism.

The doctrine of the Qur'an concurs: "Our God and your God is One" (Surah 29:46).[10] The context of the quotation clearly indicates that reference is being made to the "people of the Book," that is, to Israel and the Christians: "We believe in what has been revealed to us and to you; our God and your God is One, and we are submissive (*muslim*) to him" (Surah 29:46). And elsewhere in the Qur'an, Allah says: "There is no God but me (*illâ anâ*)" (Surah 16:2; 21:14).

Islam too traces its roots to the faith of Abraham, even though the Abrahamite covenant and the promise that goes with it are not found in the Qur'an. It teaches the existence of a single Creator God, who provides for his creation, who is almighty, all-knowing, living, and lawgiver. It also evokes the mission of the prophets of whom the Bible speaks, and that of Jesus. While it does not narrate the history of Israel in detailed fashion as the Bible does, it does evoke the high points in the lives of Abraham, Isaac, Moses, and Jesus. These high points, reported in discontinuous fashion, mark the times when God reveals himself as

---

9. It is the title of the book of Walbert Bühlmann, *All Have the Same God* (Slough, U.K.: St. Paul Publications, 1982).

10. *The Koran*, ed. Muhhamad Zafrulla Khan (London: Kurzon Press, 1975).

the one God. However, what matters for the Qur'an is not so much the history of the people as the intervention of God who, from his transcendence on high, "causes his Word to descend" on the prophets so that they can reveal him.

All three traditions, then, unequivocally claim to have their roots in the God of Abraham. They share the same God.[11] This, however, does not mean that the concept of God is identical in the three monotheistic religions. Indeed, the opposite is true, at least in terms of doctrines. The Christian tradition claims to prolong Israel's monotheism, while developing it into Trinitarian doctrine; the monotheism of the Qur'an and the Islamic tradition also traces its origin to the God of Israel's faith, while claiming to complete it and purify it from the corruption of that faith by the Christian Trinitarian doctrine. As is aptly shown by Roger Arnaldez,[12] the three founding religious communities point to quite different experiences of the same God.

For Israel, God is primarily the Almighty One who has delivered his people from slavery in Egypt and guided it throughout history; by a kind of "retrojection" the same God appears as the Creator of human beings and of the universe. Christianity internalizes the monotheistic faith of Israel, while at the same time further stressing its universal import. But while for the Jews God is primarily Savior, for Muslims he is before all else the Lord, the Almighty Creator (p. 64). Arnaldez further shows that, the identity of the one God notwithstanding, the concept of God differs vastly in the three monotheistic religions. Doctrinally, the three monotheisms are different:

> It is clear that the God of Islam who abrogates the Law of Moses and relativizes the covenant with Israel cannot be the God of the Jews. He cannot in any way either be the God of Christians since he unveils the error which faith in the Trinity and the incarnation — without which there is no Christianity — necessarily constitutes for every Muslim. On this level the three monotheisms cannot but exclude each other. But the Jew believes that God spoke through the Bible; the Christian believes that through his Word made flesh God speaks in the Gospels; the Muslim believes that God speaks in the Qur'an, or even that the Qur'an is his eternal Word. (p. 116)

For Israel, the Exodus is the paradigmatic event of salvation, wrought in the past by the God of the covenant in favor of his people; it is reenacted in history and celebrated in memorial as the promise of eschatological salvation. For Christianity, the Jesus Christ event is the hinge on which the entire history of salvation revolves as it tends toward the second coming of the Lord. For Islam, the salvific event is above all the "eternal Word" spoken by God and consigned by him through Muhammad to the Qur'an; the Qur'an is God's last word to the world, the final disclosure of his transcendent mystery and of his gracious

---

11. Cf. Karl-Josef Kuschel, *Abraham: A Symbol of Hope for Jews, Christians, and Muslims* (London: SCM Press, 1995).

12. Roger Arnaldez, *Trois messagers pour un seul Dieu* (Paris: Albin Michel, 1983).

mercy. Strictly speaking, only Islam can be called a "religion of the Book"; Israel is the religion of a covenantal bond between God and his people; Christianity, that of a personal event, Jesus Christ. However, despite such irreducible divergences between the three "faiths," their common historical foundation — God's self-disclosure to Abraham at the beginning of biblical salvation history — still stands.

More than in their doctrine of God and their respective messages, it is at the level of faith as lived by the mystics that the three monotheistic religions can be truly said to converge. The mystics of all three religions are driven by an unquenchable thirst, on a quest for union with the same one God, at once transcendent and immanent, the author of life who graciously communicates himself to unworthy creatures. Whether in the Kabbālah tradition or in Christian mysticism or in Muslim Sufism, the mystics of the three monotheistic religions witness to the same values of communion and manifest a similar relentless search for union with the one God toward whom the whole human race is tending. At that level, the "three messengers" — Moses, Jesus, and Muhammad — become the "bearers of a unique message," calling human beings to seek and to find the one God in the recesses of their hearts (p. 69).

To sum up: the three monotheistic religions appeal to the God of Abraham, considered as the only God; their experience of that same God differs vastly, however, and hence their respective doctrines of God likewise are quite different. Nevertheless, while divergence occurs on the level of doctrine, convergence obtains when faith becomes a quest for mystical union: in none of the monotheistic mystical traditions does ecstatic union with the "Absolute One" connote the fading away of the human ego into the "One" as understood in some of the Asian mysticisms. The monotheistic faiths uphold interpersonal communion between God and human persons, not the identity of the human with the Divine.

The distinction between the monotheistic or prophetic religions — although it must be handled carefully — has the merit of pointing to a common historical origin and consequently to a family resemblance between the former, and analogously between the latter, to some common traits, a strong "wisdom "or "gnostic" character which attests to reciprocal ties between them. The differences between the two are so deep as to give rise to distinct worldviews (*Weltanschauungen*).

In searching for divine revelation in the religious traditions outside the Judeo-Christian tradition, such differences must be taken into account. An existential approach to theology also makes it incumbent upon the Christian interpreter to transcend the level of the imperfect ideas of God conveyed by the religions which, as they are outside the Judeo-Christian tradition, live in the dispensation of the "cosmic covenant," in order to attain, insofar as possible, the living experience of the divine underlying these ideas and concepts.

We must indeed recognize that many women and men living under the dispensation of the cosmic covenant have encountered the true God in an authentic religious experience. For example, prayer, by its very nature, entails a personal relationship between an "I" and an infinite "Thou." One does not pray to an impersonal God.[13] Authentic prayer is always a sign that God, in some secret hidden way, has undertaken the initiative of a personal approach to human beings in self-revelation and has been welcomed by these human beings in faith. Those who entrust themselves to God in faith and charity are saved, however imperfect their conception of the God who has revealed himself to them. After all, salvation depends on the response made by sinful human beings in faith to a personal communication initiated by God.

There is a gap, however, between religious experience and its formulation. This is true even of the Christian experience; a fortiori, it will be true of the others. We never have access to the religious experience of another in its pure state, without the garment in which it is clothed by being stated in human discourse. Language, it is true, gives us access to this experience and communicates it to us; but it does so inadequately. Indeed, in transmitting it, it betrays it, inasmuch as by its very nature religious experience is beyond all expression. If we wish to reach to the religious experience of others and discover the hidden elements of truth and grace there, we shall be obliged to go beyond the concepts that enunciate that experience. Insofar as it is possible, we shall have to ascertain the core of the experience through the defective concepts through which it is expressed.

As we know, in Eastern religious traditions religious experience is not always expressed in terms of a personal relationship with God. Hindu *advaita* mysticism conceives it as an awakening to one's identity with the Brahman. As for Buddhism, even while, despite its agnostic attitude and nontheistic appearance, it does imply an (impersonal) Absolute, no personal relationship with God is professed here, either. Buddhists speak of contemplation and meditation, not of prayer. By contrast, in Christianity and the other monotheistic and prophetic religions, religious experience takes the form of an interpersonal dialogue between God (who takes the initiative) and the human being (who responds to that initiative). Thus while the mystical Asian religions cultivate "instasy" (the quest for an unknown Absolute "in the cave of the heart"), ecstasy (the encounter with the "wholly other" God, distinct from oneself) predominates with their prophetic counterparts; the former emphasize negative discourse ("extinction" — *nirvāṇa*, "emptiness" — *śūnyatā*), the latter the positive.

However, despite the limitations setting apart how those experiences are expressed, wherever there is genuine religious experience, it is surely the God revealed in Jesus Christ who thus enters into the lives of men and women, in a hidden secret fashion. While the concept of God remains incomplete, the interpersonal encounter between God and the human being — inasmuch as it is God who takes the initiative, awaiting the response of faith on the part of the human being — is authentic. Theologically we must hold that wherever and whenever human beings turn toward an Absolute that addresses them and bestows itself upon them, an attitude of supernatural faith is thereby at work, in response to a

---

13. Cf. H. Limet and J. Fries, eds., *L'expérience de la prière dans les grandes religions* (Louvain-la-Neuve: Centre d'histoire des religions, 1980).

personal divine revelation. The one at whom this attitude of faith is directed, and the one who originally arouses it, is the God of Jesus Christ who communicates himself to them.

All the differences notwithstanding, a Christian theology of religious experience cannot but interpret the experience as in all circumstances involving the self-disclosure and self-gift of the one God who fully manifested himself in Jesus Christ. The theological reason for affirming this is as simple as it is compelling. It holds to the *Shemá* of Israel, as it is found in Deuteronomy 6:4: "Hear, O Israel: The Lord our God is one Lord" (cf. Mk 12:29). God is one, and there is no other! The same God it is who performs saving deeds in human history and speaks to human beings in the secret of their hearts. The same God is at once the "Utterly Other" and the "Self at the center of the self"; the transcendent "without" and the immanent "within"; the Father of our Lord Jesus Christ and the "ground of being of all that is." And while, in Jesus Christ, God has truly become our Father, that God remains the One "Who Is," whereas we are those who "are not." In ecstasy the same God is contemplated, awareness of whom may gush forth in "instasy"; the same God is affirmed through theological "cataphaticism" and inferred in mystical "apophaticism."

This polarity and tension between distinct approaches to the reality of God is not new to the Christian tradition. God has been reached from both ends, as the "Father in heaven" and as "more deeply intimate to myself than I am" (*interior intimo meo*) (St. Augustine, *Confessions* III, 6, 11). He has been known as the Unknowable: "If you have understood it is not God" (*Si enim comprehendisti non est Deus*) (St. Augustine, *Sermo* 117, 3, 5); "We can know neither God's being, nor God's essence" (*Non possumus scire esse Dei, sicut nec eius essentiam*) (St. Thomas Aquinas, S.T. I, q. 3, a. 4, ad 2um). The "apophatic" tradition should enable Christian interpreters to reconcile the two revelations, the cosmic and the historical, respectively exemplified by the "mystical" and "prophetic" religious traditions, as ultimately springing from the same source. "We must try," writes Bede Griffiths, "to see the values in each of these revelations, to distinguish their differences and to discover their harmony, going beyond the differences in an experience of 'non-duality,' of transcendence of all dualities." And he adds:

> These two modes of experience, the cosmic and psychological on the one hand, and the personal and historical on the other, are not opposed but complementary. There is only one Reality, one Truth, whether it is known through the experience of the cosmos and the human soul or through encounter with a historic event.[14]

That one Truth is the God who revealed himself "in many and various ways" (Heb 1:1) through human history, until such time as his self-disclosure to the world culminated in Jesus Christ. The previous chapter has illustrated the Trini-

---

14. Bede Griffiths, *The Marriage of East and West* (London: Collins, 1982), 177–80; see also idem, *Return to the Center* (London: Collins, 1976).

tarian structure of God's deeds in salvation history; the same Trinitarian structure must be said to apply to God's self-revelation: whenever God has spoken in human history, he has done so through his Word, in his Spirit.

That God's speech is always through his Word is clearly implied by the reference in the Johannine Prologue to the Word of God as "the true light that enlightens every human being" by coming into the world (Jn 1:9). Vatican II refers to this passage when it speaks of the elements of truth in the doctrines of other religious traditions which "often reflect a ray of that Truth (*illius Veritatis*) which enlightens all human beings" (*Nostra Aetate* §2). The same reference seems implied in the council's repeated appeal to the "seeds of the Word" present in those traditions (*Ad Gentes* §§11, 15). Admittedly, the council did not explain in what precise sense it used the expression. Do the "seeds of the Word" refer to a human expectancy of a word spoken by God? Or is the Word of God understood to be actually present and active in the elements of truth contained in the religious traditions? One thing is clear: the council borrows the expression from the early fathers of the church, specifically from St. Justin, whose theology of the *Logos spermatikos* (the Word that sows its seeds) clearly intended to refer to different participations of human beings in the divine Logos affirmed by the Johannine Prologue. We will return to this point later.

That may serve to show that, before God's self-manifestation culminated in the incarnation of his Word (Jn 1:14), God had already "spoken" to humankind in the Word-to-become-incarnate. To the question, "Could a Christian affirm that the same divine Lord whom Christians worship in Jesus is worshipped, under other symbols, by the devotees of the Lord Krishna or of the Lord Buddha?" Avery Dulles answers in typically guarded fashion:

> It need not be denied that the eternal Logos could manifest itself to other peoples through other religious symbols . . . In continuity with a long Christian tradition of Logos-theology that goes back as far as Justin Martyr . . . it may be held that the divine person who appears in Jesus is not exhausted by that historical appearance. The symbols and myths of other religions may point to the one whom Christians recognize as the Christ.[15]

The universal significance of the incarnation of God's Word notwithstanding, room must be left for his anticipated action in history as well as his enduring influence under other symbols.

The postconciliar doctrinal statements have openly and increasingly acknowledged the activity of the Holy Spirit not only in the lives of persons belonging to the religious traditions of the world but in those traditions themselves. The active presence of the Spirit is universal. It anticipates the event of Jesus Christ and, after that event, extends beyond the confines of the church. The Spirit spreads throughout the world, vivifying all things. The cosmic revelation itself is caught up in this transformation.

---

15. A. Dulles, *Models of Revelation*, 190.

Is it true, then, that the activity of the Spirit reaches the members of other religious traditions precisely through their traditions? If so, what specific role might their sacred books play with respect to this activity? Do the nonbiblical scriptures mediate the activity of the Spirit in the religious life of others? How do these writings nourish and sustain their religious experience? How do they invite the members of these religions to the obedience of faith that saves? Can theology discover in the sacred scriptures of other religious traditions the harvest of an authentic divine revelation — a genuine word addressed by God to human beings?

To answer these and similar questions, we must continue to keep in mind the Trinitarian structure of every divine self-manifestation in history, by virtue of which the Holy Spirit is the necessary "point of entry" of divine truth and life into the human spirit. Every personal encounter of God with the human being and of the human being with God occurs in the Holy Spirit. God becomes God-for-the-human-being in the Spirit, and it is in the Spirit that we can respond to the divine advances. All "being together" of God and the human being is made possible in the Spirit, or — and this is the heart of the matter — all religious experience becomes truly personal in the Spirit. In the order of divine-human relationships, the Spirit is ultimately God rendered personally present to the human being — God felt by the human being in the depths of the human heart.

As this is an axiomatic truth in Trinitarian theology, we must say that all authentic experience of God is in the Spirit. Thus, the Spirit is present and active in all authentic experience of God, whatever be the manner in which human beings are situated in salvation history or the particular stage of this history to which they belong. The Holy Spirit is at work at every stage of salvation history. Likewise, at the various stages of the history of salvation, just as in the personal story of individual human beings, the same Spirit is at work, revealing and manifesting God. Such mediation of the Holy Spirit in God's self-disclosure is also operative in the sacred scriptures of other religious traditions.

WORDS AND WORD OF GOD

WORDS OF GOD
AND SACRED BOOKS

Can the "sacred scriptures" of other religions be acknowledged by theologians as a "word of God"? And, if so, to what extent and in what way?[16] Here we must distinguish between divine revelation, prophecy, and sacred scripture, although the realities respectively denoted by these various terms are bound together by manifold relations. God has wrought a personal self-manifestation in the history of the nations in such a manner that theology can speak of a *divine revelation,*

---

16. Cf. D. S. Amalorpavadass, ed., *Research Seminar on Non-Biblical Scriptures* (Bangalore: NBCLC, 1975).

ordered though it is to the Jewish and Christian revelation. Every divine self-manifestation implies divine revelation. In this regard, we need only recall the "holy pagans" of the Old Testament[17] and the divine covenants with humanity and the nations. At the same time, it is becoming more and more widely admitted today that the *prophetic charism* had antecedents outside Israel,[18] both before Christ and after. Indeed, the prophetic charism itself must be correctly understood. It primarily consists not of a prediction of the future but rather of an interpretation for a particular people of the sacred history being lived by that people: an interpretation of the divine interventions in their history and of the divine will for them. The source of the prophetic charism is, in effect, a "mystical experience." This has been excellently formulated in the case of the prophets of Israel: The prophet "has no doubt that the word of God has come to him and that he must pass it on to others. The source of this conviction is a mysterious, we may call it mystical, experience of a direct contact with God...The divine seizure often provokes 'abnormal' manifestations...as with the great mystics."[19] But the prophetic charism is not the exclusive privilege of Israel. Even the Old Testament acknowledged as genuine prophecy coming from God four important oracles of Balaam, a non-Hebrew (Num 22:1–24:25): "The Spirit of God came upon him, and he took up his discourse..." (Num 24:2–3). As for Christian antiquity, it sometimes regarded the ancient Greek Sibylline Oracles as prophetic.

The case of the prophet Muhammad is instructive here. On the basis of the description of the prophetic charism just cited, R. C. Zaehner thinks that Muhammad (like Zoroaster) is a genuine prophet. And comparing the Old Testament with the Qur'an, he observes: "It is impossible to read the two books together without concluding that it is the same God who speaks in both: the prophetical accents are unmistakable."[20] The acknowledgment of Muhammad as a genuine prophet of God is no longer unusual in Christian theology. Christian theologians who admit this, let us observe, are aware that the Qur'an cannot in its entirety be regarded as the authentic word of God; it is not without error. But this does not prevent the divine truth it contains from being a word of God uttered through the prophet. Seen in its historical context of widespread and assertive polytheism, Muhammad's affirmation of an uncompromising monotheism can appear as deriving from a religious experience that can be called "prophetic." This revelation will not be said to be perfect, much less complete; but it is not thereby devoid of any value.

Actually, the real problem is not that of revelation, or even of prophecy, but of the *sacred scriptures* as containing words uttered by God to human beings over the course of salvation history. From the Christian standpoint, sacred scriptures con-

---

17. Jean Daniélou, *Holy Pagans in the Old Testament* (London: Longmans, Green, 1957).
18. Cf. André Neher, *L'essence du prophétisme* (Paris: Calmann-Lévy, 1972).
19. "Introduction to the Prophets," in *The New Jerusalem Bible* (London: Darton, Longman & Todd, 1985), 1159.
20. R. C. Zaehner, *Concordant Discord* (Oxford: Clarendon Press, 1970), 23–29.

tain memories and interpretations of divine revelation; these have been recorded in writing under a special divine impulse in such a way that God himself can be called the author of this writing. This does not mean that the human authors of the sacred books, or the compilers who gathered the oral or written traditions contained therein, are bereft of the full exercise of their human faculties and cease to be the authors of their works. Rather, both God and the human being are to be credited as author, albeit on different levels. Sacred scripture is "the word of God in the words of human beings." Because God is its author, it is not reducible to a human discourse about God; rather, it is a word addressed by God to human beings. But because a human being is the author as well, this word addressed by God to human beings is authentically a human word — the only word, after all, that would be intelligible to them.

To elucidate the mystery of how God and the human being can be coauthors of the same word, Christian theology makes use of the concept of *inspiration*. Traditionally, by divine inspiration is meant that God, while respecting the human author's activity, guides and assumes this activity in such a manner that what is written is the word of God. However, it is doubtless a shortcoming of the traditional theology of sacred scripture that the proper role of the Holy Spirit therein is largely passed over in silence. That it constantly uses the term "in*spir*ation" changes nothing. The origin and deeper significance of the word seem most often to have fallen into oblivion or to have drawn little attention. The theology of sacred scriptures should once more put in full relief the personal influence of the Spirit in the inspiration of these scriptures. Only then will we be in possession of a theology of sacred scripture that will permit a more open attitude toward the scriptures of other religious traditions.

Karl Rahner has emphasized the communitarian character of the sacred scriptures. "The Bible is the book of the Church": it contains the word of God addressed to the ecclesial communion.[21] In other words, in the books that compose it, especially in those of the New Testament, the church has recognized the authentic expression of its own faith and the word of God in which that faith is grounded. Sacred scripture is thus a constitutive element of the mystery of the church, the community assembled and called into being by the word of God. But this does not require that the sacred author be aware of being moved by the Holy Spirit to write. As we know, the charism of scriptural inspiration extends well beyond the group of authors to whom various books are attributed — perhaps erroneously. These authors acted as redactors, or editors, of oral or written traditions that they had received from others.

This being the case, the question is whether Christian theology may acknowledge in other sacred scriptures a word of God inspired by the Holy Spirit and addressed by God to other religious communities — and if so, in what way this word is the word of God. To put it another way: Are the writings recognized

---

21. Karl Rahner, *Inspiration in the Bible* (New York: Herder, 1961); cf. also Karl Rahner and Joseph Ratzinger, *Revelation and Tradition* (New York: Herder, 1966).

as sacred scriptures by other religious traditions, in which Christian theology is today accustomed to see the "seeds of the Word," sacred scripture in the theological sense of the word? Are we to acknowledge in them a word of God to human beings, inspired by the Holy Spirit? Or are we to see only a human word concerning God — or, again, are we to see a human word addressed to God in the expectation of a divine response? If indeed it is a matter of a word of God, then we must further ask: What is the connection between this word, uttered by God to human beings, as contained in the sacred scriptures of various religious traditions, and the decisive word spoken by God to human beings in Jesus Christ, of which the New Testament constitutes the official record? To answer these questions we shall appeal to the notion of a progressive, differentiated revelation and to an analogical concept of scriptural inspiration.

Meanwhile, we must maintain that the religious experience of the sages and "seers" (*ṛṣi*) of the nations is guided and directed by the Spirit. Their experience of God is an experience in God's Spirit. To be sure, we must simultaneously admit that this experience is not a privilege destined to the seers alone. In the divine providence, God, to whom alone belongs the initiative of any divine-human encounter, has willed to speak to the nations themselves, through the religious experience of their prophets. In addressing the prophets personally in the secret recesses of their hearts, God has willed to be manifested and revealed to the nations in the divine Spirit. Thus God has secretly entered the history of peoples, guiding them toward the realization of the divine design. The social character of the sacred scriptures of the nations can thus be said to have been willed by God. These scriptures represent the sacred legacy of a tradition-in-becoming, not without the intervention of divine providence. They contain words of God to human beings in the words of the seers, inasmuch as they report secret words uttered by the Spirit in hearts that are human, but words destined by divine providence to lead other human beings to the experience of the same Spirit. To say anything less would seem to underestimate the realism of God's self-manifestation to the nations.

What is suggested here is not tantamount to saying that the *whole* content of the sacred scriptures of the nations is word of God in the words of human beings. In the compilation of the sacred books of other traditions, many elements may have been introduced that represent only human words about God. Still less are we suggesting that the words of God contained in the scriptures of the nations represent God's decisive word to humankind, as if God no longer had anything to say that he has not already uttered through the mediation of the prophets of the nations.

Our proposal comes down to this: the personal experience of the Spirit by the seers, inasmuch as, by divine providence, it is a personal overture on the part of God to the nations, and inasmuch as it has been authentically recorded in their sacred scriptures, is a personal word addressed by God to them through intermediaries chosen by God. In a true sense, this word may be called "a word inspired by God," provided (as will be seen later) we do not impose too narrow an understanding of the concepts and that we take sufficient account of the cosmic influence of the Holy Spirit.

THE *"FULLNESS"* OF REVELATION
IN JESUS CHRIST

The Letter to the Hebrews states (Heb 1:1) that the word uttered by God in Jesus Christ — in the Son — is God's decisive word to the world. And Vatican II comments that Jesus Christ "completes and perfects" divine revelation (*complendo perficit*) (*Dei Verbum* §4). The council adds in fact that Jesus Christ "is himself both the mediator and the sum total of revelation" (*mediator simul et plenitudo totius revelationis*) (*Dei Verbum* §2). However, in what sense, and how, is Jesus Christ the fullness of revelation? Where precisely is this plenitude? To avoid any misunderstanding, let us note that the fullness of revelation is not, properly speaking, the written word of the New Testament. The latter constitutes the official record and interpretation, the authentic memorial, of that revelation. This authentic memorial — which is part of "constitutive" tradition — is to be distinguished from the Jesus Christ event itself, to which the accredited witnesses give testimony. It is the very person of Jesus Christ, his deeds and his words, his life, his death, and his resurrection — in a word, the total Jesus Christ event itself — that constitutes the fullness of revelation. In him God has uttered to the world his decisive word.

This is the understanding of Vatican II's constitution *Dei Verbum*, when it distinguishes the fullness of revelation in the Jesus Christ event (*Dei Verbum* §4) from its "transmission" in the New Testament, which belongs to apostolic tradition (*Dei Verbum* §7). The authentic memorial transmitted by the New Testament is of course normative (*norma normans*) for the faith of the church of all times. But this does not mean that it constitutes the fullness of the word of God to human beings. The New Testament itself bears witness that this memorial reports the event of Jesus Christ only incompletely (see Jn 21:25).

Thus Jesus Christ is personally the fullness of revelation. Furthermore, let us note, this fullness is not to be understood quantitatively — as though after Christ everything related to the divine mystery were already known and there were nothing further to learn — but qualitatively. It is owing to his personal identity as Son of God that Jesus Christ is, properly speaking, the pinnacle and culmination of the revealed word. In order to understand this, we must begin with the human awareness that Jesus had of being the Son of God. Jesus lived his personal relationship to the Father in his human awareness. His human consciousness of being the Son entailed an immediate knowledge of his Father, whom he called *Abbà*. Thus, his revelation of God had its point of departure in a unique, unsurpassable human experience. This experience was actually none other than the transposition to the key of human awareness and cognition of the very life of God and of the Trinitarian relations among the persons. Thus, according to the Fourth Gospel, Jesus prayed to the Father in whom he had his origin, while he promised to send the Spirit that came from the Father through him (Jn 14:16–17, 26; 16:7).

If divine revelation attains its qualitative plenitude in Jesus, it is because no revelation of the mystery of God can match the depths of what occurred when the divine Son incarnate lived in a human key, in a human consciousness, his own identity as the Son of God. This is what took place in Jesus Christ, and it is this that is at the origin of the divine revelation that he delivers to us.

Jesus' unity with the Father confers on his human consciousness a specific and unique character: Jesus refers to the Father with a familiarity never before conceived or witnessed. What Jesus revealed of the mystery of God could not be explained by an extraordinary knowledge of the Scriptures. It was not something learned. It was something that sprang out of the lived experience of a unique intimacy. If, as the gospel attests, no one had ever spoken before like Jesus (Jn 7:46), the reason is that no other human experience of God was comparable to his. The gospel according to John provides us with a glimmer of that unity between Father and Son: "The Father and I are one" (Jn 10:30). Such unity implies reciprocal immanence (10:38; 14:11; 17:21), mutual knowledge (10:15), reciprocal love (5:20; 15:10), common action — what Jesus does, the Father does in him (5:17).

Jesus' life and human condition are therefore a human expression of the mystery of the Son of God in relation to his Father. His human words are accordingly the human expression of the Word of God. Jesus, as opposed to the prophets, does not simply speak words received from God to human beings; he himself is the Word of God made flesh. The reason why God's self-revelation in Jesus is decisive, unsurpassed and unsurpassable, is that Jesus experiences in his human consciousness the mystery of the divine life in which he participates personally. This transposition of the divine mystery into human consciousness enables it to be expressed in human language. In Jesus the revelation of this mystery thus has a qualitatively different and unique character, because as understood by the biblical witness, Jesus is himself the Son of God who expresses himself and affirms his divine origin in human terms. That revelation is central and normative for Christian faith, in the sense that no one is in a position to communicate the mystery of God to human beings with a depth equal to that with which the very Son made human did so. Jesus speaks the word because he *is* the Word.

Nevertheless, this revelation is not "absolute"; it necessarily remains limited. The human consciousness of Jesus, while it is that of the Son, is still a human consciousness and hence limited. It could not be otherwise given the mystery of the incarnation. No human consciousnesses, not even that of the Son-of-God-made-human, could "comprehend," that is, contain and exhaust, the divine mystery in its totality. No expression of the mystery in human words, not even those that sprang from the unique experience of the Son in his humanity, could exhaust the mystery in its entirety: that can be done only by the intra-divine consciousness, shared by the three persons in the mystery of the Trinity. The human knowledge and consciousness of Jesus, however, while it is the personal knowledge and consciousness of the Word, is and remains authentically and specifically human, and it cannot, through a mistaken notion of the *communicatio idiomatum*, entail a direct communication of the divine knowledge to the human. It is thus a fallacy to hold that because the person speaking is a divine person, his human words contain the whole of the divine mystery, despite the innate limitations of his human nature. Indeed human words, even if they could — hypothetically — be uttered directly by God himself, would not be able to exhaust the reality of the Divine Mystery.

On the other hand, it was precisely this human experience that Jesus had of being the Son, in relation to the Father, that enabled him to translate into human words the mystery of God, revealing it to us. Indeed, the mystery of the triune God could be revealed to human beings only by the incarnate Son who, living his own identity of Son in his human being, could express such a mystery in human words to his brothers and sisters. The mystery of the triune God was disclosed to the consciousness of Jesus' disciples when at Pentecost, the risen Lord poured over them the Spirit of the Father (Acts 2:23) as he had promised (Jn 16:7). However, the transposition of the mystery into human language imposes another specific limit on God's revelation in Jesus Christ, due to the particular language in which Jesus expressed himself, the Aramaic spoken in his day. Any human linguistic idiom has its own riches and its own limits. If Jesus had been obliged to express his divine revelation in a language from a different cultural area, would he have been able to make exactly the same discourse?

On the one hand, in fact, we must believe that God remains, even after the revelation in Jesus Christ, a God hidden in inaccessible light (cf. 1 Tim 6:16). Otherwise, faith would vanish! It remains true that "No one has ever seen God" (Jn 1:18), even after "the only Son . . . has 'revealed' (*exègèsato*, that is, interpreted) him." On the other hand, we must also believe that the words used by Jesus to reveal the mystery (*Abbà*, Spirit, etc.) correspond objectively — even if only analogously — to the reality of the divine mystery. We know that paternity and filiation are objectively in the divine mystery, but we have no positive representation of how such "personal relations" are concretely realized in the divinity: in what does the transcendent manner in which generation takes place in God consist? It must likewise be recognized that the Spirit who "proceeds" from the Father through the Son remains for us the "unknown one beyond the Word" (Hans Urs von Balthasar). The Spirit, while clearly being "person" according to the New Testament witness, does not even have a proper personal name for himself: the Father and the Son are also "spirit"!

This all shows that the "fullness" of revelation in Jesus Christ must be understood correctly and with the proper precision. It is a qualitative rather than a quantitative fullness; it is of a singular intensity, but it does not "exhaust" the mystery. Therefore, even though it is unsurpassed and unsurpassable, it remains limited. It still remains unfinished and will remain so until the completion of revelation in the eschaton. Indeed, *Dei Verbum* teaches that, "as the centuries go by, the church is always advancing towards the plenitude of divine truth, until eventually the words of God are fulfilled in her" (§8), that is, in the eschaton. Pope John Paul II is in agreement in his encyclical *Fides et Ratio* (1998), where he says that "every truth attained [by the church through revelation] is but a step towards that fullness of truth which will appear with the final Revelation of God" (§2). He then quotes St. Paul: "For now we see in a mirror dimly, but then face to face. Now I know in part; then I shall understand fully" (1 Cor 13:12). There always remains the "remainder" or the "eschatological proviso." On the one hand, revelation is already "full" in Jesus Christ; on the other, however, it remains "unfinished" until its complete manifestation in the eschaton. The language of revelation in the New Testament indeed has a strong eschatological tone. In some cases it points directly to the definitive revelation at the end of time (cf. 1 Pet 1:5, 7, 13). For the First Letter to Peter and the Letter to Titus (2:11–14), revelation in Jesus Christ, while full, nonetheless remains clearly limited and unfinished with respect to the eschaton.

The qualitative fullness — the intensity, we could say, or the depth — of revelation in Jesus Christ does not constitute, even after the historic event has taken place, an obstacle to the continuation of a divine self-revelation also through the prophets and sages of other religious traditions. Such ongoing self-revelation of God has taken place in history and continues to take place. Yet no revelation, before or after Christ, has been able or ever will be able to surpass or equal the one that has been granted in him, the Son of God incarnate. As long as the unsurpassable fullness of the revelation that has taken place in Jesus Christ is kept in mind, it can be said that God continues to speak to our world to this day. There are still prophets in the church, and St. Augustine said that there were some also among the members of other religions. Revelation in Jesus Christ continues to "become actual" in the life of the church; outside the church, it can be "sketched out" by the highlighting of authentic aspects of the divine mystery, or through incomplete "faces" of that mystery and through genuine "presentiments" of the mystery revealed in Jesus Christ.

The church, meanwhile, must continue to grow in a more profound understanding of the words uttered by God "once for all" in his Word incarnate. To this end, the church is assured of the constant assistance of the Spirit that guides it "into all the truth" (cf. Jn 16:13).[22] The church does this, furthermore, in reference to the authentic record of the event contained in the New Testament, which remains for all time the norm (*norma normans*) of an ecclesial comprehension of God and his Christ.

REVELATION, DIFFERENTIATED AND COMPLEMENTARY

Once the singular character of the Jesus Christ event and the unique place of the official record of this event by the community of the church in the mys-

---

22. Cf. Ignace de la Potterie, "Jésus-Christ, plénitude de la vérité, lumière du monde et sommet de la révélation d'après Saint Jean," *Founders of Religions, Studia Missionalia* 33 (1984): 305–24; cf. also Gerald O'Collins, *Retrieving Fundamental Theology* (New York: Paulist Press, 1993).

tery of God's revelation to the world is recognized, there remains room for an "open" theology of revelation and sacred scriptures. Such a theology will posit that, even though he spoke his decisive word in Jesus Christ, besides having spoken through the prophets of the Old Testament, God has uttered initial or seminal words to human beings through the prophets of the nations — words whose traces can be found in the sacred scriptures of the world's religious traditions. The decisive word does not preclude other words: on the contrary, it presupposes them. Nor may we say that God's initial word is the one reported in the Old Testament. No, the Old Testament itself attests that God spoke to the nations even before addressing Israel. Witness to this are the covenants of God with Adam and Noah, and the familiarity with which in both cases God engages with human beings. Thus the sacred scriptures of the nations, along with the Old and New Testaments, represent various manners and forms in which God addresses human beings throughout the ongoing process of the divine self-revelation to them.

It is possible to distinguish three stages, which, strictly speaking, do not represent a chronological sequence, but are at least partially overlapping. In the first stage, God enables seers to hear in their hearts a secret word, at least traces of which are found in sacred scriptures of the religious traditions of the world. In the second stage, God speaks "officially" to Israel through the mouth of its prophets, and the entire Old Testament is the record of this word and of human responses to it. In both of these two stages, the word of God is ordered, however differently in each, to the plenary revelation that will take place in Jesus Christ. In this third stage, God utters his decisive word in him who is "the Word," and it is to this word that the whole New Testament bears official witness.

The sacred scriptures of the nations contain initial, hidden words of God. These words do not have the "official" character that we must ascribe to the Old Testament, insofar as it represents the immediate historic preparation willed by God in view of his revelation in Jesus Christ. Much less do they have the significance and the decisive value that must be attributed to God's word in Jesus Christ, alongside which, as the constitution *Dei Verbum* says (§4), "no new public revelation is to be expected before the glorious manifestation of our Lord." Although they do not represent a "public revelation" in the sense intended by the council, such words nevertheless have a "social" function, insofar as they are addressed by God to the religious communities of the peoples through their prophets and sages; and hence they cannot be reduced to "private" revelations. Such words can be called words of God, insofar as God pronounces them through his Spirit. From a theological standpoint, the sacred books containing them deserve to be called "sacred scriptures." The problem is ultimately terminological in nature: the issue is what must be understood by *word of God, holy scripture,* and *inspiration.*

The traditional way of speaking has given to these terms a restrictive theological definition, limiting their application to the scriptures of the Jewish and Christian traditions alone. The recent document of the International Theological

Commission, titled "Christianity and the World Religions,"[23] retains that restrictive usage. Even while admitting that God "has been able to enlighten men in
different ways" (§91), that some "divine enlightenment" could be at work "in
the composition" of other sacred books (§92), and that "the religious traditions
have been characterized by 'many sincere persons, inspired by the Spirit of God'
("Dialogue and Proclamation," 30)" (§90), the commission holds that it is "much
more fitting to reserve the qualification of *inspired* to the books of the canon"
(§92). The reason is the fact that "the divine inspiration which the church recognizes in the writings of the Old and New Testaments assures us that she has
recognized in them all and only what God wanted written about him" (§91).
The reason then why the commission finds it "much more fitting to reserve the
qualification of *inspired*" to the canonical books of the Old and New Testaments
is primarily the assurance that everything that has been written in them comes
from God, and hence the privilege of "inerrancy" is attributed to the biblical
writings, which cannot be likewise affirmed of the sacred books of the other religious traditions (even though biblical inerrancy must be understood correctly).
As valid as this reason may be, it is still legitimate to ask whether the concepts
ought to be defined a priori in such a way that they can be validly applied only
to the biblical scriptures. From such an a priori definition, it will logically follow
that the biblical books are the only ones to contain an authentic word of God to
human beings: outside of the biblical books there is no word of God, nor sacred
scripture.

Yet it remains possible — in an extended context of God's personal involvement with humankind — not without valid theological grounds, to propose a
broader definition of the terms involved according to which "word of God," "sacred scripture," and "inspiration" are applicable to the scriptures of other religious
traditions. "Word of God," "sacred scripture," and "inspiration" will then not express precisely the same reality at different stages of the history of revelation and
salvation. Important as it is to safeguard the special significance of the word of
God reported by the Jewish and Christian revelation — including "scriptural inerrancy" — it is no less important to recognize the true value and meaning of the
words of God contained in the sacred books of other religious traditions. "Word
of God," "sacred scripture," and "inspiration" then are *analogical* concepts, and
they are applied differently to the various stages of a progressive, differentiated
revelation. On this matter Claude Geffré calls for "a deeper theological appreciation of revelation as differentiated revelation." He writes, "While the theology of
the non-Christian religions has not yet emerged from the stumbling, searching
stage, we must try to think how a single revelation can include different words
of God."[24]

The history of salvation and revelation is one. In its various stages — cosmic,

---

23. "Christianity and the World Religions," *Origins* 27 (1997–98): 149–66.
24. Claude Geffré, "Le Coran, une parole de Dieu différente?" *Lumière et Vie* 32 (1932): 28–29.
Also cf. idem, "La place des religions dans le plan du salut," *La mission à la rencontre des religions
Spiritus* 138 (February 1995): 78–97.

Israelite, and Christian — it bears, in different ways, the seal of the influence of the Holy Spirit. By this we mean that throughout the stages of the divine revelation, God, through the gifts of divine providence, personally guides humanity toward the divinely set goal. The positive divine disposition of the cosmic revelation, as a personal revelation of God to the nations, includes the divine disposition of the sacred scriptures of those nations. The "seeds of the Word" contained in their scriptures are seminal words of God, from which the influence of the Spirit is not absent. The influence of the Spirit is universal. It extends to the words uttered by God to humanity in all stages of the self-revelation of God to humanity. It was Thomas Aquinas who wrote, quoting Ambrosiaster: *"Omne verum a quocumque dicatur a Spiritu Sancto est"* ("Every truth, no matter by whom it is said, comes from the Holy Spirit") (S.T. I-II, 109, 1, ad 1).

REVELATION IS PROGRESSIVE and differentiated. A true complementarity may even be said to exist between revelation inside and outside the Judeo-Christian tradition — without prejudice to the decisiveness of the Christ event. And, equivalently, it may be said that an analogous complementarity may be found between the sacred books of the other religious traditions and the biblical corpus. The same God who spoke to seers in the secret of their hearts spoke in history through his prophets and "in these last days" through the Son (Heb 1:1–2). All truth comes from God who is *Truth* and must be honored as such, whatever the channel through which it comes to us. Word of God and divine revelation are not to be considered monolithically, but as a diversified and complex reality.

Naturally, a keen discernment needs to be observed to sift divine truth from untruth. For the Christian, the normative criterion for such a discernment is unmistakably the mystery of the person and event of Jesus Christ, who *is* the Truth (Jn 14:6). Whatever is in contradiction to him who is *"the* Word" cannot come from the God who sent him. But, this being firmly asserted, there remains room for a complementarity of God's word, not only between the two testaments of the Christian Bible but also between the biblical and nonbiblical scriptures. The latter may contain aspects of the Divine Mystery which the Bible, the New Testament included, do not highlight equally. To give some examples: in the Qur'an the sense of the divine majesty and transcendence, of adoration and of the human being's submission to the holiness of God's eternal decrees; and in the sacred books of Hinduism, the sense of God's immanent presence in the world and in the recesses of the human heart.

Such complementarity between biblical and nonbiblical scriptures may be considered as reciprocal insofar as the latter may bring the Divine Mystery into greater relief than the Bible, including the New Testament. The complementarity between them is, therefore, reciprocal in the sense that we may discover not only clues to or elements of a kind of natural knowledge of God that will be fulfilled in a singular way by the Jewish and Christian tradition. This was what was intended in the theory of fulfillment theology, which has not been superseded. Nor is it only a matter of aspects or scattered fragments of divine truth, the fullness of which will be found abundantly in Christian revelation. Viewed from another angle, such reciprocal complementarity does not entail the idea of a lack in Christian revelation that any other revelation would remedy, or the notion that another revelation would have a supplementary character vis-à-vis Christian revelation, as though there were some "void" to be filled in the revelation of Jesus Christ. This would contradict its unique fullness and transcendence. The revelation in Jesus Christ indeed represents the apex, the center, the key for understanding any divine revelation. Thus reciprocal complementarity is not understood to mean that anything is lacking within Christianity that it would have to receive from other religions, without which it would not enjoy the fullness of divine revelation; but rather in the sense that God has provided gifts to human beings in the other religious traditions as well, which even though they find their fulfillment in the revelation of God in Jesus Christ, nonetheless represent authentic words of God, and additional autonomous gifts from God. Such divine gifts to human beings do not in any way impede the transcendence and unsurpassability of God's gift to humankind in Jesus Christ. The complementarity between the seeds of "truth and grace" in the other religious traditions and the "fullness" of the divine manifestation in Jesus Christ, attested by the Christian sacred scriptures, is thus to be understood as *mutual "asymmetrical" complementarity*. The term "asymmetrical," as new as it might seem in this context, cannot be ignored; otherwise the complementarity might be understood in a way that is theologically incorrect. What has been said about the complementarity of divine revelation in and outside of Jesus Christ will be applied later to the relationship between the various religious traditions and Christianity in general. Even while being reciprocal, their complementarity will also have to be understood as "asymmetrical" for the same reasons.

Recognition of the complementarity of sacred scriptures is one of the elements that make an "open theology" of the religions possible without undermining Christian identity. It is therefore possible to give an answer to the question of whether the word of God contained in other religions is valid as "word of God" only for those adhering to such traditions, or whether indeed we can think that God can speak even to us Christians through the prophets and sages whose religious experience constitutes the source of the sacred books of such traditions. The answer is that the fullness of revelation contained in Jesus Christ does not contradict that possibility. It has already been pointed out that the divine covenants, whether with Abraham and Moses or the one with Noah, remain valid albeit in relation to the decisive covenant in Jesus Christ; indeed, they retain their significance and value for Christians. Analogously, it may be said that the words of God in the diverse stages of his self-revelation, and consequently the sacred books that contain traces of it, retain even for Christians their meaning as initial words directed toward the decisive word of God in Jesus Christ. To say less would amount to emptying the true sense of the "seeds of the Word" spoken of in the Christian tradition, which were taken up by Vatican II (*Ad Gentes* §§11, 15), as well as the sense of the "ray of that Truth (*illius Veritatis*) that enlightens all human beings," emphasized by the council (*Nostra Aetate* §2), implicitly referring to the Prologue to the gospel according to John (1:9).

Therefore the use in Christian prayer of words of God contained in the sacred books of other religious traditions is not necessarily ruled out in principle, even in the "liturgy of the word."[25] This is to be done certainly with pastoral prudence, with no sort of ambiguity, and with respect for the different phases of the history of divine revelation, which culminates in God's word in Jesus Christ. Under these conditions, we will be able to discover with surprise amazing convergences between the words of God and his Word in Jesus Christ. As paradoxical as this might seem, prolonged contact with nonbiblical scriptures — if practiced within their own faith — may help Christians to discover in greater depth some aspects of the divine mystery that they contemplate disclosed to them in Jesus Christ.

---

25. Cf. D. S. Amalorpavadass, ed., *Research Seminar on Non-Biblical Scriptures* (Bangalore: NBCLC, 1975).

Chapter Six

THE WORD OF GOD, JESUS CHRIST, AND THE RELIGIONS OF THE WORLD

I N CHAPTER 3 I suggested a Trinitarian and pneumatic Christology as model for an open theology of religions. It would seem that this model, while clearly holding to the full meaning of Jesus Christ with regard to the universal salvation of humankind, also opens the door to a recognition of the salvific value of ways or paths of salvation put forward by the religious traditions for their followers. The solution proposed for resolving the apparently insoluble contradiction between these two affirmations consists in putting together and emphasizing three complementary and converging aspects by which, in the divine plan for humanity, salvation reaches the persons according to their actual circumstances in history and the world.

These three elements are as follows: (1) the universal reality and the effectiveness of the event of Jesus Christ, notwithstanding the historical particularity of this event; (2) the universal operative presence of the divine Word whose action is not constrained by the human nature assumed by him in the mystery of the incarnation; (3) the equally universal work of the Spirit of God, which is neither limited nor exhausted by the effusion of the Spirit through the glorified and risen Christ. In this chapter we will limit ourselves to the problem which consists in bringing together in an adequate way the work of the Word and the effectiveness of the event of Jesus Christ.

In this regard, questions arise which have to do directly with the relationship between the Word of God and the man Jesus Christ, as well as that between the pre-Easter Jesus and the Easter Christ. Such questions, while not being new, become more acute in the context of a theology of religions; in this context they take on new accents and become more burning. The question is asked in fact who is the Savior, Jesus Christ or the Word of God? As the event of Jesus Christ is limited to a particular historical time, how can this event enjoy an effectiveness which passes beyond the limits imposed on it by time and space? Is it not perhaps necessary to reduce the salvific meaning of the historic event to the advantage of the universal work of the Word of God which knows no such limits? The conclusion which would be reached then would consist in saying that it is really the Word who saves, while the significance of the event Jesus Christ consists in witnessing to the salvific action of the Word. Otherwise, if one maintains a salvific effectiveness of the risen human being of Jesus in view of Christians, who have recognized him as sacrament of salvation in their favor, it would seem necessary that this effectiveness be limited to those who have believed in him. Thus one arrives at the point of saying that, while Christians are saved through Jesus Christ, the members of the other religious traditions reach salvation through the universal working of the Word of God.

Earlier, while I was reviewing the different positions taken today in the debate on the theology of religions, I made reference, among others, to a new paradigm, which I called "Logocentrism." This paradigm tends to separate the work of the Word of God from the event of Jesus Christ in two different ways: either the distinct action of the Word must be considered as representing an economy of salvation distinct from that in Jesus Christ and parallel to it; or, the economy of salvation remaining one, salvific action must no longer be attributed to the Word as incarnate and to his being human, but to the Word himself, independently of his being human, whatever significance this being human may have in the order of salvation.

To counter these tendencies to distance and erroneously detach the universal action of the Word from the salvific effectiveness of the event of Jesus Christ, it is important to show that, while both aspects are distinct notwithstanding the personal identity of the historical Jesus with the Word–Son of God, they remain at the same time united in the single divine plan for humanity, so that they can never be separated as though they represented two parallel economies of salvation.

The present chapter consists therefore of two parts. The first part shows that there is a salvific working of the Word as such, distinct from that of the Word operating through his human being in Jesus Christ, risen and glorified, though in "union" with it. This activity of the Word as such can be discovered by studying the data of revelation as also the tradition of the fathers. A clear result of such study is to show the relevance and importance of the action of the Word as such for a theology of religions capable of uncovering a salvific value of the other religious traditions for their followers. The second part of the chapter shows that this work of the Word as such remains related to the event of Jesus Christ in the single divine plan of salvation for humanity, which culminates in the mystery of the incarnation of the Word in Jesus Christ and in the paschal mystery of his death and resurrection. It is therefore necessary to show in which way are combined both aspects of the universal action of the Word as such and of the universal salvific meaning of the event of Jesus Christ, in the single economy of salvation willed by God for humanity. Thus we will glimpse how, while the event of Jesus Christ is "constitutive" of universal salvation, other religious ways nonetheless have a salvific significance for their own followers in the same divine plan.

THE UNIVERSAL ACTION
OF THE WORD AS SUCH

It seems opportune here to start with the affirmation from the encyclical *Redemptoris Missio* (1990) regarding the inseparability of the Word of God and

Jesus Christ according to the Christian faith. A firm holding on to the personal identity between the Word of God and Jesus Christ is necessary, as also between Jesus and the Christ. It is the unique singularity, constitutive of personal identity, which confers on Christ a universal significance. The pope rightly affirms: "To introduce any sort of separation (*separationem*) between the Word and Jesus Christ is contrary to the Christian faith," and he continues: "One cannot separate (*separare*) Jesus from the Christ" (§6). The personal identity between the Word of God and Jesus Christ in virtue of the assumption of the humanity of Jesus in the divine person of the Word of God through the mystery of the "hypostatic union" must therefore always be maintained. It follows from this that the salvific effectiveness of the Word and the salvific significance of the historical event of Jesus Christ cannot be separated one from the other, in such a way as to attribute the salvific work to the Word exclusively, to the detriment of the humanity of Jesus.

This is not to say that it is not possible to speak of an action of the Word as such, distinct from his working through the humanity of Jesus, even in his risen and glorified state. It is necessary, however, to understand correctly this action of the Word as such. It must be well understood that the Word of God with whom we are dealing is not different from the one who became incarnate in Jesus Christ. It is clear that there is no Word of God other than the one who assumed human flesh in Jesus of Nazareth. But, while the mystery of the incarnation of the Word is a historic event and therefore particular in time and space, the Word as such exists in the eternity of the divine mystery. He also exists and is present and working throughout the history of the world and humanity — which in fact becomes the history of salvation in as much as it comprehends the totality of the self-manifestations of God to humanity through his Word. The Word of God is therefore operative through the whole of history, both before and after the mystery of the incarnation. For clarity's sake it seems therefore useful to distinguish the following: the action of the Word-to-be-incarnate (*Verbum incarnandum*), that is, the Word before the incarnation; the action of the Word incarnate (*Verbum incarnatum*), either in the state of kenosis during his human life or after the resurrection in the glorified state; and the perduring action of the Word as such which continues after the incarnation of the Word and the resurrection of Christ and is not constrained by the limits of his humanity. The action of the Word-to-be-incarnate, before the incarnation, and that of the Word as such, after the incarnation and the resurrection of Christ, must be established on the data of both revelation and tradition.

THE WISDOM OF GOD
IN THE WISDOM TRADITION

A first element to recall, in Old Testament evidence, is the economy of the Wisdom of God especially stressed in the Wisdom literature. Mons. P. Rossano, with profound insight, has made us see that, in Old Testament evidence, the firmest starting point for an open theology of religions is that of divine Wisdom, operating universally through the history of humanity. This should be analysis by close attention to the whole of Wisdom literature; here, however, we are forced to limit ourselves to some of the more important examples. As reference we will make use of the recent book by Giovanni Odasso, *Bibbia e religioni: Prospettive bibliche per la teologia delle religioni* (*The Bible and Religions: Biblical Perspectives for a Theology of the Religions*),[1] to which reference has already been made. Speaking of the Wisdom literature, this author notes that it develops "an understanding of revelation as a divine gift of Wisdom, which culminates in the canonization of the Torah. At the same time, tradition develops its own virtuality to the highest point, reaching an understanding of Wisdom as the plan itself of God, at the base of creation, of human history and the existence of Israel. It is a matter of the phenomenon known as 'hypostasizing' or 'personification' of Wisdom" (p. 200).

The author gives close examination to four important texts from Wisdom literature in order to show the development through biblical revelation of the theology of the Wisdom of God, of its universal presence and effectiveness, and its relevance for a theology of religions. The four texts are the following: Job 28:1–28; Prov 8:22–31; Sir 24:1–32; Wis 9:1–18. In the text from Job, Wisdom appears as "the personified expression of the divine plan, which transcends the whole of creation, even if it is accomplished in it, and consequently in human history" (p. 203). "The whole of humanity is reached by the gift of divine Wisdom and, therefore, of the light of the Word" (p. 205). Turning to the text from Proverbs, Wisdom "appears as a person who calls, making her voice heard, inviting people to listen and learn" (p. 206). "Wisdom, therefore, the eternal divine design hypostasized, in as far as she is the indefectible source of life and hope, places God himself in a relationship of security, trust and love with creation and, thus, most importantly, with humankind" (p. 207). "In this view religions present themselves as the historic-cultural expression of the experience through which humankind lives when it opens itself to the gift of divine Wisdom" (p. 209). The text from Sirach represents the next step in the personification of Wisdom. "In Israel, Wisdom exercises in the supreme way her *exousia*" (p. 210), but "The people of the Torah is qualified to perceive the fruit of the action of Wisdom, the illumination of her salvific *exousia*, and the epiphany of divine communication with men in the cultural and religious heritage of peoples" (p. 211). "Even the history of peoples . . . is the making concrete in time and space of the Word of the Most High, and of his eternal design of love and salvation" (ibid). In the text from Wisdom, "Wisdom and the Spirit of God are placed in a close mutual relationship. Where there is Wisdom, there also is the Spirit. Conversely, when God sends his Spirit he communicates his Wisdom to humankind" (p. 212). "Wisdom becomes the permanent salvific gift of God to humankind"; this gift is universal (p. 213). In consequence, "religions present themselves as the fruit of

---

1. Giovanni Odasso, *Bibbia e religioni: Prospettive bibliche per la teologia delle religioni* (Rome: Urbaniana University Press, 1998).

the activity of Wisdom in the life of people" (p. 215). Summarizing the result of his research in the Wisdom tradition, the author writes:

> From the perspectives which appear to our eyes it results that through Wisdom reflection, Scripture develops a new understanding of peoples and their histories, and of man and his destiny. We have here one of the greatest contributions of biblical faith, capable of giving vigor and new impulse to the knowledge of man in our own times and, in particular, to theology. In this field it seems legitimate to affirm that, for whoever looks at them from the perspective revealed by Wisdom reflection, religions present themselves as the context by antonomasia where man allows himself to be taught by Wisdom and guided by her towards the destination of the whole of humanity: full, invigorating and eternal communion with the living God. (p. 222)

THE WORD OF GOD IN THE PROLOGUE TO ST. JOHN'S GOSPEL

Turning to the New Testament, it is important to show that the message of the Wisdom literature of the Old Testament regarding the presence and the working of the Wisdom of God in the world's religions is continued and deepened. In the Old Testament there exists a close relationship, sometimes almost an identification, between the Wisdom of God and his Word. The same ambivalence can be found in the Christology of the New Testament in which Jesus Christ is considered as both Wisdom and as the Word of God. The emphases of Wisdom literature are not missing in the Christology developed in the Prologue to the Gospel according to John, though the author of the Fourth Gospel has privileged the concept of the Word of God to explain who is the one "with God" of whom he is speaking, and who became man in Jesus Christ. What is to be seen here is the Prologue's affirmation of a universal action and presence of the Word of God already in human history before the incarnation, as also the permanence of this action of the Logos as such after the incarnation of the Word and the resurrection of Jesus Christ.

Some exegetes read from the very first verses of the prologue, or at least from v. 6 (for example, R. Brown), a direct and explicit reference to Jesus Christ as the Word incarnate; others, however, insist, vv. 6–8 notwithstanding, that from the beginning until v. 14 (that is, from v. 1 to v. 13 inclusive) the prologue is referring to the Word-of-God-to-be-incarnate, considered before his incarnation as already present in the mystery of God and working from the very beginning of human history. This must be shown following some authoritative exegetes.

In his commentary on John's Gospel, X. Léon-Dufour[2] explains that the Logos was working from the beginning of creation (vv. 2–5) as the source of light and of life, setting up a personal relationship between God and men: as such, "coming into the world" in the way of the Wisdom of God in Sirach 24, he is the source

---

2. X. Léon-Dufour, *Lecture de l'Evangile selon Saint Jean*, vol. 1 (Paris: Seuil 1988), 62–144.

of light for all men and to those who have received him he gave "power to become children of God" (vv. 9, 12). Léon-Dufour writes, in fact, about the synergy that takes place between God and human beings as they welcome the Logos: "This enlightening action, insofar as it is welcomed, produces divine sonship. And this is so, even before the Logos takes a human face, that is independently from any explicit reference to Jesus Christ" (p. 109). He adds: "The 'coming' of the Logos has already been spoken of in 1:10f: he 'was in the world' and 'he came to his own home.' If it is true that the Logos is God communicating himself, this communication has begun not with the incarnation but since creation, and it has continued through the whole history of revelation. However, the incarnation of the Logos marks a radical change in the mode of communication" (p. 112). The change consists in the fact that "henceforth [revelation] happens through the language and the existence of a man among others: this phenomenon of concentration in a man will make it possible for the revelation of God to be formulated directly in an intelligible way, and for all people to have access to a definitive communication with God" (p. 124). Léon-Dufour goes on, however, to insist that, notwithstanding the novelty introduced by the incarnation, "this new stage does not supersede the previous one. The Logos continues to express himself thanks to creation of which he is the author and the witness given to the light: many can receive him and become children of God. Henceforth, however, revelation is also and mostly concentrated in him who will be designated by his name: Jesus Christ (v. 17)" (p. 124). According to Léon-Dufour it is therefore clear that we must speak not only of the universal action of the Word-to-be-incarnate before the incarnation, but also of the continuing action of the Word as such after the incarnation of the Word and after the resurrection of Jesus Christ.

Other exegetes who can serve as witnesses for a universal action of the Logos before the incarnation and of the Logos as such after the incarnation, according to the Prologue of John, are R. Schnackenburg,[3] J. Dupont,[4] A. Feuillet,[5] and M.-E. Boismard.[6] It suffices to mention the firmly held opinion of D. Mollat, who, referring explicitly to John 1:9, clearly affirms that the universal action of the Logos as such obtains even today. In his introduction to the exegesis of John[7] he writes, in fact, with reference to John 1:9: "In this verse...this coming of the Word into the world, implicitly referred to in vv. 4 and 5, is explicitly revealed." He continues:

It is said that this true light "enlightens all men." The present tense, "enlightens"...signifies that this is its proper task and its constant work.

3. R. Schnackenburg, *The Gospel according to St. John* (New York: Crossroad, 1987), 253–54.

4. J. Dupont, *Essais sur la christologie de Saint Jean* (Bruges: Editions de l'Abbaye de Saint-André, 1951), 48.

5. A. Feuillet, *Le prologue du quatrième évangile* (Bruges: Desclée de Brouwer, 1968), 62–76.

6. M.-E. Boismard, *Le prologue de Saint Jean* (Paris: Cerf, 1953), 43–49.

7. D. Mollat, *Introductio in Exegesim Scriptorum Sancti Johannis* (Rome: PUG, 1961), 21–24.

This work is to be understood in the supernatural sense of the enlightening which in v. 4 was declared to be the salvific illumination through which man is instructed and freed, transfigured and sanctified, and also judged. It must be stated that the illuminating virtue of this true light extends to all men. There is no one who is not reached or touched by it. A personal relationship between all men and the Word must therefore be affirmed. (pp. 23–24)

It seems therefore possible to talk of an action of the Word of God, not only before the incarnation of the Word but also after the incarnation and the resurrection of Jesus Christ, distinct from the salvific action through his humanity, provided that this continued action of the Word be not "separated" from the event in which the insuperable "concentration" of the self-revelation of God according to the one divine plan for the universal salvation of humankind takes place.

This vision agrees with the Christological dogma of the Council of Chalcedon (Denzinger, nos. 301–2). The council teaches that the two natures of Jesus Christ, the human and the divine, while being "inseparable," remain "distinct." The same thing is true of the two "actions" or "operations" as was later explained by the Third Council of Constantinople (Denzinger, nos. 635–37). Notwithstanding the personal identity, there is neither "confusion" nor "change" between the divine action of the Word and the human action of Jesus Christ. Historical monophysitism conceived the union of both natures and actions in such a way as to allow the human nature to be absorbed by the divine; what resulted from this view was that the human being and doing of Jesus Christ lost its human integrity, authenticity, and specificity. This monophysitism was condemned by both the councils referred to above. But we must be equally attentive to the real possibility, even today, of an "inverse monophysitism," that is, a way of reducing the divine nature on the part of the human; in this case, while the human nature of Jesus becomes united to the divine Word, the divine attributes and the divine actions of the person of the Word would be lessened, or, at least, reduced in some way and made commensurate with the human nature. Against this "inverse monophysitism," a clear affirmation of the permanent integrity of the divine nature and of the action of the Word, and of their continuing "distinction," is needed. It is from this permanent integrity and continued "distinction" of the divine action of the Word that the possibility of a continuing action of the Word as such is derived, distinct from that which takes place through the humanity of Jesus Christ.

In other words: the Word of God, as incarnate, remains the Word of God; God remains God. The Word continues, therefore, to be the one who "was in the beginning with God" and by means of whom "everything was made" (cf. Jn 1:1–3), without the human historical being of Jesus, which was not yet in existence, being able to serve as instrument for the divine act of creation. Similarly the Word remains still the true light, that which "enlightens every man coming into the world" (Jn 1:9) beyond the salvific action of the Word incarnate through his humanity. That means that the Word as such continues to share, according to his personal character in the mystery of the Trinity, the divine action in the world. The Word remains God: his divine eternity is not absorbed by his temporality as man; his creative function is not suppressed by his creatureliness as man; his "illuminative" power is not reduced to his revelation of God in human words. In short, it means that the Word remains that which he is in the mystery of the Trinity, though, being united in the person of the Word through the historic mystery of the incarnation, the very humanity of Jesus has become part, in a mysterious way, of the mystery of God himself. And this is why the continuing and invigorating action of the Word as such is "related" to the "concentration" of the divine salvation in the Word insofar as he is incarnate in Jesus Christ, and to the permanent actuality of the historic event through the risen condition of his humanity.

Passing from the exegesis of the New Testament and from the Christological dogma to theology, one can refer to different theologians who agree to see the salvific action of the Word incarnate in Jesus Christ as the sacrament of a broader action, that of the eternal Word of God which embraces the whole religious history of humanity. Claude Geffré writes explicitly on this:

> Jesus is the icon of the living God in a unique manner, and we need not wait for another "mediator." But this does not lead us to identifying the historically contingent aspect of Jesus with his "Christic" or divine aspect. The very law of God's incarnation through the mediation of history leads [us] to think that Jesus does not put an end to the history of God's manifestations... In conformity with the traditional view of the fathers of the church, it is, therefore, possible to see the economy of the Son incarnate as the sacrament of a broader economy, that, namely, of the eternal Word of God which coincides with the religious history of humankind.[8]

And he insists: "Without producing a ruinous dissociation between the eternal Word and the Word incarnate, it is legitimate... to consider the economy of the Word incarnate as the sacrament of a broader economy, that of the eternal Word of God, which coincides with the religious history of all humanity."[9]

Other authors affirm the same, with reference to the meaning of this working of the Word for the salvation of members of other religious traditions and the salvific value of their traditions. One recent author emphasizes the permanence of the action of the Word, with explicit reference to the exegesis of John 1:9 proposed by Léon-Dufour. He writes: "By not identifying straightaway the Logos with Jesus-the-Christ, it is easy to conceive a broad revealing action of the Logos

---

8. Cl. Geffré, "La singularité du christianisme à l'âge du pluralisme religieux," *Penser la foi: Recherches en théologie aujourd'hui: Mélanges offerts à Joseph Moingt,* ed. J. Doré and C. Theobald (Paris: Cerf-Arras, 1993), 365–66.

9. Cl. Geffré, "Théologie chrétienne et dialogue interreligieux," *Revue de l'Institut Catholique de Paris* 38, no. 1 (1992): 72.

throughout the history of salvation, not only before, but also after the incarnation."[10] The same idea has been expressed by Y. Raguin, also with reference to John 1:9. To give account of the real possibility of salvation for all, both before and after the incarnation, he explains that whoever has not been able to know the Word as incarnate can be saved through his/her knowledge of the Word as such. He writes:

> Those who will not have known the Father through the Incarnate Word will be able to know him through his non-incarnate-Word. Thus, all human beings can know the Word of God, even without knowing him in his incarnation...We read in the Prologue of the Gospel of John that the Word of God is the life of all things and that this life becomes the light of human beings. Now, every human being can make in oneself this experience of life become light and thus enter, through union with the Word, in the intimacy of the Father. This is how the greatest part of humankind can enter into relationship with God, source of all life and of all love, through the mediation of the Word, without having encountered Jesus and without having known him.[11]

This is also the meaning of the Final Declaration of the twenty-first annual meeting of the Indian Theological Association (April 1998), where it says:

> Celebrating the gracious and living mystery of God, we are not only aware of the Spirit of God "who blows where he wills," but also of the Word of God who speaks to peoples through various manifestations in different ways (Hebrews 1:1) and whom we profess as the one who became incarnate in Jesus. We gratefully acknowledge that it is our experience of the incarnate Jesus that leads us to the discovery of the cosmic dimensions of the presence and action of the Word. We realise that we can "neither confuse nor separate" these different manifestations of the Word in history, and in various cultures and religions. We joyfully proclaim our own experience of the Word in Jesus, on one hand, and on the other we also seek to relate in an open and positive way to the other manifestations of the Word as they are part of one divine mystery (5, 14–5, 15).[12]

These different testimonies converge in the affirmation of a salvific action of the Word as such even after the incarnation of the Word and after the resurrection of Jesus Christ. It remains to ask if this biblical affirmation was continued in the theology of the fathers of the church. The principal element to bear in mind is

---

10. B. Senécal, *Jésus à la rencontre de Gautama le Bouddha* (Paris: Cerf, 1998), 213.

11. Y. Raguin, *Un message de salut pour tous* (Paris: Vie chrétienne, n.d.), 31.

12. "Significance of Jesus Christ in the Context of Religious Pluralism in India," Final Statement of the Twenty-First Meeting of the Indian Theological Association, April 1998, in *What Does Jesus Christ Mean? The Meaningfulness of Jesus Christ amid Religious Pluralism in India*, ed. E. D'Lima and M. Gonsalves (Bangalore: Indian Theological Association, 1999), 182.

the doctrine of the *Logos spermatikos* in the theology of the fathers of the second century.

THE DOCTRINE OF THE LOGOS SPERMATIKOS IN THE EARLY FATHERS OF THE CHURCH

At the beginning of the Christian era, the concept of Logos or *Dabar* occupied a preeminent place in the minds of the intelligentsia in both Hellenistic philosophy and in Semitic thought. In the mind of the Hellenistic philosopher, Logos represented a principle of intelligibility immanent in the world; for the Jews it recalled by way of a literary personification the manifestation and personal revelation of Yahweh. When the Gospel of John described the man Jesus as the Word of God incarnate this must have appeared as a revolutionary innovation. The Christian Logos appeared as a "person" distinct from Yahweh and a divine person. Notwithstanding, however, the originality of his personal character in the mind of the early fathers, the Logos also exercised the functions attributed by Hellenism to the impersonal Logos. Paul had spoken of the cosmic significance of Christ. In what way, it was asked, does the Logos exercise this universal cosmic function? Did the eternal Logos manifest himself to all human beings, or was knowledge of him limited to the Jewish-Christian tradition? Did those who lived before or outside this tradition have part in him, or was it restricted solely to those who received him when he came into the world? These were questions of enormous import: creation and history; revelation and incarnation; Christianity, religions, and philosophy; nature and the supernatural: all these important theological themes were involved, one way or another, in the theology of the Logos. Not all the fathers shared the same approach. Some, however, approached these questions with an open mind, laying down the basis for a theology of history. They distinguished different ages of the universe, which in turn gave rise to a concept of successive stages of the self-manifestation of the divine Logos: the Word of God was active in the cosmos from the very beginning, even if the mystery of his self-manifestation had to pass through various stages before reaching its culmination in the incarnation. These are the theologians who interest us here. Concentrated principally in the second century, they can be swiftly listed: the philosopher Justin, the most important of the Greek apologists; Irenaeus, who, notwithstanding his strong diffidence when confronted with the futility of Gnostic speculation, became, if one can put it that way, the founder of the theology of history; and, in the city of Alexandria, where systematic theology was born, Clement, the first speculative theologian. All these fathers shared a common vision. Nevertheless we will deal with each of them separately in such a way as to better show their specific contributions.

St. justin and the logos-sower

In the writings of Justin, the Logos has a cosmological function. The divine efficacy from which the world proceeds is concentrated in him. He is the *dunamis* of God, an "energetic Word" (*logikhè dunamis*), the creator and organizer of the cosmos. One could think of him as the platonic soul of the world. The difference, however, is clear: Justin speaks of the existence of the divine Word with God; all the cosmological functions and all the interventions of God in the world are attributed specifically to the Logos. It is, in fact, the Logos of the Prologue of John. The cosmological function of the Logos is, in effect, the basis of the theology of revelation of Justin. The Father works through the Son: all divine manifestations in the world have taken place through him. And this is true of the personal manifestations of God as well as of the divine act of creation. The manifestation of God through his Word is not, however, limited to the Christian economy. It took place, before the incarnation of the Word, among the Jews and the Greeks: wherever there have been people living according to the Word, they have merited the name of Christians. Justin writes:

> We have been taught that Christ is the first-begotten of God, and have previously testified that he is the Logos (*Logos*) of which every race of humans partakes (*metechein*)...Those who have lived in accordance with the Logos (*meta logou*) are Christians, even though they were called godless, such as, among the Greeks, Socrates and Heraclitus and others like them; among the Barbarians, Abraham, Ananias, Azarius, Misael, and Elijah, and many others, whose deeds and names I forbear to list, knowing that this would be lengthy. So also those who lived contrary to the Logos were ungracious and enemies to Christ, and murderers of those who lived by the Logos. But those who lived by the Logos and those who live so now, are Christians, fearless and unperturbed. (1 *Apol.* XLVI, 1–4)[13]

It would be possible to quote many texts, but space does not allow here. What follows are some of the clearest: "Our doctrine surpasses all human teaching, because we have the Word in his entirety in Christ, who has been manifested for us, body, reason and soul (*sòma, logos, psychè*). All the right principles that philosophers and lawgivers have discovered and expressed they owed to whatever of the Word they have found and contemplated in part (*kata meros*). The reason why they have contradicted themselves is that they have not known the entire Word which is Christ" (2 *Apol.* X, 1–3) (p. 41). And again: "It is not, therefore, that the teaching of Plato is alien to that of Christ, but it is not like it in all points, any more than is that of other men, Stoics, poets, or writers. Each of them, indeed, because he saw in part (*kata meros*) that which derived from the divine Word and was sown by him (*tou spermatikou theiou logou*), was able to speak well; but by contradicting themselves on essential points they show that they do not possess the higher learning and the knowledge which is irrefutable" (2 *Apol.* XIII, 2–3) (p. 41). And he explains: "These writers were able to perceive the Truth obscurely (*anudròs*) thanks to the sowing (*spora*) of the Word which had been implanted within them. But it is one thing to possess a seed (*sperma*)

---

13. All citations from Justin are taken from J. Daniélou, *Gospel Message and Hellenistic Culture* (Philadelphia: Westminster Press, 1973); here 40–41.

and a likeness proportioned to one's capacity, and quite another to possess the reality itself, both the partaking and the imitation of which are the results of the grace which comes from him" (2 *Apol.* XIII, 4–6) (p. 42).

Trying to put some order in these ideas, Justin's thinking can be summarized in the following points: (1) There exist three kinds of religious knowledge: that of the nations, the Jewish, and the Christian. (2) The Logos is the unique source of all religious knowledge in its different kinds. (3) The difference between the various kinds of religious knowledge corresponds to various forms of participation in the Logos: extending to the whole cosmos and to all human beings, the intervention of the Logos in Israel becomes more incisive; it is only completed with the advent of Christ in human flesh. (4) All who have known the Truth and lived rightly are Christians insofar as they have participated in and lived in conformity to the Logos who is all Truth.

The key to the whole system is in the differentiated participation in the Logos: all people share in him, but while others have received from him only partially (*apo merous*), we to whom the Logos revealed himself in his incarnation have been blessed with his complete manifestation. In all persons a seed of the Logos (*sperma tou logou*) may be found, for the Logos-sower (*spermatikos logos*) sows in all; yet to us only the entirety of the Logos has been made manifest. The expressions of Justin must not be emptied of their true meaning. The Logos which he attributes to all people is not the "product of human reason," but the participation in the person of the Word, from whom all truth, however partial and uncertain, is derived: that of which we all have partaken is "the *dunamis* of the ineffable Father, not just a product of human reason" (2 *Apol.* X, 8). Daniélou writes pointedly: "He [Justin] is not in the least tempted by the idea of an order of natural truth which is the proper object of reason on the one hand, and of an order of supernatural truth, the object of revelation, on the other. There are only an obscure knowledge and a clear knowledge of the one truth, which is the Word."[14] The implications of the texts quoted are clear: all possession of religious truth as well as all right conduct, in whomever they are found, come from a personal manifestation of the eternal Word of which the incarnation is the full manifestation. Christianity exists beyond its visible boundaries and prior to its historical appearing, but up to the incarnation, it is fragmentary, hidden, ambiguous, and even mixed with error. It may be asked if this is not, but for the expression, the theology of "anonymous Christianity," eighteen centuries before K. Rahner.

St. Irenaeus and the Revealing Word

Irenaeus can be said to be the founder of the theology of history. Not only did he bring out the historical significance of the Mosaic and Christian dispensations, but he also integrated the pre-Mosaic dispensation in the history of salvation, thus making room for a salvific value of prebiblical religions. Irenaeus organized

---

14. Ibid., 44.

systematically his theology of history around his idea of the revealing Logos. In a well-known passage is contained in a condensed form the whole of his theology:

> Since it is God who works all things in all, he is, by virtue of his nature and his greatness, invisible and ineffable to all his creatures, but not therefore unknown; for, through his Word, all learn that there is one sole God and Father who contains all things, who gives being to all things, as it is said in the gospel: "No one has seen God at any time; the only-begotten Son, who is in the bosom of the Father, he has made him known" (Jn 1:18). Thus from the beginning the Son of the Father is the one who makes him known, since it is he, who from the beginning is with the Father, who has shown to the human race both the visions of the prophets and the various kinds of charismatic gifts and his own ministries and the glorification of his Father, all in their right order and arrangement and at the same time most useful for them... Moreover, the Word was made the dispenser of his Father's grace for the benefit of people, for whose sake he carried out such great divine plans (*dispensationes=oikonomias*), showing God to people, presenting them to God and preserving the invisibility of his Father so that the human being should never come to despise God, and that he should always have a goal toward which to advance; on the other hand, showing God to people in many ways, lest they, wholly lacking God, should cease to exist. For the glory of God is the living human being; but the life of the human is the vision of God. For if that manifestation of God which comes through the creation gives life to all who live on the earth, how much more does the manifestation of the Father which is performed by the Word give life to those who see God. (*Adv. Haer.* IV, 20, 6–7)[15]

The whole theology of Irenaeus is found in this dense text: the divine philanthropy which creates human beings, that they may live; the economy of the divine manifestations through the Logos who, present to creation from the beginning, reveals the Father progressively. The fundamental principle of this theology is *Visibile Patris Filius* ("The Son is the visible of the Father"), not precisely the sacramental sign of the Father — for Irenaeus is not thinking only of the incarnate Logos — but more generally the manifestation, visible or invisible, the revelation, the knowability of the Father. In himself, the Father is and remains through all economies the unknown; but he manifests himself in the Son: *Invisibile etenim Filii Pater, visibile autem Patris Filius:* "The Father is the invisible [aspect] of the Son and the Son is the visible [aspect] of the Father" (*Adv. Haer.* IV, 6, 6). Irenaeus, who never tires of commenting on John 1:18 and on the "Johannine" logion of Matthew (11:27) (see, e.g., *Adv. Haer.* IV, 6–7), explains that

---

15. Quotations from *Adv. Haer.* are taken, wherever possible, from Daniélou, *Gospel Message and Hellenistic Culture*. Otherwise they are taken from *The Ante-Nicene Fathers* (ANF), vol. 1, ed. A. Cleveland Cox (Grand Rapids, Mich.: Eerdmans, 1977) or translated from *Contre les hérésies* III, Sources chrétiennes 211, ed. A. Rousseau and L. Doutreleau (Paris: Cerf, 1974). Here Daniélou, 359.

all divine manifestations take place through the Logos: "Through the Son who is in the Father and who has in him the Father, the God 'who is' (cf. Ex 3:8) manifested himself, the Father giving witness to the Son and the Son announcing the Father" (*Adv. Haer.* III, 6, 2; SC 211:71). The first of these divine manifestations is creation itself. It is already a revelation of the Logos since creation itself is a divine manifestation: *per conditionem ostensio Dei* (*Adv. Haer.* IV, 20, 7); and all divine manifestations are Logos-manifestations:

> The Son, controlling all things for the Father, guides all things to their goal from beginning to end, and without him none can know God. For the knowledge of the Father is the Son (*agnitio enim Patris Filius*); and the knowledge of the Son in the Father is also revealed by the Son. That is why the Lord said: "No one knows the Father save the Son, and those to whom the Son has revealed him (*revelaverit*)." The word "has revealed" was not spoken referring only to the future, as though the Word began to make the Father manifest only when he was born of Mary; but he is present at every point in time. For from the beginning the Son, present to the creatures whom he has formed, reveals the Father to all those to whom the Father wills, and at the time and in the way he wills; and therefore in all things and through all things there is one God and Father, and one Word, his Son, and one Spirit, and one salvation to all who believe in him. (*Adv. Haer.* IV, 6–7; Daniélou 361–62)

Irenaeus finds in the order of creation itself a historical and personal manifestation of the Logos. In his view, the human person's knowledge of God is already a response to a personal initiative of God as the infinite person who graciously addresses himself to us. Such an encounter is, however, an encounter with the Logos: through creation, it is in fact the Logos who speaks to people. In other words, the order of creation itself is part of God's historical and personal manifestation. Irenaeus writes: "For by means of the creation itself, the Word reveals God the Creator; and by means of the world [does he declare] the Lord, the Maker of the world; and through that which is moulded, the artisan who moulded it; and by the Son the Father who begat the Son" (*Adv. Haer.* IV, 6, 5–6; ANF 1:468–69).

The revelation of the Father by the Son constitutes a permanent dispensation. The order of creation was only the first stage of God's manifestation through the Logos. The Jewish and Christian dispensations follow after. Thus, after considering creation, Irenaeus goes on to write: "But by the law and the prophets did the Word preach both himself and the Father alike [to all]; and all the people heard him alike, but all did not alike believe. And through the Word himself who had been made visible and palpable, was the Father shown forth, although all did not equally believe in him; but all saw the Father in the Son: for the Father is the invisible of the Son, but the Son the visible of the Father" (*Adv. Haer.* IV, 6, 6; ANF 1:469). Irenaeus is unequivocal in attributing to the Logos God's self-disclosure in the old dispensation. All the Old Testament theophanies are applied to the Word: they are theophanies insofar as they are Logophanies. In Irenaeus's own expressions, the Word was "present in," "descended in," or "passed through" the Old Testament economies; in the theophanies he was present "rehearsing" his future coming in the flesh.

One can in fact ask if the theology of the universal revelation of the Word, so brilliantly exposed by Irenaeus, shows sufficient awareness of the unique and irreplaceable significance of his coming in the flesh. If the history of Israel is already full of the personal interventions of the Word, what becomes of the *ephapax* character of the Christ event? If the Word in some way anticipates his incarnation in the typological events of the Old Testament, then is not the newness of his coming in the flesh seriously impaired? The answer is no: for there remains the whole difference between Christ heralded and Christ given. Irenaeus writes: "Know this, that he brought something completely new, by bringing himself (*omnem novitatem attulit seipsum afferens*) who had been heralded" (*Adv. Haer.* IV, 34, 1; Daniélou 172). Irenaeus has no doubt that the universal revelatory function of the Logos makes him present to humankind from the beginning; again, the Old Testament Logophanies are for him authentic anticipations of the Christophany. Yet the human manifestation of Christ which took place once for all in space and time is in his mind ample guarantee of the newness of historical Christianity. For if in the old dispensation the Logos in a certain sense was already made visible — visible to the mind, in as far as he is the revelation, the manifestation, of the Father (*visibile Patris*) — to the eyes of the flesh he became visible only by his advent in the flesh. Irenaeus distinguishes two ways of visibility of the Word. They correspond to each other in the sense that he, to whose nature it belongs to manifest the Father to the minds of people, once incarnate demonstrates him to their eyes. The two manifestations remain however essentially distinct. If in fact the Logos from the beginning reveals the Father, he becomes — to use a recent idiom — the "sacrament of the encounter with God" by his incarnation. The historical Christ is a sacramental Logophany. The assumption of human flesh constitutes the decisive mission of the Son, the climax of the Father's manifestation through the visibility of the Logos.

CLEMENT OF ALEXANDRIA AND THE LOGOS OF THE COVENANT
The first feature which distinguishes Clement's theology of the Word is the emphasis it lays on the term "Logos." The basic principle of his Christology remains that of Irenaeus: all personal manifestation of the Father takes place through the Logos: "We understand the Unknown by divine grace, and by the Word alone that proceeds from him" (*Strom.* V, 12).[16] More exactly, Clement distinguishes in the Father that which is entirely unknowable and that which can be known once it has been manifested in the Son (cf. *Excerpta* 23, 5). A significant difference must, however, be mentioned: while Justin and Irenaeus

---

16. Quotations are from *The Ante-Nicene Fathers*, vol. 2, ed. A. Roberts and J. Donalson (Grand Rapids, Mich.: Eerdmans, 1979) (ANF 2); here ANF 2:464.

seemed to attribute all knowledge of God to the action of the divine Word, Clement distinguishes two distinct levels. A common, elementary knowledge of God can be acquired through the use of reason (*logos,* which means here human reason); it is accessible to all human beings and is called natural: "There was always a natural (*phusikès*) manifestation of the one Almighty God, among all right-thinking people" (*Strom.* V, 13; ANF 2:465). At another level, it is the personal action of the Logos which introduces people into God's secrets, otherwise inaccessible. How far does the influence of the Logos extend? Beyond the boundaries of the Judeo-Christian tradition, for the "pagan" world has had its own prophets. Greek philosophy — to be understood in Clement's rich meaning of the term, according to which human wisdom and religiosity are included — witnesses to a special divine assistance. Philosophy comes from God; it constitutes for the Greek world a divine economy, parallel, if not in all things equal, to the Jewish economy of the Law. Both were designed by God to lead people to Christ. In effect, for the Greeks philosophy was an instrument of salvation given to them by God. Clement has no hesitation in calling philosophy a covenant (*diathèkè*) made by God with people, a stepping-stone (*hupobathra*) to the "philosophy" which is according to Christ. He writes: "Truly we are not mistaken if, generally speaking, we say that all things necessary and profitable for life come to us from God and, better, that philosophy was given to the Greeks as a covenant (*diathèkè*) peculiar to them, which served as a stepping-stone (*hupobathra*) to the philosophy which is according to Christ" (*Strom.* VI, 8; ANF 2:495).

But, as is the case for the Jewish law itself, the function of philosophy is a transitional one. Having prepared people for Christ's coming, it must finally make room for him: as a lamp loses its raison d'être once the sun is up, so too does philosophy in Christ's advent (*Strom.* V, 5). Philosophy is a partial knowledge; Christ alone is the whole truth. What was for Clement true for Greek philosophy is a fortiori true for Eastern wisdom. The authentic guides of humankind are the ancient philosophers who, truly inspired by God and acted upon by the Logos, have taught the nations divine truths. Clement mentions among others: "... the Indian gymnosophists. Of these there are two classes, some of them called Sarmanae, and others Brahmins ... Some, too, of the Indians obey the precepts of Buddha, whom, on account of his extraordinary sanctity, they have raised to divine honour" (*Strom.* I, 15; ANF 2:316). This amounts to affirming, together with the presence of partial Christian truth in the Hindu and Buddhist traditions, a positive significance of these traditions in the history of salvation.

Before the *Stromata,* Clement had written the *Protreptikos* (Exhortation to the heathens), in which he developed a Logocentric theology, asserting that the Logos at work in Judaism, and in the best of what the Greek philosophers and poets had to offer, is that very Logos who became incarnate in Jesus Christ. Clement stresses the identity between the not-yet-incarnate Logos and the Logos-made-flesh, while at the same time asserting the entire newness which the incarnation of the Word brings about, as compared to his earlier manifestations to humankind.

The perception of the truth which the philosophers have had through the Logos remained partial; it is in Jesus Christ, the Logos incarnate, that the truth about God is fully revealed to human beings, as well as true life in God, who through his Word-made-flesh shares with us his own incorruptibility and immortality.[17] For Clement, "The Word of the Father, the benign light, the Lord who brings light, faith to all, and salvation" (*Protrept.* VIII, 80) has been active everywhere, bringing light and truth. The Logos is "the light of humans" (*Protrept.* IX, 84); he "is not hidden to any one; he is the common light, that shines for all humans" (*Protrept.* IX, 88). But whatever manifestation of the Word there may have been in the truth perceived by philosophers, the fact remains that the fullness of the manifestation of God in his Word is found in Jesus Christ, the Word made man. Indeed, Clement writes: "The Word of God became human, that [we might] learn from a man how human beings may become God" (*Protrept.* I, 8).

INTERPRETATION OF THE THEOLOGY OF THE LOGOS IN THE EARLY FATHERS
The theology of the Logos of the early fathers of the church is not without raising questions of interpretation. This is not the place to raise them all. One question, however, particularly attracts our attention here in the context of this study. Does the Logos, everywhere present among humans in the works of the three authors, refer back to the immanent *logos* (or "reason") of the Stoa and of Philo the Jew? Or is it to be identified with the Word of God of the Prologue of the Gospel according to St. John, present and active everywhere in human history and finally incarnate in Jesus Christ? The answer to this question has important consequences for the theology put forward by the three authors. If the first interpretation turns out to be correct, all that can be read in the texts is the attainment of some "natural" truth through the philosophical use of reason. If the second interpretation is to be retained, what is being affirmed is the universal presence and action of God's immanent Logos in human history; there would then be a reference, through the Prologue of the Fourth Gospel, to the "literary personification" of the Word of God (*dabar*) which, in the Old Testament, stood for God in as much as he manifests himself through deeds and words in history, and in the New Testament refers to the person of the Word, eternally "with God," and present and operative through the entire history of salvation.

This question cannot be answered by an either-or statement. The Prologue of the Gospel according to John already integrates features of the *logos* of Stoic philosophy into its concept of the Word of God acting in history; the early fathers of the church continued to do likewise. Thus they gave to the Logos a complex meaning, seeing the Word of God as the principle of intelligibility of creation, world, and history. But this function was attributed by them to the personal Logos present in the divine mystery and operating through the whole of history, of which the Prologue of John spoke. The early fathers thus courageously combined the Stoic concept of reason immanent in the universe with the biblical

---

17. Quotations are from ANF 2.

tradition of the Word which had sown its seeds among men. In this way they invite us to affirm the presence of the Word of God among humankind outside the Jewish-Christian tradition.

But it is also necessary to ask what theological relevance these authors attributed to the influence of the divine Logos, in Greek wisdom and elsewhere, outside the Christian dispensation. We must moreover ask whether such an efficacy was understood by them to apply exclusively to pre-Christian times or could, on the contrary, be viewed as extending to the period following the Christ event. In this last case, what value did the active presence of the Word of God among human persons have in terms of bestowal upon them of divine grace and justification by faith? It is certain that the fathers considered the pre-Christian active presence of the Logos as a divine "pedagogy" toward things to come, or — to use the expression which Eusebius of Caesarea would illustrate later — as a "preparation for the gospel" (*praeparatio evangelica*). Clement writes explicitly that philosophy was given to the Greeks as a first gift, until the Lord would call the Greeks. For it would serve as a schoolmaster (*epaidagogei*) to bring the Hellenic mind to Christ, just as the Law did for the Hebrews (*Strom.* I, 5, 3). But was the role of Greek wisdom as an "educator" for the gospel exhausted with the historical event of Jesus Christ? Or did it continue afterwards, until the time when individuals would be personally challenged by the Christian message? It would seem that the second interpretation must be maintained. According to our authors, Greek philosophy and other similar wisdom bestowed upon humans by the Word of God did not forfeit their role in the economy of salvation, even after the Lord's historical coming: their providential role endured until such time as individual persons would be directly challenged by the Christian message.

There still remains, however, the decisive question of the theological significance of the pre- and pro-Christian divine pedagogy operative through the Logos in terms of the bestowal upon persons of divine life and grace, whether before the Christ event or after it, outside the boundaries of the Christian fold. Against the interpretations according to which there is a "qualitative" difference between pre-Christian justification and Christian grace, in the sense that the immanent presence of the Holy Spirit, which characterizes the grace of the New Testament, is not present in the former, it should be stated that, if it is true that divine grace is in every historical situation the self-giving of the triune God, it must be substantially identical in every case. The difference, in fact, between the two "regimes" of the self-communication of God in grace, before and after the Christ event, consists in the intervention in the second case of the glorified humanity of Jesus Christ, as universal channel of grace through his resurrection from the dead, and, therefore, of the communication through it of the indwelling of the Spirit.

This all makes it clear how important and relevant the early theology of the divine Logos, both in the Bible and in the tradition of the early fathers, is today for an open theology of religions, in which the universal presence and action of the Logos of God in persons belonging to other religious traditions and in those traditions themselves can be affirmed. The Logos of God has sown his seeds through the entire history of humanity and continues today to sow them outside the Christian tradition. An illuminating and salvific action of the Logos exists, therefore, even after the incarnation of the Word and the resurrection of Jesus Christ, which makes it possible to discover a positive value of the religions of the world in the order of salvation according to the divine plan for humanity. The theology of the Word sowing his seeds is by itself capable of leading toward a theology of the history of salvation and of the religions of the world, in their relationship to the Christ event in which the self-manifestation of God to humanity culminates.

The fact that over the centuries theology lost the profound significance of the theology of the Word-sower, reducing the meaning of his universal presence to the possibility of some sort of inherent natural knowledge of God within humankind, is a matter for regret. This being the case, a rich source for positively valuing religious traditions outside the Jewish-Christian tradition was lost. The "seeds of the Word" were reduced to gifts of human nature "capable of God," without their indicating any longer the universal presence and action of the Word of God as the personal self-communication of God to humankind. The Second Vatican Council appropriated the patristic expression the "seeds of the Word" and went on to say, "which lie hidden among them" (*Ad Gentes* §11, see also §15), but did not indicate the meaning that should be given to the traditional expression. Does it refer to something belonging to nature or to personal gifts of God through his Word? The continuing ambiguity with regard to the meaning intended results in it being impossible — as noted earlier — to attribute safely to the council the idea of a positive significance for religious traditions in the order of salvation of their members. It belonged to postconciliar theological reflection to develop such a positive evaluation of religions, partly through a rediscovery of the theology of the universally present and active Word of God. There remains to show in the second part of this chapter how this universal action of the Word of God combines, in the unique divine plan for humanity, with the historic event of Jesus Christ in which the history of the personal commitment of God toward men reached its culmination.

THE UNIVERSALITY OF THE WORD AND THE CENTRALITY OF THE EVENT OF JESUS CHRIST

It must therefore be shown that there is no contradiction between the universal and operative presence of the Word of God and the unique salvific meaning of the historical event of Jesus Christ. The whole matter depends on the use of three words: separation, distinction, identification. The universal action of the Word and the historical event of Jesus Christ are neither identified nor separated; they remain, however, distinct. Both elements must be mutually harmonized in the divine plan for humanity. While it is true that the work of the Word extends beyond the limits of space and time and therefore cannot be reduced, by way of a wrong identification, to the historical happening of Jesus Christ, it is at the same time true that the personal insertion of the Word of God into the history of humanity through the mystery of the incarnation has, in the development of the history of salvation, a totally unheard-of meaning, as "constitutive" of salvation.

We must affirm, following the Prologue of John, a universal presence of the Logos before his incarnation in Jesus Christ (Jn 1:1–4). He is the "true light that enlightens every human being" (Jn 1:9) coming into the world. The anticipated presence and action of the Logos before the incarnation — which continues after the incarnation — do not, however, prevent the New Testament from seeing in the Word incarnate, of whom the Prologue of the Johannine Gospel also speaks (1:14), the universal "Savior" of humankind, the one "mediator" between God and humankind (1 Tim 2:5). Christianity has traditionally understood this to mean that, whichever might be the divine manifestations through the Word as such, the event of Jesus Christ remains the climax of God's plan for humankind and of the history through which this plan unfolds. The Word as such and the Word incarnate belong together to the one history of salvation. Logocentrism and Christocentrism are not mutually opposed; they call for each other in a unique dispensation. The following will make this clearer.

THE CENTRALITY OF THE EVENT OF JESUS CHRIST

The "constitutive" uniqueness and salvific universality of the event of Jesus Christ must be based on his personal identity as the Son of God. In recent years Christology has rightly shown — as we mentioned earlier — that the starting point for the Christological discourse must be the human reality, even the human history, of Jesus of Nazareth. It means that — following the development already operative in the Christological reflection of the New Testament — Christology must start "from below," not "from above," that is, not from the person of the Word preexisting in the mystery of God. But, at the same time, it is also true that, in order to be whole and entire, Christology "from below" must lead through the intrinsic dynamism of the faith toward a christology "from above," that is, a Christology that does not rest at the human being of Jesus, in whom "God is present and working" (see Acts 2:22), but which with the Johannine Christological reflection ascends toward the mystery of the preexisting person of the Word of God, made man in Jesus Christ (Jn 1:1–14).

It must be said clearly that no other consideration except the personal identity of Jesus Christ as the only-begotten Son of God provides an adequate theological foundation for his salvific uniqueness and universality. The "gospel" values which Jesus upholds, the Kingdom of God which he announces, the human project or "program" which he puts forward, his option for the poor and the marginalized, his denouncing of injustice, his message of universal love: all these, no doubt, contribute to the difference and specificity of Jesus' personality; none of them, however, would be decisive for making him or recognizing him as "constitutively unique" for human salvation. The theological foundation of the unique meaning of the Jesus Christ event rests, therefore, on the fact that through the mystery of the incarnation the Word of God became, once for always (*ephapax*), personally inserted in human reality and in the story of the world. Through him God has established an unbreakable bond of union with the whole of humanity. As the constitution of the Second Vatican Council, *Gaudium et Spes* puts it, "By his incarnation, he, the Son of God, has in a certain way united himself with each man" (§22). The incarnation represents the most profound and immanent way in which God personally committed himself to humanity in history. It follows from this that the Jesus Christ event in its entirety, from the incarnation to the resurrection and glorification, seals the decisive pact which God institutes with humanity. It is, and remains, throughout history the sacrament and seal of that pact. In this quality the Jesus Christ event obtains, in the history of salvation, a unique and irreplaceable place. It is a truly "constitutive" element in the mystery of salvation for the whole of humanity.

The personal identity between the Word of God and Jesus Christ must therefore be clearly affirmed before all else. Jesus Christ is none other than the Word of God made man in human history. Therefore no separation between them can ever be affirmed which would deny the personal identity. This is the essential meaning of the mystery of the "hypostatic union," that is, of the union of the humanity of Jesus in the divine person of the Word. This union is realized independently of the kenotic or glorified state of Jesus' human being. It is true that the transition from the kenotic state to the glorified state implies a real and profound transformation of the whole human being of Jesus. But, in both situations we are dealing equally with the humanity of the Word of God incarnate. This humanity began to exist in time with the mystery of the incarnation, being submitted to the conditions of time and space; but it perdures beyond death, in the glorified and risen state, having become henceforth "metahistorical" or "transhistorical," that is, having reached beyond the conditioning of time and space. Due to this real transformation the salvific meaning of the Christ event and of the paschal mystery of the death and resurrection of Jesus remains present through all times and in all places.

It is to this Word of God incarnate in Jesus Christ that Pauline and deutero-Pauline theology attributes "primacy" in the divine plan for humanity, both within the order of creation and in that of re-creation. According to the Christological hymns of the letters to the Ephesians (1:3–14) and to the Colossians (1:15–20), Jesus Christ stands at the center of the eternal divine plan for humanity and the world. God has never thought of either the world or humanity without willing them in his Word which would become incarnate, to whom belongs the "primacy" in both the created and the re-created order. In him we have been "chosen before the creation of the world" (Eph. 1:4), predestined to be his adopted sons (Eph 1:5), according to his "plan to 'gather up' (*anakephalaiòsasthai*) all things in Christ" (Eph 1:10). "For in him it pleased God to make all the fullness (*plèròma*) to dwell, and through him to reconcile to himself all things, whether on earth or in heaven, making peace by the blood of his cross" (Col 1:19–20). Jesus Christ stands eternally at the center of God's intention in his act of creating the world.

Notwithstanding all this, however, it still remains true that the historic event of Jesus Christ, of itself and of necessity, is particular and circumscribed by the limits of space and time. The human life of Jesus belongs to a particular time and to a precise location; the mystery of the resurrection is itself an event registered punctually in history, even though it introduces the human being of Jesus into a "metahistoric" condition. And, while it is true that, in the glorified state of the Risen one, the historic salvific event becomes present and actual for all times and in all places, it remains also true that this event does not by itself exhaust — nor can it exhaust — the revelatory and salvific power of the Word of God. While Jesus' human being can never be separated from the person of the Word of God, neither can the two ever be identified, as the two natures remain distinct in the personal union.

The way in which the early fathers expressed themselves when they affirmed that in the incarnation the "entirety" of the Word had been manifested to us must therefore be understood correctly. For example, Justin Martyr, as we have noted earlier, wrote that, while otherwise, that is, outside the incarnation, the Word was only "partially" (*kata meros*) communicated, "the complete Word appeared to us" in Jesus Christ (2 *Apol.* VIII, 1). The Word was undoubtedly manifested in Jesus Christ in the most complete way possible in history, indeed in the most profoundly human way that it is possible to conceive, and therefore in the way best adapted to our human nature. But, paradoxically, this very human way of self-manifestation implied by itself its own limitations and incompleteness. The Word of God remains beyond whatever can be manifested and revealed in the human being of Jesus, assumed personally by him. In his humanity, therefore, Jesus Christ is the "universal sacrament" — the efficacious sign — of the mystery of the salvation which God offers to the entire humankind through his Word; but the God who saves through him remains beyond the human being of Jesus, notwithstanding his personal identity with the Word, even when he has reached his glorified state. Jesus Christ risen and glorified does not substitute for the Father; neither does his glorified humanity exhaust the Word himself, which is never totally contained in any historical manifestation.

THE UNIVERSALITY OF THE WORD

We see therefore how the universal salvific value of the historical event of Jesus Christ leaves space for an illuminating and salvific action of the Word as such, both before the incarnation and after the resurrection of Jesus Christ. The basis of this action of the Word in biblical revelation and tradition was set out in the first part of this chapter. It remains now to show how the universal action of the Word is organically combined with the salvific value of the Christ event in the unique divine plan for humanity.

We noted earlier a diversity and multiplicity of divine manifestations by means of the Word through history. Not all these divine manifestations and revelations have the same weight, or the same value and meaning. They are, however, all Logophanies in the sense that they are divine manifestations through the Word. Irenaeus, as noted earlier, could see the entire economy of salvation as made up of various divine manifestations through the Word; it remained true, however, that the incarnation of the Word in Jesus Christ involved "something totally new" (*omnem novitatem attulit seipsum afferens*) (*Adv. Haer.* IV, 34, 1), owing to his personal coming into the flesh.

This means that the salvific action of God, which always works within the framework of a single design, is unique and, at the same time, multifaceted. It never abstracts from the Christ event, in which its highest historical density is found. Yet the action of the Word of God is not exclusively linked to his becoming man historically in Jesus Christ. The mediation of the salvific grace of God to humanity takes on different dimensions which have to be combined and integrated.

The Christ event, while it is inclusively present and actual in different times and places, does not exhaust the power of the Word of God which became flesh in Jesus Christ. The working of the Word goes beyond the limits which mark the working presence of the humanity of Jesus even in his glorified state, just as the person of the Word goes beyond the human being of Jesus Christ, notwithstanding the "hypostatic union," that is, the union in the person. In this way one is able to catch a glimpse of how seeds of "truth and grace" (*Ad Gentes* §9) can be present in other religious traditions of the world, which serve, for their followers, as "ways" or "paths" of salvation. It is the Word of God who sowed his seeds in the religious traditions. And these are not to be understood as simply human "stepping stones" (*pierres d'attente*), gifts of nature, awaiting a divine self-manifestation to take place in some indeterminate future, but as true divine self-manifestation and self-giving in their own right, however initial and germinal.

The incomparable enlightening force of the divine Word — which was "the true light that enlightens every human being," by coming into the world (Jn 1:9) — was universally operative before its manifestation in the flesh, and remains operative through the whole history of salvation, even after the event of Jesus Christ and beyond the boundaries of Christianity. As the first apologists had already seen, people could, in fact, be "illuminated" by the Word, the source of divine Light. And not only individual persons — Socrates, Buddha, and others — were able to receive some divine truth from the Word; human enterprises — "philosophy," Greek wisdom, and the wisdom of the East — were also channels through which the divine light reached persons.

It follows from this that religious traditions, in which experiences with the divine truth of followers and prophets of peoples all over the world are recorded, contain seeds of "truth and grace" (*Ad Gentes* §9) sown in them by the Word, by means of which his illuminating virtue and strength remain operative. The divine Word continues even now to sow his seeds among peoples and religious traditions: revealed truth and salvific grace are present in them through his action.

It is important, without doubt, to safeguard the unity of the divine design for the salvation of humanity, which embraces all human history. The becoming-man of the Word of God in Jesus Christ, his human life, death, and resurrection, are the climax of the historical process of divine self-communication, the cornerstone which supports the whole process, its interpretative key. The reason for this is that the "humanization" of the Word marks the unsurpassed — and unsurpassable — depth of the self-communication of God to human beings, the supreme mode of immanence of his being-with-them.

We must not, however, allow the centrality of the incarnation in the salvific economy of God to overshadow the permanent presence and action of the divine Word. The illumination and the salvific power of the Word are not circumscribed by the particularity of the historical event. They transcend every barrier in space and time. The historical event of Jesus Christ, constitutive of salvation, and the universal working of the divine Word, do not, however, constitute two different, parallel economies of salvation; they represent complementary and inseparable aspects of a single but diversified divine plan for humanity.

WE HAVE TRIED TO SHOW the importance and the relevance of a theology of the Word of God for an open theology of religions. From what has been said, it seems clear that there exists a continuing action of the Word as such, which is combined, in the divine plan for humanity, with the universal salvific value of the historical event of Jesus Christ. The historical event of Jesus Christ retains its universal salvific value, working through the risen humanity of Jesus in all times and in all places; but it is part of a wider context of the divine manifestations in the Word as such through the entire history of humanity. A twofold title accounts, therefore, for the possibility of divine salvation for members of other religious traditions: the inclusiveness of the event of Jesus Christ, on the one hand, and the universality of the active presence of the Word as such, on the other. Both aspects are combined in the single divine plan of salvation.

The theology of the Word of God also helps to see the positive role which the other religious traditions can exercise in the mystery of divine salvation for their members. With it the theology of religions makes a qualitative leap forward toward a new problematic. As has been explained earlier, theology has passed in recent decades from the problematic of the possibility of Christian salvation for members of other religions to that of the possibility of a positive role exercised by these religions in the mystery of the salvation of their members. Now, the problematic is making a further step forward which consists in asking whether or not the other religious traditions have by themselves a positive significance in the divine plan for humanity. The question is whether the religious pluralism in which we live is simply a pluralism *de facto,* or also *de principio.* If, as is being suggested here, all religions have their original source in a self-manifestation of God to human beings through his Word, the principle of plurality finds its primary foundation in the superabundant richness and variety of the self-manifestations of God to humanity.

In this way we reach a different conclusion from that which in the past has often been taken for granted and affirmed traditionally by theology. The traditional negative evaluation of the other religions rested, among other things, on forgetting the theology of the Word of God, witnessed to in the Bible, already in the Old Testament, and prolonged in the theology of the early fathers of the church. The rediscovery of this theology seems to open the door for a positive revalorization of religions. It is, however, well understood that the solution offered here is a tentative proposal for theological reflection. Its merit consists in the combination of two profound convictions: the universality of Jesus Christ the Savior, on the one hand, and, on the other, the salvific value and positive meaning of the other religious traditions in the divine plan for humanity. A proposal remains, nonetheless, provisional and open to improvement. Theology must always maintain a strong sense of the mystery and transcendence not only of God, but also of his plan of salvation. In this case, it must not claim to describe or define the "how" and "in which way" (*quomodo sit*) of the essential relationship between the universal action of the Word — and the Spirit — and the historical event of Jesus Christ. Theological apophatism suggests silence where, though being able to underline the fact (*an sit*), we cannot and need not explain the "how." It behooves theology to be reserved and humble.

Chapter Seven

THE "ONE MEDIATOR" AND "PARTICIPATED MEDIATIONS"

T HE "SYMPHONY" of the preceding chapter has remained incomplete. What remains to be shown more clearly insofar as possible is the relationship between the universal saving value of the Christ event which reaches its apex in the paschal mystery of the death and resurrection of Jesus, on the one hand, and the operative presence of the Word of God as such and the equally universal activity of the Spirit of God, on the other. Without wishing to enter into the various theories about the mystery of "redemption" in Jesus Christ, already adumbrated in the New Testament, the universal saving value of the event is maintained here uncompromisingly, on the theological grounds of the personal identity of Jesus Christ as the "only begotten" Son of God made man and of the real transformation of his human being from the historic condition of kenosis to the "metahistoric" condition through his resurrection and glorification. However, that mystery of salvation in Jesus Christ must be situated and placed in the ambit of the commitment of the triune God, Father, Son, and Holy Spirit, to humankind through the entire history of salvation. To that end the Trinitarian Christology proposed earlier will be employed as the model and key for the interpretation of the entire mystery. We then inquire what the relationship is between the activity of the Father in the mystery of salvation and that of the Son in his humanity; and likewise where and how the Holy Spirit enters into the mystery of salvation. This is also the problem of the reciprocal "relationship" between the historic Christ event and the universal activity of the Word as such and of the Holy Spirit, in the single divine plan of salvation and its unfolding throughout the entire history of humankind.

In reviewing the current debate on the theology of the religions, we emphasized that the Christological question is of utmost importance for a Christian theology of the religions. The saving role to be attributed (or not) to other "ways" and other "saving figures" within God's overall plan for humankind is intrinsically and inextricably connected—from a Christian standpoint—to how the person and event of Jesus Christ are understood and interpreted. What is at stake in the debate between the Christocentric and theocentric paradigm, as we said earlier, is the choice between a "high," ontological Christology that unambiguously recognizes the personal identity of Jesus Christ as Son of God, and a "low" Christology, which, deliberately remaining on the functional level, opens for discussion and ultimately denies the validity of such ontological claims for Jesus Christ. The choice is between a Christology of the unique sonship and a Christology of "degree." The reappraisal of the person of Jesus Christ advocated by the pluralists is based on various considerations, which can be grouped under three headings: philosophical, historical-critical-exegetical, and theological. Here it suffices to take note of the theological considerations offered by the pluralists in arguing their thesis. The exegetical considerations will be noted inside the chapter.

Theologically, the pluralists set up a dichotomy between the particularity of the Jesus event, located in space and time and thereby irremediably limited, and the Christian claim of a universal significance for that event. The argument is that no historical event could claim the "uniqueness" and "universality" that Christianity attributes to the Jesus Christ event. Nor does such a claim find support in the history of religions, which rather attests to a multiplicity of "ways" to salvation, having similar credentials, all endowed with equal value in their variety; all of them moreover put forward mutually conflicting claims of universality, if not of "absolutism."

Our aim is to show that a well-pondered assertion of the uniqueness and universality of Jesus Christ which unambiguously maintains his personal identity as the "only begotten" Son of God leaves space for an "open" theology of the religions and of religious pluralism. A Trinitarian Christological perspective, in particular, allows us to recognize the ongoing presence and activity of the Word of God and of the Spirit of God. Such a perspective makes it possible to affirm a multiplicity of "ways" and "routes" toward human liberation/salvation, in keeping with God's plan for humankind in Jesus Christ; it likewise opens the way for recognizing other "saving figures" in human history.

Before proceeding further, the meaning of some terms has to be clarified. First of all, here we are speaking of the "uniqueness" of Jesus Christ, not of Christianity. The question of the "absoluteness of Christianity" has often been raised in the past. Hegel affirmed such an absoluteness in the framework of his idealistic philosophy; Ernst Troeltsch relativized it from the standpoint of the history of the religions.[1] Karl Barth admitted it insofar as Christianity is the incarnation of saving faith in Jesus Christ, as distinct from the Christian religion;[2] Paul Tillich objected to any self-absolutization of the religions.[3] Karl Rahner used the expression "absoluteness of Christianity" in the sense of "uniqueness,"[4] and he repeatedly spoke of Jesus Christ as "absolute Savior."[5] In these pages, however,

---

1. Ernst Troeltsch, *The Absoluteness of Christianity and the History of Religions* (Richmond: John Knox Press, 1971).

2. Cf. Reinhold Bernhardt, *Christianity without Absolutes* (London: SCM Press, 1994), 83–85.

3. Ibid., 113–14.

4. Karl Rahner, "Christianity's Absolute Claim," in *Theological Investigations* (London: Darton, Longman & Todd, 1961–88), 21:171–84; "Church, Churches, and Religions," in *Theological Investigations*, 10:30–49.

5. Karl Rahner, *Foundations of Christian Faith: An Introduction to the Idea of Christianity* (London: Darton, Longman & Todd, 1978), 193–96, 204, 298–99, 318–21.

we will steadfastly avoid speaking of "absoluteness" in reference to Jesus Christ, and a fortiori in reference to Christianity. We note in passing that official church teaching hardly ever adopts this term, and not without good reason. The reason is that strictly speaking, "absoluteness" is an attribute of the Ultimate Reality or Infinite Being, and it should not be predicated in the proper sense of any finite reality, even of the human existence of the Son-of-God-made-man, which is indeed created and contingent. Only the "Absolute" is "absolutely"; he alone is infinite and necessary. Everything created, by contrast, is finite and contingent, including the humanity of the incarnate Word. It may be noted in passing that although he had written of an "absolute and universal meaning" of Jesus Christ in the encyclical *Redemptoris Missio* (§6), Pope John Paul II has written more recently in *Fides et Ratio* (§80) that "God alone is the Absolute." In his book *Sign of Contradiction,* he had earlier explained at length the infinite distance between the uncreated Absolute and the created finite. Specifically, he wrote:

> The status of creature and the status of an *ens contingens* are concepts dif-
> fering from one another, but each traces the direction of human thought *"ad
> Deum."* The key of this journey is being in its aspect of existence . . . The
> contingency of being means its limitation in terms of its existence. Ac-
> cordingly, contingency implicitly points to the Absolute, not only as its
> opposite pole in the dialectical sense, but as the real basis, the fundamental
> reason, for a contingent being, which explains the existence of a world that
> is composed of contingent beings and is itself contingent and relative. The
> Absolute is a necessary being in the sense that it is *"Ipsum esse subsistens."*[6]

If, then, the term "absoluteness" is used (less accurately) to refer to realities that are not intrinsically divine, it will be necessary to make distinctions that it would be preferable to avoid altogether. The fact that Jesus Christ is "universal" Savior does not make him the "absolute Savior," who is God in himself. Not everything universal is absolute: the risen humanity of Jesus has universal saving significance, but that does not therefore make it "absolute." On this point, one quote from among numerous others may be cited. Adolphe Gesché writes: "Any Christianity that would absolutize Christianity (including the Christ) and its revelation would be idolatrous. It is not only 'others' who are affected by 'idolatry'; it can also be present among us. If Christianity absolutized itself, it would be idolatrous, and such falsification would turn against it and its own logic."[7]

That having been said, there are still many ambiguities in the terminology with which theologians express what distinguishes Jesus Christ from other "saving figures" and Christianity from other traditions. It need only be recalled, with regard to "uniqueness" and "universality," that both terms can be understood in a "relative" or a "singular" sense. "Relative uniqueness" indicates the original

---

6. Karol Wojtyla, *Segno di contraddizione* (Milan: Vita e Pensiero, 1977), 22.
7. Adolphe Gesché, "Le christianisme et les autres religions," *Revue Théologique de Louvain* 19, no. 3 (1988): 339.

character of any person or tradition in its being different from the others; "singular uniqueness" is predicated of Jesus Christ as "constitutive" Savior of humankind. Likewise, "relative universality" indicates the universal attractiveness that various saving figures may exercise in representing different ways of salvation; "singular universality" implies yet again that Jesus Christ is the constitutive universal Savior. As conceived here, the uniqueness and universality of Jesus Christ are neither "relative" nor "absolute." They are "constitutive," that is, they belong to the essence of salvation insofar as Jesus Christ has saving significance for all of humankind, and insofar as the Christ event — in particular the paschal mystery of his death and resurrection — is truly "cause" of salvation for all human beings.[8] The Christ event seals a bond of union between the Divinity and humankind that can never be broken, and it constitutes the privileged channel through which God has chosen to share the divine life with human beings. Such an event is "relational" insofar as it is inserted into an overall plan of God for humankind that has many facets and whose realization in history is composed of different times and moments. As we will suggest further on, Jesus Christ, by contrast with the various "saving figures" within whom God is present and operating in a hidden manner, is the only "human face" in which God, while remaining invisible, is "fully" — if not "in a final way" — disclosed and revealed and the mystery of human salvation achieved. In the course of history, God has willed to be "in different ways" (Heb 1:1) a God-of-human-beings; in Jesus Christ he has become God-of-human-beings-in-a-fully-human-way (cf. Jn 1:14): the Em-manu-el (Mt 1:23). The term "relational" is especially intended to affirm the relationship existing in the single divine plan of salvation between the "way" that is in Jesus Christ and the various "ways" of salvation that the religious traditions offer to their adherents.

From what has been said before, it is clear that when the expression "ways of salvation" is applied to the religious traditions, it refers not simply to a search for God, universally present in human beings, albeit never satisfied through their efforts, but rather primarily to the search *of* God for them, and the gracious initiative taken by God in inviting them to share in his own life. The ways of salvation are prepared by God rather than by human beings themselves. The question to be raised accordingly is what relation there is in God's providence between the "only way" and the "many paths" — that is, how Christian faith in the universal efficacy of the Christ event does not contradict a positive value and a saving significance of the ways opened in other religious traditions.

To put it another way: the question is whether the Christian character of the economy of salvation leads to the conclusion that the members of other religious traditions are saved through Christ outside, or even despite, the religious tradition to which they belong and that they practice with sincerity. Or should it be said, on the contrary, that they are saved within and through such traditions? And if the latter alternative is true, how is the saving power of these other ways to be

---

8. Karl Rahner, "The One Christ and the Universality of Salvation," in *Theological Investigations,* 16:199–224.

explained by a Christian theology of the religions? Would such a saving power enter into competition with the saving power of Jesus Christ to the point that it must be denied a priori as the exclusivist thesis in fact does? Or on the contrary will it, as the pluralists say, simply manifest the variety of the ways in which God can be found in human cultures and traditions — a variety that nullifies any theological claim of an orderly and single plan? From a Christian standpoint, how can the saving power of the various "ways" be inserted into the divine plan of salvation?

Before responding to such questions, some terminological clarifications are required. First, with regard to the "paths" or "ways" of salvation, from a Christian standpoint it must be stressed that God — and only God — saves. That means that no human being is his or her own savior; it likewise means that only the "Absolute" is the primary and ultimate agent of human salvation. In the Hebrew Bible, the title "Savior" has to do primarily with God; in the New Testament it is applied to God, and only secondarily to Jesus Christ — without gainsaying that God remains the ultimate cause and original source of salvation. The object of faith, according to New Testament theology, remains primordially God the Father; likewise, according to that theology, is it primarily God who saves, and not primarily but conjointly, Jesus Christ: God saves through his Son (cf. Jn 3:16–17). The primary cause of salvation is still the Father: "In Christ God was reconciling the world to himself" (2 Cor 5:19); "This is right and acceptable in the sight of God [the Father] our Savior, who desires everyone to be saved and to come to the knowledge of the truth" (1 Tim 2:3–4); ". . . we have our hope set on the living God, who is the Savior of all people" (1 Tim 4:10). Pierre Grelot rightly notes: "It would be wrong to say that after the resurrection of Christ the nature and object of faith has changed: it remains faith in God as before. But a new aspect of the mystery of God is being revealed: 'Jesus Christ and Lord' (Acts 2:36) is associated with God as Son with his Father." And with regard to the necessary relationship between faith and salvation in the New Testament, he adds: "The words of Jesus, who never puts himself forward, are about faith in God [who saves], except when Jesus gives orders in God's name for exorcisms or healings. The words of the apostles are about faith in the Lord Jesus, because God saves through his name."[9] After all, it is always primarily God who saves. The fact that God is primarily the Savior, however, does not prevent Jesus Christ himself from being called Savior, but he is so secondarily, insofar as the Christ event is the efficacious expression of the divine saving will and action. That he is called "constitutive" rather than "absolute" Savior does not "relativize" the saving work of Christ; that which is "constitutive" belongs to the essence.

To say that the religions save or even that "Christianity" saves is therefore a misuse of language. It is worth noting that early Christian literature pointed to that which will be later called "Christianity" as the "way" of Jesus (Acts 9:2; 19:9; 19:23; 22:4; 24:14; 24:22). Nor should it be thought that "the other religions

---

9. Pierre Grelot, *Dieu le Père de Jésus-Christ* (Paris: Desclée, 1994), 137, 131.

save" any more than Christianity actually does. What is intended is that they can become "ways" or "means" that communicate God's saving power: "ways" of salvation for those who "journey" through them. The "how" remains to be seen.

Second, with regard to the concept of salvation: it varies a great deal from one religion to another, as is well known. Here it is neither necessary nor possible to go into long discussions on such differences.[10] Suffice it to note that all religions present themselves to their followers as routes to salvation/liberation. The two concepts are combined for more than one reason, especially because the joint notion applies more easily to various traditions, regardless of the diversity of their respective conceptions. The double concept also has the advantage of combining complementary aspects, which are too often kept separate within Christianity itself: aspects such as the spiritual and the temporal, the transcendent and the human, the personal and the social, the eschatological and the historic. The considerable differences running between the various traditions notwithstanding, one could hazard the proposal of a universal and expressly neutral concept of salvation/liberation defined as follows: salvation/liberation has to do with seeking and reaching fullness of life, wholeness, self-fulfillment, and integration.

The term "mediation" likewise calls for clarification. The New Testament uses the term *mesitès* referring to Jesus (1 Tim 2:5; Heb 8:6; 9:15; 12:24) and Moses (Acts 7:38; Gal 3:19–20). Moses was mediator between God and the chosen people in the covenant of Sinai; Jesus is the "mediator of a new covenant" (Heb 12:24). The term *mesitès* does not have the same meaning in both cases. According to the Christological faith of the Christian tradition, Jesus Christ is "mediator" between God and humankind inasmuch as he unites divinity and humanity in his person in such a way that in him the Divinity and humankind have become united in a permanent bond: "For, by his incarnation, he, the Son of God, has in a certain way united himself with each human being" (*Gaudium et Spes* §22). As for Moses, he acted as "intermediary" between God and his people in the initiative of the covenant struck by God vis-à-vis Israel. The theological content of the concept is quite different from one case to the other. The Christian tradition sees the "mediation between God and human beings" present in Jesus Christ as the "unique": "there is one God: there is also one mediator between God and humankind, Christ Jesus, himself human" (1 Tim 2:5). Yet that does not prevent speaking of "participated mediations" as attested by the encyclical *Redemptoris Missio* where, after having clearly affirmed the "unique and universal mediation" of Christ, Pope John Paul II continues: "Although participated forms of mediation of different kinds and degrees are not excluded, they acquire meaning and value *only* from Christ's own mediation, and they cannot be understood as parallel or complementary to his" (§5). According to this passage, any "participated mediation" — including that of other religious traditions — must be seen

---

10. See G. Iammarrone, *Redenzione: La liberazione dell'uomo nel cristianesimo e nelle religioni universali* (Rome: Edizioni Paoline, 1995); Hans Küng et al., *Christianity and World Religions: Paths of Dialogue with Islam, Hinduism, and Buddhism* (Maryknoll, N.Y.: Orbis Books, 1993).

as essentially connected to the unique mediation of Jesus Christ and as deriving its power from it. In what sense, then, will a theology of the religions apply the concept of "mediation" to the ways of salvation traced by other traditions?

The chapter consists of two main parts. In the first part, the "constitutive" uniqueness of Jesus Christ is reaffirmed in the face of the current challenge by the pluralist theologians, on the basis of data provided by the Christian sources and an interpretation of Christological faith in the context of religious plural- ism. The "relational" character of the uniqueness and universality of Jesus Christ as the "human face" of God is accordingly clarified within a Trinitarian and pneumatological Christological perspective. Jesus Christ is thus seen as the "con- crete universal" in whom are assumed and "gathered up" (cf. Eph 1:10) all the approaches of the triune God to human beings in history. The second part asks more directly in what sense the other "ways" and saving figures presented in them can act as "mediations" and lead to divine salvation as it is traditionally perceived in Christian faith.

UNIVERSAL SAVIOR AND UNIQUE MEDIATOR

NEW TESTAMENT CHRISTOLOGY REVISITED AND INTERPRETED

In the field of biblical and New Testament exegesis, the argument of the pluralists is that a valid use of historical criticism leads inevitably to a reappraisal of Jesus Christ for a number of reasons: the context of the New Testament claims about the person and work of Jesus, the literary genre of such claims, the unbridgeable gap and complete discontinuity between the claims of the historical Jesus, and the interpretations of his person made by the apostolic church. Jesus, it is said, was completely centered on God, and proclaimed God and God's Reign; the Christocentric proclamation of the apostolic church falsified his message. The apostolic church was primarily responsible for the "paradigm shift" that marked the shift from theocentrism to Christocentrism; the task now is to reverse the situation, by returning to theocentrism.

The theocentric paradigm of the theology of religions is plainly based on a "revisionist" Christology, which may be characterized as a "low" Christology or one of "degree." Without attempting an in-depth critical study of the various considerations on which revisionist Christology is based, we must nevertheless make a quick overview and appraisal of the historico-critical and exegetical con- siderations on which it is supported. Two basic stances among the advocates of the pluralist paradigm must be distinguished. There are some who simply state in general terms the need to "relativize" the claim to uniqueness in the New Tes- tament, insofar as the context of the relevant passages refers to the Jews, or at least can be understood as referring solely to them: Jesus is claimed to be the sole Savior for the Jews. Others do not shrink from acknowledging that the New Testament firmly asserts the uniqueness of Jesus Christ the Savior, but they ask whether such a claim can or should be maintained today, in the current context of religious pluralism.

The main texts directly concerned are Acts 4:12, 1 Timothy 2:5–6, and John 14:6. To them may be added, among others, the Christological hymns of the Pauline and deutero-Pauline letters, such as Ephesians 1:1–13 and Colossians 1:15–20. How should such texts be interpreted in our context? Various reasons are proposed for relativizing the claims of uniqueness. Recent hermeneutical research is said to show that such claims are actually the result of a historically conditioned view of the world and of linguistic modes dependent on a particular historic context. We can no longer consider such uniqueness as the exact "referent" of the gospel message — as the untouchable core of the Christian kerygma.[11]

It is also pointed out that in the context of the Jewish apocalyptic mentality, impregnated as it was with an eschatological expectancy, it was natural for the early church to interpret the experience of God in Jesus Christ as final and un-surpassable. But this "apocalyptic" mentality was and is culturally limited. The finality it implies for the Jesus Christ event, therefore, cannot be regarded as pertaining to the essence of Christianity; it belongs rather to the fortuitous cultural context in which it was first experienced and presented. If Jesus had been encountered and interpreted in some other cultural context, involving some other philosophy of history, he would have been considered neither final nor unique.[12]

St. Paul is often held to bear the responsibility for the explicit assertion of the uniqueness of Jesus Christ. It is suggested that if the apostle had entered into contact with the rich mystical traditions of the oriental religions, he would have softened his absolute, unnuanced assertions. Or again, this time with regard to St. John, it is observed that the uniqueness of Jesus Christ is articulated in terms of "incarnation," but this is a mythical modality of thought, like the concept of preexistence with which it is bound up. Mythical language ought to be taken for what it is — "poetry, not prose" (John Hick) — and thus understood not "literally" but "metaphorically" (John Hick). The incarnation must therefore be "demythologized." The result would be the demythologization of Jesus Christ as universal Savior, a concept now recognized as belonging to a mythic mode of thought and hence not having a literal meaning.[13]

Finally, it is remarked that, in the historical context in which Christianity arose, and in the face of the opposition it encountered, it was natural for the disciples to present Jesus' "way" as unique. This absolute language is historically conditioned. It is "survival language." Or, in Paul F. Knitter's interpretation, it

---

11. Cf. Paul F. Knitter, *No Other Name? A Critical Survey of Christian Attitudes toward the World Religions* (Maryknoll, N.Y.: Orbis Books, 1985), 182–86.

12. Cf. John Hick, *God and the Universe of Faiths: Essays in the Philosophy of Religion* (London: Macmillan, 1973), 108–19.

13. Cf. Hick, *God and the Universe of Faiths*, 148–79; idem, *The Metaphor of God Incarnate* (Louisville: Westminster/John Knox Press, 1993); *The Myth of God Incarnate* (London: SCM Press, 1977).

is "action language" or "performative language" — that is, language designed to invite disciples to earnest following.[14]

Apocalyptic, mythical-metaphorical, survival, performative — there has even been talk about "love language." Bernhardt sums it all up under the rubric of "confession and doxology." He writes:

> So the Bible's supposed claims to absoluteness are simply public prayers of confession addressed to the oppressors and the oppressed alike and ultimately to God himself. In theological terms, they have the character of confession and doxology. Anyone who tears them from their historical foundation, generalizes them and uses them to condemn non-Christian religions is thus falsifying their original character.[15]

In ending this review of pluralistic interpretations toward the uniqueness of Jesus Christ as universal Savior in the New Testament texts, it should be noted that to assert the "constitutive" uniqueness of Jesus Christ — as the Christian tradition seems to require — does not necessarily lead to the result of "condemning" the other religions and their "saving figures." A persistent flaw in the pluralist paradigm is that of imagining that the only real possible alternative to its own viewpoint is a dogmatic, exclusivist dismissal of the other religions. Such a black-or-white alternative is justifiable neither biblically nor theologically. Far from contradicting the multiplicity of ways, faith in Jesus Christ requires being open and committed to encountering them, as will be seen further on.

What answer can be given to the criticisms and questions raised by the "pluralists"? After misleading language has been eliminated, especially the misuse of the terms "absolute" and "absoluteness," there still remains the Christian claim about Jesus Christ as it has traditionally been understood: faith in Jesus Christ does not simply consist in trusting that he is the way of salvation "for me": it means believing that the world and humankind have been saved and find their salvation in him and through him. Nothing less than this is sufficient to do justice to the firm claims of the New Testament.

But this is where, in the current pluralistic context, and not least, for the sake of interreligious dialogue, a new interpretation of the New Testament seems necessary. An inductive way of doing theology, as was stated in the introduction to this study, shows theology to be an "interpretation in context." That means that the "first act" consists of a "praxis," from which one turns to the "datum" of Christian revelation to get light and direction — in order to then return to praxis, following the "hermeneutic circle." Whereas in a context of human oppression, the "first act" is a praxis of liberation — as shown by liberation theology — in a context of religious pluralism the praxis of interreligious dialogue comes into play. It must, however, be asked what doctrinal and moral authority are attributed to

---

14. Cf. Paul F. Knitter, *Jesus and the Other Names: Christian Mission and Global Responsibility* (Maryknoll, N.Y.: Orbis Books, 1996), 68–69.
15. Bernhardt, *Christianity without Absolutes*, 59–60.

the source of revelation, if turning to it in pursuit of guidance follows as "second act" a praxis of interreligious dialogue. Does the source of revelation still function as the *norma normans* of Christian thought and practice? Or is it on the contrary downgraded to a mere secondary norm, as though it were a kind of checkpoint?

We may begin by answering that the first act of praxis is itself inspired and informed by Christian faith as its proper starting point. In the context of religious pluralism, this means that the practice of dialogue does not bracket the faith of the practitioner, through a kind of *epochè;* on the contrary, the authenticity of dialogue requires that the partners, whether Christian or not, enter into it with the integrity of their faith.[16] There is no interreligious dialogue in a space devoid of any religious conviction.

That does not decide everything, however. Indeed, there is an urgent question of whether the shock of encounter between two living faiths may not be so great that it forces Christians into a "reinterpretation" of long held certainties, affecting the core of their faith.

In the context of liberation theology, biblical hermeneutics does not consider the sacred book to be a mere memory of a past word. The word is being "re-actualized" in present history, thus making present history part of the ongoing history of salvation. Some theologians speak, in this connection, not only of a "fuller sense" (*sensus plenior*) of scripture, but of a "surplus of meaning," insofar as God's original word is becoming actualized anew in the present.[17] The "paradigmatic" event of the Exodus is not merely a *kairos* of the past; it is being reactualized by God in the history of peoples even today; and while the Jesus Christ event has happened once for all (*ephapax*) (Rom 6:10; Heb 7:27; 9:12; 10:10), it remains contemporary to all generations and operative in their ongoing history. The presence of the life-giving Word of God in history extends, therefore, beyond the "foundational revelation" recorded in the sacred book; it makes divine revelation an ongoing reality.

As this scheme attests, the word of God does remain, for a hermeneutical theology of liberation, the *norma normans;* but it is a dynamic rather than static norm. The word is not confined to the dead letter; it abides with its creative power (see Isa 5:11), spurring salvation history to forge ahead to fulfillment. The same is true in the context of religious pluralism. Here too the word of God stands as the *norma normans,* for the "first act" of dialogic praxis as well as for the "second act" of theologizing. But an inductive theology of religions ought to see the word of God as a dynamic reality, calling for interpretation in the specific context of interfaith encounter.

This requires that the revealed message not be treated as a monolithic statement of truth. The "constitutive" uniqueness of Jesus Christ will stand as an affirmation of Christian faith, but it will not be "absolutized" by relying merely

---

16. R. Panikkar, *The Intrareligious Dialogue* (New York: Paulist Press, 1978).

17. Cf. especially, J. Severino Croatto, *Exodus: A Hermeneutics of Freedom* (Maryknoll, N.Y.: Orbis Books, 1981); idem, *Biblical Hermeneutics: Towards a Theory of Reading as the Production of Meaning* (Maryknoll, N.Y.: Orbis Books, 1984).

on a unilateral grounding in a few isolated texts: Acts 4:12; 1 Timothy 2:5; John 14:6. The word of God will be seen as a complex whole, with the tensions involved between apparently contradictory, yet complementary, elements of truth. The Word "pitched his tent among human beings" (Jn 1:14) in Jesus Christ; but Wisdom had previously taken possession of every people and nation, seeking among them a resting place (Sir 24:6–7), and "pitched her tent" in Israel (Sir 24:8–12). Likewise, Jesus Christ is "the way, the truth, and the life" (Jn 14:6); but the Word who was before him was "the true light that enlightens every human being" by coming into the world (Jn 1:9). Again, "in these last days" God "has spoken to us by a Son"; but he had previously spoken "in many and various ways" (Heb 1:1). The Spirit "had not been given" before Jesus was glorified (Jn 7:39); but he had been present in "all things" that exist, well before (Wis 11:24–12:1). Jesus Christ is "the faithful witness" (Rev 1:5; 3:14); but God did not "leave himself without a witness" at any time (Acts 14:17). Interfaith encounter must help Christians to discover new dimensions to the witness which God has given to himself in other faith-communities.

THE HUMAN FACE OF GOD

What has been stated does not dispense us from showing, in response to the "revisionist" or "degree" Christologies on which the pluralistic paradigm of the theology of religions rests, that the Christian claim to a "constitutive" uniqueness of Jesus Christ rests on solid ground and has a valid foundation. Admittedly, a faith-conviction, by its very nature, lies beyond the purview of an empirical or scientific proof. Were it otherwise, it would cease to be a witness of faith and become merely the result of academic and historical research. What, however, can and needs to be done is to show the merits and the credibility of the Christian faith-claim for Jesus Christ.

The main historical-critical-exegetical argument put forward by the pluralistic Christologies can be reduced to the trite contention that there is an unbridgeable gap between the historical Jesus and the Christ of the church apostolic and thereafter. The allegation takes on different forms: Jesus was entirely centered on God, whereas the church after him became Christ-centered; he announced the coming of God's Reign, whereas the church proclaimed him; he affirmed God's universal fatherhood, whereas the church asserted his unique sonship. In brief, whereas Jesus was "a man attested . . . [to the Jews] by God with mighty works and wonders and signs which God did through him in [their] midst" (Acts 2:22) — as the early kerygma simply acknowledged — the church soon raised him, through a process of "deification," to the rank of a divine person. Or else, under the widespread impact of Hellenistic thought-patterns, the church transposed into "ontological language" what was meant as purely "functional." What should have been taken as "mythical" or "metaphorical" language was interpreted "literally": "poetry" was construed as "prose" (John Hick).

In this context, the Christological task must consist in showing that the Christian faith in Jesus-the-Christ is firmly grounded in the historical person of Jesus of Nazareth — in other words, the church's explicit Christology is grounded in the implicit Christology of Jesus himself. Continuity-in-discontinuity must be made to stand out at every stage: between the messianic expectation of the Jewish scripture and its coming to fulfillment in Jesus; between the prepaschal Jesus and the Christ of the apostolic kerygma; between the Christology of the early kerygma and later biblical enunciations between New Testament Christology and that of the church tradition; and so forth. This vast task has been attempted elsewhere and need not be repeated here.[18]

The expression "continuity-in-discontinuity" merits some explanation, however, for it takes on different meanings at different stages of Christological development. There is a real discontinuity between Jesus and the Christ, inasmuch as the human existence of Jesus was transformed when he passed from the state of kenosis to the glorified state through the resurrection (cf. Phil 2:6–11); nevertheless, continuity persists insofar as the personal identity remains. The one who is glorified is he who has died: Jesus is the Christ (Acts 2:36). The historical Jesus *is* the Christ of faith (pp. 58–65).

The expression "continuity-in-discontinuity" takes on a different meaning when it concerns the relation between the "functional" Christology of the early kerygma and the later "ontological" Christology of the New Testament. The transition from the "functional" to the "ontological" level takes place through the dynamism of faith, inasmuch as the personal identity of the Son of God is presupposed, in the order of being, to the "divine condition" that shows forth in the glorified humanity of Jesus. The transition from the one to the other is a homogeneous development (pp. 65–76).

The meaning of "continuity-in-discontinuity" differs again where the relation between the ontological Christology of the New Testament and the church's Christological dogma is concerned. Here the expression refers to a continuity of content in the discontinuity of idiom. The Christological dogma does not "Hellenize" the content of faith; rather, it represents a de-Hellenization of content in a Hellenization of terminology (pp. 77–101). It is a question of "inculturation," to use the contemporary expression.

Pluralists, John Hick in particular,[19] dismiss the term "incarnation" as mythical and metaphorical language. If, however, the term is properly demythologized, it is seen by them to affirm — correctly — that God makes himself manifest and can be encountered through the man Jesus: understood as metaphorical parlance, the Word "becoming flesh" in Jesus Christ (see Jn 1:14) is then seen as equivalent to "Jesus of Nazareth, a man attested . . . by God" (see Acts 2:22). It is true that the concepts of preexistence and incarnation are both open to misunderstanding. Preexistence is not existence in a fictitious time before time. However, the fact remains that the incarnation of the Son of God involves, in a very real way, the

---

18. Jacques Dupuis, *Who Do You Say That I Am? Introduction to Christology* (Maryknoll, N.Y.: Orbis Books, 1994).

19. Hick, *The Metaphor of God Incarnate.*

becoming-human in history of the Word, who, independently of this becoming, exists eternally in the mystery of God.[20] Such is the real meaning conveyed through the symbolic language of incarnation.

Writing on the Christology of the Gospel according to John, Rudolf Schnackenburg shows well the difference between any mythological speculation and the real language of preexistence, which seeks to substantiate the saving power of God's incarnate Son. He writes:

> Johannine Christology is not modeled on a set pattern of mythological speculation about a redeemer descending from heaven and returning there again. It is rather the desire to establish clearly the Christian redeemer's power to save that leads to the emphasis on his pre-existence, so that now his way is seen more clearly to begin from "above" and to return there once more.[21]

One witness will suffice. In a thoroughly documented and critical study, Karl-Josef Kuschel writes about St. John's Christology:

> John's concern is the confession that the Word of God which is with God from eternity, God's Word and thus God himself, has become man in Jesus of Nazareth. Jesus is the eternal Word of God in person, not because people believe in him or because he asserts it of himself, but because this is what he is from God. Jesus is the eternal Son of God, not because human beings have understood this to be the case or because he has made it plausible, but because this is what he is, and always was from God. So what stands in the foreground is not the speculative question how the man Jesus could have had glory with God but the confession that the man Jesus of Nazareth is the Logos of God in person. And he is the Logos as a mortal man. However, he is the Logos only for those who are prepared to believe, trusting God's word in his word, God's actions in his actions, God's history in his career, and God's compassion in his cross.[22]

We have insisted that the constitutive uniqueness and universality of Jesus Christ must be made to rest on his personal identity as the Son of God. The universality of Jesus-the-Christ cannot, however, be allowed to overshadow the particularity of Jesus of Nazareth. It is true that Jesus' human existence, transformed by his resurrection and glorification, has reached beyond time and space and become "transhistorical"; but it is the historical Jesus who has become that. The universality of the Christ who, "being made perfect," became "the source of eternal salvation" (Heb 5:9) does not cancel out the particularity of Jesus, "made like his brothers and sisters in every respect" (Heb 2:17). A universal Christ, severed from the particular Jesus, would no longer be the Christ of Christian

---

20. Karl Rahner, "On the Theology of the Incarnation," in *Theological Investigations*, 4:105–20.

21. Rudolf Schnackenburg, *The Gospel according to St. John* (New York: Crossroad, 1987), 555–56.

22. Karl-Josef Kuschel, *Born before All Time? The Dispute over Christ's Origin* (London: SCM Press, 1992), 389.

revelation. To stress the historical particularity of Jesus is not, in fact, without implications for an open theology of religions. Nor is it indifferent in a context of interreligious dialogue.

The historical particularity of Jesus imposes upon the Christ event irremediable limitations. This is necessarily part of the incarnational economy willed by God. Just as the human consciousness of Jesus as Son could not, by its very nature, exhaust the mystery of God, and therefore God's revelation in him remains limited, likewise the Christ event does not — and cannot — exhaust God's saving power. God remains beyond the man Jesus as the ultimate source of both revelation and salvation. The revelation of God by Jesus is a human transposition of God's mystery; his saving action is the channel, the efficacious sign or sacrament, of God's saving will and action. The liturgy rightly calls Jesus Christ the "universal sacrament of salvation" (cf. in the Roman Missal, the prayer for Tuesday of the second week after Easter) — a title that could never be used for God himself. It is understood that he is the universal "primordial" sacrament of salvation; the church is referred to "as the universal sacrament of salvation" (*ut universale salutis sacramentum, Lumen Gentium* §48), derivatively. The personal identity of Jesus as Son of God in his human existence notwithstanding, a distance continues to exist between God (the Father), the ultimate source, and he who is God's human icon. Jesus is no substitute for God.[23]

If this is true, it will also be seen that, while the Christ event is the "universal sacrament" of God's will to save humankind and of his saving action, it need not be thereby and exclusively the only possible expression of that will. God's saving power is not exclusively bound by the universal sign God has designed for his saving action. In terms of a Trinitarian Christology, this means that God's saving action through the Word before the incarnation, of whom the Prologue of John's Gospel states that he "was the light that enlightens every human being," by coming into the world (Jn 1:9), continues even after the incarnation, as does a saving action by God through the universal presence of the Spirit, both before and after the historical event of Jesus Christ, as will be noted below. The mystery of the incarnation is unique; only the individual human existence of Jesus is assumed by the Son of God and united to him in person. But while he alone is thus constituted the "image of God," other "saving figures" may nonetheless be "enlightened" by the Word or "inspired" by the Spirit, to become pointers to salvation for their followers, in accordance with God's overall design for humankind.

Certainly, in the mystery of Jesus-the-Christ, the Word cannot be separated from the flesh that it has assumed. But, inseparable as the divine Word and Jesus' human existence may be, they nevertheless remain distinct. Thus, while the human action of the incarnate Word is the universal sacrament of God's saving action, it does not exhaust the action of the Word. A distinct action of the Word as such continues — not, to be sure, as constituting a distinct economy

---

23. Christian Duquoc, *Messianisme de Jésus et discrétion de Dieu* (Geneva: Labor et Fides, 1984).

of salvation, parallel to that realized in the flesh of Christ, but as the expression of God's superabundant graciousness and absolute freedom.

The particularity of the Jesus Christ event in relation to the universality of God's plan of salvation opens, as it were, new ways of approaching a theology of religious pluralism that would make room for diverse "paths" to salvation. Claude Geffré sees the paradox of the incarnation as lying in the simultaneity of the "particular" and the "universal": Jesus Christ is, according to an expression of Nicholas of Cusa that has been taken up by Paul Tillich and Hans Urs von Balthasar, the "concrete universal." The particularity of the event, however, leaves room for holding together, within the one divine plan, the universal significance of Jesus Christ and the saving value of other traditions.[24] He has written:

> The very *incarnational principle,* that is, the manifestation of the Absolute in and through a historic particularity, encourages us not to absolutize Christianity. If the Christ is universal, he is so as Jesus of Nazareth, dead and risen. The man Jesus is not a sort of divine emanation. His humanity is relative because it is historic, though having an absolute [?] and universal meaning. Jesus is the concrete element through which human beings have access to God. But... he himself is subject to the judgment of the *unconditioned,* should he ever seek to identify himself with the Absolute.[25]

For his part, Edward Schillebeeckx asks how Christianity can maintain the uniqueness of Jesus Christ and at the same time attribute positive value to the different religions. He notes that "Jesus is indeed a *'singular and unique,'* but nevertheless 'contingent,' i.e., historical and thus limited, manifestation of the gift of salvation from God for all men and women." But he continues:

> The revelation of God in Jesus, as the Christian Gospel preaches this to us, in no way means that God absolutizes a historical particularity... We learn from the revelation of God in Jesus that no individual particularity can be said to be absolute, and that therefore through the relativity present in Jesus anyone can encounter God even outside Jesus, specially in our worldly history and in the many religions which have arisen in it. The risen Jesus of Nazareth also continues to point to God beyond himself. One could say: God points via Jesus Christ in the Spirit to himself as creator and redeemer, as a God of men and women, of all men and women. God is absolute, but no religion is absolute.[26]

Earlier Schillebeeckx had written: "For even Jesus not only reveals God but also conceals him, since he appeared among us in non-godlike, creaturely hu-

---

24. Claude Geffré, "La singularité du Christianisme à l'âge du pluralisme religieux," in *Penser la foi: Recherches en théologie aujourd'hui: Mélanges offerts à Joseph Moingt,* ed. J. Doré and C. Theobald (Paris: Cerf-Arras, 1993), 53; idem, "Paul Tillich et l'avenir de l'oecuménisme interreligieux," *Revue des Sciences Philosophique et Théologique* 77 (1993): 3–22; idem, "La place des religions dans le plan du salut," *La mission à la rencontre des religions, Spiritus* 138 (February 1995): 78–97.
25. Claude Geffré, "Pour un christianisme mondial," *Recherches de Science Religieux* 86 (1998): 63.
26. Edward Schillebeeckx, *Church: The Human Story of God* (London: SCM Press, 1990), 165–66.

manity. As man he is a historical, contingent being, who in no way can represent the full riches of God...unless one denies the reality of his real humanity."[27] More recently he has added: "A Christian may never lose sight of the fact that Christianity, and the man Jesus himself, are neither absolutes nor are they absolutely unique. The only one who is so is the God of Jesus, the Creator, he who is the God of all human beings. What Christian faith witnesses is that in Jesus the Absolute, that is, the one God, is reflected as such in the relativity of history under a unique form."[28]

We may also quote Christian Duquoc where he similarly warns against absolutizing the particularity of God's manifestation in Jesus Christ. He writes:

> By revealing himself in Jesus, God has not absolutized a particular event ...on the contrary,...no particular historical event is absolute and..., in virtue of this relativity, God can be met in real history...The fundamental particularity of Christianity requires, therefore, that differences be allowed to endure, and be not abolished as if God's manifestation in Jesus had brought "religious" history to an end.[29]

THE UNIVERSAL PRESENCE OF THE HOLY SPIRIT

Thus the historic particularity of the Christ event, combined with its universal saving significance, leaves room for a saving action of the Word as such. It should be added that the Trinitarian perspective prompts observations about a universal presence of the Holy Spirit, similar to those about the ongoing action of the Word as such. A Spirit Christology helps make it clear that the Spirit of God is universally present and active, before and after the Christ event. The Christ event both derives from the working of the Spirit in the world and gives rise to it. There is a "relationship of mutual conditioning" between the two aspects by virtue of which the Spirit in the course of the entire history of salvation may properly be called the "Spirit of Christ."[30] God's economy of salvation is only one; the Christ event is both its apex and universal sacrament; but the God who saves is three-personed: each of the three is personally distinct and remains active distinctly. God saves "with two hands," the Word and the Spirit, wrote St. Irenaeus in the second century (*Adv. Haer.* IV, 7, 4).

Recent church teaching has insisted on the universality of the active presence of the Spirit. It may be asked, however, whether after the Christ event the communication of the Spirit and his active presence in the world take place solely

---

27. Edward Schillebeeckx, *Jesus in Our Western Culture: Mysticism, Ethics, Politics* (London: SCM Press, 1987), 2.

28. Edward Schillebeeckx, "Universalité unique d'un figure religieuse historique nommée Jésus de Nazareth," *Laval Théologique et Philosophique* 50, no. 2 (1994): 273.

29. Christian Duquoc, *Dieu différent* (Paris: Cerf, 1977), 143.

30. Cf. Karl Rahner, "Jesus Christ in the Non-Christian Religions," in *Theological Investigations*, 17:39–50.

through the glorified humanity of Jesus Christ, or, on the contrary, can also go beyond that limit. In other words, has the "Spirit of God" become the "Spirit of Christ" to such an extent that he can no longer become present and active beyond the communication of him that takes place through the risen Christ, in such a manner that his activity is henceforth circumscribed to that of the risen Christ, and in that sense limited?

In the New Testament, and particularly in Paul, the Spirit is called either "Spirit of God" or "Spirit of Christ." The expression "Spirit of Christ" (Rom 8:9) seems to refer to the communication of the Spirit made by the risen Christ, which corresponds to the promise made by Jesus to the disciples in the gospel of John (Jn 15:26; 16:5–15) and to its realization in Pentecost (Acts 2:1–4). It is likewise understood that the work of the Spirit consists of establishing between human persons and the Lord a personal bond by which they are incorporated into Christ: "Anyone who does not have the Spirit of Christ does not belong to him" (Rom 8:9). In that sense it has been noted that the Spirit is God's "point of insertion" through Christ in people's lives and that its work consists of making them children of the Father in the Son through the risen humanity.

It remains true, however, that the Spirit is more often called the "Spirit of God": "The Spirit of God dwells in you" (Rom 8:9); "If the Spirit of him who raised Jesus from the dead dwells in you, he who raised Christ from the dead will give life to your mortal bodies also through his Spirit who dwells in you" (Rom 8:11); "All who are led by the Spirit of God are children of God" (Rom 8:14); cf. also 1 Cor 2:11; 2:14; 3:16; 6:1; 12:2; 2 Cor 3:3 and so forth. The Spirit who is communicated is fundamentally the "Spirit of God." If, then, from God's manifestation in history one reaches out to the triune communication within the very mystery of God, the Spirit is presented to us as the person who "proceeds" primordially from the Father, the "principle without a principle," through the Word or the Son. In line with the biblical data just mentioned, it can be asked whether there can take place a saving activity of the Holy Spirit after the Christ event beyond that which takes place through the risen humanity of Jesus, just as before the historic event of the incarnation, a saving action of the Spirit was exercised without the humanity of Jesus.

The metaphor of God's two hands used by St. Irenaeus can help clarify the distinct activity of the Spirit by virtue of his distinct personal identity. Underlying that metaphor is probably the image of God as a potter (cf. Isa 64:6–7), who with two hands produces a single work, namely, the one economy of salvation. God's two hands, the Word and the Spirit — we may add — are paired hands. That means that, while they are united and inseparable, they are also distinct and complementary in their distinction. The activity of each is different from that of the other; indeed it is the concurrence or "synergy" of the two distinct activities that produces God's saving effect. Neither one nor the other can be reduced to representing a mere "function" of the other; rather both activities converge in achieving a single economy of salvation. God acts with both God's hands. This metaphor may make it easier to understand that the communication of the Spirit through the risen Christ does not necessarily exhaust the activity of the Spirit after the Christ event.

It is well known that the Eastern Orthodox tradition has often accused the Western tradition of promoting a theological "Christomonism" in which the Holy Spirit is reduced to being a "function" of Christ. Although Yves Congar regards the accusation as exaggerated, he nevertheless recognizes that it is not entirely without a basis: indeed it offers Western theology the chance to reflect on the inadequacy of its pneumatology.[31] While certainly no "autonomous" economy of the Spirit can be construed detached from that of the Word, neither can the Spirit be reduced to a "function" of the risen Christ, to the point of being, as it were, his "vicar." The fullness of the personal saving activity of the Spirit would thereby be lost. Paul Evdokimov felicitously highlights the personal character of the Spirit's "mission" from the Father, as distinct from that of the Word, when he writes:

> The Word and the Spirit, "God's two hands" in the expression of St. Ire-naeus, are inseparable in their action manifesting the Father, and yet ineffably distinct. The Spirit is neither subordinate to the Son, nor a function of the Word; he is the second Paraclete. In the two economies of the Son and the Spirit can be seen reciprocity and mutual service, but Pentecost is not simply the consequence or continuation of the Incarnation. Pentecost has its full value in itself, *it represents the Father's second act:* the Father sends the Son and now sends the Holy Spirit. With his mission complete the Christ returns to the Father so that the Holy Spirit may descend in person.[32]

Vladimir Lossky indeed accuses the Latin tradition, because of its concept of the "procession" of the Spirit from the Father and the Son (*filioque*), of reducing both the personal identity of the Spirit in the inner mystery of God and his saving activity in the divine economy of salvation:

> Reduced to the function of a bond between two persons and subordinated one-sidedly to the Son in his very existence, to the detriment of authentic perichoresis, the Spirit loses, along with the hypostatic independence, the personal fullness of his economic activity. That activity will henceforth be regarded as a mere means placed at the service of the economy of the Word, on the plane of both the church and the person.[33]

Certainly no "subordination" of the Spirit to the Son in the inner mystery of God may be assumed, the "order" of the intra-Trinitarian "processions" notwith-

---

31. Yves Congar, "Pneumatologie ou 'christomonisme' dans la tradition latine?" in *Ecclesia a Spirito Sancto edocta: Mélanges théologiques* (Gembloux: Duculot, 1970), 41–63; idem, *The Word and the Spirit* (London: G. Chapman, 1986).

32. Paul Evdokimov, *L'Esprit Saint dans la tradition orthodoxe* (Paris: Cerf, 1969), 88–89.

33. See A. de Halleux, in *Revue Théologique de Louvain* 6 (1975): 13–14, referring to Vladimir Lossky, *Essai sur la théologie mystique del l'Orient* (Paris: Aubier, 1944), 242–43; see also 155–56, 163, 166, 185, 193.

standing. The risk in the Latin tradition of reducing the saving activity of the Spirit in the divine "economy" is not, however, imaginary; it must be taken seriously. Indeed, it seems that there are various ways in which the Spirit can be unduly reduced to a "function" of Christ. One such way would consist in simply identifying the Spirit with the risen Christ; such an opinion is based on an erroneous understanding of the Pauline statement: "The Lord is the Spirit" (2 Cor 3:17).[34] More discreet and subtler, but perhaps just as unsatisfactory, would be the position that the saving and vivifying action of the Spirit consists entirely in the communication of the Spirit made by the risen Lord. That is the position being discussed here.

Vatican II affirms clearly (*Ad Gentes* §4) and recent church teaching insistently reaffirms (cf. in particular the encyclical *Dominum et Vivificantem* §53) that the Spirit was already present and operative before the glorification of Christ, even before the Jesus Christ event, throughout all of history from creation onward. It is understood that "this is the same Spirit who was at work in the Incarnation and in the life, death, and resurrection of Jesus, and who is at work in the church. He is therefore not an alternative to Christ, nor does he fill a sort of void which is sometimes suggested as existing between Christ and the Logos. Whatever the Spirit brings about in human hearts and in the history of peoples, in cultures and religions serves as a preparation for the Gospel and can only be understood in reference to Christ" (*Redemptoris Missio* §29). Nevertheless, it is not apparent why, whereas before the Christ event the Spirit was at work in the world and in history, without being communicated through the risen humanity — which did not yet exist — its activity after the Christ event would have to be so tied to such communication as to be limited to it. It must certainly be kept in mind that in both cases — whether before or after the historic event — the outpouring of the Spirit is always in relation to the event in which the expansion of the divine plan of salvation through history reaches its culminating point. In that sense it can and must be said that the gift of the Spirit before the incarnation takes place "in view" of the Christological event. But that does not allow saying that after that event no action whatever of the Spirit as such, albeit in relation to that event, may be conceived — in a way similar to what it has been possible to affirm regarding an action of the Word as such, according to the explanations given earlier. There are not two economies of salvation. But both of God's "hands" have and keep their own personal identity in the divine activity. The Word is the light "which enlightens everyone" (Jn 1:9); for his part, the Spirit "blows where he wills" (Jn 3:8).

The central position of the Jesus Christ event in the single divine plan must always be kept in mind. That event — as has been said many times — represents the high point of God's commitment to humankind, and as such, it is the interpretative key of the entire extension of personal dealings between God and

---

34. See Donald L. Gelpi, *The Divine Mother: A Trinitarian Theology of the Holy Spirit* (Lanham, Md.: University Press of America, 1984), 136; also Elizabeth A. Johnson, *She Who Is* (New York: Crossroad, 1992), 211.

human beings. That is why in the explanation of the different paradigm shifts proposed in the current debate on religions, the new paradigms of logocentrism and pneumatocentrism have been clearly rejected. But it is one thing to affirm different economies of salvation parallel to that of the Christ event, and another matter to distinguish without separation different complementary aspects of a single economy of salvation willed by God for humankind.

MEDIATION AND MEDIATIONS

VARIOUS PATHS
TO A COMMON GOAL

"Various rivers flowing to the same ocean": this and other similar expressions have often served as catchwords for a pluralistic theology of religions. As various rivers flowing to the same ocean, so too the various religions tend to the same Divine Mystery. Paths differ, but the ultimate end is common to all. The pluralistic model of "God-centeredness," and later of "Reality-centeredness," proposed by John Hick, fits into the axiom; the more recent "pluralism of orientation" of S. Mark Heim,[35] on the contrary, contradicts it. According to Heim, if it is to be authentic, pluralism must recognize that a real multiplicity of different religious ends is objectively characteristic of the various traditions. As he sees it, the recognition of such a multiplicity of religious ends does not appear to contradict Christian tradition. Without wishing to enter into debate with such an opinion, which is scarcely compatible with Christian tradition, suffice it to say that for us, the expression "various paths to a common goal" is used within the Christian conviction that the ultimate goal intended by God for all human life in any historic and religious context is personal union and sharing of life with the God who revealed Godself in Jesus Christ. Yet the various religious traditions represent various paths leading, though differently, to that common goal. That is what we still must show.

"It is possible to hold," Keith Ward writes, "that, in an important sense, many faiths may offer different paths to a common goal, conceived in a number of rather different ways."[36] He goes on to explain that the specific Christian beliefs in the incarnation, atonement, and the Trinity can be interpreted in a number of distinctive ways, which already constitute diverse doctrines within the Christian spectrum; other religious traditions introduce further diversification in the way of conceiving the final goal of human beings. The goal, however, remains common, and this makes it possible to speak of a true "convergence" in a common quest (p. 339). Differences in theological concepts do not necessarily prevent the real commonality of the end.

---

35. S. Mark Heim, *Salvations: Truth and Difference in Religion* (Maryknoll, N.Y.: Orbis Books 1995); idem, *The Depth of the Riches: A Trinitarian Theology of Religious Ends* (Grand Rapids, Mich.: Eerdmans, 2001).

36. Keith Ward, *Religion and Revelation* (Oxford: Clarendon Press, 1994), 338; cf. 310f.

Traditional Christian thinking has often been reluctant, even in recent years, to see in the other religious traditions valid "paths," "ways," or "channels" through which the goal of union with the God of Jesus Christ may be reached; or, to put it the other way round — as is more appropriate — through which the God of Jesus Christ communicates personally and shares his own life with the followers of those traditions. Vatican II, notwithstanding its openness to the positive values contained in those traditions, did not venture to call them "ways" of salvation, though it may be asked whether this is not — at least partly — implied in the council's recognition of elements of "truth and grace" contained in them "as a sort of secret presence of God" (*Ad Gentes* §9).

The central texts of the postconciliar magisterium have already been considered previously and need not be reviewed again here; what they affirm is limited. The document that comes closest to saying that the other religions constitute paths to salvation for their adherents is the already quoted text from "Dialogue and Proclamation" (1991):

> Concretely it will be in the sincere practice of what is good in their own religious traditions and by following the dictates of their conscience that the members of other religions respond positively to God's invitation and receive salvation in Jesus Christ, even while they do not recognize or acknowledge him as their Savior. (§29)

Other documents, although they are admittedly less authoritative, display a greater openness toward the other religious traditions. God is seen as present and active in them, drawing people to himself; their plurality itself witnesses to "the manifold ways in which God has related to peoples and nations." The statement published by the Thirteenth Annual Meeting of the Indian Theological Association (December 28–31, 1989) under the title "Toward an Indian Christian Theology of Religious Pluralism"[37] already noted says: Whereas we deal with the problem of pluralism "from our own faith perspective" (§9), we also "understand the purpose and meaning of the wonderful religious variety around us and its role and function in the attainment of salvation" (§8). There follows an important statement:

> The religions of the world are expressions of the human openness to God. They are signs of God's presence in the world. Every religion is unique and through this uniqueness, religions enrich one another. In their specificity, they manifest different faces of the supreme Mystery which is never exhausted. In their diversity, they enable us to experience the richness of the One more profoundly. When religions encounter one another in dialogue, they build up a community in which differences become complementarities and divergences are changed into pointers to communion. (§32)

---

37. Cf. K. Pathil, ed., *Religious Pluralism: An Indian Christian Perspective* (Delhi: ISPCK, 1991), 338–49.

Other similar testimonies can be found, such as the "Guidelines for Inter-religious Dialogue," published in 1989 by the CBCI (Catholic Bishops' Confer-ence of India) Commission for Dialogue and Ecumenism. The text states:

> The plurality of religions is a consequence of the richness of creation itself and of the manifold grace of God. Though all coming from the same source, peoples have perceived the universe and articulated their awareness of the Divine Mystery in manifold ways, and God has surely been present in these historical undertakings of his children. Such pluralism therefore is in no way to be deplored but rather acknowledged as itself a divine gift. (§25)[38]

Two years earlier, the Theological Advisory Commission of the Federation of Asian Bishops' Conferences (FABC) had published a document entitled "Theses on Interreligious Dialogue" (1987), in which a positive evaluation of the role of other religious traditions in the divine economy of salvation was clearly expressed. There we read the following:

> Its experience of the other religions has led the Church in Asia to [a] positive appreciation of their role in the divine economy of salvation. This appreciation is based on the fruits of the Spirit perceived in the lives of the other religions' believers: a sense of the sacred, a commitment to the pursuit of fullness, a thirst for self-realization, a taste for prayer and commitment, a desire for renunciation, a struggle for justice, an urge to basic human goodness, an involvement in service, a total surrender of the self to God, and an attachment to the transcendent in their symbols, rituals and life itself, though human weakness and sin are not absent.
>
> The positive appreciation is further rooted in the conviction of faith that God's plan of salvation for humanity is one and reaches out to all peoples: it is the Kingdom of God through which he seeks to reconcile all things with himself in Jesus Christ. (§§2, 2–2, 3)[39]

In comparison to the foregoing witnesses, the recent document of the Inter-national Theological Commission titled "Christianity and the World Religions" expresses extreme caution and apparent reluctance to recognize some "saving function" in the other religious traditions. The relevant passages, while admitting the presence of the Spirit in the religions, which is affirmed in recent official church teaching, are much more reserved in drawing positive conclusions:

> Given [the] explicit recognition of the presence of the Spirit of Christ in the religions, *one cannot exclude the possibility* that they exercise as such a certain salvific function, that is, despite their ambiguity, they help people

---

38. Cf. CBCI Commission for Dialogue and Ecumenism, *Guidelines for Interreligious Dialogue*, 2d rev. ed. (New Delhi: CBCI Centre, 1989), 29.

39. FABC Theological Advisory Commission, *Theses on Interreligious Dialogue, FABC Papers* no. 48 (Hong Kong: FABC, 1987), 7.

achieve their ultimate end. In the religions is explicitly thematized the relationship of man with the Absolute, his transcendent dimension. *It would
be difficult to think* that what the Holy Spirit works in the hearts of persons
taken as individuals would have salvific value, and think that what the Holy
Spirit works in the religions and cultures would not have such value. *The
recent magisterium does not seem to authorize such a drastic distinction.* (§84;
emphasis added)

The religions can therefore be, in the terms indicated, a means (*mezzo*)
helping the salvation of their followers; but they cannot be compared
(*equiparare*) to the function that the Church realizes for the salvation of
Christians and those who are not. (§86)[40]

In the next chapter we will come back to the role of the church toward the
members of other religious traditions and toward those traditions themselves.
Meanwhile, what strikes the eye in comparing this last text with those from Asia
is the different perception of those who have extensive daily interaction with
the members of the other religious traditions with regard to the meaning and
value of these latter in God's design for humankind, as compared to the reserved
assessment coming from the document from the church center with a dogmatic
a priori approach. The documents connected to the central teaching authority
find it hard to admit in theory what for others is a lived experience. However,
it still must be shown how the religious traditions mediate salvation for their
adherents; or to put it in other terms, how within them and through them God
communicates Godself to their adherents in various differentiated ways. Even
more specifically: in just what sense are the traditions "channels" of salvation?
What causality is operative within them to justify calling them (univocally or
analogously) ways or paths of salvation?

PARTICIPATED MEDIATIONS
OF SALVATION

A Trinitarian model of Christology lays the groundwork for various considerations which, while they are closely connected, can still be clearly distinguished.
Grace or divine salvation "bears within itself both a Christological aspect and a
pneumatological one" (*Dominum et Vivificantem* §53). This is true in any historic
situation or circumstance, whether before or after the Jesus Christ event. As a
recent author has written:

It must ... be emphasized that this understanding of the universality of
God's presence to his creation and of the universality of God's reconciling
and saving love for his creation is for Christian theology never independent of God's self-disclosure in the particularity of the Christ event as the
particular Trinitarian God — Father, Son, and Spirit. A Christian theology

40. Text in *Origins* 27 (1997): 149–66.

of religion loses its particular identity if it attempts to base its understanding of the religions not on the universality of God, who is disclosed in Christ, but on some supposedly universal anthropological constant such as an alleged "religious a priori."[41]

God's saving action, which always operates in the framework of a unified design, is one and yet multifaceted. It never prescinds from the Christ event in which it reaches its greatest intensity in history. Nevertheless, the action of God's Word is not limited to being expressed solely through the humanity of Jesus Christ; nor is the work of the Spirit in history limited to its outpouring from the risen and exalted Christ. God's saving grace can reach humankind in different ways which must be combined and brought together.

That the historic event of Jesus Christ, culminating in the paschal mystery of the death-and-resurrection, has universal saving significance has no need of further explanation. What still must be explained is how his saving power reaches the adherents of other religious traditions. Does this take place solely through an invisible action of the glorified humanity which through his resurrection/ glorification has become "transhistoric," removed from the constraints of space and time? Or does God's saving action in Jesus Christ reach the members of the other religious traditions through a certain "mediation" of their own traditions? Are these latter then somehow "channels" of Christ's saving power — and in what sense? Do the traditions confer a certain visibility and social character on the saving power of Christ when it reaches their adherents? Are they signs, albeit perhaps incomplete, of his saving activity?

In order to see that that is what the traditions really are it is crucial to highlight the historic and social character of the human being. Against the "fulfillment theory" which sets up a division between the religious life of the individual person and the community of faith in which that life is experienced, the theory of the "presence of the mystery of Christ" shows rightly that such a sharp division is not theologically feasible.

Human existence is essentially historic. That means two things. First, the human person, incarnate spirit, is a becoming that is expressed in time and space, in history and in the world. The person exists only in this self-expression. That which we call our body is precisely that expression. Such is the deep significance of the Thomistic theory of the "substantial" union of soul and body. That the soul is the "substantial form" of the body means that soul and body do not constitute two elements so distinct as to be independently existing entities and thus easily separable, as though the union between them were merely accidental. Quite the contrary: human beings are persons only to the extent that as spirits, they are incarnate. Modern existential philosophy has recognized and said it better than Thomism. In any case, what is true of the life of a human being in general is also

---

41. Cf. Ch. Schwöbel, "Particularity, Universality, and the Religions: Toward a Christian Theology of Religions," in *Christian Uniqueness Reconsidered: The Myth of a Pluralistic Theology of Religious,* ed. Gavin D'Costa (Maryknoll, N.Y.: Orbis Books, 1990), 39.

true of his or her religious life. This life is not composed of purely spiritual states of the soul — nor could it be. In order to exist, religious life must be expressed in religious symbols, rites, and practices. In the light of the essentially composite nature of the human being, such symbols, rites, and practices are necessary for the very existence of the religious life, insofar as they function as the expression and support for the aspirations of the human spirit. There is no religious life without religious practice. Nor is there, in this sense, any faith without religion.

The anthropological principle proposed here means, next, that the human being is not an isolated "monad," but a person living in a human society. Any human being becomes person by virtue of his or her interpersonal relationships with other human beings. While it is true that one must exist as person in order to have interpersonal relationships with others, it is also true that the human being becomes person and grows as such through such relationships. This is what the philosophy of personalism has made clear. It is also true of the human being's religious life. Religious human beings subsist not as separated individuals but as members of a particular religious community having particular traditions. They grow and are transformed by sharing in the religious life of their respective religious communities, personally entering into the respective historic religious traditions in which they have been placed, and taking on their social manifestations, doctrine and teaching, moral code, and ritual practices.

If all this is true and if many members of other religious traditions have an authentic experience of God, the unavoidable conclusion is that in their institutions and social practices these traditions contain traces of the encounter of these human beings with grace, "components due to a supernatural influence of grace."[42] No dichotomy can be set up between the subjective religious life of human beings and the religion they profess, between personal religious experience and the historico-social religious phenomenon, that is, the religious tradition made up of sacred books and worship practices to which they adhere. Nor may it be said that while the persons belonging to these traditions may obtain salvation through the sincerity of their subjective religious life, their religion itself has no saving value for them.

Clearly the dichotomy on which such negative judgments are based is gravely inadequate. Subjective religion and objective religion must be distinct, but they cannot be separated. The religious traditions of humankind derive from the religious experience of the persons or groups that established them. Their sacred books contain the memory of concrete religious experiences with Truth. Their practices in turn derive from the codification of such experiences. Thus it seems infeasible and theologically unrealistic to hold that while the members of the various religious traditions can attain salvation, their religion does not play any role in that process. Just as there is no purely natural concrete religious life, there is no such thing as a purely natural historic religion.

---

42. Karl Rahner, "Christianity and the Non-Christian Religions," in *Theological Investigations,* 5:121, 130.

To show how the various religious traditions may function as mediations of the mystery of salvation for their members, we must take as our point of departure the mystery of Christ itself, and then go on to consider Christ's presence to human beings. In Christ God enters into a personal relationship with human beings — becomes present to them. Any genuine experience of God, by Christians as well as others, is an encounter of God in Jesus Christ with the human being. God's presence to the human being, insofar as it constitutes — like any personal presence — a "being with" in the intentional order, situates God in relationship to the human being in an interpersonal exchange between a "Thou" and an "I." The order of faith or salvation consists precisely in this personal communication of God with the human being, a communication whose concrete realization takes place in Jesus Christ, and whose effective sign is the humanity of Jesus.

Yet God is infinite Person, beyond any finiteness, and God's transcendence deeply marks the nature of the personal divine presence to human beings. Insofar as the Infinite is infinitely distant from the finite, God's personal presence to the human being — and a fortiori to the sinful human being — can only be gratuitous. The initiative of God's relationship to the human being must come from the side of the Divine. God's indulgence to human beings stands at the center of the mystery of Christ.

In Christianity, God's personal presence to human beings in Jesus Christ reaches its highest and most complete sacramental visibility through the word revealed in him and the sacraments based on him. However, this complete mediation of the mystery of Christ reaches only Christians, members of the sacrament-church, from which they receive the word and whose sacramental economy they share. Can other religions contain and signify in some fashion God's presence to human beings in Jesus Christ? Does God become present to them in the very practice of their religions? The answer has to be "yes." Their religious practice is indeed what gives expression to their experience of God and of the mystery of Christ. It is the visible element, the sign, the sacrament of that experience. This practice expresses, sustains, supports, and contains — as it were — their encounter with God in Jesus Christ.

The religious tradition of others is accordingly for them — in this particular sense — a way and a means of salvation. To reject that conclusion would be tantamount to mistakenly drawing an undue separation between personal, subjective religious life and objective religious tradition — made up of words, rites, and sacraments — in which that life finds expression. Such a separation is, as we noted, theologically infeasible.

Reaching a clear determination of exactly in what sense the historic religions function as mediations of the presence of the Christic mystery for their members may be elusive. We must, however, distinguish between various modalities of the sacramental presence of the mystery. The mediation of the mystery of Christ takes place in a variety of ways. While God's grace is certainly one, it is visibly mediated in different ways — differing from one another not only in degree but in nature. This means that the religious practices and sacramental rites of other religions are not on the same level as the Christian sacraments deriving from Jesus Christ; but it does also mean that we must attribute to them a certain mediation of grace.[43] There is only one mystery of salvation in Christ. But this mystery is present to human beings outside the bounds of Christianity. In the church, eschatological community, it is present to them openly and explicitly, in the full visibility of its complete mediation. In the other religious traditions, it is present hiddenly and implicitly, through a modality of incomplete, but no less real, mediation, constituted by such traditions.

As theologically obscure as the difference between the various modalities of the mediation of the mystery of salvation may be, that difference must be clearly affirmed. In this regard, some twelve years ago I wrote:

> It is one thing to receive the word spoken by God to human beings by the mediation of sages who have heard it in the depths of their hearts and conveyed their experience to others. It is another to hear the decisive Word that God speaks to human beings in God's incarnate Son who is the fullness of revelation...
>
> Again, it is one thing to enter into contact with the mystery of Christ through the symbols and ritual practices that have sustained and given visible form throughout the centuries to the faith response of women and men and to their commitment to God; it is another thing to encounter that mystery as represented in the full sacramentality of the symbolic acts instituted by Jesus Christ and entrusted by him to the church...
>
> Finally, it is one thing to have the experience of the mystery of Christ and live by it unconsciously, in a hidden way without a clear awareness of the infinite condescension shown to us by God in the divine Son, without full knowledge of the earnestness and authenticity of God's descent to us in that Son; and it is another thing to recognize the mystery in the humble condition of the human Jesus, in his human life, his death, and his resurrection, with full awareness that, in this human being, who is a member of our race, God has personally come to meet us on our own level. Apart from Christianity, God encounters human beings in Christ, but the human face of God remains unknown. In Christianity, God encounters women and men in the human face of the human Jesus, who reflects for us the very image of the Father. While every religion contains an approach to the human being on the part of God, in Christianity God's advance toward the human being becomes fully human.[44]

But it must be recalled once more that the Christ event, while present inclusively, still does not exhaust the power of the Word of God who became flesh in Jesus Christ. The illuminating and saving power of the Word is universal,

---

43. On the question of sacramental rites, cf. N. Abeyasingha, *A Theological Evaluation of Non-Christian Rites* (Bangalore: Theological Publications in India, 1984).

44. Jacques Dupuis, *Jesus Christ at the Encounter of World Religions* (Maryknoll, N.Y.: Orbis Books, 1991), 149–50.

reaching all times and all people. His incomparable illuminating force operating throughout human history contributes to the salvation of human beings, both before and after his manifestation in the flesh. As he did before the incarnation, the divine Word still continues sowing his seeds within peoples and religious traditions: divine truth and grace are present in them through his activity. Similar observations must be made with regard to the universal presence of the Holy Spirit, both before and after the incarnation of the Word. The Spirit's presence and activity "affect not only individuals but also society and history, peoples, cultures and religions" (*Redemptoris Missio* §28). Elements of "truth and grace" are therefore present in human cultures and religions by virtue of the combined action of the Word of God and of God's Spirit. Again we are led to recognize a saving function of those religions in communicating to their adherents the offer of God's grace and salvation and in giving expression to their positive response to God's gracious self-gift. The Word and the Spirit — God's "two hands" (St. Irenaeus) — work together through their universal action to confer "truth and grace" on the religious life of people and to inscribe "saving values" into the religious traditions to which they belong. Can the "saving values" contained in those religious traditions be discerned theologically? On what criterion should such a work of discernment be based?

DISCERNMENT OF SAVING VALUES

The specifically Christian criterion for such discernment is: "a religion is true and good if and insofar as it allows us to perceive the spirit of Jesus Christ in its theory and practice."[45] This consists of asking whether and to what extent the "Christian spirit" can be found in other religions. "Jesus Christ is for Christians the *deciding regulative factor*" (p. 251). One thinks here spontaneously of the fruits of the Spirit mentioned by St. Paul (Gal 5:16–24), on which Christians and the Christian tradition do not have the monopoly. The matter can be summed up in one word: love (*agapè*); for "God's central revelation, which is given in Jesus Christ, is *agapè*."[46]

A distinction must be made, however, between the subjective faith-commitment of the individual person and the objective, historical religious tradition to which the person belongs and from which he or she derives religious life and inspiration. Christian theologians will agree that anyone who normally abides by what Christian revelation calls the law of love has heard God speaking in the secrecy of his or her heart and responded to that call within a faith-commitment. *Ubi caritas et amor, Deus ibi est.* The New Testament makes it clear that *agapè*, though made up of two dimensions, is one, and that the love of God necessarily passes through the love of neighbor (1 Jn 4:20). Recent theology expresses this mediation in terms of the "sacrament of the neighbor." The New Testament also insists that the empowering love of *agapè* is a gift of the Spirit, who has been poured into

---

45. Hans Küng, *Theology for the Third Millennium* (New York: Doubleday, 1988), 248.
46. Cf. Peggy Starkey, "Agapè: A Christian Criterion for Truth in the Other Religions," *International Review of Mission* 74 (1985): 433.

our hearts (Rom 5:5). *Agapè* is the overflow in us of the love by which God loved us first. That is why the practice of love is the sure criterion for recognizing that a person has listened to the word of God and opened his or her heart to it. The practice of *agapè* is the reality of salvation, present and operative in human beings in response to God's self-disclosure and revelation.

But how far the habitual practice of *agapè* and the ensuing mystery of personal salvation are inspired by the religious tradition to which a person belongs is more difficult to ascertain. Nor is it easy to evaluate if, to what extent, and how clearly saving charity is enjoined as a precept by the sacred books considered in other religious traditions as divine revelation. Do the scriptures of those traditions offer an equivalent to the Christian precept of love as it is disclosed in the New Testament? How far is the mystery of subjective salvation, present and operative in the lives of those who adhere to those scriptures, a response to a divine revelation about love contained in them?

What conditions must love of neighbor fulfill, according to the gospel norms, in order to be saving *agapè*? The first is that it be disinterested and unconditional. Such an attitude involves a recognition, at least nonthematic, of the personal worth of the "other" and an implicit acknowledgment of a transcendent Absolute upon which this personal worth is based — whatever the name given to this transcendent Absolute.

The gospel further requires that love be universal. Jesus is clear about what has been called the "radicalism" of the gospel. Love of God and of fellow humans go hand in hand (Mt 22:34–40; Lk 10:25–28); it is by that latter love that people shall be judged (Mt 25:31–46). *Agapè* extends not only to neighbors and friends ("Even the tax collectors do as much, do they not? . . . Even the Gentiles do as much, do they not?"), but to enemies as well (Mt 5:43–48). *Agapè* is universal, for "you must be perfect, as your heavenly Father is perfect" (Mt 5:48).

How do the sacred scriptures of other religious traditions stand in relation to the radical demands of *agapè* contained in the gospel message? Do they provide such incentive for and invitation to outgoing love as can be recognized, from a Christian viewpoint, as divine revelation inspiring and sustaining in the followers of those traditions a commitment to saving *agapè*? In the article referred to above, Peggy Starkey reviews the evidence available in the various religious traditions in favor of a divine revelation inviting their followers to commit themselves to the practice of *agapè*. Her findings are being followed here, first with regard to the monotheistic religions (Judaism and Islam) and thereafter to some of the Asian traditions (Hinduism, Buddhism, and Confucianism).

The precept of the love of neighbor is very clearly taught in Jewish scriptures, where it is based on God's own attitude of covenantal love and faithfulness toward God's people. It is divine *agapè* extending as it were to human relationships. Is that love, however, universal? According to the gospel tradition, Jesus sternly observed: "You have learned how it was said: *"You shall love your neighbor* and hate your enemy. But I say to you: Love your enemies" (Mt 5:43–44). Exegetes note that the second part of the old command is not found in this abrupt form in the law, and that the brusque expression attributed to Jesus comes from the original Aramaic, which recognized few half-tones. The equivalent meaning would be: there is less obligation to love one's enemies. Starkey observes: "The command to love one's neighbor is central to the Tanakh and to the Talmud" (cf. Lev. 19:17–18). But she goes on to say: "Since antiquity, the problem that has risen among the rabbis is not the centrality of the command but the meaning of the word neighbor (*rēá*)" (p. 437). However, she remarks, "today the idea of neighbor is universalized by many Jewish writers" (p. 439). And she sums up:

> A Christian can conclude from the examination of the Scriptures and traditions of Judaism, that Jews are called to live a life characterized by deeds of compassion, charity, loving kindness, respect, justice towards all . . . According to the criterion of *agapè*, Judaism contains truth. (p. 441)

The Qur'an's message about love seems in many ways similar to that of the Jewish scriptures. It is based on the attitude of God — as merciful and compassionate — toward humankind. A certain universalism also characterizes that precept of charity: it extends at least to all Muslims and, according to some traditional interpretations, even to all people (pp. 441–46).

Paradoxically, the universal demand of love seems to be more clearly formulated in the Asian traditions, Hinduism, Buddhism, and Confucianism, than in the two great monotheistic religions other than Christianity. Speaking of Hinduism, Starkey writes: "The Hindu Scriptures call for the action of *agapè* described as acts of compassion, justice, respect, generosity, uprightness, and selflessness towards all" (p. 451). Similarly, of Buddhism: "The Buddhist must not only treat friends and neighbors with *metta* (love), but also 'one's enemies should be treated with loving kindness'" (p. 454); and again, quoting E. A. Burtt,[47] *metta* is "an unlimited self-giving compassion flowing freely towards all creatures that live" (p. 455). Finally, having reviewed the evidence concerning Confucianism, the author concludes: "In the Confucianist tradition, *jen* is love that is universal and active in human relationships" (p. 461).

What, however, in those Asian traditions is the foundation for universal, compassionate love? Can it be said to be based on God's prevenient love for humankind, the divine love being as it were reproduced in and extended to human relationships? Speaking of Hinduism, Starkey rightly points out: "The reason for [the] actions [of *agapè*] . . . is often different from the Western Christian view" (p. 451). Such is the case when altruistic behavior is based, as in the *Upanishadic* tradition, on the identity of *Brahman-Ātman*. By contrast, in the *bhakti* tradition altruistic love finds its foundation in the personal dignity of human beings in relation to a personal God. Of Buddhist compassion for all living creatures, the question has often been asked whether it can be equated with Christian charity. It must, however, be admitted that the theological foundation for an altruistic

---

47. Cf. E. A. Burtt, ed., *The Teachings of the Compassionate Buddha* (New York: The New American Library, 1955), 46.

attitude differs on both sides, as Buddhism's agnostic and neutral stand toward the existence of a "self" and a personal Divine Reality suffices to show. Similarly, in Confucianism, even though it may be correct to observe that *jen* (human heartedness) stands in "close resemblance to the Christian concept of *agapè*," this does not necessarily mean that it has a theological foundation equivalent to that of the Christian attitude of *agapè*.

However, it remains true that acts of love or *agapè* in action are, from a Christian standpoint, the sign that God has entered into the life of a person in self-disclosure and manifestation — no matter how "anonymously" or secretly, no matter how imperfect the awareness of the God who has thus intervened may remain in the subject. They are also the sign that the person has responded positively to God's intervention in his or her life, no matter how unthematic the knowledge of the self-revealing God may remain. Nor is it to be thought that God's initiative in manifesting God's being to a person and the positive response that the person gives to God's initiative are totally unrelated to the religious tradition to which he or she belongs and to what that tradition has taught him or her about the Absolute, no matter how limited this doctrine may be. Subjective faith-commitment expressed in *agapè* and the objective doctrine and practice of the faith-community to which one belongs cannot be severed without doing violence to both.

What, then, is the conclusion? That *agapè* is indeed the sign of the operative presence of the mystery of salvation in every man and woman who is saved: "God is love, and those who abide in love abide in God, and God abides in them" (1 Jn 4:16). But there is yet a further conclusion. The various religious traditions contain elements of divine revelation and moments of divine grace, even though these remain incomplete and open to a fuller self-gift and disclosure on the part of God. The gracious moments enshrined in the religious traditions of humankind open their followers — through faith and *agapè* — to God's grace and salvation. They do so insofar as in God's providence they anticipate God's fuller disclosure and decisive self-gift in Jesus Christ. In Christ, who is God's Son made man, God has united with humankind in an irrevocable bond of love. This is why saving *agapè* finds in Christ its decisive theological foundation. If love is salvific, the reason is ultimately that it imitates and reproduces in us that love with which God has loved us in the first place in the incarnate Son.

IT SEEMS LEGITIMATE, in concluding, to point to a convergence between the religious traditions and the mystery of Jesus Christ, as representing various though not equal paths along which, through history, God has sought and continues to seek human beings in God's Word and God's Spirit. Jesus Christ, it has been said, is the "integral figure (*la figure intégrale*) of God's salvation"; the other religious traditions represent "particular realizations of a universal process, which has become preeminently concrete in Jesus Christ."[48] Salvation is at work every-

---

48. Cf. Jeremiah S. O'Leary, *La vérité chrétienne à l'âge du pluralisme religieux* (Paris: Cerf, 1994), 253.

where; but in the concrete figure of the crucified Christ the work of salvation is seen to be accomplished. Jesus Christ, then, is the "unique Savior," not as the unique manifestation of the Word of God, who is God himself (pp. 261–65); not even in the sense that God's revelation in him would be exhaustive and already achieved — which it is not and cannot be; but in relation to the universal process of divine revelation which occurs through concrete, historical, limited manifestations:

> The contingency of the incarnation goes hand in hand with the universality of the manifestation of the Absolute. The incarnate *Logos* is searching for himself through history. Evangelization and dialogue are the encounter of the incarnate *Logos*, in the contingency of history, with the universal *Logos* sown in every human heart...The fullness — to be realized only in the eschaton — of what we call revelation and incarnation can only be found in the accomplishment of this dialogue. (p. 280)

The convergence between the religious traditions will reach its goal in the eschaton with the "recapitulation" (*anakephalaiòsis:* Eph 1:10) of all things in Christ. This eschatological recapitulation will coincide with the final "perfection" (*teleiòsis*) of the Son of God as "source of eternal salvation" (Heb 5:9), whose influence remains subject, up to this final fulfillment, to an "eschatological remainder." When the Reign of God is achieved, then will come the end when Christ will "hand over the Kingdom to his Father," and the Son himself being "subjected to the one who put all things in subjection under him," God will be "all in all" (1 Cor 15:24–28). The eschatological fullness of the Reign of God is the common final fulfillment of Christianity and the religions. While they tend together toward that fulfillment, the religions must continually be converted to God and his Reign, through a mutual action of testing, of encouraging, and of brotherly and sisterly correction. Human foresight is not privy to the goals toward which such a road will lead through history; rather they must be left to the future ongoing action of the Spirit of God.

Chapter Eight

THE REIGN OF GOD, THE CHURCH, AND THE RELIGIONS

IN THE INTRODUCTION to this work, we spoke of the "purification of theological language" that must go along with the "purification of memory." In the context of the theology of religions and of interreligious dialogue, the expression "Reign of God" in both traditional and more recent theology poses problems. Is it restricted to the hope of Israel and, in its historic realization in the world, to Christianity and the church? Are the "others" excluded from it? Or are they fully members of it, even while remaining outside the church? Or, otherwise, do they belong to it "in some manner" that could be qualified as implicit or invisible? In short, should Christianity and the church be identified with the Reign of God insofar as it is present in the world and history? Or is that Reign a universal reality that extends far beyond the confines of the church and those of the Christian churches? In that case, what is the relationship of the church, on one side, and the religions, on the other, to the universal Reign of God? And what is their relationship to one another? Are Christians and the "others" equally members of the Reign of God?

There are no unanimous responses to these questions. The theology of the Reign of God certainly developed during the precouncil period. Vatican II was able to benefit from this contribution. The council, however, did not resolve all the questions being raised, let alone draw the consequences for a theology of the religions. Our aim in this chapter is to rapidly show the development of the theology of the Reign of God in postconciliar theology and, more importantly, to show its relevance for a theology of the religions in relation to the church. This task will be pursued in two parts. The first part will show the slow rediscovery of the universality of the Reign of God, in which Christians and the "others" are co-members; the second will spell out further the relationship of the church and the other religious traditions to the universal reality of the Reign of God. Thus it will be noted that a regnocentric perspective on ecclesiology and the mission of evangelization seems more suited to the pluralistic religious world in which we are now living, and which will no doubt continue to characterize the new millennium now begun.

Before going further, some clarifications on the meaning of concepts are required, starting with the Reign of God itself. Suffice it to recall, with regard to the Old Testament, that whereas the term "Reign of God" is seldom used as such, the "lordship" of God over his people, and over all peoples, is one of the main themes of Hebrew revelation. According to the New Testament, John the Baptist came announcing that the Reign of God was coming, but he saw it as divine judgment (cf. Mk 1:9–11). Jesus, by contrast, announced the Reign of God as "good news" for all human beings. The "gospel" (*euanggelion*), that is, the "good news," is the breaking into history of the "lordship" of God, the fulfill-ment of the divine promises, and the renewal of the relationship between God and human beings and among human beings themselves. The Reign is "symbol" of the new lordship that God will establish in the world, thereby renewing all things and reestablishing all relationships. In addition, as we already said in chap-ter 1, in Jesus' thought and actions the Reign of God and his imminent coming — through his own life — are the main concern, and indeed the necessary reference point. That Reign is universal, with no limits whatsoever of ethnic, religious, or other ties.

More problematic is the concept of the church to be adopted by a theology of the relationship between the Reign of God, the church, and the religions. In the ancient tradition, specifically in St. Augustine, there has been a tendency to identify the "church" with the totality of all those people who are de facto saved in Jesus Christ, including those who lived before him: *Ecclesia ab Abel,* the first "just man." The legitimacy of such an extended concept of the church is questionable, however; it is indeed more problematic than any modern theory of "implicit" or "anonymous" Christianity which seeks to directly affirm a relationship of all the saved with Christ rather than with the church. From time to time, an even wider — and more problematic — conception of the church has been proposed, by which it would be identified with all of humankind, saved in principle through the Christ event.

Such undue extensions of the church do not seem very useful for our purpose; nor do they correspond to the concept of church officially proposed by recent church teaching. Thus here we are employing the concept of the church affirmed and explained by Vatican II in the constitution *Lumen Gentium* §8, according to which the church is constituted by two inseparable elements, one invisible and the other visible: it is both a spiritual communion and a human institution. The council teaches: "the visible society and the spiritual community...are not to be thought of as two realities. On the contrary, they form one complex reality comprising a human and a divine element." It then adds by way of explanation, "the church is compared, in no mean analogy, to the mystery of the incarnate Word. As the assumed nature, inseparably united to him, serves the divine Word as a living organ of salvation, so, in somewhat similar fashion, does the social structure of the church serve the Spirit of Christ who vivifies it, in the building up of the body" (*Lumen Gentium* §8). Thus while both aspects of the mystery of the church may be distinct, they may not be separated as though they constituted two different realities. There are not two churches: one institutional and visible to which "Christians" belong, and another one spiritual and invisible to which the "others" would also belong. The question will thus be what relationship the "others" can have toward the one church.

REIGN OF GOD AND CHURCH:
IDENTITY OR DISTINCTION?

RECENT HISTORY OF RELATIONSHIPS
BETWEEN CHURCH AND REIGN OF GOD

It was not so long ago that the theology of the Reign of God was character-ized by a double identification. On the one hand, the church was identified quite simply with the Reign of God; on the other hand, the Roman Catholic Church was thought to be fully identical with the church itself. The encyclical *Mystici Corporis* (1943) of Pope Pius XII affirmed this second identification in no un-certain terms.[1] In it the Mystical Body of Christ, the mystery of the church, was identified with the Roman Catholic Church. As for the identification of the church with the Reign of God, this was commonly affirmed or presupposed by theologians at a time when theology was not overly concerned with distinctions which would be later called for by further studies in eschatology.[2] The result was a double identification between the Reign of God and the church, on the one hand, and between the church and the Roman Catholic Church, on the other hand. A single example will suffice. A few years before Vatican II, Timotheus Zapelena wrote in his treatise *De Ecclesia Christi:* "The whole of ecclesiology could be summarized and put in the form of a rectangle: Reign of God=Church of Christ=Roman Catholic Church=Mystical Body of Christ on earth."[3]

Without going into the genesis of Vatican II's Constitution *Lumen Gen-tium*, it is clear that the council distanced itself from identifying the mystery of the church with the Roman Catholic church by adopting the formula: *"Haec Ecclesia . . . subsistit in Ecclesia catholica"* — "This church . . . subsists in the Catho-lic Church" (*Lumen Gentium* §8). The new formula broke with the identification and agreed to recognize in the other Christian churches the existence of "many elements of sanctification and of truth" (*Lumen Gentium* §8), and thus of real elements of the mystery of the church. The mystery is unquestionably present in the Catholic Church, and is indeed so in a privileged way; but it is also present elsewhere, albeit incompletely.[4] What about the identification, made by tradi-tional theology, of the Reign of God with the church? Did Vatican II adopt this

---

1. *AAS* (1943): 199.
2. Examples can be given almost at random. Among others, see Yves de Montcheuil, *Aspects de l'Eglise* (Paris: Cerf, 1949), 29–30; Lucien Cerfaux, "L'Eglise et le Règne de Dieu d'après Saint Paul," in *Recueil Lucien Cerfaux*, vol. 2 (Gembloux: Duculot, 1954), 386.
3. Timotheus Zapelena, *De Ecclesia Christi (Pars apologetica)* (Rome: Pontificia Università Gregoriana, 1955), 41.
4. Cf. Francis A. Sullivan, "The Significance of the Vatican II Declaration That the Church of Christ 'Subsists in' the Roman Catholic Church," in *Vatican II: Assessment and Perspectives*, ed. René Latourelle, vol. 2 (New York and Mahwah, N.J.: Paulist Press, 1989), 272–87.

position, or did it, on account of a renewed eschatology, somewhat distance itself from it? Various distinctions must be made.

Recent theology has rediscovered the Reign of God as an eschatological reality. Consequently, it has now become essential to distinguish between the Reign of God in its eschatological fullness and the Reign of God as it is present in history, that is, between the "already" and the "not-yet." God has instituted his Kingdom in the world and in history through Jesus Christ; but it must still keep developing until it reaches the eschatological fullness at the end of time. Thus, while Israel's eschatological expectation was entirely turned toward a definite but indeterminate future, in Christian faith this expectation follows a twofold rhythm: the "already" of the Reign of God in history and the "not-yet" of its fulfillment at the end of time.[5] Vatican II of course adopted this by now indispensable distinction. In dealing with the institution of the Reign of God in history, the constitution *Lumen Gentium* specifies that this Reign is advancing toward its fulfillment at the end of time (*Lumen Gentium* §5; cf. §9). However, there remains the question of whether the council identified the Reign of God in history with the church.

After examining the council documents,[6] I thought it could be concluded that the constitution *Lumen Gentium* still retains the identification between the two, as was commonly maintained before the council. This seems clear from passages such as those where the constitution, speaking of the church, declares that it is "on earth, the seed and beginning of that kingdom" (*huius Regni in terris germen et initium constituit*) (*Lumen Gentium* §5), and likewise that the church is the Reign of Christ "already present in mystery" (*Ecclesia, seu Regnum Christi iam praesens in mysterio*) (*Lumen Gentium* §3). If this presence is qualified as "mysterious," it is so insofar as the Reign — or the church identified with it — while already present in the world, must yet grow until it reaches its eschatological fullness.

Furthermore, after examining the postconciliar church documents — including those of the "International Theological Commission" and the *Catechism of the Catholic Church* — I have likewise thought that it could be concluded that the first document of the central magisterium to clearly affirm a distinction between church and Reign of God already present in the world is John Paul II's encyclical *Redemptoris Missio* (1990).[7] The pope states that "The Kingdom aims at transforming human relationships; it grows gradually, as people slowly learn to love, forgive and serve one another" (*Redemptoris Missio* §15). "The Kingdom's nature, therefore, is one of communion among all human beings — with one another and with God." He explains: "the Kingdom is the concern of everyone: individuals, society, and the world. Working for the Kingdom means acknowledging and promoting God's activity, which is present in human history and transforms it. Building the Kingdom means working for liberation from evil in all its forms. In

5. Oscar Cullmann, *Christ and Time: The Christian Concept of Time and History* (London: SCM Press, 1952).

6. Jacques Dupuis, *Toward a Christian Theology of Religious Pluralism* (Maryknoll, N.Y.: Orbis Books, 1997), 334–36.

7. Ibid., 336–40.

a word, the Kingdom of God is the manifestation and the realization of God's plan of salvation in all its fullness" (ibid.). The pope further explains — we will return to this further on — that the church is "effectively... at the service of the Kingdom." It plays this role, among others, by spreading throughout the world "the 'Gospel values' which are an expression of the Kingdom and help people to accept God's plan" (*Redemptoris Missio* §20). But the encyclical then adds:

> It is true that the inchoate reality of the Kingdom can also be found beyond the confines of the Church among peoples everywhere, to the extent that they live "Gospel values" and are open to the working of the Spirit who breathes when and where he wills (cf. Jn 3:8). But it must immediately be added that this temporal dimension of the Kingdom remains incomplete unless it is related to the kingdom of Christ present in the Church and straining towards eschatological fullness. (*Redemptoris Missio* §20)

This is tantamount to saying that while the Kingdom is present in a special way in the church, as will be explained further ahead, it extends beyond the limits of the church, and the adherents of other religious traditions can belong to it, provided they live its values and help to spread it in the world.[8] This text is decisive for our present concern. It contains an explicit recognition that the Reign of God in its historical reality extends beyond the church to the whole of humankind, that it is present where gospel values are at work and are lived, and where people are open to the action of the Spirit. The text also affirms that the Kingdom in its historical dimension remains oriented toward its eschatological fullness, and that the church is in the world at the service of the Reign throughout history. Thus, a distinction is made, on the one hand, between the Reign in history and its eschatological dimension and, on the other hand, between the Reign and the church.

The recognition that the Reign of God in history is not restricted to the dimensions of the church but extends beyond them to the world is not without bearing and importance for a Christian theology of religions. Vatican II recognized the presence and action of the Spirit in the world and among members of other religious traditions. It also spoke about the "seeds of the Word" among the nations. As regards the Reign of God, while distinguishing between the historical and eschatological aspects, it continued to identify the Reign in history with the church. The encyclical letter *Redemptoris Missio* is the first document of the Roman magisterium to distinguish clearly, while keeping them united, between the church and the Reign of God in their pilgrimage through history: the Reign present in the world is a reality which is broader than the church; it extends

---

8. A passage with very similar content is found in the document "Dialogue and Proclamation" (1991), which reads: "... the inchoate reality of the Kingdom can be found also beyond the confines of the church, for example in the hearts of the followers of other religious traditions, insofar as they live evangelical values and are open to the action of the Spirit. It must be remembered, nevertheless, that this is indeed an inchoate reality, which needs to find completion through being related to the Kingdom of Christ already present in the church, yet realized fully only in the world to come" (§35). Text in Pontifical Council for Interreligious Dialogue, *Bulletin* n. 77; 26, no. 2 (1991): 225.

beyond its boundaries and includes — even if modalities may differ — not only the members of the church but also the "others."

What the recent encyclical on the church's missionary mandate has now recognized — with great caution and not without reservations — had already appeared in other expressions of the church's magisterium, where it was presented simply as a fact to be affirmed without hesitation. By way of example, a document of the Federation of Asian Bishops' Conferences (FABC), dated November 1985, may be cited. It contains the following passage:

> The Reign of God is the very reason for the being of the Church. The Church exists in and for the Kingdom. The Kingdom, God's gift and initiative, is already begun and is constantly being realized, and made present through the Spirit. Where God is accepted, where the Gospel values are lived, where the human being is respected . . . there is the Kingdom. It is far wider than the Church's boundaries. This already present reality is oriented towards the final manifestation and full perfection of the Reign of God. (§II, 1)[9]

The universality of the Reign of God and its presence, wherever the gospel values, i.e., the values of the Reign, are lived, has been expressed in an even livelier and more concrete manner in the final conclusions of a theological consultation, titled "Evangelization in Asia," organized by the Office for Evangelization of the Federation of Asian Bishops' Conferences (FABC), held in Hua Hin, Thailand, in 1991. The text reads:

> The Kingdom of God is therefore universally present and at work. Wherever men and women open themselves to the transcendent Divine Mystery which impinges upon them, and go out of themselves in love and service of fellow humans, there the Reign of God is at work . . . "Where God is accepted, where the Gospel values are lived, where the human being is respected . . . there is the Kingdom." In all such cases people respond to God's offer of grace through Christ in the Spirit and enter into the Kingdom through an act of faith . . .
>
> This goes to show that the Reign of God is a universal reality, extending far beyond the boundaries of the Church. It is the reality of salvation in Jesus Christ, in which Christians and others share together; it is the fun-

---

9. Final declaration of the Second Institute of Bishops for interreligious affairs, on the theology of dialogue (Pattaya, Thailand, November 17–22, 1985), in *For all the Peoples of Asia: Federation of Asian Bishops' Conferences Documents from 1970 to 1991*, ed. G. Rosales and C. G. Arevalo (Maryknoll, N.Y.: Orbis Books, 1992), quote from p. 252. The text may be compared with another one published by the Theological Advisory Commission (TAC) of the FABC. The "Theses on Interreligious Dialogue" (1987) declared, "The focus of the Church's mission of evangelization is building up the Kingdom of God and building up the Church to be at the service of the Kingdom. The Kingdom is therefore wider than the Church. The Church is the sacrament of the Kingdom, visibilizing it, ordained to it, promoting it, but not equating itself with it" (§6.3). The text is found in *FABC Papers*, no. 48 (Hong Kong: FABC, 1987), 16.

damental "mystery of unity" which unites us more deeply than differences in religious allegiance are able to keep us apart.[10]

JOINT MEMBERS AND BUILDERS
OF THE REIGN OF GOD

The universality of the Reign of God consists in the fact that Christians and the "others" share the same mystery of salvation in Jesus Christ, even if the mystery reaches them in different ways. To recognize that the Reign of God in history is not confined to the boundaries of the church but extends to those of the world is relevant to a Christian theology of religions. Vatican II, we have recalled earlier, recognized the presence and action of the Spirit in the world and in the members of other religions; it likewise spoke of positive values contained in the traditions themselves. Its undeclared intention was to affirm a positive role of those traditions in the order of salvation, without explicitly declaring them to be "means" or "ways" of salvation.

It has been pointed out that the "others" have access to the Kingdom of God in history through obedience in faith and conversion to the God of the Kingdom. It has also been said that the Reign is present in the world wherever the "values of the Reign" are lived and promoted. According to the encyclical letter *Redemptoris Missio,* the inchoate reality of the Kingdom is present in all people "to the extent that they live 'gospel values' and are open to the working of the Spirit" (§20).

Liberation theology has laid stress on the role which the "gospel values" — or "values of the Kingdom" — play in the coming of the Reign of God among people. The Kingdom of God, as Jon Sobrino has shown, was for Jesus "the truly ultimate objective," which gave meaning to his life, his action, and his fate. Now this Ultimate Reality, to which all else is subordinated, is at work and comes close to human beings wherever, following Jesus himself, they share the values of the Kingdom — love and justice.[11]

The theology of religions, for its part, must show how, through opening themselves up to the action of the Spirit, the "others" share in the reality of the Reign of God in the world and in history. For this purpose a Kingdom-centered model will be adopted. This does not mean — as was observed above following the encyclical *Redemptoris Missio* (§§17–18) — that the Christocentric perspective can be set aside. In fact, one cannot separate the Reign of God in history from the Jesus of history, in whom it was instituted by God, nor from Christ, whose present kingship is its expression. Through sharing in the reality of salvation which the Reign of God is, the "others" are by this very fact subject to the saving action of God in Jesus Christ, in whom the Reign of God has been established. Far from being mutually exclusive, the Kingdom-centered and Christocentric perspectives are necessarily interconnected.

---

10. Text in *FABC Papers,* no. 64 (Hong Kong: FABC, 1992), 31.

11. Jon Sobrino, *Jesus in Latin America* (Maryknoll, N.Y.: Orbis Books, 1987); idem, *Jesus the Liberator: A Historical-Theological Reading of Jesus of Nazareth* (Maryknoll, N.Y.: Orbis Books, 1993).

The Reign of God to which the believers of other religious traditions belong in history is then indeed the Kingdom inaugurated by God in Jesus Christ. It is that Kingdom which God, in raising Jesus from the dead, has put into his hands; under the kingship of Christ, God has destined it to grow toward its final plenitude. While believers of other religious faiths perceive God's call through their own traditions and respond to it in the sincere practice of these traditions, they become in all truth — even without being formally conscious of it — active members of the Kingdom. In the final analysis, then, a theology of religions following the Kingdom-centered model cannot bypass or avoid the Christocentric perspective.

Through sharing in the mystery of salvation, the followers of other religious traditions are thus members of the Kingdom of God already present as a historic reality. Does it thereby follow that the religious traditions themselves contribute to the construction of the Reign of God in the world? To see that this is so, it must be recalled — as has been said earlier — that the personal religious life of the followers of other traditions cannot in fact be separated from the religious tradition to which they belong and through which they give it concrete expression. If, as must be affirmed, their response to the divine invitation takes form in, and is upheld by, objective elements which are part of these religious traditions, such as their sacred scriptures and their "sacramental" practices, then it must also be admitted that these traditions themselves contain "supernatural, grace-filled elements"[12] for the benefit of the followers of these traditions. It is in responding to these elements of grace that they find salvation and become members of the Reign of God in history. It follows that the religious traditions contribute, in a mysterious way, to the building up of the Reign of God among their followers and in the world. They exercise, for their own members, a certain mediation of the Kingdom — doubtless different from that which is operative in the church — even if it is difficult to define this mediation with theological precision.

This explains how Christians and "others" are called to build together the Reign of God in the world down the ages. They can and must build together this Reign, in which they already share, through conversion to God and the promotion of gospel values, until it achieves, beyond history, its eschatological fullness (cf. *Gaudium et Spes* §39).

Building the Reign together extends, moreover, to the different dimensions of the Reign of God, which can be called "horizontal" and "vertical." Christians and others build together the Reign of God whenever they commit themselves by common accord to the cause of human rights, and whenever they work for the integral liberation of each and every human person, but especially of the poor and the oppressed. They also build the Reign of God by promoting religious and spiritual values. In the building of the Kingdom the two dimensions, human and religious, are inseparable. Indeed, the former is the sign of the latter.

---

12. Karl Rahner, "Christianity and the Non-Christian Religions," in *Theological Investigations*, 21 vols. (London: Darton, Longman & Todd, 1961–88), 5:121, 130.

"OUTSIDE THE CHURCH NO SALVATION"?

What then must be said about the age-old adage, "Outside the church there is no salvation," which obviously assumed the identification between the Reign of God and the church? Without intending to reconstruct the genesis of the adage here, it will suffice to recall in a few words what I have presented at length elsewhere.[13] The adage has its origin in some of the fourth- and fifth-century church fathers, particularly Cyprian of Carthage and Fulgentius of Ruspe. Later it was incorporated into official church documents, especially in Lateran Council IV (1215) (Denzinger 802), in the Bull *Unam Sanctam* of Boniface VIII (1302) (Denzinger 870, 872, 875), and in the Decree on the Copts of the Council of Florence (1442) (Denzinger 1351). This last document states that the church "firmly believes, professes and preaches that 'no one remaining outside the Catholic Church, not only pagans' [citing Fulgentius of Ruspe], but also Jews, heretics and schismatics, can become partakers of eternal life; but they will go 'to the eternal fire prepared for the devil and his angels' (Mt 25:41), unless before the end of their life they are joined [*aggregati*] to it . . . " (Denzinger 1351). I have explained how the adage was understood over the centuries and how it must be interpreted today.[14] That does not have to be entirely repeated here.

However, it is important to remember that originally the adage referred explicitly solely to heretics and schismatics, to those therefore who had culpably separated themselves from the church — which was compared to the ark of Noah in the time of the flood — and for whom there no longer was a way of salvation. Only gradually was the adage extended to include not only the case of Jews but also "pagans" who were indeed thought to be at fault for not having become Christians. Such a position, which can only seem strange today, was based on the persuasion running through the entire middle ages that the gospel had been "proclaimed" everywhere in the world (known to them); that belief continued untroubled until the "discovery" of the "new world" in 1492. With the discovery of the Americas, theologians began to develop various theories about "implicit" faith, which in their view would now suffice for the salvation of those who had not come in contact with the gospel. Such theory got under way in the decree on justification of the Council of Trent, with the doctrine of "baptism *in voto*" (Denzinger 1524), and later was taken up and further explained by Pius XII in the 1949 letter of the Holy Office (Denzinger 3866–72) mentioned earlier, in chapter 3.

It has become clear today that the traditional adage, even though it was called a "dogma" of the church by Pius XII, can no longer be taken in the literal sense. Indeed, as Yves Congar explains, a correct interpretation of it requires such lengthy explanations that it seems preferable to forget it. He writes: "There is no longer a question of applying the formula to any concrete person . . . [The axiom] is no

---

13. Dupuis, *Toward a Christian Theology of Religious Pluralism*, 86–99; cf. also Francis A. Sullivan, *Salvation outside the Church?* (New York and Mahwah, N.J.: Paulist Press, 1992).

14. Dupuis, *Toward a Christian Theology of Religious Pluralism*, 99–102.

longer regarded as answering the question '*Who* will be saved?,' but . . . the question: '*What* is it that is commissioned to discharge the mystery of salvation?' "[15] The church is the institution willed by God to discharge that ministry.

We in turn may conclude that the abiding value of the axiom consists in the affirmation made by Vatican II — which, this time, is formulated positively — according to which the church is "necessary for salvation" (*Lumen Gentium* §14). This is repeated many times in the council documents. The constitution *Lumen Gentium* states that the church is "in Christ in the nature of sacrament — a sign and instrument, that is, of intimate union with God and of the unity of the entire human race" (§1); or that it has been set up as the "universal sacrament of salvation" (§48). The constitution insists on the fact that this pilgrim church is "necessary for salvation" (*Lumen Gentium* §14), being constituted by Christ to be "the instrument for the salvation of all," or "that it may be for each and everyone the visible sacrament of this saving unity" which is in Christ (*Lumen Gentium* §9). Referring to this last passage, the encyclical *Redemptoris Missio* (§9) states that the church is taken up by Christ "as the instrument of salvation for all." The decree on ecumenism *Unitatis Redintegratio* for its part, while recognizing that "the Spirit of Christ has not refrained from using them [separated churches and Christian communities] as means of salvation," also states that the Catholic Church is constituted as "general help (*generale auxilium*) toward salvation" (*Unitatis Redintegratio* §3). The question remains, however, in what sense the universal need and instrumentality of the church in the order of salvation must be understood. We will turn to that below.

Meanwhile it seems legitimate to dissent from the opinion of the International Theological Commission in its recent document titled "Christianity and the World Religions," where it states that "Vatican Council II makes its own the sentence *Extra ecclesiam nulla salus*" (§67). That statement is made in reference to *Lumen Gentium* §14, where what is being discussed is in fact the necessity of the church for salvation; but there is a great distance from one statement to the other. It can be supposed that the commission thought that it ought to speak as it did, in continuity with the 1949 document of the Holy Office, which continued to speak of the "infallible pronouncement that teaches us that 'outside the church there is no salvation'" (Denzinger 3866–72), thus calling this pronouncement a "dogma." However it is clear that what belongs to the content of faith is the necessity of the church, as taught by Vatican II, while "explicit," public, and visible belonging to it, as members, is not necessary. Certainly, there can be no return toward the very restrictive understanding that the adage gradually took on through the centuries so as to arrive at the clear, but very narrow and negative, pronouncement of the Council of Florence, recalled earlier (Denzinger 1351).

Nor is the International Theological Commission convincing when it states

---

15. Yves Congar, *The Wide World My Parish: Salvation and Its Problems* (London: Darton, Longman & Todd, 1961), 98, cf. 112; cf. also idem, "Hors de l'Eglise pas de salut," in *Sainte Eglise: Etudes et approches ecclésiologiques* (Paris: Cerf, 1963), 417–32; Josef Ratzinger, *Das Neue Volk Gottes* (Düsseldorf: Patmos, 1970), 339–61.

that where Vatican II takes up the adage, "it explicitly directs itself to Catholics and limits its validity to those who know the necessity of the church for salvation" (§67). That would mean that the commission is taking the adage in the original meaning given to it by the ancient tradition, according to which it was addressed to heretics and schismatics, not to Jews and "pagans," and thus it has a "parenetic" character, namely to dissuade those members of the church who are tempted to leave it. However, it is not clear how it can be affirmed as a doctrine of faith that a Catholic who, after having heard and learned the teaching of the church according to which the church is necessary for salvation, is converted to another religious tradition — assuming that his or her conversion is based on the sincere following of his or her own conscience, albeit erroneous — no longer has a possibility of salvation. It is God who judges conscience, not we. Could not the International Theological Commission have been content to speak, as the council had done, of the necessity of the church for salvation, without appealing to the traditional adage that by now has become very difficult to comprehend? It does not seem that fidelity to the doctrine of Pius XII required making explicit reference to the adage as such, any more than the council had thought it so. Indeed, the Theological Commission has followed the example of the council in the care with which it speaks — as we will see later — of an "ordering" toward the church of those who are not members of it, rather than of them being "members *in voto*" (§68). Would it not have been well advised to have the same discretion toward the adage that has become controversial?

There is no escaping the fact that John Paul II has retained the use of the traditional axiom; but it must be noted that he has used it with various nuances, and has even proposed a new version, stating that "*without* the church there is no salvation." This happened especially in the public audience on May 31, 1995. Here is the main passage on the matter:

> And as Christ effects salvation through his mystical Body, which is the church, the way of salvation is essentially linked to the Church. The adage *extra ecclesiam nulla salus* — "outside the church there is no salvation" — belongs to the Christian tradition... The adage means that for those who know that the Church which has been founded by God through Jesus Christ is necessary, there is the obligation to enter and persevere in it in order to attain salvation (cf. *Lumen Gentium* §14)... In order to operate, saving grace requires an adhesion, a cooperation, a "yes" to God's self-gift, and such adhesion is, at least implicitly, oriented toward Christ and the church. Hence, it is also possible to say *sine ecclesia nulla salus* — "*without* the church there is no salvation*": adhesion to the church, mystical body of Christ, no matter how implicit and indeed mysterious, constitutes an essential condition for salvation. It [the Church] therefore exercises an *implicit* mediation also vis-à-vis those who are unaware of the gospel.[16]

---

16. *Osservatore Romano*, June 1, 1995, 4.

Various nuances are apparent here: the adage is not called a dogma of faith but it is said to be part of Christian tradition; moreover the new version of the adage fits more discreetly with the affirmation of the need of the church for salvation, made in *Lumen Gentium* §14.

Moreover, a number of recent authors have pointed out that the traditional adage represented a very "ecclesiocentric" concept of the church as sole means of salvation. The evolution of theological thinking today requires that correctives be placed on the rigoristic interpretation of the adage. In this regard, Jean Rigal has recently written:

> Not only does Vatican II no longer cite this formula, but it distances itself from the ecclesiocentrism of the past. While it declares that the Church is necessary for salvation (*Lumen Gentium* §14), the council, leaving aside the defensive positions of the past, strives to bring out the positive conditions of the acceptance of salvation by people of good faith and good will (cf. *Lumen Gentium* §16). The terms of "belonging" to the Church have been put aside; the council is content to say that "Those who have not yet received the Gospel are ordained, in various ways, to the people of God" (*Lumen Gentium* §16). This is why some are astonished by the fact that the International Theological Commission...has thought to do well in declaring — twenty years after the council — that "belonging to the Reign cannot but constitute a belonging — at least implicitly — to the Church."[17] John Paul II seems to display more prudence and more flexibility, when he is content to speak of "a mysterious relationship with the Church" (*Redemptoris Missio* §10).[18]

THE CHURCH AND THE RELIGIONS
IN THE REIGN OF GOD

NECESSITY OF THE CHURCH

The necessity of the church in the order of salvation is clearly affirmed by Vatican II, as noted above. The terms "universal sacrament," "sign and instrument," "general help," and "necessary" are in themselves sufficiently clear; the encyclical *Redemptoris Missio* recalls them when it speaks of the "specific and necessary role" of the church in relation to the Reign of God (§18). However, the council does not explain the exact nature of the universal necessity of the church; as for the encyclical, it seems somewhat embarrassed about determining the church's "specific and necessary role." Hence, some questions arise. Has the universality of the church in the order of salvation the same meaning, the same force, as the Christian tradition

---

17. There are questions about the document published by the International Theological Commission in view of the extraordinary synod on the occasion of the twentieth anniversary of the closing of Vatican II. See Commission Théologique Internationale, *L'unique Eglise du Christ* (Paris: Centurion, 1985), 7.

18. Jean Rigal, *L'Eglise en chantier* (Paris: Cerf, 1995), 49.

attributes to Jesus Christ, the universal Savior? Is the necessity of the church for salvation of the same order? How can we understand that the church is not only a sign but also a means, a universal instrument of salvation, that it is assumed by Christ "as instrument of salvation for all" (*Redemptoris Mission* §9)? Must a universal "mediation" be assigned to it — though one necessarily "participated" in relation to that of Jesus Christ, which is unique (1 Tim 2:5), a mediation, that is, endowed with "meaning and value *only* from Christ's own mediation" (*Redemptoris Missio* §5)? What is understood when one speaks, as the pope has done, of "*implicit* mediation . . . vis-à-vis those who are unaware of the gospel"?

Two extreme positions must be avoided here. The first would place the necessity and universality of the church on the very same level as that of Jesus Christ. This position would take us back to an excessive interpretation of the ancient axiom *Extra ecclesiam nulla salus*. The other would minimize the necessity and universality of the church by simply reducing its function and operation to the salvation of its own members. This would amount to introducing two parallel ways of salvation without any mutual relationship — both derived from the unique mediation of Jesus Christ, yet one operative for the members of the church while the other comes into play for people who are saved in Jesus Christ outside of it. Is there a middle way between these two equally unsustainable extreme positions? This difficult point remains open to theological discussion, and there is no common opinion among theologians. Two questions need to be distinguished: (1) that of "belonging" to the church or of being "oriented" toward it; and (2) that of the church's universal "mediation" vis-à-vis people living outside of it.

BELONGING TO, OR ORIENTATION TOWARD, THE CHURCH?

We have recalled that a traditional, preconciliar ecclesiology identified the Reign of God, already present in history, with the church. This theology considered the people saved by Christ outside the church as belonging to it in some way. Distinctions were made: between actual members (*reapse*) and members in desire (*voto*); between belonging visibly and invisibly, explicitly and implicitly, to the soul and to the body of the church; and so forth. The Council of Trent employed this kind of distinction when it spoke of baptism *in voto* of people saved outside the church (Denzinger 1524). It was further explained that the desire necessary for salvation outside the church was not the "explicit" desire of catechumens but the "implicit" desire of those who, while finding themselves outside the church, had the dispositions required for receiving salvation.

Vatican II, as we have noted, seems to have maintained the identification between the Reign of God present in history and the church. It did not, however, repeat the existing terminology about being members. On the contrary, it has established some precise distinctions concerning the relation to the church of persons finding themselves in different situations. The term "members" is not used everywhere; that of "*votum*" is applied only to catechumens (*Lumen Gentium* §14). In general terms, it is said that "all are called to this Catholic unity of the people of God ... and in different ways belong to it or are ordained to it: the Catholic faithful, others who believe in Christ, and finally all humankind, called by God's grace to salvation" (*Lumen Gentium* §13). This is explained and specified in detail: Catholics are fully incorporated (*plene incorporantur*) (*Lumen Gentium* §14) into the church; catechumens are united (*coniunguntur*) to the church by virtue of their desire (*voto*) to join it (*Lumen Gentium* §14); the church is "joined" (*coniuncta*) for many reasons to non-Catholic Christians (*Lumen Gentium* §15), who are in turn incorporated (*incorporantur*) into Christ. Finally, "those who have not yet received the gospel are ordained (*ordinantur*), in various ways, to the People of God" (*Lumen Gentium* §16). This "orientation" toward the church is realized under different forms, but in no case is mention made of a desire, explicit or implicit, of belonging.[19]

The expression *ordinantur* is, in fact, taken from the encyclical *Mystici Corporis* (1943). The encyclical affirmed that all those who do not belong to the Catholic Church are "oriented toward [it] by a certain unconscious desire and wish" (*inscio quodam desiderio ac voto ad mysticum Redemptoris Corpus ordinari*) (Denzinger 3821), while only Catholics are members of it actually (*reapse*). Karl Rahner notes that most likely this 1943 formulation has been intentionally substituted for Bellarmine's "being in the church in desire" (*voto esse in Ecclesia*): "The encyclical did everything in its power to avoid giving the impression that the yearning for membership is already a 'being-in-the-church' or a proper actual membership."[20]

Be that as it may, it is certain that for persons outside the church Vatican II intentionally used the term of orientation (*ordinantur*) to the church, while leaving out the language of a membership in desire or wish. According to the council, the members of the other religious traditions can be saved through Jesus Christ without belonging to the church in any manner; they are, however, "oriented" toward it, inasmuch as in it is found the fullness of the means of salvation. The encyclical *Redemptoris Missio* would seem to continue and extend this view when it says of those who do not have explicit faith in Jesus Christ and are not members of the church: "For such people, salvation in Christ is accessible in virtue of a grace which, while having a mysterious relationship to the church, does not make them formally part of the church but enlightens them in a way which is accommodated to their spiritual and material situation" (§10).

In what does this "orientation" consist? We have already said that they are oriented toward the church inasmuch as the risen Lord has entrusted to it "the fullness of the means of salvation," which fullness is not available to them outside it (*Redemptoris Missio* §18). But it must still be asked what the church is doing for their salvation in Jesus Christ; that is, what is the "specific and necessary role" (*Redemptoris Missio* §18) that it is playing for them as well as the "implicit mediation" that the pope speaks about. The documents of the magisterium do not

---

19. Giaccomo Canobbio, *Chiesa perché: Salvezza dell 'umanità e mediazione ecclesiale* (Cinisello Balsamo: San Paolo, 1994), 142–47.

20. Karl Rahner, "Membership in the Church according to the Teaching of Pius XII's Encyclical 'Mystici Corporis,'" in *Theological Investigations*, 2:54.

seem to be entirely clear on this matter; indeed they observe a certain discretion that is intentional. *Redemptoris Missio* is content to speak about such people of a "mysterious relationship with the church" (§10) and of a "specific and necessary role" of the church (§18) which, however, do not prevent a certain "participated" mediation of their own religious tradition which derives its "meaning and value *only* from Christ's own mediation" (*Redemptoris Missio* §5).

The International Theological Commission, for its part, in the document already considered, states that while the possibility that the religious traditions "exercise as such a certain salvific function" toward their members is not a priori excluded (§84), and thus they "can ... be, in the terms indicated, means helping the salvation of their followers," yet they "cannot be compared to the function that the Church realizes for the salvation of Christians and of those who are not" (§86). Unfortunately, no further explanation is given about what the church might be doing for them, "more" than the other religious traditions can do for their members; or, in the terms of the text cited from the pope, about the church's "implicit mediation" on their behalf. The positive influence that the sacred books and traditions of the other religions in the religious life of their members and in helping them to give a positive response to the divine offer of grace may not be underestimated a priori. Nor must the superiority of the "function that the Church realizes" for the salvation of those who are not its members be claimed a priori, without explaining in what that function consists.

The encyclical *Redemptoris Missio* speaks of a "mysterious relationship to the church" (§10) of persons saved in Jesus Christ outside of it, as well as of a "specific and necessary" role of the church (§18) in the order of salvation for all persons. It must certainly be held that the church is "indissolubly united" to Christ as his Body, in a "singular and unique relationship" from which flows its "specific and necessary role" (§18) for all. In a more recent public audience, Pope John Paul II explained this relationship of the role of the church to that of Christ toward the members of other religious traditions. He said:

> There cannot be ... admitted other *autonomous* sources or ways of salvation, alongside Christ. Therefore, in the great religions, which the church views with respect and admiration in the line indicated by Vatican II, Christians recognize the presence of saving elements, which however work in dependence on the influence of the grace of Christ. Thus such religions, by virtue of the mysterious action of the Holy Spirit, who "blows where he wills" (cf. Jn 3:8), can contribute to helping human beings on the road to eternal happiness, but this role is itself a fruit of Christ's redemptive activity. Even in relationship to the religions therefore Christ the Savior is mysteriously at work and in this work *he unites to himself the church,* constituted "as sacrament ... of intimate union with God and of the unity of the entire human race."[21]

---

21. *Osservatore Romano*, February 5, 1998, 4 (emphasis added).

It must thus be said that the church is universally united to Christ in the work of salvation. This is true for all people regardless of where they find themselves in relation to the church. There nevertheless remains the fact that the expressions used to express the specific role of the church on behalf of the "others" are deliberately so imprecise that further questions are raised: how must the "mysterious relationship" with the church of the members of other religious traditions on the one side and the "specific and necessary" role of the church toward them on the other be conceived? This is the question whether or not there exists a "universal mediation" of the church; that is, a true and proper mediation by it vis-à-vis the adherents of other religions for salvation. There is no denying an "implicit mediation" — albeit difficult to conceive — of the church; the question is rather in what may consist an "explicit mediation" by it on their behalf. Can we, must we, speak of a universal "mediation" of the church in the order of salvation, even while — as is necessary — considering it subordinated to the sole mediation of Jesus Christ, and "participated" in it?

Explicit universal mediation?

It is, therefore, necessary to ask in what consists the "mediation" of the church, understood in the strict theological sense. The church exercises its salvific mediation primarily by announcing the word and through the sacramental economy, at the center of which is the eucharistic celebration ("the table of the word and of the bread"); cf. *Apostolicam Actuositatem* §6: "chiefly (*principaliter*) with the mystery of the word and the sacraments." The proclamation of the word and the celebration of the sacraments constitute a true mediation of the action of Jesus Christ in the ecclesial community. But, it must be added, those factors do not — by definition — reach out to the members of the other religious traditions who receive salvation in Jesus Christ. It is true, indeed, that in its eucharistic celebration the church fulfills all the ancient sacrifices. However, the *grace* of the Eucharist which it celebrates is not the salvation of people outside of it but the unity in the Spirit of its own members — as the eucharistic liturgy clearly indicates: "May all of us who share in the body and blood of Christ be brought together in unity by the Holy Spirit" (*epiclesis,* that is, invocation of the Holy Spirit, in the Eucharistic Prayer Two of the Roman liturgy); and likewise: "Grant that we, who are nourished by his body and blood, may be filled with his Holy Spirit, and become one body, one spirit in Christ" (*epiclesis* of Eucharistic Prayer Three). Is it possible, then, to speak in proper terms of a mediation of grace on the part of the church toward those who are not its members? Efforts have been made to respond positively to this question, by pointing to the intercession and prayers of the church and to the witness, the life, and the merits of its members, for the salvation of all.[22]

The church unquestionably intercedes and prays for the salvation of all, especially in the eucharistic celebration: "Lord, may this sacrifice, which has made

---

22. Cf. among others Sullivan, *Salvation outside the Church?*

our peace with you, advance the salvation of all the world" (prayer of intercession of Eucharistic Prayer Three). Such intercession, insofar as the church is united to Christ as his body, is certainly ecclesial missionary action. Yet it must be asked whether this intercession can be considered as "mediation" in the proper theological sense. The universal mediation of Christ in the order of salvation concretely refers to the fact that his risen humanity is the channel, the instrumental efficient cause, of grace for all people. Karl Rahner has stressed the perduring role of mediation of the humanity of Jesus Christ, even in the beatific vision.[23] As for the church, it exercises its derived participated mediation in the strict sense through the proclamation of the word and the sacramental economy celebrated in and by the church communities. To borrow the terminology of scholastic theology, this entails an instrumental efficient causality in the strict sense. Things are different where the church's intercession is concerned; for the causality at work here seems to be of the moral rather than the efficient order. The church prays and intercedes with God for all people that the grace of salvation in Jesus Christ may be granted to them. The church intercedes and God saves. In this case, it would not seem legitimate to speak of "mediation" in the strict, theological sense. The causality involved is not of the order of efficiency but of the moral order and of finality.

Some recent theologians did not fail to note this. Among these, Yves Congar may be mentioned in the first place. He wrote:

> Every Catholic must admit and admits that there have existed and exist gifts of light and grace working for salvation outside the visible boundaries of the Church. We do not even deem it necessary to hold, as is nonetheless commonly done, that these graces are received *through* the Church; it is enough that they be received in view of the Church and that they orient people toward the Church.[24]

As stated here, the relationship between the church and nonmembers is not of the order of efficiency but of finality: nonmembers are oriented toward (*ordinantur*) the church. Congar concludes that the axiom *Extra ecclesiam nulla salus* should be abandoned, for it can neither be taken in the literal sense nor be understood correctly without long explanations. This does not mean that it is altogether meaningless, for it contains, in effect, a biblical truth, namely that the church is the institution commissioned by God to lead people to God's salvation in Jesus Christ: "The Catholic Church remains the only institution (*sacramentum*) divinely instituted and commissioned for salvation, and whatever grace exists in the world is referred to it in finality, if not in efficiency."[25] If the formula is to be preserved, it must be given an "entirely positive" meaning: "There is, therefore, in the world *one* reality which represents the gift which God has destined for the world and

---

23. Karl Rahner, "The Eternal Significance of the Humanity of Christ for Our Relation to God," in *Theological Investigations*, 3:35–46.

24. Yves Congar, "L'Eglise, sacrement universel du salut," *Eglise Vivante* 17 (1965): 351; also idem, *This Church That I Love* (Denville, N.J.: Dimension Books, 1969).

25. Cf. Yves Congar, *Sainte Eglise: Etudes et approches ecclésiologiques*, 431–32.

which he has made to save it, that is, to make it reach to life and communion with God: this is Jesus Christ . . . dead and risen for us, Master of truth, who has entrusted to the church, his Spouse and his Body, the deposit of the word and the sacraments that save."[26]

The traditional axiom thus takes on a positive meaning. The council affirms the necessity of the church for salvation (*Lumen Gentium* §14), as the "universal sacrament of salvation" (*Lumen Gentium* §48). This necessity does not, however, imply a universal mediation in the strict sense, applicable to every person who is saved in Jesus Christ. On the contrary, it leaves room for "substitutive mediations" (*des médiations de suppléance*),[27] among which will be found the religious traditions to which the "others" belong. One may accordingly infer that the causality of the church in relation to the "others" is of the order not of efficiency but of finality. However, according to the recent magisterium, the church remains the "ordinary way" for people's salvation (*Evangelii Nuntiandi* §80) inasmuch as it possesses the "ordinary means" of salvation (ibid.) or the "fullness of the means of salvation" (*Redemptoris Missio* §55), even though the members of the other religious traditions can be saved in Jesus Christ "in a way known to God" (*Ad Gentes* §7; cf. *Gaudium et Spes* §22). Saving grace must be called "Christic": it may be called "ecclesial" (*gratia ecclesialis*) insofar as it is tending toward the mystery of the church, in virtue of the orientation toward it (*ordinati*) (*Lumen Gentium* §16) of people saved in Christ outside of it. The "universal instrumentality" of the church in the order of salvation mentioned in *Lumen Gentium* §9 and *Redemptoris* §9 is understood, in the case of nonmembers, as expectation and hope, based on their orientation to it.

The thought of Karl Rahner is similar.[28] Rahner's "anonymous Christianity" — it is important to note it — points to a relationship to Jesus Christ in the order of grace and salvation, not to a relationship directly to the church. In principle, the entire human family is already saved in Jesus Christ; accordingly, the whole of humanity already constitutes the "people of God." People saved in Jesus Christ outside the church are objectively oriented toward it (*ordinati*) but without being members of the church. It is true that the church is in a privileged way "the locus of the sending of the Spirit," in which the grace of salvation consists.[29] The Spirit is not, however, so bound to the church, to its ministry and institutions, that its presence and work of salvation are impaired outside of it. What Cardinal Manning wrote in the nineteenth century should be kept in mind: "It is true to say with St. Irenaeus, *Ubi ecclesia ibi Spiritus* — Where the church is, there is the Spirit — but it would not be true to say: Where the church is not, neither is the Spirit. The works of the Holy Spirit have always pervaded the entire history of human beings from the beginning, and they are still fully at

26. Congar, *Vaste monde ma paroisse* (Paris: Témoignage chrétien, 1959), 131–32.
27. Dupuis, *Toward a Christian Theology of Religious Pluralism*, 133–47, cf. 144.
28. Rahner, "Membership in the Church."
29. Karl Rahner, "Die Kirche als Ort der Geistsendung," *Geist und Leben* 29 (1956): 94–98.

work among those who are outside the Church."[30] The church cannot be said to be the "only place" where the Holy Spirit is operating. Grace has no "station," because it works everywhere. Salvation outside the church through the Spirit implies, nevertheless, an orientation, a reference, to the church which, if it comes to full effect, emerges as belonging to the church through membership.

As privileged locus of the Spirit, the church must, therefore, be understood as the point toward which the grace obtained outside it is tending; that grace is destined to find its visible expression in the church. Such orientation toward the church exists wherever the Spirit is present and working. However, orientation does not imply a universal mediation of the church already operative by way of efficient causality. As we will see in the final section of this chapter, the necessity of the church is ultimately to be viewed in terms of its function as sacramental sign of the presence of God's grace among people. Divine grace is operative where the church is not present, but the church is the universal sacramental sign of the presence of divine grace in the world.

THE CHURCH, SACRAMENT OF THE KINGDOM

Vatican II defined the church as the "universal sacrament of salvation" (*Lumen Gentium* §48). Subsequently, there has developed a theology which considers the church as the "sacrament of the Reign of God." We have recalled that, while Vatican II seemed to still identify the Reign of God present in the world with the church, the encyclical *Redemptoris Missio* (§20) has been the first official document of the central magisterium to distinguish them clearly by affirming that the Reign of God is a wider reality than the church, indeed a universal reality.

Once the universality of the Reign of God is affirmed, the question of the sacramentality of the church in relation to the Reign of God is necessarily posed differently. It is no longer simply a matter of stating that the church, God's Reign in history, is the "sacrament" of its own fullness to be achieved in the eschatological future (*sacramentum futuri*). Rather it entails showing that the church is the "sacrament" in the world of the universal reality of salvation in Jesus Christ, already present and at work in history. Between the church and the Kingdom there is, according to the encyclical *Redemptoris Missio*, "a unique and special relationship which, while not excluding the action of Christ and the Spirit outside the church's visible boundaries, confers upon her a specific and necessary role" (§18). How is this role to be understood? More specifically, how can it be understood that the church is in history the sacrament of the Kingdom already present? The "sacramental theory" can be extremely helpful here. Rahner has applied it with great clarity to the relationship between the church in the world and the Reign of God in history.[31]

---

30. Quoted by Yves Congar, *I Believe in the Holy Spirit,* vol. 2 (London: G. Chapman, 1983).

31. Karl Rahner, "Church and World," *Sacramentum Mundi: An Encyclopedia of Theology* I (New York: Herder and Herder, 1968), 346–57.

The classical distinction made in sacramental theology between the *sacramentum tantum*, the *res et sacramentum*, and the *res tantum* — that is, between the sacramental sign, the first ecclesial effect of the sacrament, and the second effect of grace — which applies directly to the seven sacraments, is here applied analogously to the relationship between the historic sign of the church and the reality of grace signified and produced; or to state it more exactly, in three terms: between the sign of the church, becoming members of the church, and being members of the Reign of God. The church, in its visible aspect, is the sacrament (*sacramentum tantum*); the reality signified (*res tantum*), which it both contains and confers, is belonging to the Reign of God — that is, the sharing in the mystery of salvation in Jesus Christ; the intermediate reality, the *res et sacramentum*, is the relationship established between the members of the ecclesial community and the church, by virtue of which they participate in the reality of the Reign through their belonging to the church as its members. Nevertheless, as the sacramental theory implies, it is possible to attain to the *res tantum* without passing through the mediation of the *res et sacramentum*. This means that the "others" can attain the reality of the Kingdom of God present without belonging to the body of the church. They can be members of the Reign of God without becoming part of the church as its members. This does not mean that the church ceases to be the efficacious sign, willed by God, of the presence in the world and in history of the reality of the Reign of God. It must bear witness to it, serve its growth, and announce it.

It can thus be seen how, by considering the formulations provided by the council in a new light, the church can be understood to be the sacrament of the Kingdom in history. The council said that in the church the Reign of God is "already present in mystery" (*in mysterio*) (*Lumen Gentium* §3). According to the sacramental theory, this does not refer directly to the presence inchoate in the church of the Reign of God ordered toward its final completion. Rather, what is meant is the church as the mysteric or sacramental (*in mysterio*) presence of the reality of the Reign of God already present in the world and in history. The church is "the sacrament of the Reign already present." This means — to adopt the formulation used in the final document of the episcopal conference at Puebla (1979) — that in it "we find the visible manifestation of the project that God is silently carrying out throughout the world. The church is the place where we find the maximum concentration of the Father's activity" (§132).[32]

The presence of the church-as-sign of the Reign of God in the world bears witness, therefore, that God has established in this world his Reign in Jesus Christ. Furthermore, as efficacious sign, the church contains and effects the reality which it signifies, giving access to the Reign of God through word and sacrament. However, the necessity of the church is not of such a nature that access to the Reign of God would be possible only through being members of

32. John Eagleson and Philip Scharper, eds., *Puebla and Beyond* (Maryknoll, N.Y.: Orbis Books, 1979), 152.

it; the "others" can be part of the Reign of God and of Christ without being members of the church. The presence of the Reign of God in the church is, nevertheless, a privileged one, for it has received from Christ "the fullness of the benefits and means of salvation" (*Redemptoris Missio* §18). It is the "universal sacrament" (*Lumen Gentium* §48) of this Reign. This is why those who have access to salvation and to the Reign outside of it, though they are not incorporated into it as members, are nevertheless "oriented" (*ordinantur*) to it — as is noted in the constitution *Lumen Gentium* (§16), which does not in fact resume the earlier teaching about "members in desire." A recent author already cited makes the point clearly:

> To say that the Church is "sacrament of salvation" means that it witnesses to a reality that runs through it but that extends beyond its borders; that it has at the same time an inevitable relationship with that reality. If it is the sacrament (sign and instrument) of salvation it cannot be its origin or the only place where salvation is achieved; it is rather its humble handmaid... To say that the church is like "the [universal] sacrament of salvation" (*Lumen Gentium* §48) serves to emphasize that it cannot be sign of itself, but of that salvation that comes from God. It reveals salvation, but it does not possess it. If it is permanent, it is so in order to be able to signify the permanence of God's gift through Christ in the Spirit.[33]

That the church is sacrament of the Reign of God, universally present in history, does not necessarily mean that it carries out an activity of universal mediation, in the strict theological sense, of grace in favor of the members of other religious traditions who have entered the Reign of God by responding to God's invitation through faith, conversion, and love. That is why, in the preceding chapter, we could argue for a participated and derived "mediation" of the religious traditions for their members. While not being in any way members of the church or subject to its mediation (in the theological sense), the "others" are, nevertheless, oriented toward it; its causality on their behalf is of the order not of efficiency but of finality.

Such is the meaning of the expression *sacramentum mundi*, from which the theological encyclopedia edited by Karl Rahner draws its title. The church is the sign willed by God to signify what his grace in Jesus Christ has accomplished and continues to accomplish in the world. Schillebeeckx specifies matters: "The Church *is* not the Kingdom of God, but it bears symbolic witness to the Kingdom through its word and sacrament, and in its praxis effectively anticipates the Kingdom."[34] And Rahner explains equivalently:

> That the Church is the sacrament of the world's salvation... means this: that the Church is the concrete historical *appearance* in the dimension of history become eschatological, in the dimension of society, for the unique

---

33. Jean Rigal, *L'Eglise en chantier*, 58–59.
34. Edward Schillebeeckx, *Church: The Human Story of God* (London: SCM Press, 1990), 157.

salvation which occurs, through God's grace, across the length and breadth of humankind.[35]

In that sense one can transform the ancient controversial axiom and say: "No salvation outside the world" (*Extra mundum nulla salus*). Jerome P. Theisen sums up well this understanding of the church-sacrament when he writes:

> The Church as sacrament may mean only that the Church exists in the world as the visible sign of the saving grace that God is effecting through Christ at a distance from the visible Church. The Church mirrors, articulates, and makes intelligible the process of salvation that is being accomplished anywhere in the world... In this sense the Church as sacrament exists to show forth the riches of God's mercy in Christ. It is a universal sacrament of salvation in that it becomes a sign of God's salvific activity in Christ wherever this occurs in the world. The thrust of the sacrament model of the Church leads to an understanding of the Church as visible event and concrete manifestation of God's grace effecting salvation of people anywhere in the world.[36]

The sacrament of the Reign of God, the church is also at the service of the Reign. As has been recalled earlier, the encyclical *Redemptoris Missio* distinguishes various ways in which the church is at the service of the Reign of God. Among other ways, it states: "The church serves the Kingdom by spreading throughout the world the 'gospel values' which are an expression of the Kingdom and which help people to accept God's plan." The church also contributes to the promotion of the Reign of God "through her witness and through such activities as dialogue, human promotion, commitment to justice and peace" (§20).

In a Christocentric and regnocentric perspective which overcomes a too narrow ecclesiocentric perspective, the mission of the church will be seen in a new light. It will be kept in mind that the New Testament applies the term "mediator" to him who is "the one Mediator between God and humankind, Christ Jesus, himself human" (1 Tim 2:4–5). He is the *analogatum princeps* for any participated and derived mediation that may exist (cf. *Redemptoris Missio* §5), including that of the church. The task of the church will not be conceived in terms of some universal function of mediation, but rather as witness, service, and proclamation. The church must display to all the presence in the world of the Reign which God has inaugurated in Jesus Christ; it must serve the growth of the Reign and proclaim it. The assumption is that the church is to be entirely "decentered" from itself, to be entirely centered on Jesus Christ and the Reign of God.[37]

The church does not find in itself its own reason for being; it is not an end in itself. As Jesus was entirely oriented to the Father, who was establishing his

---

35. Karl Rahner, *The Church after the Council* (New York: Herder and Herder, 1966), 53–54.

36. Jerome P. Theisen, *The Ultimate Church and the Promise of Salvation* (Collegeville, Minn.: St. John's University Press, 1976), 134.

37. Cf. Ignacio Ellacuría, *Conversión de la Iglesia al Reino de Dios: Para anunciarlo y realizarlo en la historia* (Santander: Editorial Sal Terrae, 1982).

Reign in him, so also the church must be oriented entirely to Jesus Christ and to the Reign established by the Father in him. It must then be entirely related to Christ and to God's Reign. Since it is the "sacrament" of the Reign, it must "signify" it, making its mystery visible and tangible. However, being a sign is a difficult and dangerous position, because a sign must point toward that which it signifies and which is beyond it and surpasses it; in this instance, the church must point toward Jesus Christ and the Reign of God. It must always take care to avoid becoming turned in on itself and forgetting its signifying function. If it should do so, and to the extent that it did so, it would become "insignificant," even a "countersign." The church thus must give witness to the Reign through its own life, making it visible and tangible for human beings, reproducing in itself its values, promoting it through various endeavors, and in sum proclaiming its active presence in the world as "good news" for all people. In short, only a self-evangelized church can serve the Reign of God and announce it. Therein lies the credibility of its witness as sign and sacrament.

Nor does the church have any monopoly on the Reign of God. We have seen that the members of the other religious traditions share truly in the Reign of God present in history, and that the religious traditions can contribute to the building up of the Reign of God, not only among their followers but in the world. While the church is the "universal sacrament" of the Reign of God in the world, the other traditions too exercise a certain sacramental mediation of the Reign, different, no doubt, but no less real.

Chapter Nine

INTERRELIGIOUS DIALOGUE
IN A PLURALISTIC SOCIETY

R ELIGIOUS PLURALISM, as we have said before, is nothing new. Early Christianity from apostolic times onward had to situate its message first in relation to Judaism, from which it emerged, and then in relation to the other religions that it encountered along its way. What is actually new is the acute awareness attained by our world of the pluralism of cultures and of religious traditions, and of the right that each has to its own difference. There is no need to develop here the many reasons for this realization. They are well known, and are political and economic — and indeed human, cultural, and religious — in nature.

Our concern in this chapter is to ask what this new awareness of the surrounding religious pluralism has to tell us about Christian praxis. What attitudes toward the "others," whoever they may be — Muslims, Buddhists, Hindus, or others — does Christian faith lived in such an environment require of us? It seems clear that a new attitude on the part of the church toward the religions is linked to the recognition on its part of the positive values that can be found in them. No wonder then that there is something new in contemporary discourse on interreligious dialogue; it was not spoken of before Vatican II. We know, however, that Paul VI's encyclical *Ecclesiam Suam* published during the council (1964) helped give it a powerful impulse forward. The pope described the church as destined to extend the dialogue of salvation that God has sustained with humankind over the centuries. As we noted, he traced four concentric circles of such dialogue on the part of the church: dialogue with the whole world; dialogue with members of other religions; dialogue with other Christians; and finally, dialogue within the church itself. These four concentric circles are taken up — moving in the opposite direction — in the conclusion of Vatican II's constitution *Gaudium et Spes* (§92).

Let us note, however, that while encouraging interreligious dialogue, Paul VI did not take a position on the exact place that such dialogue might occupy in the church's mission. The reason is that the pope's own diagnosis of the value of these religions remained quite negative. Indeed, as we have noted before, in his later apostolic exhortation *Evangelii Nuntiandi* (1975), Paul VI still retained a negative evaluation of other religious traditions (§53): they represented the "natural" religiosity of human beings, whereas Christianity was the only "supernatural" religion. Consequently, the "others" were seen only as "beneficiaries" of the church's evangelizing mission, still conceived primarily in terms of the "proclamation" of the gospel and of the church's activities related to it. Paul VI, who had become the pope of dialogue with *Ecclesiam Suam*, did not mention dialogue at all in the later document.

Nor did the council make any statement to the effect that dialogue belongs to the mission of the church. Throughout the council documents, the evangelizing mission remains strictly identified with announcing or proclaiming Jesus Christ to "non-Christians" in order to invite them to "conversion" to Christianity. The council positively commends interreligious dialogue (cf. *Nostra Aetate* §2; *Gaudium et Spes* §92); but as important as dialogue might seem, it is never said to belong to the mission of the church as such. However significant and commendable it may be in terms of its relationship to evangelization, dialogue represents only a first approach to the "others," to which the preconciliar theological term of "preevangelization" could still be applied.

The foregoing may serve to show that viewing dialogue as something intrinsic to "evangelization" marks a significant qualitative change in the postconciliar theology of mission. It is part of the working out, during the post–Vatican II years, of a broad and comprehensive notion of "evangelization," of which dialogue represents — together with other elements — a constitutive dimension. The decisive step forward in official teaching took place with some documents in the 1980s and 1990s.

Before proceeding further, some clarifications of a terminological nature must once more be provided. The definitions proposed here are largely borrowed from the document "Dialogue and Proclamation" (1991), which has been cited many times. The term "evangelization" or "evangelizing mission" of the church "refers to the mission of the Church in its totality" (§8), in the various elements of which it is composed. "Dialogue," an integral part of that mission, indicates "all positive and constructive interreligious relations with individuals and communities of other faiths which are directed at mutual understanding and enrichment . . . in obedience to truth and respect for freedom" (§9). "Announcement" or "proclamation" is "the communication of the gospel message, the mystery of salvation realized by God for all in Jesus Christ by the power of the Spirit. It is an invitation . . . to entry through baptism into the community of believers which is the Church" (§10). Given these definitions, it becomes clear that "dialogue" and "mission" should not be opposed as though they were mutually in opposition, or even adequately distinct from one another, because dialogue is an integral part of the evangelizing mission to which proclamation belongs. At the same time, while dialogue is already in itself evangelization, evangelization cannot be reduced to dialogue — as will be seen below in opposition to some contemporary theological tendencies. The two elements are different in scope: as a specific element in evangelization, dialogue does not seek the "conversion" of others to Christianity but the convergence of both dialogue partners to a deeper shared conversion to God and to others; by contrast, proclamation invites others to become disciples of Christ in the Christian community.

The postconciliar documents of the magisterium in which a broad concept of the church's evangelizing mission is clearly developed so as to include in it, as constitutive and integral elements, both full human promotion and liberation on the one hand, and interreligious dialogue on the other, are the document "Dialogue and Mission" (1984), the encyclical *Redemptoris Missio* (1990), and the document "Dialogue and Proclamation" (1991). In the 1984 document of the Secretariat for Non-Christians, the church's evangelizing mission is presented as a "single, but complex and articulated reality" (§13), of which the "principal elements" are listed. They are the following: (1) witness; (2) "the concrete commitment to the service of humankind and all forms of activity for social development and for the struggle against poverty and the structures which produce it"; (3) liturgical life, prayer, and contemplation; (4) "the dialogue in which Christians meet the followers of other religious traditions in order to walk together towards truth and to work together in projects of common concern"; (5) finally, announcing [the *kerygma*] and catechesis [*didachè*]. "The totality of Christian mission embraces all these elements" (§13).[1] The significance of this text is considerable: interreligious dialogue on the part of the church is already evangelization; Christians and others are together on their way toward the truth. Part of the endeavor of a theology of religion is to render an account of such claims.

The document "Dialogue and Mission" further explains that interreligious dialogue as a specific task of evangelization — which "finds its place in the great dynamism of the Church's mission" (§30) — can itself assume various forms. There is the dialogue of life, open and accessible to all (§§29–30). There is the dialogue of a common commitment to works of justice and human liberation (§§31–32). There is intellectual dialogue in which scholars engage in an exchange about their respective religious legacies, with the aim of promoting communion and fellowship (§§33–34). Finally, on the deepest level, there is the sharing of religious experiences of prayer and contemplation, in a common search for the Absolute (§35). All these forms of dialogue are, for the Christian partner, so many ways of working for the "evangelical transformation of cultures" (§34), so many opportunities of sharing existentially with others the gospel values (§35).

The encyclical *Redemptoris Missio* says of the relationship between dialogue and proclamation:

> These two elements must maintain both their intimate connection and their distinctiveness; therefore, they should not be confused, manipulated (*nec immodice instrumentorum instar adhibenda*) or regarded as identical, as though they were interchangeable. (§55)

That dialogue cannot be "manipulated" means emphatically that it cannot be reduced to an *instrument* for proclamation; it has value in itself as an authentic expression of evangelization. In interreligious dialogue the church seeks to discover the "seeds of the Word," and a "ray of that Truth which enlightens all

---

1. See Secretariatus pro Non-Christianis, "Dialogue and Mission," *Bulletin* n. 56, 19, no. 2 (1984): 126–41.

human beings," that are found in the persons and in the religious traditions of humankind. The church is stimulated "both to discover and acknowledge the signs of Christ's presence and of the working of the Spirit, as well as to examine more deeply her own identity and to bear witness to the fullness of revelation which she has received for the good of all" (§56).

The document "Dialogue and Proclamation"[2] echoes the encyclical when it states:

> Interreligious dialogue and proclamation, though not on the same level, are both authentic elements of the Church's evangelizing mission. Both are legitimate and necessary. They are intimately related, but not interchangeable...The two activities remain distinct, but...one and the same local Church, one and the same person, can be diversely engaged in both. (§77)

However, the document also observes that dialogue, while representing an authentic expression of evangelization, does not exhaust it but remains oriented toward proclamation. The scope of both activities is different. That of interreligious dialogue is "a deeper conversion of all towards God"; as such, it possesses "its own validity" (§41). Proclamation, on the other hand, "aims at guiding people to explicit knowledge of what God has done for all men and women in Jesus Christ, and to invite them to be disciples of Jesus through becoming members of the Church" (§81). The document states:

> dialogue...does not constitute the whole mission of the Church...it cannot simply replace proclamation, but remains *oriented* towards proclamation, in so far as the dynamic process of the Church's evangelizing mission reaches in it its climax and its fullness. (§82)

Both elements are conceived as in a dialectical relationship within the same evangelizing mission, which represents a dynamic process: proclamation and its sacramentalization in the life of the church represent the peak of the evangelizing mission. The "orientation" of dialogue toward proclamation in fact corresponds to the "orientation" (*ordinantur*) of the members of other religious traditions toward the church, spoken of in *Lumen Gentium* §16. They are "oriented" to it because to it is entrusted "the fullness of the benefits and the means of salvation" (*Redemptoris Missio* §18). Similarly, dialogue remains "oriented" toward proclamation through which the "others" are invited to share that fullness in the church.

If the question of whether and to what extent these three postconciliar documents go beyond what the council had said previously is raised, the following may be said: Vatican II encouraged dialogue with the other religious traditions, but did not declare it to be part of the church's evangelizing mission. The latter point is indeed stated clearly by the subsequent three documents. Moreover, all

---

2. Pontifical Council for Interreligious Dialogue, "Dialogue and Proclamation," *Bulletin* n. 77, 26, no. 2 (1991): 210–50.

three documents develop a "broad" concept of evangelization that is not yet discernible in Vatican II; they assert, albeit in different ways, that dialogue cannot be reduced to an "instrument" of proclamation, but has value in itself. In these and other ways, they constitute, with different accents and nuances, a step forward in the church's doctrine on evangelization, dialogue, and proclamation.

Our aim in this chapter is to take into account the reciprocal interaction existing between interreligious dialogue and the theology of the religions. First, it must be shown that, in its deep meaning, dialogue is based on an open theology of the religions; it must therefore be asked what the theological foundation for dialogue is. In a second step, the question is in what sense dialogue in turn influences theology, and what are its challenges, as well as its fruits and benefits.

THE THEOLOGICAL FOUNDATION
OF DIALOGUE

"MYSTERY OF UNITY"

To lay the foundation for the "relations between the church and non-Christian religions" and especially for interreligious dialogue, Vatican II's Declaration *Nostra Aetate* stated that "Humanity forms but one community. This is so because all stem from the one stock which God created to people the entire earth, and also because all share a common destiny, namely God. His providence, evident goodness, and saving designs extend to all humankind" (§1). Dialogue is thus established on a double foundation: the community which has its origin in God through creation, and its destiny in him through salvation in Jesus Christ. Nothing is said about the presence and action of the Spirit of God operating in all people and all religious traditions themselves.

Indeed, it is well known that the council only gradually rediscovered the activity of the Spirit, and the fruits of that rediscovery are found primarily in the constitution *Gaudium et Spes*. It must also be recognized that the council took note of the universal activity of the Spirit of God in the midst of all human beings in the earthly aspirations of all humankind, such as peace and brotherhood, work and progress, rather than in their properly religious aspirations and endeavors.

That the Spirit of God is universally present and operative in the religious life of the "others" and in the religious traditions to which they belong just as among Christians and in the church would also be a postconciliar rediscovery. The importance of such a vision for the theological foundation of interreligious dialogue cannot be ignored: it constitutes a third element of its foundation. But that vision gained ground only slowly. There are no traces of it in the official teaching of Paul VI. To make this clear it suffices to note that in the apostolic exhortation *Evangelii Nuntiandi* (1975), which resumes the work of the synod of bishops on evangelization in the modern world, the Spirit appears only as driving the church and empowering it for fulfilling its evangelizing mission (§75), which as noted earlier, consists primarily and principally in the proclamation of the gospel.

The presence and universal action of the Spirit of God among the "others" and in their religious traditions represent John Paul II's most important contribution to the theological foundation of interreligious dialogue. There is no need to cite again the prominent texts, which have been noted earlier. It suffices to recall the main ideas. The pope says that the "firm belief" of the followers of other religions is "an effect of the Spirit of truth operating outside the visible confines of the Mystical Body" (*Redemptor Hominis* §6). In the important speech given by the pope to members of the Roman Curia on December 22, 1986, already noted, the pope wished to justify theologically the "event" of the world day of prayer for peace, held in Assisi two months previously. Hence, taking the theological foundation of dialogue which was presented by the council — the unity of origin and of destiny of the human race through creation and redemption — he sees it as a "mystery of unity" which unites all human beings, whatever the differences in the circumstances of their lives might be: "The differences are a less important element than the unity which, by contrast, is radical, basic, and decisive" (§3).[3] He further insists: In the light of this twofold "mystery of unity," "differences of all kinds, and first of all religious differences, to the extent to which they diminish God's design, are shown to pertain to another order... They must be surmounted in progress toward the realization of the great design of unity guiding creation." Despite their differences, which are sometimes perceived as insuperable divisions, all human beings "are included in the grand and single design of God in Jesus Christ" (§5). "The universal unity based on the event of creation and redemption cannot but leave a trace in the reality lived by human beings, even those belonging to different religions" (§7). These "seeds of the Word" sown among the others constitute the concrete foundation of interreligious dialogue encouraged by the council.

To that "mystery of unity," the foundation of dialogue, the pope added yet a third element, namely the active presence of the Spirit of God in the religious life of the "others," especially in their prayer: "We may think," he wrote, "that any authentic prayer is aroused by the Holy Spirit, who is mysteriously present in the heart of every human being" (§11).

The text of the encyclical *Dominum et Vivificantem* (1986) on the Holy Spirit could be cited at length. In it the pope extends his discourse with a far-reaching theological treatment of the universal presence of the Spirit throughout the entire history of salvation from the beginning and after the Jesus Christ event, well beyond the confines of the church. Suffice it to again evoke the encyclical *Redemptoris Missio* (1990), where it is explicitly said that the presence of the Spirit extends not only to the religious life of individuals but also to the religious tra-

---

3. See Pontifical Commission "Justitia et Pax," *Assise: Journée mondiale de prière pour la paix (Octobre 26, 1986)*, 1987: 147–55.

ditions to which they belong. "The Spirit's presence and activity affect not only individuals but also society and history, peoples, cultures and religions" (§28).

Through these texts there gradually emerges the same teaching: the Holy Spirit is present and active in the world, in the members of other religions, and in their religious traditions themselves. Every authentic prayer (even if addressed to a God still unknown), the human values and virtues, the treasures of wisdom hidden in the religious traditions, and thus also the dialogue and authentic encounter between their members, are so many fruits of the active presence of the Spirit.

The document "Dialogue and Proclamation" (1991), following John Paul II, again invokes the "mystery of unity," the threefold theological foundation of interreligious dialogue, based on the common origin and the single destiny of the human race in God, universal salvation in Jesus Christ, and the active presence of the Spirit in all (§28). The fundamental reason for the church's commitment to dialogue "is not merely anthropological but primarily theological" (§38). The church should enter into a dialogue of salvation with all human beings in the very same way in which God entered into an age-long dialogue of salvation with humankind, a dialogue still taking place. "In this dialogue of salvation, Christians and others are called to collaborate with the Spirit of the Risen Lord who is universally present and active" (§40).

In pursuing the theological foundation of interreligious dialogue, emphasis must also be given to the universality of the Reign of God, in which members of other religious traditions are fully members and in which they participate together with Christians. This fourth element is not explicitly mentioned as such in the documents mentioned here earlier. "Dialogue and Proclamation," however, makes an implicit hint at it in a text already cited: "From this mystery of unity it follows that all men and women who are saved share, though differently, in the same mystery of salvation in Jesus Christ through his Spirit. Christians know this through their faith, while others remain unaware that Jesus Christ is the source of their salvation. The mystery of salvation reaches out to them, in a way known to God, through the invisible action of the Spirit of Christ" (§29).

In the previous chapter, we explained that the Reign of God universally present in the world represents the universal presence of the mystery of salvation in Jesus Christ. That all are co-members in the Reign of God means that all share in the same mystery of salvation in him. The importance of this for a theology of the religions and dialogue may be easily grasped. The universally present and shared Reign of God constitutes the fourth element of the theological foundation of interreligious dialogue. All have access to the Reign of God in history through obedience to the God of the Reign in faith and conversion. The theology of the religions and dialogue must show how the "others" are sharers in the reality of the Reign of God in the world and history, by opening themselves to the action of the Spirit. By responding in the sincere practice of their religious tradition to God's call addressed to them, believers of other religious faiths truly become — albeit without being formally conscious of it — active members of the Reign. Through participation in the mystery of salvation, they are members of the Reign of God already present in history, and their religious traditions themselves contribute in a mysterious manner to the construction of the Reign of God in the world. All this has already been shown, and needs no further explanation.

From that, however, there follow important consequences for interreligious dialogue. This dialogue takes place between persons who are already bound to each other in the Reign of God inaugurated in history in Jesus Christ. The differences in their religious allegiances notwithstanding, such persons are already in communion with one another in the reality of the mystery of salvation, even if there remains a distinction between them on the level of the "sacrament," that is, in the order of the mediation of the mystery. Communion in the reality is, however, more fundamental and of greater weight than differences on the level of sign. That explains the deep communion in the Spirit that interreligious dialogue is able to establish, if it is sincere and authentic, between Christians and other believers.[4] That also shows why interreligious dialogue is a form of sharing, of giving and receiving, why it is not, in a word, a one-way process: it is not a monologue but a "dialogue." The reason is that the reality of the Reign of God is already shared in mutual exchange. Dialogue makes explicit this communion preexisting in the reality of salvation, which is the Reign of God that has come for all in Jesus.

Probably nothing provides interreligious dialogue with so deep a theological basis and a motivation so true as the conviction that despite the differences that set them apart, those who belong to the different religious traditions are walking together — joint members of the Reign of God in history — toward the fullness of the Reign, toward the new humanity willed by God for the end of time, of which they are called to be co-creators under God.

DIALOGUE AND PROCLAMATION

We have noted that dialogue and proclamation are in a dialectical relationship in the dynamic process of the church's evangelizing mission. Between them there is, and there must remain, a certain tension. As I have written elsewhere, the tension "is between the 'not yet' of the Church who, together with the 'others' is in history a pilgrim toward the fullness of the Kingdom, and the 'already' of the Church who is in time and in the world the 'sacrament' of the Kingdom."

> The tension between the "already" and the "not yet" is reflected in the Church's evangelizing mission and, markedly so, in the relationship within it between interreligious dialogue and proclamation: Insofar as the Church remains on her pilgrimage, together with the "others," towards the fullness of the Kingdom, she engages with them in dialogue; insofar as she is the sacrament of the reality of the Kingdom already present and operative in

4. Cf. Abhishiktananda (Henri Le Saux), "The Depth-Dimension of Religious Dialogue," *Vidyajyoti* 45 (1981): 202–21.

history, she proclaims to them Jesus Christ in whom the Kingdom of God has been established by God.[5]

In similar fashion, the "Theses on Interreligious Dialogue" of the FABC Theological Advisory Commission — mentioned above — bases the bipolarity of dialogue and proclamation in the church's evangelizing mission on the universal presence in the world of God's work of salvation (the Reign of God), of which the church is the sacrament. In those theses we read:[6]

> The one divine plan of salvation for all peoples embraces the whole universe. The mission of the Church has to be understood within the context of this plan. The Church does not monopolize God's action in the universe. While it is aware of a special mission of God in the world, it has to be attentive to God's action in the world, as manifested also in other religions. This twofold awareness constitutes the two poles of the Church's evangelizing action in relation to other religions. While proclamation is the expression of its awareness of being in mission, dialogue is the expression of its awareness of God's presence and action outside its boundaries. The action of the Church finds itself in a field of forces controlled by these two poles of divine activity. Proclamation is the affirmation of and witness to God's action in oneself. Dialogue is the openness and attention to the mystery of God's action in the other believer. It is a perspective of faith that we cannot speak of the one without the other. (§6.5)

> The Spirit calls all peoples to conversion which is primarily a free turning of the heart to God and his Kingdom in obedience to his word. Dialogue as a mutual challenge to growth toward fullness involves such a call to conversion. Dialogue, however, does not aim at conversion, understood as a change of religion. But proclamation includes a further call to discipleship to Jesus Christ in the Church. It is not proselytism but a mystery of the call of the Spirit and the free response of the person. Because of this double movement of freedom in the Spirit, proclamation itself is dialogical. (§6.6)

It is not possible, therefore, to agree on this question with Paul F. Knitter's recent book *Jesus and the Other Names.*[7] Knitter proposes simply to identify mission with dialogue, from which proclamation must not be distinguished as a further element of mission. The received opinion according to which "dialogue *is* mission" — insofar as in itself it constitutes an intrinsic dimension, a genuine expression, of evangelization — is being reversed to become "mission *is* dialogue," whereby evangelization is simply reduced to dialogue and the witness to one's faith that dialogue implies (pp. 142–47). Proclamation as a distinct expression

---

5. Jacques Dupuis, "A Theological Commentary: Dialogue and Proclamation," in *Redemption and Dialogue,* ed. William R. Burrows (Maryknoll, N.Y.: Orbis Books, 1993), 155.

6. Text in *FABC Papers* no. 48 (Hong Kong: FABC, 1987): 16.

7. Paul F. Knitter, *Jesus and the Other Names: Christian Mission and Global Responsibility* (Maryknoll, N.Y.: Orbis Books, 1996), 125–64.

of evangelization is thereby done away with. In Knitter's view, a "constitutive" Christology, even if "inclusivist," rules out the possibility of a genuine and sincere dialogue. On the contrary, once a "pluralist" Christology which denies the constitutive character of salvation in Jesus Christ has been adopted, mission is reduced to dialogue and to the witness of one's own faith entailed in it (pp. 134–35). For Knitter, then, a constitutive Christology, even if it is inclusivist, renders the practice of interfaith dialogue impossible; it likewise nullifies any effort to build an ecclesiology and a theology of mission oriented toward the Reign of God. It can neither honestly visualize mission *as dialogue* nor foster readiness to learn anything genuinely new from the "others" through the practice of dialogue. Knitter writes: "Simply stated, it is impossible to develop a Kingdom-centered understanding of the Church that will coherently and persuasively present the Church as the Servant of the Kingdom on the basis of a Christology that insists that Jesus is the only cause of and the unsurpassable criterion for the salvation to be realized in the Kingdom" (p. 135).

For our part, we would hope that we have succeeded in showing in the previous chapters of this book that a "constitutive" Christology is not necessarily "exclusive" and that a constitutive and inclusive Christology is genuinely open to a Kingdom-centered theology of mission and to a sincere dialogue that leaves room for announcing the gospel. The universal saving impact of Jesus Christ, as "constitutive" of the salvation of the world as it might be, leaves space, as we said earlier, for other "saving figures" and other religious traditions, where God is present and at work through God's Word and Spirit. The Reign of God is thus truly broader than the church, and destined to be built by Christians and the "others"; dialogue, which entails learning new aspects of the truth, is an authentic expression of the evangelizing mission. Dialogue does not, however, exhaust that mission, in which there remains space — where God so wills — for inviting the others to become disciples of Jesus in the church. Everything hangs together and must be taken in its entirety: all the rest stands or falls with Christology — considered as constitutive or not. As Claude Geffré says incisively: a "constitutive" Christology leaves room for other mediations and divine revelations. He writes:

> Why should it be thought that only a radical theocentrism can meet the demands of interreligious dialogue? It seems that a deepened Christology can open more fruitful avenues, capable of doing justice at once to the demands of a true pluralism and to the Christian identity.[8]

Perhaps the best way to conclude these clarifications is to quote "Dialogue and Proclamation" where it explains what ultimately constitutes the deepest motivation of the church's drive to announce Jesus Christ:

---

8. Claude Geffré, "Théologie chrétienne et dialogue interreligieux," *Revue de l'Institut Catholique de Paris* 38, no. 1 (1992): 63–82, cf. 72; idem,"Le fondement théologique du dialogue interreligieux," *Chemins du Dialogue* 2 (1993): 73–103.

[How] could [Christians] not hope and desire to share with others their joy of knowing and following Jesus Christ, Lord and Savior? We are here at the heart of the mystery of love. Insofar as the Church and Christians have a deep love for the Lord Jesus, the desire to share him with others is motivated not merely by obedience to the Lord's command, but by this love itself. It should not be surprising, but quite normal, that the followers of other religions should also desire sincerely to share their faith. All dialogue implies reciprocity and aims at banishing fear and aggressiveness. (§83)

THE CHALLENGES AND FRUITS OF DIALOGUE

COMMITMENT AND OPENNESS

The conditions for the possibility of interreligious dialogue have occupied an important place in the debate on the theology of religions. It was in order that dialogue be practicable that Paul F. Knitter advocated the paradigm shift from Christocentrism to theocentrism, that is, from inclusivism to "pluralism." Indeed how, as he thought, could dialogue be sincere and simply honest if the Christian party engages in it with a preconceived idea, an already fixed bias toward a "constitutive" uniqueness of Jesus Christ, universal Savior of humankind? In the view of the "pluralists," a "constitutive" and "inclusivist" Christology, in which all of humankind is saved by God in the Jesus Christ event, leaves no room for genuine dialogue. Dialogue, it is observed, can only be sincere if it takes place on an equal footing between partners. Can the church and Christians accordingly be sincere in their professed will to enter into dialogue if they are not prepared to give up the traditional claims about Jesus as "constitutive" Savior of humankind? The problem of religious identity in general, and of Christian identity in particular, is bound up with this question as is that of the openness to the "others" required by dialogue.

First of all, one may not, on the pretext of honesty in dialogue, bracket one's faith (practicing an *epochè*), even temporarily, against the expectation, as has been suggested, of eventually rediscovering the truth of that faith through the dialogue itself. On the contrary, honesty and sincerity in dialogue specifically require that the various partners enter it and commit themselves to it in the integrity of their faith. Any methodical doubt, any mental reservation, is out of place here. Otherwise, one could no longer speak of interreligious or interfaith dialogue. After all, at the basis of an authentic religious life is a faith that endows that life with its specific character and proper identity. This religious faith is no more negotiable in the interreligious dialogue than it is in one's personal life. It is not a commodity to be parceled out or exchanged; it is a gift received from God, of which one may not dispose lightly.

By the same token, just as sincerity in dialogue authorizes no bracketing of faith, even a provisional one, so its integrity in turn forbids any compromise or reduction of faith. Authentic dialogue does not accommodate such expedients. It admits neither the "syncretism" that, in the quest for a common ground, attempts to surmount opposition and contradictions among the faiths of different religious traditions through some reduction of their content; nor the "eclecticism" that, in the search for a common denominator among the various traditions, chooses scattered elements among them and combines these into a shapeless, inconsistent amalgam. If it is to be true, dialogue may not seek the easy way, which in any case is illusory.

Rather, without wishing to conceal any contradictions among religious faiths, it must admit them where they exist and face them patiently and responsibly. To conceal differences and possible contradictions would amount to cheating and would actually end by depriving the dialogue of its object. After all, dialogue seeks understanding in difference, in a sincere esteem for convictions other than one's own. Thus it leads both partners to question themselves on the implications for their own faith of the personal convictions of the others.

If then it goes without saying that in the practice of the interreligious dialogue, Christians may not dissimulate their own faith in Jesus Christ, they in turn will acknowledge in their partners who do not share their faith the inalienable right and duty to engage in dialogue while maintaining their own personal convictions — even claims to universality that may be part of their faith. It is in this fidelity to personal, nonnegotiable convictions, honestly accepted on both sides, that the interreligious dialogue takes place "between equals" — in their differences.

As the seriousness of dialogue forbids toning down deep convictions on either side, so its openness demands that what is relative be not absolutized, whether by incomprehension or intransigence. In every religious faith and conviction there is the danger, and a real one, of absolutizing what is not absolute. A concrete example of this in terms of Christianity and faith in Jesus Christ is the way in which the "fullness" of God's self-revelation in Jesus Christ is understood. This fullness, we pointed out earlier, is not "quantitative" but qualitative: it is not an extensive fullness, comprehending, that is, the entirety of the divine mystery, as though there would no longer remain anything to discover in the "eschatological remainder," but a fullness of intensity, inasmuch as in his human consciousness Jesus experienced his interpersonal relations with the Father and the Holy Spirit, which constitute the intrinsic mystery of the divine life. The transfer that was taking place in Jesus' human consciousness of the divine mystery, while it enabled him to speak of God in an unprecedented and unsurpassable way, does not contradict the limited character of that consciousness, much less the limited and particular character of Christian revelation, which starting from the testimony of Jesus is expressed in a necessarily relative particular culture. Christian revelation does not exhaust the mystery of the Divine, nor could it; nor does it nullify the truth of a divine revelation that may take place through prophetic figures of other religious traditions. The risk of unduly absolutizing what is not absolute goes far beyond the case of revelation in Jesus Christ. We earlier insisted on the unsuitability of using the terms "absolute" and "absoluteness" for Christianity as a historic religion and indeed for the historic humanity of Jesus. While the humanity of Jesus is the personal human being of the Son of God, it remains by its very nature created, limited, contingent. God alone is the Absolute and must be called such.

Commitment to one's own faith and openness to the "other" must therefore be combined. A "constitutive" Christology which professes universal salvation in the Jesus Christ event seems to allow for both. Christian identity, as it has been understood through the centuries, is linked to faith in the "constitutive" mediation and in the "fullness" of divine revelation in Jesus Christ, but they must be understood without either reductionism or exclusive absolutism.

PERSONAL FAITH AND
THE EXPERIENCE OF THE OTHER

If dialogue supposes the integrity of personal faith, it also requires openness to the faith of the other in its difference. Each partner in the dialogue must enter into the experience of the other, striving to grasp that experience from within. In order to do this, he or she must rise above the level of the concepts in which this experience is imperfectly expressed, to attain, insofar as possible, through and beyond the concepts, the experience itself. It is this effort of "com-prehension" and interior "sym-pathy" — or "em-pathy" — that Raimon Panikkar calls the "intra-religious" dialogue, an indispensable condition for true interreligious dialogue.[9] This has been described as a spiritual technique consisting of "passing over and returning." "Passing over" means encountering both the other and the religious experience which that other carries internally, together with his or her worldview, or *Weltanschauung:*

> To know the religion of another is more than being cognizant of the facts of the other's religious tradition. It involves getting inside the skin of the other, it involves walking in the other's shoes, it involves seeing the world in some sense as the other sees it, it involves asking the other's questions, it involves getting inside the other's sense of "being a Hindu, Muslim, Jew, Buddhist, or whatever."[10]

Under these premises, we must ask ourselves whether and to what extent it is possible to share two different religious faiths, making each of them one's own, and living both at once in one's own religious life. From a totalizing viewpoint, this seems impossible. Even apart from any interior conflict that might arise in the individual, every religious faith constitutes an indivisible whole and calls for a total commitment of the person. It seems impossible that such a total engagement might be divided, as it were, between two objects. To be a Christian is not only

9. Cf. R. Panikkar, *The Intrareligious Dialogue* (New York: Paulist Press, 1978).

10. F. Whaling, *Christian Theology and World Religions: A Global Approach* (London: Marshall Pickering, 1986), 130–31.

to find in Jesus Christ values to be promoted or even a meaning for one's life; it is to be totally committed and dedicated to his person, to find in him one's way to God.

Does this mean, however, that the concept of the "hyphenated Christian" is self-contradictory — that one cannot be Hindu-Christian or Buddhist-Christian or the like? This is the issue of what is now called religious "double allegiance," to use a more satisfactory expression. To assert this would contradict experience, as such cases are not rare or unknown. Here it is well to recall that the theology of religions cannot be satisfied with a priori deductions from traditional doctrinal principles, but rather must follow a method that is primarily inductive, that is, take its cue from lived experience and then pursue its meaning in the light of the revealed datum. Indeed, there is no denying that a significant number of people, whose sincerity and trustworthiness are beyond suspicion, have undergone and are undergoing the experience of combining in their own life of faith and religious practice their Christian faith and total devotion to the person of Jesus with elements from another experience of faith and another religious commitment. Both these elements can be combined in personal experience in various degrees and in different ways, which we need not pursue at this point.

Some attention must be paid, however, to the various possible meanings of the concept of double belonging. To be a "Hindu-Christian" can mean combining in oneself Hindu culture and Christian faith. Hinduism would then not be a religious faith, strictly speaking, but a philosophy and a culture, which, with the necessary adjustments, could serve as a vehicle for Christian faith. Then the problem of the "Hindu-Christian" would be that of the "inculturation" of Christian faith and doctrine in a Hindu cultural context. In this case, obviously, the concept of a Hindu-Christian will offer no difficulty in principle. But does this explanation fully correspond to reality? Hinduism, while it is not primarily and uniformly doctrinal, nevertheless involves, in the concrete lives of men and women, a genuine religious faith. For that matter, the distinction between religion and culture is difficult to manage, especially in Asian traditions. Representing as it does the transcendent element in culture, religion is scarcely separable from culture.

Can one nevertheless combine and make one's own Hindu (or Buddhist) faith and Christian faith? In this regard, we must exercise discernment. Surely there are elements of other faiths that are in harmony with Christian faith and can be combined and integrated with it. These will serve to enrich it, if it is true that other faiths contain elements of divine truth and revelation. There may be other elements, however, that seem to formally contradict the Christian faith and cannot be assimilated.

In any case, with the cautions that we have indicated, in order to be true, interreligious dialogue certainly requires that both partners make a positive effort to enter into each other's religious experience and overall vision, insofar as possible. We are dealing with the encounter, in one and the same person, of two ways of being, seeing, and thinking. This "intrareligious dialogue" is an indispensable preparation for an exchange between persons in interreligious dialogue.

MUTUAL ENRICHMENT

The interaction between Christianity and the Asian religions, Hinduism and Buddhism in particular, has been conceived differently by various promoters of interreligious dialogue. Aloysius Pieris sees the Christian tradition, on one side, and the Buddhist tradition, on the other, as "two religious models which, far from being contradictory, are in fact, incomplete each in itself and, therefore, complementary and mutually corrective." They represent "poles of a tension, not so much geographical as psychological. They are two instincts emerging dialectically from within the deepest zone of each individual, be he Christian or not. Our religious encounter with God and human beings would be incomplete without this interaction."[11] Pieris calls these two complementary poles the *agapeic* (Christianity) and the *gnostic* (Buddhism). A parallel between the two historic founders, Jesus-the-Christ and Gautama-the-Buddha, naturally suggests itself. The question being raised is that of a possible complementarity between the saving values represented by both that can be found in the religious traditions bearing their name. Pieris understands it as complementarity between Buddhist *gnosis* and Christian *agapè*, or, more precisely — exchanging the words — between the *"agapeic gnosis"* of Christians and the *"gnostic agapè"* of Buddhists.[12] The mutual complementarity between the two traditions — their differences notwithstanding — is based on the inadequacy of the basic "medium" of each one, which leaves them open to mutual fulfillment.[13]

John A. T. Robinson, for his part, speaks of two "eyes" of truth and reality: Western Christianity represents one eye, Hinduism the other; more generally, the West stands for the first, the East for the second. Robinson sees the polarity of the two "centers" as that between the male and female principles. He too calls for a mutual complementarity between the two centers.[14]

John B. Cobb, in turn, advocates a "mutual transformation," beyond dialogue, between Christianity and Buddhism; such a mutual transformation will result from the osmosis between the complementary approaches to reality, that is, between the worldviews characteristic of both traditions.[15]

Raimon Panikkar's focus is somewhat different. He insists that the various religious traditions differ and must keep their distinct identity. He rejects a facile "eclecticism" which would destroy the respective identities; faith cannot be "bracketed" (*epochè*) to ease the dialogue. But, while the "cosmotheandric mystery," the

---

11. Aloysius Pieris, "Western Christianity and Asian Buddhism: A Theological Reading of Historical Encounters," *Dialogue* n.s. 7, no. 2 (1980): 64; idem, *Love Meets Wisdom: A Christian Experience of Buddhism* (Maryknoll, N.Y.: Orbis Books, 1988).

12. Aloysius Pieris, "The Buddha and the Christ: Mediators of Liberation," in *The Myth of Christian Uniqueness: Towards a Pluralistic Theology of Religions*, ed. J. Hick and P. F. Knitter (Maryknoll, N.Y.: Orbis Books, 1987), 162–77; idem, *An Asian Theology of Liberation* (Maryknoll, N.Y.: Orbis Books, 1988).

13. Aloysius Pieris, "The Buddha and the Christ: Mediators of Liberation," 163; idem, *Love Meets Wisdom*, 110–35.

14. John A. T. Robinson, *Truth Is Two-Eyed* (London: SCM Press, 1979).

15. John B. Cobb, *Beyond Dialogue: Toward a Mutual Transformation of Christianity and Buddhism* (Philadelphia: Fortress Press, 1982).

object of faith, is common to all religious traditions, "beliefs" differ in each. Between these "beliefs" Panikkar advocates a "cross-fertilization"—which he terms "syncretism"—for the sake of mutual enrichment.[16]

Panikkar has returned to this topic several times. Recently he has described what he regards as the profile and the horizon of interreligious dialogue for the future. Moving now beyond the problematic of "cross-fertilization," he calls for a further stage in which, transcending the static doctrinal identity of their respective traditions, the dialogue partners will be able to contribute mutually to a deeper self-understanding.[17]

Not everything seems clear or easy in the midst of this range of opinions, nor does it seem that everything should be readily accepted at face value. To the comparison of two eyes that work together in a single vision, it would be easy to oppose, for example, that of a prism whose different facets cannot be encompassed in a single view. What can, however, be concluded regarding the fruits of dialogue, if we base ourselves on the principles enunciated above? We must first remember that the principal agent of interreligious dialogue is the Spirit of God who animates people. The Spirit is at work in both traditions involved in the dialogue, the Christian and the other; thus the dialogue cannot be a monologue, i.e., a unilateral process. It is also the same God who performs saving works in human history and who speaks to human beings in the depths of their hearts. The same God is, as has been said earlier, both the "Wholly Other" and the "ground of being" of everything that is; the transcendent "beyond" and the immanent "deep down"; the Father of our Lord Jesus Christ and the Self at the center of the self. The same God is present and acting in both dialogue partners.

The Christian partners will not only give but will receive as well. The "fullness" of revelation in Jesus Christ does not dispense them from listening and receiving. They possess no monopoly on truth; they must rather let themselves be possessed by it. Indeed, their dialogue partners, even without having heard God's revelation in Jesus Christ, may be more deeply submitted to this truth that they are still seeking, but whose rays shine on their religious traditions (cf. *Nostra Aetate* §2). One can in all certainty say that, through dialogue, Christians and others "walk together towards truth" ("Dialogue and Mission" §13).

CHRISTIANS HAVE SOMETHING to gain from dialogue. They will benefit in two ways. On the one hand, their own faith will be enriched. Through the experience and testimony of the others, they will be able to discover at greater depth certain aspects, certain dimensions, of the Divine Mystery that they had perceived less clearly and that have been communicated less clearly by Christian tradition. At the same time, they will gain a purification of their faith. The shock

---

16. Panikkar, *The Intrareligious Dialogue.*
17. Raimon Panikkar, "Foreword: The Ongoing Dialogue," in *Hindu-Christian Dialogue: Perspectives and Encounters,* ed. H. Coward (Maryknoll, N.Y.: Orbis Books, 1990), ix–xviii.

of the encounter will often raise questions, force Christians to revise gratuitous assumptions, and destroy deep-rooted prejudices or overthrow certain overly narrow conceptions or outlooks. The benefits of the dialogue constitute a challenge to the Christian partner at the same time.

The fruits and challenges of the dialogue thus go hand in hand. However, above and beyond these sure benefits, we must say that the encounter and exchange have value in themselves. They are an end in themselves. While from the outset they presuppose openness to the other and to God, they also effect a deeper openness to God of each through the other.

Thus dialogue does not serve as a means to a further end. Neither on one side nor on the other does it tend to the "conversion" of one's partner to one's own religious tradition. Rather it tends toward a deeper conversion of each to God. The same God speaks in the heart of both partners; the same Spirit is at work in both. It is the same God who calls and challenges the partners through one another, by means of their mutual witness. Thus they become, as it were, for each other and reciprocally, a sign leading to God. The proper end of the interreligious dialogue is ultimately the common conversion of Christians and the members of other religious traditions to the same God — the God of Jesus Christ — who calls them together with one another, challenging them through each other. This reciprocal call, a sign of God's call, is surely mutual evangelization. It builds up, between members of various religious traditions, the universal communion which marks the advent of the Reign of God.

A word may be added regarding the benefit which will accrue to Christian theology from the praxis of interreligious dialogue. We have stressed, from the beginning of this work, that the theology of religions must be "dialogical theology," that is, built on the praxis of interreligious dialogue. Christian theology is given the opportunity to renew itself through its encounter with the other religions. The question of deciding what basic elements and religious insights can be shared by Christian theology and other religious traditions, as they come in contact with each other, is, however, a difficult one which admits of no easy solution. For each religious tradition constitutes a whole from which the various elements cannot be easily isolated. We are faced with distinct, global worldviews within which, as within living organisms, each part plays its specific function, with the result that a "dynamic equivalence" between the components on either side cannot be easily attained.[18]

Granted that among symbols there exist universally valid archetypes, is there strict equivalence in the various religious traditions between such basic theological concepts as God, creation, world, grace, freedom, salvation-liberation, and so forth? We know that such is not the case. The experience of the Ultimate Reality as the Christian Father/Mother, the Jewish Yahweh, the Muslim Allah, the Hindu Brahman, the Buddhist Nirvāṇa, the Taoist Tao, and so on, is not the

---

18. Cf. Charles H. Kraft, *Christianity in Culture: A Study in Dynamic Biblical Theologizing in Cross-Cultural Perspective* (Maryknoll, N.Y.: Orbis Books, 1979).

same. Is then every religious faith, and consequently every theology, so bound to a particular worldview that it can hardly express itself in, and be transposed to, another? Dialogical theology cannot ignore these problems.

Does not, for instance, the Christian experience of faith presuppose a density of the historical, not found as such in other traditions, without which it cannot be fully understood? What, however, is certain and needs to be fully recognized is that history and interiority are two equally valid channels for a true experience of the Divine: he who acts in history according to the Judeo-Christian tradition is he who is experienced in the "cave of the heart" according to the Hindu. The God of history is also the "ground of being."

Regardless of the questions that may remain about the limits of mutual assimilation and "cross-fertilization" between religious and theological traditions, one thing seems clear, and it is this: harmony between religious communities will not be served by a "universal theology" which would claim to bypass differences and contradictions; rather, it will be served by the development within the various traditions of theologies which, taking the mutual differences seriously, will assume them and resolve to interact in dialogue and cooperation.

Chapter Ten

INTERRELIGIOUS PRAYER

Aworld day of prayer for peace was held on October 27, 1986. Four days before the event, Pope John Paul II explained its significance, importance, and procedure during his Wednesday general audience:

> What is going to happen in Assisi will not be some kind of religious syncretism, but a sincere attitude of prayer to God in mutual respect. This is why the motto chosen for the Assisi gathering is: "being together to pray." Praying together, that is, saying a common prayer, is out of the question, but it is possible to be present when others are praying; in this manner we manifest our respect for the prayer of the others and for the stance of the others toward the divinity: at the same time, we offer them the humble and sincere testimony of our faith in Christ, Lord of the Universe.
>
> That is what will be done in Assisi, where at one point in the day, there will be separate prayers by the different religious representations in different places. But then in the square of the lower Basilica of St. Francis, there will follow, at suitable intervals, one after the other, the prayers of the representatives of each religion, while all others will attend with a respectful internal and external attitude, attesting to the supreme effort of other men and women who seek God.
>
> This "being together to pray" takes on a particularly deep and eloquent meaning insofar as all will be the ones next to the others to implore God for the gift that all of humankind most needs today in order to survive: peace.[1]

These words of the pope became the official formula given by church authority for the meaning and procedure of the Assisi event: Together to pray, not praying together. The formula was confirmed by the pope during the event, and by those in the Vatican Curia who were responsible for organizing the day both before and afterwards, and particularly Cardinal Etchegaray. *L'Osservatore Romano* published a number of articles on the event in which that same formula was repeated, and various theological reasons why a common prayer between Christians and members of other religions is not theologically acceptable were spelled out.[2] That

---

1. Pontifical Commission "Justitia et Pax," *Assise: Journée mondiale de prière pour la paix* (October 27, 1986): 25–26.
2. See especially the presentation by Archbishop Jorge Mejia, "Réflexion théologique sur la journée mondiale de prière pour la paix," *L'Osservatore Romano*, September 17, 1986. The presentation is reprinted in *Assise: Journée mondiale de prière pour la paix*, 31–38.

same paper, however, carried a more nuanced article signed by Father Marcello Zago, former Secretary of the Secretariat for Non-Christians, in which, while justifying the procedure at Assisi, he affirmed the possibility of common prayer by Christians and members of other religious traditions. He wrote:

> There have been experiences of common prayer and religious sharing. In most cases they are carried out prudently, and syncretism is avoided. Sharing an experience of meditation is the most common. There are serious theological reasons for this...Being together to pray, and sometimes to pray together, is a recognition of this essential fact of the relationship of all human beings with God.[3]

The pope's words recalled above and the explanations often repeated after the Assisi event by those in charge — "We went together to Assisi to pray, we did not go to Assisi to pray together" — might give the impression that common prayer between Christians and the "others" is, if not utterly impossible, in any case not advisable because of the danger of doctrinal and practical relativism and syncretism. That such a danger must clearly be avoided is beyond discussion. But that does not mean that prayer in common must be regarded as something that cannot be done. Attesting to it, among other doctrinal and pastoral instances in the church, are the "Guidelines for Interreligious Dialogue" of the Catholic Bishops' Conference of India (CBCI). They present prayer in common with members of other religions as not only possible, but recommended — it is even a duty — provided it be done correctly. Having distinguished between various kinds of interreligious dialogue, the Guidelines continue as follows:

> A third form of dialogue goes to the deepest levels of religious life and consists in sharing in prayer and contemplation. The purpose of such common prayer is primarily the corporate worship of the God of all who has created us to be one large family. We are called to worship God not only individually but also in community, and since in a very real and fundamental manner we are one with the whole of humanity, it is not only our right but our duty to worship him together with others (§82).[4]

Further on, the document explains the discernment required (§84), gives specific directives for prayer gatherings (§85), and explains the preparation required on the part of participants (§86). In terms of this document, the practice of prayer in common is neither unheard of nor impracticable.

To avoid misunderstandings, it must be said clearly that in the circumstances of the World Day of Prayer for Peace in Assisi it was not even possible to think about a common prayer shared by all together. That was so for several reasons:

---

3. Marcello Zago, "Les religions pour la paix," *L'Osservatore Romano*, October 15, 1986; reprinted in *Assise: Journée mondiale de prière pour la paix*, 63–72.

4. CBCI Commission for Dialogue and Ecumenism, "Guidelines for Interreligious Dialogue," 2d rev. ed. (New Delhi: CBCI Centre, 1989), 68.

the very high level of the official gathering, the lack of a common preparation, the diversity of religions represented, and the fact that people did not know one another in advance and were not jointly involved in choosing prayers acceptable to all and significant for all. However, it would be wrong to think that the formula used in Assisi is the only one possible, and to deduce from it rigid and restrictive rules. Instead, concrete situations must be taken into account, and pastoral judgments must be made on what stances are possible and advisable.

Such discernment is made from occasion to occasion. That is not our task here. Rather, our task is to show what theological considerations can serve as the basis for a practice of common prayer shared between Christians and members of other religious traditions. To that end, however, some distinctions between the various religious traditions that may be involved must be made. The theological foundation in question is not completely the same in all cases.

First of all, the distinction already mentioned between the three so-called monotheistic or prophetic religions on the one hand and the so-called mystical religions of the East must be kept in mind. Let us note in passing that that distinction must not be misunderstood or pressed in an exclusive and rigid way. The aim is not to deny that Asian religions can turn to an Absolute who is also personal or have a prophetic dimension; nor does it seek to deny to the monotheistic religions a mystical dimension. Rather what is intended is that the three so-called monotheistic religions go back to a common historical origin in the faith of Abraham; they thus belong to a common family. That belonging, as will be seen further on, offers an important element for the theological basis for prayer together.

Further distinctions would have to be made about the other religions. There are different currents among the various religions, and even within a single religion (if one follows the received terminology, which is of rather recent origin, created by Western scholars, in the case of Hinduism): theistic or nontheistic, theistic or agnostic, theistic or atheistic currents. It is plain that the differences between the Hindu *bhakti* which addresses a personal God and the Hindu mysticism of *advaita* (nonduality) are noteworthy; and likewise between the devotional attitude of Hindu *bhakti* and Buddhist meditation or contemplation, and so forth.

Here we will not enter into all the distinctions that would have to be made. It will suffice to show the theological basis for sharing in prayer and contemplation or meditation, depending on the religious families involved. Our overall thesis entails asserting two basic principles: (1) in itself and generally speaking, common prayer between Christians and members of other religions is possible and desirable, and indeed to be positively encouraged in the context of contemporary interreligious dialogue; (2) the various situations must, however, be kept in mind with regard to the religious families involved, the concrete circumstances, and the choice to be made of prayers that can be sincerely shared between the different participants, and so forth.

A clear distinction must accordingly be made between the question in principle of common prayer, and the question of fact: the first question is not problematic, but the second poses various problems.[5] This chapter will accordingly unfold in two main sections. In the first section, the theological reasons that in principle recommend the praxis of common prayer between Christians and the "others" will be set forth; the second part will take into account the various situations of dialogue between Christianity and the other religions and will inquire what concrete possibilities the various situations open up for the practice of common prayer. Thus in the first part, the question is "praying together: why?" and in the second part, the question is: "praying together: how?"

PRAYING TOGETHER: WHY?

FROM DIALOGUE TO COMMON PRAYER

In order to establish the theological foundation for interreligious dialogue in the preceding chapter, we spoke of a "mystery of unity" in which we distinguished various elements. The declaration *Nostra Aetate* had spoken of a twofold element, namely of the origin of the entire human race in God through creation and of their common destiny in God through the mystery of redemption. In his speech to the Roman Curia in late December 1986, Pope John Paul II explained and justified theologically the event of Assisi, with a reference to the church's new stance toward the other religions called for by Vatican II and expressed in *Nostra Aetate*. The considerations proposed by the pope on that occasion can serve as the foundation not only for interreligious dialogue in general, but also for common prayer between members of different religious traditions. The pope spoke of the "mystery of unity" that unites the entire human family:

> There is but a *single* divine design for every human being who comes into
> this world (cf. Jn 1:9), a single beginning and end, regardless of his or her
> skin color, the historic and geographical horizon in which he or she lives,
> the culture in which he or she has grown and finds self-expression. The
> differences are something that is less important than the unity, which by
> contrast is radical, basic, and decisive. (§3)[6]

> Human beings may not even be conscious of their radical unity of origin,
> destination, and incorporation into the same divine plan: and when they
> profess different mutually incompatible religions, they may feel that their
> divisions are insuperable. But nevertheless, they are included in God's one
> great design in Jesus Christ, who "has in a certain manner united him-
> self with each individual" (*Gaudium et Spes* §22) even if he or she is not
> conscious of it. (§5)

In this same speech, the pope also referred to a third aspect of the "mystery of unity," namely the universal active presence of the Holy Spirit, in all persons, in

---

5. See H. Küng, "Prayer of the Religions in the World Context," *Concilium* (1990/6): xi–xiii.
6. The text of the speech of John Paul II on December 22, 1986, is found in *Assise: Journée mondiale de prière pour la paix*, 147–55.

all religions, and especially in every sincere prayer that springs from the heart of any human being, whether Christian or "other." Among other things, the pope said: "We may indeed maintain that any authentic prayer is raised up by the Holy Spirit, who is mysteriously present in the heart of every human being" (§11). Even though it is not stated explicitly, John Paul II's insistence on the presence of the Holy Spirit in the religious life of the members of other religious traditions, and specifically in every sincere prayer, no matter what people's religious tradition may be, serves as the third element in the theological foundation, not only for a theology of religions and interreligious dialogue, but also for the practice of common prayer.

Through the various texts there emerges a constant teaching: The Holy Spirit is universally present and active, also in the members of other religious traditions. Every authentic prayer, even if addressed to an Unknown God, is fruit of the Spirit's active presence in human beings; it is the work of the Spirit in them. Through prayer, Christians and members of the other religious traditions are thus profoundly united in the Holy Spirit. Although it is not stated explicitly in the texts, it seems that it can be concluded (in principle) that common prayer is both possible and desirable; such a prayer will simply be the common expression of such communion in the Spirit of God. Through common prayer, the activity of the Spirit of God in both partners will meet together in a common witness.

To the considerations made thus far, we ourselves have added others that help to highlight the unity and anticipated communion existing between Christians and others, which can find a privileged expression in common prayer. The first is the universality of the Reign of God, established by God in Jesus Christ. We have noted repeatedly the universality of the Reign of God, in which Christians and the "others" are co-participants and co-members. The establishment of the Lordship of God in the world and history, which is expressed in symbolic language as the present Reign of God, is nothing else than the universal presence of the mystery of salvation in Jesus Christ, active in all humankind. We have shown its importance for a theology of the religions and dialogue; it must be added that it serves as the fourth element for the theological basis of the practice of prayer shared between Christians and "others."

Dialogue takes place between persons who are already jointly sharing in the Reign of God, begun in history in Jesus Christ. Despite the difference of adhering to different traditions, such persons are already in communion in the reality of the mystery of salvation, even if there remains a distinction between them in terms of "sacrament," that is, of the mediation of the mystery. The reality of the Reign of God is lived in anticipation in a mutual exchange between Christians and the "others." Dialogue makes explicit this prior communion in the reality of salvation, which is in fact the Reign of God arrived for all in Jesus. Such communion indeed finds its deepest expression in the sharing of common prayer between members of different faiths.

THE RELIGIONS, GOD'S GIFTS
TO HUMANKIND

Creation; redemption; universal presence of the Holy Spirit; joint sharing in the Reign of God: there is yet a fifth element for theologically grounding common prayer between Christians and "others," namely the religions of the world as God's gifts to the peoples. Traditional Christian thought has often been resistant, even recently, to seeing in other religious traditions valid "paths," "ways," or "channels" through which the goal of union with the God of Jesus Christ may be reached; or rather, to put it the other way around (as is more appropriate), through which the God of Jesus Christ personally communicates his own life and shares it with the followers of such traditions. Despite its openness and the positive values that it recognized within such traditions, Vatican II did not venture to call them "ways" of salvation, even though it can be asked whether this is not at least partly implicit in the council's recognition of elements of "truth and grace" contained within them "through a hidden presence of God" (*Ad Gentes* §9).

There are, however, other documents, as previously noted, which while not having the unique authority of the council, are more notably open to the other religious traditions. In those documents, God is viewed as being present and active in those traditions, drawing people to himself; the very multiplicity of the other religious traditions attests to the varied ways in which God has established ties with peoples and nations. The religions are "gifts of God to the peoples."

Such positive assessments of the religions as "gifts of God to the peoples" and to humankind are not so unheard of and surprising as is often thought. Attesting to it is the recent study of religions according to the Bible in the Old and New Testaments, by Giovanni Odasso, which was mentioned in chapter 1.[7] Odasso clearly distinguishes between the religions in themselves or as such, and the corruption of the religions at the hands of human beings. The harsh judgments of the prophets, for example, toward the polytheism and the idolatry of the peoples are not denied; but these corruptions of the religions are attributed to human beings and to the perverse use that they have made and are making of God's gifts. Even today religion and the religions in the hands of human beings may become ideology and be abused in support of injustice and idolatry, i.e., of power and money, Caesar and Mammon. The religions in themselves and as such are nevertheless "gifts of God to the peoples." Odasso summarizes his research in the form of several theses. His fourth thesis reads as follows: "The religions are on earth the expression of God's design, which in the eyes of the Church has been realized in the risen Christ and which finds fulfillment for all human beings in the glory of the Reign of God" (p. 371). The author explains the meaning of his thesis in a passage that deserves to be quoted again:

> That the religions are so many expressions of God's design is by now established, indeed because as can be seen from the perspective disclosed

---

7. Giovanni Odasso, *Bibbia e religioni: Prospettive bibliche per la teologia delle religioni* (Rome: Urbaniana University Press, 1998).

by the texts of the Old and New Testament, they are on earth *a gift of God to all peoples,* and therefore, a sign of the salvifically operative presence of Wisdom. Hence, the religions, as expressions of the divine design, are necessarily related to the resurrection of Christ, precisely because the resurrection represents the ultimate fulfillment of God's saving design. (372; emphasis added)

I have suggested in this book that the religions of the world do not represent solely or primarily the effort of human beings and peoples to seek God throughout the entire history of humankind, while they can never reach him with their own efforts. Rather they are the different modes and diverse ways by which God himself has first set out in search of them and found them before they sought him, even before he united them to himself in an unbreakable decisive bond in his Son made flesh among them. If it is indeed true that the religions have their originating source in a divine self-manifestation to human beings, the multiplicity of the religions is grounded in the superabundant riches and variety of God's self-manifestations to humankind.

Would not that meaning of the various religious traditions in the divine plan of salvation be the ultimate and deepest foundation for the validity and desirability of common prayer between the diverse religious traditions? Would not common prayer ultimately consist in recognition of and gratitude to God, by the diverse communities of faith, for the overwhelming gifts that God has given and keeps giving to humankind through history? Indeed it seems so.

PRAYING TOGETHER: HOW?

At the beginning of the chapter we stated that in the search for a valid theological solution to the problem of common prayer between Christians and the "others," some important distinctions must be made with regard to the concrete dialogue situations between the various religious traditions. Not all traditions are situated in the same dialogical relationship toward Christianity. Hence, while we have thus far based the possibility and indeed the appropriateness of common prayer with the members of other religious traditions in a general way on theological considerations that are universally valid, we must now distinguish between the various traditions in order to highlight the specific reasons that should regulate the practice and specific modality of prayer of Christians with the followers of each of those traditions.

Let us assume that in order for a prayer to be "universalizable," that is, shared by members of the diverse communities of faith, there must be a sensitive pastoral discernment that takes into account the various components of diverse situations and the circumstances involved. That means taking into account not only the doctrinal content of the prayer, that is, the words pronounced together by all, but also the place where the prayer is said, the times, and also the gestures accompanying it.[8] However, what especially interests us in this second part of the chapter is above

---

8. See François Boespflug, "Prier en commun et prière commune: Les limites de l'oecuménisme

all the situation and the specific theological relationship between the traditions involved in the prayer that give rise to the possibility of sharing specific prayers. It is agreed that such commonality notwithstanding, for each community of faith, in accordance with its own faith, the "universalizable" prayers will take on different accents, and indeed different understandings. Such different understandings, however, will retain a common irreducible substrate on which is grounded the validity of sharing in prayer. On the basis of those doctrinal elements, some concrete suggestions will be made for the practice of a common prayer between the members of the various communities of faith involved with one another.

COMMON PRAYER BETWEEN CHRISTIANS AND JEWS

As we have said before, the three monotheistic religions place equal emphasis on the oneness of the God whom they adore. The God of Jesus Christ, like that of the Qur'an, is the God of the faith of Abraham, who revealed his name to Moses. The *Shemá* of Israel emphasizes the oneness of the living God: "Hear, O Israel: The Lord our God is one Lord" (Deut 6:4). The same message is repeated in the Christian New Testament: "Hear, O Israel: the Lord our God, the Lord is one" (Mk 12:29). Christian monotheism claims to be in direct continuity with Hebrew monotheism.

Certainly, there is no ignoring the fact that Christian monotheism has developed into a Trinitarian monotheism by which the three "persons" of the Father, the Son, and the Holy Spirit are the same God, revealed potentially through the "First" Testament and explicitly in Jesus Christ. It remains true, however, that the God of Jesus is the very same as that of Moses, whom he calls his "Father." Between Jewish and Christian monotheism there is continuity rather than discontinuity, deepening rather than separation. Christians and Jews adore the same God.

That one God established through Moses a covenant with Israel, his chosen people. That alliance, we also noted, was never revoked, despite the infidelity of a portion of the chosen people. Here we touch a key element regarding the dialogue between Christians and Jews and the possibility of a common prayer between them. In noting the "great spiritual heritage common to Christians and Jews," Vatican II speaks of the "old covenant" established by God with the Jewish people, to whom, as Paul says, "belong the sonship, the glory, the covenants, the giving of the Law, the worship, and the promises . . ." (cf. Rom 9:4) — a God whose "gifts and call are irrevocable" (cf. Rom 11:29) (*Nostra Aetate* §4). More clearly, John Paul II, in the speech he made in 1980 in Mainz (Germany), refers explicitly to the "people of God of the old covenant, which has never been revoked."[9]

Such statements run contrary to what has long been the Christian persuasion on which relations between Christians and Jews were based. The issue is whether with the Christ event and the "new covenant" established in him, the "old covenant"

---

planétaire," in *Assise: 10 ans aprés 1986–96,* ed. François Boespflug and Yves Labbé (Paris: Cerf, 1996), 217–42.

9. Text in *AAS* 73 (1981): 80.

with Israel has become obsolete and has been abrogated, as the Christian tradition has often said. How then should the relation between the Mosaic covenant and the Christic covenant be understood? We noted how St. Paul struggled with that problem in the letter to the Romans (chaps. 9–11). We followed the rethinking on it in the recent context of the Jewish-Christian theological dialogue, with special reference to the work of Norbert Lohfink, *The Covenant Never Revoked.*[10] The argument need not be repeated here. It suffices to present the conclusions with regard to common prayer. Lohfink concludes, "I lean therefore to a 'one covenant' theory which however embraces Jews and Christians, whatever their differences in the one covenant, and that means Jews and Christians of today" (p. 84). We also cited a more recent author who likewise writes, "This ['new covenant'] is not another covenant that would have replaced that of Sinai. It is one and the same covenant of grace, in which the Jewish people and the people brought together in the Church participate, albeit differently of course."[11]

We ourselves concluded that Israel and Christianity are unbreakably joined together in salvation history under the arc of the same covenant, though shared differently. There is no substitution, we added, of another people as a "new" people of God, henceforth declared to be "old," but rather an expansion of the people of God to the ends of the earth.

Everything that has been said has important consequences for the possibility of a common prayer between Christians and Jews. Despite the differences in how the two groups share in the single divine covenant, both have the same God, and stand under the arc of the same divine covenant; indeed, together they constitute the same people of God. Joint prayer between them will be a matter of recognizing the common bond that unites them with one another in the divine plan of salvation for humankind, their differences and contradictions notwithstanding. It will consist in giving thanks to God for his gratuitous and irrevocable gifts.

With regard to the way in which common Christian-Jewish prayer can proceed, it cannot be forgotten that Jesus was a Jew and regularly went to the synagogue, where he participated in its prayer. The apostolic church continued to do the same in the first decades of its existence until it separated from its Jewish matrix. Even after that separation, Jewish prayer continued to provide substantial nourishment to that of Christians. The psalms in particular even today constitute an enormous portion of the "Christian prayer book." It is clear that most of the psalms can be shared by Christians and Jews in a common prayer. Likewise acceptable to all should be the prayer taught by Jesus to his disciples, whose content and wording are deeply inspired by the spirituality of the Hebrew Bible. It has been noted by biblical scholars that the only characteristically Christian tone in the "Lord's Prayer" is the intimacy and familiarity with which the disciples are invited to address God as "Father" with the use of the term *"Abbà"*; yet, it should

---

10. Norbert Lohfink, *The Covenant Never Revoked: Biblical Reflections on Christian-Jewish Dialogue* (New York: Paulist Press, 1991).

11. Erich Zenger, *Il Primo Testamento: La bibbia ebraica e i cristiani* (Brescia: Queriniana, 1997), 133–34.

never be forgotten that the fatherhood of Yahweh vis-à-vis Israel is a theme of Old Testament spirituality, based on the central event of the Exodus.

COMMON PRAYER BETWEEN CHRISTIANS AND MUSLIMS

The Vatican Secretariat for Non-Christians has presented directives on this matter in its *Guidelines for a Dialogue between Christians and Muslims*. The second edition of the Guidelines (1988)[12] states as follows:

> It happens that Christians and Muslims feel the need of praying together and they realize immediately how difficult it is. It seems that both sides must fully respect that which constitutes the ritual prayer and official worship of their partners, without ever seeking to participate directly, but willingly agreeing to be witnesses, if they are invited to attend, or if they ask to be present, in the name of the hospitality of Abraham. True dialogue demands that invitations under pressure or facile confusions be avoided: some would see there masquerading forms of self-serving proselytizing, and others would deduce from it an intention of practical syncretism.
>
> The same thing will have to be applied to the sacred books and the official texts that flow from the authentic expression of the faith of both sides: the Koran belongs primarily to Muslims and the *"fatiha"* is the prayer proper to them, as the New Testament belongs primarily to Christians and the "Our Father" is the prayer that best corresponds to their faith. Demonstrating proof of respect for the faith of others here means avoiding any intention of annexation and any attempt at recuperation. Even so, it may be thought that both sides may find in the example of the mystics and the saints the boldness needed to create common forms of praise and supplication that will reunite them in an experience of jointly lived prayer. (p. 152)[13]

While not ruling out the possibility of a common prayer between Christians and Muslims, the Guidelines are very careful to preclude any kind or appearance of syncretism or undue recuperation. It must, however, be asked in the context of dialogue with Muslims whether there may not be a specific basis that may justify, and indeed even perhaps encourage, such a practice.

In speaking of the esteem with which the church views Muslims "who adore the one God," Vatican II insists on the fact that they seek to submit themselves

---

12. Cf. Maurice Borrmans, *Orientamenti per un dialogo tra cristiani e musulmani* (Rome: UUP, 1988).

13. It can be noted that in the first edition (1971) the Guidelines seemed less rigid. While ruling out active participation in the worship of the other religion, they left the door open to spontaneously joining, at least on special occasions, in prayers belonging to the legacy of the other religion. However, they regarded it as more appropriate to use prayers composed for the specific occasion based on common beliefs as expressions of religious feelings shared by all the participants. Some well-chosen psalms or texts drawn from Muslim mystics could express such sentiments well. See Secretariatus pro Non-Christianis, *Guidelines for a Dialogue between Muslims and Christians*, Indian edition (Cochin: K. C. M. Press, 1979), 128, n. 1.

to his "hidden decrees... just as Abraham submitted himself to God's plan, to whose faith Muslims eagerly link their own" (*Nostra Aetate* §3). It should be noted that the council is content to state that Muslims connect their faith to that of Abraham, without explicitly saying that they indeed share in that faith together with Jews and Christians. The church's official documents have become gradually more explicit in this regard.[14] On a number of occasions, Pope John Paul II has removed the ambiguity remaining in the council documents. A few examples will suffice. Speaking to the Catholic community in Ankara (December 3, 1979), he said unequivocally, "They [Muslims], like you, have the faith of Abraham in one, almighty, merciful God."[15] In Lisbon (May 14, 1982), the pope referred to "Abraham, the common ancestor of Christians, Jews, and Muslims." Perhaps the clearest and most explicit text is found in John Paul II's speech to young Muslims in Casablanca (August 19, 1985), where he said, "For us, Abraham is a common model of faith in God, of submission to his will and of confidence in his goodness. We believe in the same God, the one God, the living God, the God who created the world and brings his creatures to their perfection."[16] All three so-called monotheistic religions have a common historic foundation in the faith of Abraham.

We previously showed that Christian monotheism claims direct continuity with Jewish monotheism. The God of Moses is the God of Jesus Christ — and also the God of the Qur'an and Islam. The teaching of the Qur'an, as we said in an earlier chapter, is in agreement: "Our God and your God are one" (Sura 29:46).[17] All three traditions therefore unequivocally claim to be rooted in the God of Abraham. They share the same God.[18] That does not mean, however, as was noted earlier, that the three monotheistic religions have the same notion of that God. Doctrinally speaking at least, the opposite is the case. The Christian tradition claims to extend the monotheism of Israel, while developing it into Trinitarian doctrine; that of the Qur'an and the Islamic tradition also highlights its origins in the monotheism of Israel, while claiming to complete it and purify it of the corruption it suffered at the hands of the Christian doctrine of the trinity. However, such irreducible divergences among the three "faiths" notwithstanding, their common historic foundation still remains, namely God's self-revelation to Abraham at the beginning of the Hebrew-Christian-Muslim biblical tradition, along with the identity of that same God, the God of Abraham, Isaac, and Moses, whom Christians call the Father of the Lord Jesus Christ.

With regard to the basis for a common prayer between Christians and Muslims, it will further have to be asked what precise significance Christians can

---

14. See Thomas Michel, "Islamo-Christian Dialogue: Reflections on the Recent Teaching of the Church," Secretariatus pro Non-Christianis, *Bulletin* n. 59, 20, no. 2 (1985): 172–93.

15. *Origins* 26, no. 9 (1979): 419.

16. *Islamochristiana* 11 (1985): 201.

17. *The Koran*, ed. Muhammad Rafrulla Khan (London: Curzon Press, 1975).

18. Karl-Josef Kuschel, *La controversia su Abramo: Ciò che divide — e ciò che unisce ebrei, cristiani e musulmani* (Brescia: Queriniana, 1996); Roger Arnaldez, *Trois messagers pour un seul Dieu* (Paris: Albin Michel, 1983).

attribute to the Qur'an and Muslims to the Hebrew and Christian Bible, as word of God. Without going into the merits of that discussion,[19] let it suffice to recall what was noted in chapter 5, namely, that the same God can speak, albeit differently, in all three scriptures of the monotheistic traditions. The Qur'an may also contain some word given by God to human beings, albeit different and incomplete, and not without admixture of human errors.[20]

Thus, there is a theological foundation on which to base the possibility, even the desirability, of a common prayer between Christians, Jews, and Muslims. On this point, Karl-Josef Kuschel writes:

> If they take seriously the fact that Muslims adore the same God, Christians can address their prayers to this God, the creator of heaven and earth, the merciful and benevolent who leads human history, the judge and perfector of the world and humankind. The same thing must be said of the Jews; if they can recognize the presence of the patriarch Abraham in the other brothers and sisters, they can pray to the God of Abraham, not only together with Christians, but even with Muslims.[21]

In such common prayers there must only be expressed convictions common to the diverse traditions involved. Specifically, the same author suggests that from the sacred scriptures of the various traditions, the following may be used: the psalms of the Hebrew Bible; the prayer of Jesus, i.e., the "Our Father"; the *"fatiha,"* that is, the Sura which opens the Qur'an by way of invocation of Allah, which represents the key prayer of the Islamic tradition, as the "Our Father" does in the Christian tradition, and has accordingly been called the "Our Father of Islam." Here is the text:

> In the name of Allah, Most Gracious, Ever Merciful.
>
> All types of perfect praise belong to Allah alone,
> the Lord of all the worlds,
> Most Gracious,
> Ever Merciful,
> Master of the Day of Judgment.
> Thee alone do we worship and Thee alone do we implore for help.
> Guide us along the straight path —
> the path of those on whom Thou has bestowed Thy favours,
> those who have not incurred Thy displeasure, and
> those who have not gone astray. (Sura 1).[22]

Moreover, in ecumenical gatherings for prayer between Jews, Christians, and Muslims, many spontaneous prayers may also be formulated. Kuschel concludes,

---

19. See Groupe de recherches Islamo-Chrétien, *Ces écrites qui nous questionnent* (Paris: Centurion, 1987).

20. Cf. Claude Geffré, "Le Coran, un parole de Dieu différente?" *Lumière et Vie* 32 (1983): 21–32.

21. Kuschel, *La controversia su Abram*, 418.

22. *The Koran*, ed. Muhammad Rafrulla Khan.

"One thing is indeed certain: without prayer there is no true and spiritually deep ecumenism, *without spirituality there is no ecumenicity*" (p. 422). Common prayer between the three monotheistic religions is simply the embodiment of a true "Abrahamitic hospitality."

COMMON PRAYER BETWEEN CHRISTIANS AND THE "OTHERS"

In this section, the word "others" is understood to mean the members of other religious traditions who do not belong to the Abrahamitic "family"; that is, those traditions, primarily in the East, that we earlier called "mystical" religions. Among them two world religions deserve special mention, namely Hinduism and Buddhism.

In their case, the issue of common prayer is even more complex. That is so for a number of reasons — not least the luxuriant variety and enormous complexity of the data that they present and the different overall worldview (*Weltanschauung*) on which they are based. Without going into particular considerations on the different religious traditions and currents, we must note the following: whereas in the encounter with theistic currents which are quite widespread in Hinduism, sharing in a common prayer is conceivable, when it comes to those currents that profess to be "nontheistic" such as Buddhism, for example, what will be proposed is sharing in meditation, that is, in common contemplation. Be that as it may, here we will limit ourselves to some general theological considerations, which may serve to reinforce what was said earlier in the first part of this chapter. The aim is to situate the issue of common prayer or meditation in the framework of a Christian theology that is broad and open to the religions, highlighting the positive significance of the other religious traditions in God's overall plan of salvation for humankind.

The issue of the relationship between the "Absolute Reality" affirmed by Asian religions and the God of the monotheistic religions, who according to Christian faith has been revealed decisively in Jesus Christ, must be raised theologically. Is it legitimate to think, from the standpoint of a Christian theology, that the "Ultimate Reality" to which those religions point is, the great diversity of their mental constructs notwithstanding, the same as that which the monotheistic religions affirm to be the God of Abraham, Isaac, and Jacob? Is there an "Ultimate Reality" common to all religious traditions, albeit experienced differently and conceived variously by the different traditions? A single divine mystery with many faces?

We gave a positive response to that fundamental question in a previous chapter. It suffices here to recall these conclusions insofar as they have a bearing on common prayer or contemplation. "All have the same God," wrote Walbert Bühlmann,[23] having in mind the "God Father of our Lord Jesus Christ." For our part, we thought it possible to hold that wherever there is a genuine religious

---

23. Cf. the work already cited, Walbert Bühlmann, *All Have the Same God* (Slough, U.K.: St. Paul Publications, 1982).

experience, surely the God revealed in Jesus Christ enters in a hidden, secret manner into the lives of men and women. Despite the contrasting concepts of the "Ultimate Reality" (Paul Tillich's *ultimate concern*) involved in the religious experience lived in the other religious traditions, Christian theologians, holding to a Trinitarian monotheism — in continuity with Jewish revelation and their own tradition — cannot but interpret that Reality in terms of the universal presence and self-manifestation of the one tri-personal God. For them the divine mystery with many faces is unequivocally the God and Father who has revealed his face for us in Jesus Christ. He is also the God toward whom every sincere prayer is addressed, whether consciously or not, through the action of the divine Spirit, who is present and at work in every sincere human prayer. Whenever people open up in faith and entrust themselves to an Absolute on whom they depend absolutely, present there in self-manifestation and self-revelation is the one God, the God of all human beings.

Such being the case, it is legitimate to think that Christians and the "others," the conceptual differences about the divine Absolute notwithstanding, can together address their prayer or meditation toward that Absolute who in any case is beyond any adequate mental representation. Thus we turn to what has been said previously about the active presence of the Spirit of God in every sincere prayer, whether by Christians or by the "others." Praying together will simply make it possible for them in a certain sense to meet together with one another in the Spirit of God, present and at work on both sides. On the Christian side, it also indicates an acknowledgment that all belong to the same God, creator and universal end of all peoples. As Vatican II says:

> All peoples form but one community. This is so because all stem from the same stock which God created to people the entire earth, and also because all share a common destiny, namely God. His providence, His evident goodness, and saving designs extend to all humankind till the day when the elect will be gathered together in the Holy City which is illumined by the glory of God, and in whose splendor all peoples will walk. (*Nostra Aetate* §1)

It was previously noted that as all peoples constitute a single community, likewise they belong together to the Reign of God present in history; that Reign is growing through history toward its eschatological fullness. That Christians and the "others" together are members of the Reign of God means that they share, whether consciously or not, in the same mystery of salvation in Jesus Christ. Joint members of the Reign, they are also co-creators of it under God. That means that they are called to promote together the values of the Reign of God, namely justice and peace, freedom and brother- and sisterhood, faith and charity. Christians have no monopoly on such gospel values. In the context of the Reign of God which is to be built in history through the common engagement of the members of the various religious traditions, it can be better understood how commendable and desirable it becomes that there be common prayer between Christians and "others" for peace and justice in the world, for freedom and universal brother-

and sisterhood between the peoples of the world. In short, despite the deep doctrinal differences between Christianity and the Asian mystical religions, there remains a common theological substrate and an anticipated communion, which is destined to grow through the practice of dialogue and can be expressed uniquely in common prayer and contemplation.

With regard to the choice of prayers that can be shared between Christians and the "others" there may be suggested, by way of example and beside those noted earlier, the "Canticle of the Creatures" of St. Francis of Assisi, in which he blesses God for the entire creation; the hymn to the unknown God attributed to St. Gregory Nazianzen; in Hinduism some passages of the *Upanishads* and of the *BhagavadGītā*, and of religious mystics and poets; as well as other texts borrowed from other Eastern traditions.[24] By way of examples, some texts borrowed from the *Upanishads* and the *BhagavadGītā* will be quoted here, followed by the famous hymn attributed to Gregory Nazianzen. All these texts give voice to the impenetrability of the divine mystery, which remains and will ever remain beyond full human comprehension. All religious traditions indeed share that sense of the incomprehensibility of the Absolute Mystery.

One well-known passage is that of the *Bṛhadāraṇyaka Upaniṣad* (I, 3, 28) which was cited by Paul VI in his address to representatives of the various religions during his visit to Bombay for the 1964 Eucharistic Congress:

> From the unreal lead me to the real!
> From darkness lead me to the light!
> From death lead me to immortality![25]

Another passage, drawn from the *Kena Upaniṣad* (I, 3–8), insists on the fact that the *Brahman* which is both transpersonal (*nirguṇa*) and personal (*saguṇa*) is situated beyond all human knowledge: It is *neti, neti* ("not this, not that"); it is "different from that which is known and also from that which is unknown":

3. There no eye can penetrate,
No voice, no mind can penetrate:
we do not know, we do not understand
How one should teach it.

Other It is, for sure, than what is known,
Beyond [the scope of] the unknown too.
So have we heard from men of old
Who instructed us therein.

4. That which cannot be expressed by speech,
By which speech [itself] is uttered,
That is *Brahman* — know thou [this] . . .

---

24. See Boespflug and Labbé, eds., *Assise: 10 ans après 1986–96*, 242–47; Kuschel, *La controversia su Abramo*, 420–24.

25. *Hindu Scriptures*, ed. R. C. Zaehner (London: Dent, 1966), 34.

5. That which thinks not by the mind,
By which, they say, the mind is thought,
That is *Brahman* — know thou [this] . . . [26]

In the *BhagavadGītā*, addressing the Supreme God in adoration, Arjuna sings his praise expansively and devotedly as follows:

36. Full just it is that in praise of Thee
The world should find its pleasure and its joy,
That monsters by terror [tamed] should scatter in all directions,
And that all who've won perfection should do Thee homage.

37. For why should they not revere Thee, great as is thy Self,
More to be prized art Thou than *Brahmā*, [Thou] the first Creator,
God's Lord, the world's [abiding] home, unending,
Thou art the Imperishable, Being, Not-Being and what surpasses both.

38. Thou art the Primal God, Primeval Person,
Thou of this universe the last prop and resting-place,
Thou the knower and what is to be known, [Thou our] final home
    [*dhāma*],
O Thou whose forms are infinite, by whom the whole [universe] was spun.

39. All hail [to Thee] when I stand before Thee,
[All hail] when I stand behind Thee,
All hail to Thee wherever I may be,
[All hail to Thee], Thou All![27]

And here is the *Hymn of Gregory Nazianzen*, which contains accents similar to those expressed in the passages from Hindu mysticism just cited:

> By what name shall I call upon you,
> Who are beyond all name?
> You are beyond all; what name shall I give you?
> What hymn can sing your praises
>   or what word tell of you?
> No mind can probe your secret,
>   no intelligence comprehends you.
> All that is spoken proceeds from you,
> But you remain beyond the reach of speech.
> All that is thought stems from you,
> But you are beyond the power of thought.
> All things proclaim you,
> The mute and those with the power of speech.
> All things celebrate you,

26. Ibid., 161.
27. Ibid., 298.

The unconscious and those endowed with consciousness.
The longings of the universe,
The groanings of the entire creation,
Are turned toward you in silent prayer.
All who know to interpret the world you have created
Sing to you a hymn of praise.
All that subsists you uphold;
All that moves you draw.
You are the goal of all that is;
you are one, O God.
You are all the things that are and you are none;
You are not the part and you are not the whole.
All names are given to you and none comprehends you.
How shall I name you, who are beyond all name?[28]

IN SHORT, IT CAN BE SAID that common prayer between Christians and the "others" has a sure theological foundation, even if that foundation has not been adequately highlighted in the past. Obviously, such prayer requires on the part of all participants involved a great sensitivity and a deep respect for the differences existing between the various religious traditions, together with an attitude of openness to them. The practice of common prayer is based on a communion in the Spirit of God shared in anticipation between Christians and "others," which in turn grows and is deepened through such practice. Through common prayer, Christians and the "others" grow together in the Spirit. Common prayer seems then to be the soul of interreligious dialogue, the deepest expression of dialogue and at the same time the guarantee of a deeper common conversion of the partners to God and to the others.[29]

---

28. PG 37, 507–8. Translation in J. Dupuis, I. M. Echaniz, and J. Volckaert, *Give Praise to the Lord: Community Prayer Book* (Gamdi-Anand: Anand Press, 1971), 67–68.

29. Cf. François Boespflug, "De l'horizon multiple où les religions peuvent se rencontrer," in Boespflug and Labbé, eds., *Assise: 10 ans après,* 296.

CONCLUSION

A S EXPLAINED IN THE INTRODUCTION to this work, the overarching question asked in recent theology of religions is whether and in what sense it can be said that the different religious traditions of the contemporary world have a positive meaning in God's single but complex plan for humankind. Such a question goes beyond the earlier question about the mere possibility of salvation in Jesus Christ for members of other religious traditions, or that of a possible recognition of positive values, whether "natural" or "of truth and grace," that might be found inside those traditions. By contrast, the new perspective entails asking whether such religious traditions find their justification in God's universal plan of salvation and accordingly have a positive value as "ways" or "routes" of salvation for their followers foreseen or intended by God.

In order to avoid possible misunderstandings, a clear distinction must be made between the proposal made here and the "pluralist" paradigm postulated by the "pluralist" theologians. The "paradigm shift" from inclusivism to "pluralism" pursued and promoted by the "pluralists" is based on the a priori rejection of the universal saving significance of the person and event of Jesus Christ, as it has been traditionally professed by the Christian faith. Jesus Christ is reduced by the "pluralists" to being one saving figure among many offered by the other religious traditions as "ways" leading toward the ultimate Mystery. All these ways are in principle of equal value; no "singular" uniqueness need or can be attributed to Jesus Christ as universal Savior of humankind. By contrast, the challenge that the theological perspective sustained here seeks to meet entails simultaneously holding and combining, albeit in dialectical tension, both the central claim of Christian faith on the unique significance of the person of Jesus Christ as universal constitutive Savior of all of humankind, and a salvific value, within the sole divine plan intended for humankind, for the "ways" of salvation proposed by the other religious traditions. Such is the meaning of the "religious pluralism in principle" sustained here, which has nothing to do with the "paradigm shift" toward a neutral and indifferent "pluralism" of the "pluralists." Jesus Christ is indeed the constitutive Savior of humankind, and the Christ event is the cause of the salvation of all human beings; but this does not prevent the other traditions from serving as "mediations" of the mystery of salvation in Jesus Christ for their followers within God's design for humankind.

RELIGIOUS PLURALISM IN PRINCIPLE

Over the various chapters of this work we have assembled different elements that seem to justify the claim of a "religious pluralism in principle." We have seen that God has manifested and revealed Godself in saving words and deeds throughout the entire history of humankind since creation. "Salvation history" encompasses the entire history of the world and humankind. It is "salvation in history" and throughout all of history. God has made various covenants with humankind in history, before making a "new covenant" with it in Jesus Christ. These different covenants in Adam and Noah, and in Abraham and Moses, are in God's providence directed toward the "new" covenant in Jesus Christ, but they are not thereby provisional, nor have they ever been abolished or revoked. They remain valid and operative in their relationship to the Christ event in the overall framework of God's design for humankind. God has thus spoken "in many and various ways" to humankind before speaking his decisive word "through the Son" (Heb 1:1), through the one who is the Word. We concluded that all peoples are "peoples of God," and that they all live "under the arc of the divine covenant."

The Jesus Christ event must be seen in the overall framework of God's design running through the entire history of humankind. That event is unquestionably the center, apex, high point, and interpretive key of the entire historic saving process; as such, it has universal saving significance. But it must never be isolated from the entire process, as though by itself it represented and exhausted God's entire saving power. Rather, the historic (and as such particular) saving event of Jesus Christ leaves room for a saving action by God, through his Word and his Spirit, that goes beyond even the risen humanity of the incarnate Word. The universal inclusive presence over the centuries of the Christ event through the risen humanity of the Jesus of history become "metahistoric," the universal operative presence of the Word of God, and that of the Spirit of God: all three elements are combined and together they represent the totality of God's saving action toward human beings and peoples. God's self-manifestation and self-communication have taken place in different ways throughout history. At every step God has taken the initiative in the encounter between God and human beings. This is why it seems that it can and must be said that the world's religious traditions are "ways" or "routes" of salvation for their followers. They are such because they represent "ways" traced by God himself for the salvation of human beings. It is not human beings who have first set out in search of God through their history; rather God has set out first to approach them and to trace for them the "ways" over which they may find him. If, as has been suggested, the world's religions are in themselves "gifts of God to the peoples of the world," the foundation for a "religious pluralism in principle" as understood here need not be sought far away.

However, such pluralism must be established on a sure theological foundation. The question raised by the term "in principle" is whether the religious pluralism in which we are living today is simply to be accepted or tolerated as a de facto reality of our current world that must be taken into account, rather than as something welcome; that is, received gratefully as a positive factor that at the same time attests to the sovereign generosity with which God has manifested himself in many ways to humankind and to the manifold response that human beings have made to God's self-revelation in different cultures. It would be presumptuous to pretend to sound out God's design for humankind; no human consciousness will ever be able to claim the divine vision of reality. That having been admitted, however, it can be asked whether the way that "God knows" (mentioned in *Gaudium et Spes* §22) through which the Spirit of God gives to all human beings the possibility of coming into contact with the Christic mystery of salvation, may not be the religions of the world as "paths" initiated by God in pursuit of human beings.

On what basis, then, can the affirmation of a religious pluralism "in principle" be based? The appeal to faith in a plurality of persons in the one God is not in itself a sufficient reason for it; a simple appeal to the "plural" character of all reality (the multiplicity of elements in nature, of the seasons of the year, of the dimensions of space and time, and the like) would be even more inadequate. Nor will it do simply to point to the variety of ways in which human beings, in the diversity of cultures in the world, have given expression to their search for the divine Mystery, and to the innate, inevitable limits of any human grasp of the Mystery. To stop at that point would be the same as seeking to found a plurality in principle on a truncated view of religion and of the religions as nothing but a human search for God.

If, however, religion and the religions originate in a self-manifestation of God to human beings, the primary foundation for the principle of multiplicity is the superabundant riches and variety of God's self-manifestation to humankind. God's initiative of self-communication, "in many and various ways," and its "reception" and codification in different traditions lie at the origin of the plurality of the religions. It forms part of the nature of the overflowing communication of the tri-personal God to humankind to extend beyond the divine life the plural communication inherent in that very life. Religious pluralism in principle is then based on the immensity of a God who is Love and communication.

If the perspective of "religious pluralism in principle" must be expressed in the usual terminology in the debate over the theology of religions, the most suitable expression, as was suggested earlier, will be that of a "pluralistic inclusivism" or of an "inclusive pluralism," which upholds both the universal constitutive character of the Christ event in the order of salvation and the positive saving significance of the religious traditions within the single manifold plan of God for humankind.

MUTUAL ASYMMETRICAL COMPLEMENTARITY

The model of a Trinitarian and Spirit-based Christology used in this book has allowed for a deeper understanding and a more positive appraisal of the other religious traditions. Such a model, used as an interpretive key, has made it possible to put the accent on the universality of the active presence of the Word of God and of his Spirit as source of "illumination" and "inspiration" of the religious founders and of the traditions that have issued from their experience. That interpretive key has been brought to bear at various stages of the inquiry, including the treatment of divine revelation and of God's self-gift in salvation, the various "faces" of the divine Mystery, and the "saving figures" and "ways of salvation" proposed by the various traditions. That has led to a view of the overall process of God's self-revelation throughout human history and finally in Jesus Christ — in whom it culminates — as an organic process in which the different stages are essentially related to one another and find their intelligibility and inner coherence on the basis of the entire process and in their relationship to its center and culmination, the Christ event.

The Trinitarian and pneumatic theological model of Christology thus makes it possible to overcome not only the "exclusivist" but also the "inclusivist" paradigm, without, however, resorting to the "pluralist" paradigm which is based on the negation of "constitutive" salvation in Jesus Christ. One thus arrives at a position which combines what must be retained from Christological inclusivism with what may be said theologically with regard to a certain pluralism of the religions in God's design. The inclusive efficacy of the Christ event through the risen humanity of Jesus, the universal "illumination" by the Word of God, and the equally universal "enlivening" by the Spirit make it possible to discover in other saving figures and traditions, truth and grace not made explicit with the same force and clarity in the revelation and manifestation of God in Jesus Christ. In the entire history of God's relations with humankind, there is more truth and grace than available and discoverable in the Christian tradition alone. Hence, the question emerges of a possible complementarity between the Christian tradition and the other religious traditions. We touched on this issue in chapter 5 of this book when we spoke of divine revelation and revelations, of words of God and of his Word. There remains to apply the principles to the question of complementarity between Christianity and the other religious traditions in general.

Jesus Christ, as "human face" or "icon" of God — the Word of God made flesh — has a specific, unique and singular, constitutive and universal character of truth and grace. But, while it is true that he is constitutive of salvation for all, and indeed cause of their salvation, he neither excludes nor includes other saving figures or traditions. That he does not exclude them is understood in the sense that elements of divine "truth and grace" are at work also outside the Christian tradition springing from Jesus Christ, though not unrelated to his person and his work. That he does not include them, on the other hand, means that whatever truth and grace are found in other religious traditions are not absorbed and as it were expropriated from them by the Christian tradition. Such elements "of truth and grace" rather constitute additional and autonomous benefits.

The various religious traditions of the world contain therefore elements of "truth and grace" (*Ad Gentes* §9); the decisive character of the Christ event notwithstanding, it is not possible to think that Christianity — and the Christian religion — possesses the entirety of the truth or has the monopoly of grace. God is Truth and Love. His Truth and Love take possession of human beings in a way "known to God" (*Gaudium et Spes* §22), often beyond our calculations. One can therefore speak of a certain *complementarity* between Christian truth and grace and those outside Christianity. But this complementarity must be correctly determined.

The truth and grace that can be found elsewhere ought not to be reduced to "seeds" or "stepping stones" (*pierres d'attente*) that must simply find completion by way of substitution in Christian revelation. If that revelation brings salvation history to its culmination, it is not by way of substitution or replacement, but through confirmation and accomplishment. The Christ event, culmination of saving history, does not cancel out but confirms all that God has done for humankind before that event and in view of it. The complementarity in question is not to be understood unilaterally as though the values scattered outside Christianity by way of fragmentary truths should univocally find "fulfillment" — in a unilateral process — in Christian values and should be destined to be simply "integrated," assumed, and absorbed into Christianity, thereby losing their self-consistency. Rather it is a *mutual complementarity* whereby an exchange and a sharing of saving values, a dynamic interaction, can take place between Christianity and the other traditions, such that it can result in mutual enrichment. Because the complementarity between them is reciprocal, their interaction is not one-way, a "monologue," but an interreligious dialogue. Any authentic dialogue necessarily involves receiving and giving, listening and testifying, by both parties. Christian tradition can be enriched by contact and interaction with other religious traditions, if it is true, as said earlier, that there are true and authentic aspects of the divine Mystery that are more deeply accented in other traditions than they are in the Christian tradition.

It must also be added that the mutual complementarity between the Christian tradition and the other religious traditions as sources of divine truth and grace is *asymmetrical*. This means that the acknowledgment of additional and autonomous values of truth and grace in the other traditions does not cancel out the unsurpassable transcendence of God's revelation and self-communication in the person and work of Jesus Christ. Such transcendence, as has been clearly stated earlier, is based on the personal identity of Jesus Christ as the only-begotten Son of God made man. He is personally, in the sense explained, the "fullness" of revelation and the accomplishment of the mystery of human salvation. Thus, whereas other religious traditions can find, and are destined to find, in the Christ event their fullness of meaning — but without being absorbed or dispossessed — the reverse is not true: God's self-manifestation and self-giving in Jesus Christ are not in need of a true completion by other traditions, even though they are interrelated with the other divine manifestations in the overall realm of God's self-revelation to humankind, and can be enriched by mutually interacting with other religious traditions. By contrast, the other religious traditions are oriented toward the mystery of Jesus Christ in whom they can find their fullness; however, that orientation does not prevent the germs of "truth and grace" contained in them, as gifts granted by God to the nations, endowed with their own intrinsic value, from contributing positively to the enrichment of Christianity through dialogue, albeit not in the sense of filling a void which the fullness of Jesus Christ would have left open and which would remain to be filled.

A QUALITATIVE LEAP

In order to develop relationships of mutual openness and collaboration between Christianity and the other religious traditions there is need, as we noted in the very introduction to this book, for a purification of memories. That does not mean forgetting the often contentious past which has marked those relationships, let alone forgetting the crimes against humankind that have often been perpetrated in the name of God and religion; rather it means a change of mindset and spirit in all, in effect a "conversion" (*metanoia*) to God and to the "others," that will allow for a healing of relations. We added that a purification of theological language is likewise needed, in terms of the often offensive and harmful way in which we spoke about other religious traditions and their members in the past. We offered some examples which need not be repeated. But a linguistic purification is still not enough. What is sought is actually a purification of theological understanding itself, and a fresh comprehension of how to think about the "others" and their cultural and religious legacy. It should not be forgotten that deeds follow thought; and hence, that the negative and often offensive attitudes toward other religions that have characterized the past have issued from the often unjust and defamatory assessments that have been made of them. To give a pressing example: it is true that a clear distinction must be made between religious "anti-Judaism" and "anti-Semitism" as an atheistic ideology; however, it may be asked whether traditional Christian "anti-Judaism" has not to some extent nourished and aided the development of that inhuman ideology.

Be that as it may, it cannot be forgotten that over many centuries, Christianity has taken on the aspect of a religion that is "exclusive" of others — an exclusivism whose clearest symbol was the axiom "outside the church there is no salvation," understood narrowly; we noted that for centuries that axiom was maintained as official church teaching. Christianity was seen as the "only true religion," which, since it possessed the entire truth, was the only possible way of salvation for all human beings, or even the only religion that had the right to exist. The exclusion of any positive significance of the other religions in the order of salvation remained in fact the opinion shared by most theologians until the decades just before Vatican II, when some began to recognize in them not only positive "natural" values, but even elements "of truth and grace."

It cannot be forgotten that Vatican II was the first council in the two-thousand-year history of church councils to speak positively of the religions, recognizing positive values in them. Whether it was a "watershed" or not remains open to discussion, depending on the meaning that the council intended to give to the expressions that it used in reference to the religious traditions:

"seeds of the Word" (*Ad Gentes* §§11, 15), "a ray of that Truth which enlightens all men and women" (*Nostra Aetate* §2), elements of "truth and grace" (*Ad Gentes* §9). One thing is certain: the council never intended to give the impression that it regarded the other religions as "ways" of salvation for their followers, though in relationship with the Christ event of salvation. While the council's openness represented something new in official teaching, it ultimately remained limited and scant. That having been said, however, the often prophetic gestures and often remarkably open words of Pope John Paul II, which encourage new steps forward to be taken toward a broader theological opening and more courageous concrete stances, cannot be ignored. Like all councils in the life of the church, Vatican II does not represent a last word but rather a first word; it points the direction in which to walk in order to reach a broader understanding of God's design for humankind, which will always remain beyond our complete comprehension.

In this context, the aim of this book was to propose some guidelines for reflection which could lead to a "qualitative leap" by the Christian and Catholic theology of the religions toward a more positive theological assessment of them and a more open concrete stance toward their followers. It goes without saying that the proposals advanced here are deliberately set within the framework of ecclesial faith and remain open to theological discussion. Yet we are persuaded that such a "qualitative leap" — which, to say it once more, has nothing to do with the "paradigm shift" toward theological pluralism — is required in order for the Christian message to retain its credibility in today's multicultural and multireligious world; or better, so that such credibility may grow in proportion to the adaptation of the message to the broader horizons of the contemporary world. What must be avoided are the ways of "defending the faith" that turn out to be counterproductive, by making it appear to be restrictive and narrow. I am convinced that a broader approach and a more positive attitude, provided that they be theologically well grounded, will help us to discover, to our surprise, new breadths and new depths in the Christian message.

POSTSCRIPT

A s THE INTRODUCTION STATES, this book was completed on March 31, 2000. Two documents have been published since then by the Congregation for the Doctrine of the Faith, to which it has not been possible to refer in the course of the redaction of the book. The first document is the Declaration *Dominus Iesus*, published by the Congregation on September 5, 2000, the full title of which is "Declaration *Dominus Iesus* on the Unicity and Salvific Universality of Jesus Christ and the Church." This document has been published in different languages in booklet form by the Libreria Editrice Vaticana. Its official Latin text is found in *AAS* 92 (2000/10) (October 7), pp. 742–65. The second document is a *Notification* about my previous book, *Toward a Christian Theology of Religious Pluralism* (Maryknoll, N.Y.: Orbis Books, 1997), which bears the title "Notification on the Book *Toward a Christian Theology of Religious Pluralism* by Jacques Dupuis." It was originally published in Italian in *Osservatore Romano* on February 27, 2001. The official text of the *Notification* notes the existence in the book of "notable ambiguities and difficulties on important doctrinal points, which could lead a reader to erroneous or harmful opinions" (preface). Such potentially harmful ambiguities ought to be dispelled.

Both documents are closely related to several themes developed in the previous book as well as in the present one. The *Declaration* establishes at length the doctrinal principles on the matters concerned, as these are found either in the divine and Catholic faith or in Catholic doctrine; it goes on to refute doctrines and opinions which it considers to contradict either the faith or the church's teaching. The *Notification*, as is explicitly stated in a note, "draws from the principles expressed in *Dominus Iesus* in its evaluation of Father Dupuis' book" (note 1). The connection between the two documents is clear and in no need of being elaborated: the subject matter is the same; the general themes are similar; the same elements of divine faith are stressed and the same points of Catholic doctrine are emphasized; the errors and false opinions refuted in both cases coincide. Though being a much shorter document which omits all extensive developments of the doctrine, the *Notification* follows the same method and carries the same material as the *Declaration*. It is divided into eight main propositions. In six of these it begins by stating clearly the content of the faith or of Catholic doctrine, thereafter to refute, in a second step, the opinions which are considered errors against the faith or against Catholic doctrine.

In a situation in which I find myself directly concerned, the question arises about the present new book abstaining from making any explicit reference to either of the two documents. Is it enough to say that the manuscript of the book was completed, as has been noted above, before the publication of the two documents? Should the manuscript have been revised seriously in the light of what the two documents affirm or deny? Or at least should abundant references to the documents have been included to discuss and justify possible points of disagreement? A deeper explanation is required to justify the apparent silence observed in the book about the two documents. Several elements must be considered here.

First, it must be remembered that, as has been stated in the introduction, the publishing houses had requested from the author a text which would be more adapted to a broader public than its predecessor had been. *Toward a Christian Theology of Religious Pluralism* had in view theologians by profession and specialists on the theology of religions. It was bound therefore to enter into detailed discussions which a broader public would not need in order to grasp the main argument of the book, and would be ill-equipped to follow. In order to produce a text more readable for many, the new book has deliberately left out some subtle discussions; notes have been reduced to the minimum required, and a more pastoral orientation has been given to the entire treatment. It is this new orientation that suggests not overloading the new text with long discussions with the two recent documents of the Congregation for the Doctrine of the Faith. It seems preferable to keep the text of the book as originally written.

It would be wrong, however, to conclude that the content of the two documents is thereby ignored in this new book. In what sense and under what shape the two documents are in fact everywhere present in the text needs, however, to be explained. Account must be taken of the fact that as early as June 1998, *Toward a Christian Theology of Religious Pluralism* — which had been originally published in September 1997 — had been submitted to investigation by the Congregation for the Doctrine of the Faith. Over a period that lasted for almost three years the author had to answer questions addressed to him by the Congregation. This long procedure, however burdensome it may have been, provided the author with the opportunity to consider more closely some important issues, to revise some positions, to clarify concepts, to avoid ambiguities in the expression of his thought. The three substantial articles written during that long period — two of which have been published in Italian and English — to which reference has been made in the introduction, witness to this continuous process of rethinking and rewording. Though these articles addressed themselves to questions asked by fellow theologians in some book-reviews and other studies, published in different languages, not to those formulated by the Congregation for the Doctrine of the Faith — to which no public reference could be made in writing — it is clear that the answers contained in them respond to both audiences. This is not surprising, as both the theologians and the Congregation often addressed themselves to the same problems and formulated similar doubts or misgivings. By responding explicitly to the theologians, the articles implicitly had in mind the Congregation as well. It can then be said that a continuous process of rethinking and rewording of the ideas contained in the previous book has been going on for almost three years, not without reference to the previous questioning, wherever it came from.

Compared to its predecessor, the present book has then, in the mind of the author, the merit of clarifying ideas in the light of prolonged discussions, of avoiding some ambiguities which had not been altogether absent in its predecessor, of reinforcing the foundation in the Christian revelation and tradition of some affirmations, of providing further explanations where some doctrines could seemingly have lacked in theological foundation. All this had to be and was in fact combined with the deliberate intention of being open to a large public and pastorally oriented.

How then does the new book relate to the content of the two recent documents from the Congregation for the Doctrine of the Faith? It goes without saying that it agrees without restriction with the documents wherever these assuredly profess the doctrine of divine and Catholic faith. There can be no dissent on the content of the faith, even while different enunciations of this content are possible in different contexts. Moreover, while the faith is one, distinct perceptions of that faith are also possible, due to different perspectives in which the faith is approached and different contexts in which it is expressed.

The documents of the Congregation approach the faith in a dogmatic perspective, based on select quotations from Scripture, from conciliar documents, and from pronouncements of the church's magisterium. This approach, while legitimate, is not necessarily exclusive. Another perspective consists in developing what has been called in this book a "Trinitarian and pneumatological Christology." Such a perspective has the merit of stressing the interrelationships with the Father, on the one hand, and with the Spirit, on the other, which are intrinsic to the mystery of Jesus Christ. God's dealings with humankind throughout history will then appear at once Trinitarian and Christological. The approach will also combine an inductive a posteriori method with the a priori deductive one, thus professing explicit reference to the concrete reality of de facto religious pluralism. The task of theology in this context will consist in asking whether the religious pluralism which characterizes our present world may or may not have a positive significance in God's one plan of salvation for humankind — whether, that is, the Christian faith in Jesus Christ, universal Savior of humankind, is compatible with the affirmation of a positive role of other religious traditions in the mystery of salvation of their followers.

The fact cannot be overlooked that some positions in the book either do not coincide in all respects with those expressed in the documents or enunciate the doctrine in a different manner. An effort has, however, been made in the book to clarify the divergences and to show which reasons seem to justify retaining a different way of expressing the doctrine, thereby dispelling the misunderstandings and misinterpretations to which the previous book has sometimes given rise. It goes without saying that divergences never imply a difference in the content of the faith but a distinct perception of the same faith in a different context. Such divergences are proposed in a spirit of constructive fidelity to Christ's revelation and to the church's doctrinal authority.

I have been aware of suggesting what I have called a "qualitative leap," which would open new horizons in what is even today the official teaching of the church's magisterium, though I meant and mean these new horizons to be deeply anchored in the church's living tradition and to build upon it. I was and remain convinced that the official teaching of the church does not intend to fix rigid and frozen boundaries beyond which theological research is forbidden to venture, but, while determining authoritatively what is of divine faith, draws up guidelines and indicates pointers along which theology may think and reflect anew, on the ineffable divine mystery which has been progressively disclosed to humankind throughout history and, "in these last days," "fully revealed" in Jesus Christ. The outcome has been what I have called an "inclusive pluralism" which, while having nothing in common with the pluralistic paradigm of the "pluralist theologians," would attempt to show how the Christian faith and doctrine can combine the faith-affirmation of the uniqueness of Jesus Christ as universal Savior and the theological understanding of a positive role and significance in the divine plan for humankind of the other religious traditions. I once more submit my efforts and endeavors to the consideration of my theological peers and to the judgment of the church's doctrinal authority.

There can be no doubt that the Christian identity must be preserved in its integrity in the process of encountering and entering into dialogue with the other religious traditions. There is no dialogue in a void or in a flux of personal religious persuasions. But the sincere affirmation of the Christian identity need not entail exclusivist statements by which any positive significance in God's eternal design for humankind, assigned to other traditions by God himself, is a priori denied. Absolute and exclusive statements about Christ and Christianity, which would claim the exclusive possession of God's self-disclosure or of the means of salvation, would distort and contradict the Christian message and the Christian image. Our one God is "three," and the communion-in-difference which characterizes God's inner life is reflected and operative in the one plan which Father, Son, and Spirit have devised for their dealings with humankind in revelation and salvation. The plurality of religions, then, finds its ultimate source in a God who is Love and communication.

In conclusion, I may express once more the conviction with which I ended the present book. I am deeply convinced that the teaching church would do well, in keeping with its oft-stated desire and claim to reproduce in its own life and practice the divine approach in the dialogue of salvation, to abstain from any ways of proposing the Christian faith which may imply insensitive or exclusivist evaluations of the others. Such an approach in "defending" the faith can only be counterproductive; it presents it with a "face" that is restrictive and narrow. I am convinced that a more positive approach and a more open attitude than is often enough in evidence even today, provided such an approach and attitude be theologically well founded, will strengthen the credibility of the Christian faith and help Christians themselves to discover in the Christian message new dimensions and a new depth.

INDEX

A WORD ON "THE CHRIST MANDALA"
OF NALINI JAYASURIYA

The strikingly strong painting of the Sri Lankan artist Nalini Jayasuriya, reproduced on the cover of this book, is entitled "The Christ Mandala." It is one of a several paintings by Ms. Jayasuriya that concretize a Sri Lankan Christian's imagination of Jesus as the Christ, God-among-us.

Mandala in the ancient Sanskrit language means both "center" and "circle" — a moving center that radiates endlessly in infinite circles, returning to the center of supreme, holy power. The Tibetan Buddhist mandala is a cosmic visual form used as a meditational diagram to rally and unify the senses in the intellectual and spiritual oneness required in Buddhist meditation practice.

Ms. Jayasuriya uses the mandala to express the universal power and presence of Christ. In the center of the mandala is Christ offering the eucharistic host symbolizing and realizing human communion in his paschal mystery, the ultimate point from which the circles are generated. Three red disks symbolize the Trinity revealed by Christ. The four evangelists are on either side of Christ and their symbols are in the four squared corners of the diagram. Word and sacrament reinforce one another for those who follow Jesus.

Nalini Jayasuriya is artist-in-residence at the Overseas Ministries Study Center in New Haven, Connecticut, and has displayed her work there and at the Yale Divinity School. She has also lived, taught, and painted in her native Sri Lanka, as well as in Japan, Israel, and Europe, seeking to express her vision of the "inner icon" and ways of seeing in Eastern and Western art. A collection of Ms. Jayasuriya's paintings with accompanying text to articulate her vision is being prepared for publication.